DATE DUE

HISPANIC FOUNDATION

BIBLIOGRAPHICAL SERIES NO. 14

latin america, spain, and portugal

an *Annotated Bibliography of*

paperback books

Compiled by
GEORGETTE MAGASSY DORN
Latin American, Portuguese, and Spanish Division

LIBRARY OF CONGRESS   /   WASHINGTON   /   1976

Library of Congress Cataloging in Publication Data

Dorn, Georgette M.
  Latin America, Spain, and Portugal.

  (Hispanic Foundation bibliographical series; no. 14)
  Originally compiled in 1964 by D. H. Andrews under
title: Latin America; a bibliography of paperback books.
  Supt. of Docs. no.: LC 24.7:14
  1. Latin America—Bibliography. 2. Spain—
Bibliography. 3. Portugal—Bibliography. 4. Bibliog-
raphy—Paperback editions. I. United States. Library
of Congress. Latin American, Portuguese, and Spanish
Division. II. Andrews, David H. Latin America; a
bibliography of paperback books. III. Title.
IV. Series.
Z2685.H5 no. 14 [Z1601] [F1408]   016.98   75-619187

ISBN 0-8444-0210-9

ISSN 0083-1581 *Key title:* Hispanic
Foundation bibliographic series

For sale by the Superintendent of Documents, U.S. Government Printing Office
Washington, D.C. 20402 - Price $3
Stock Number 030–013–00007–7

contents

ıntroduction

This edition lists over 2,200 titles relating to the Hispano-Luso-American world that are currently available in paperback editions. It is a second edition of a bibliography issued in 1971 and bearing the same title. Before that date, two somewhat similar bibliographies of paperback books had been issued. The first, published in 1964 as a joint effort of the Hispanic Foundation (now the Latin American, Portuguese, and Spanish Division) and the State Education Department of the University of the State of New York, contained no annotations and was designed for the use of teachers and students of secondary schools, colleges, and universities. The second, which appeared in 1967, was annotated but limited to titles on Latin America. Thus, the present edition is the second to include annotations and titles concerning Spain and Portugal together with those concerning Latin America.

The use of paperback books for class assignments and outside reading continues to be extensive. This demand and general public interest account for the variety, quality, and quantity of works listed. All fields in the humanities and the social sciences are covered; many standard works have been kept in print, some at higher prices. Literature and history are best represented, and the increasing emphasis on social sciences reflects the growing interest in social and economic affairs on a regional as well as on a worldwide scale.

Trends and specific events have led to the publishing of a number of works on particular subjects. In the 1960's a proliferation of books on the Cuban Revolution followed Castro's rise to power. Recent titles reflect continued interest in the subject but are based on deeper study of a society that has reached a new stage of development. A massive response to the rise and fall of Allende's government can similarly be discerned in the substantially higher number of titles on Chilean politics appearing in this bibliography. The prevailing concern for social and economic conditions and issues and the increasingly active role of the Church is apparent in works that mirror many viewpoints and theoretical approaches. New Latin American novels and works of poetry, some in bilingual or annotated editions, have become more numerous; they add to the educational and literary value of bibliographical resources now available in paperback form.

The bibliography is divided into three alphabetically arranged sections: Latin America; Spain and Portugal; and Dictionaries, Grammars, Readers, and Textbooks. A subject index and a list of publishers are also included.

A variety of sources were used in the compilation of the list, including *Paperback Book in Print, Publisher's Weekly,* and publishers' catalogs. A number of persons have aided Mrs. Dorn in preparing this work, painstakingly weeding out titles no longer in print and gathering new titles.

Mary Ellis Kahler, Chief
Latin American, Portuguese, and
Spanish Division

latin america

1

Acosta, Maruja, and Jorge E. Hardoy. *Urban reform in revolutionary Cuba.* Translated by Mal Bochner. New Haven, Conn., Antilles Research Program, Yale University, 1973. xii, 111 p. illus. (Antilles Research Program, occasional papers, 1) $2

> Richard Morse states in the foreword,"What distinguishes urban reform in Cuba within the Western and Latin American context is not the ecological goal but the political objectives and social assumptions." Includes many statistical tables.

2

Adams, Richard N., and others. *Social change in Latin America today; its implications for U.S. foreign policy.* New York, Random House, 1961. xiv, 353 p. $1.95

> Includes essays by six scholars, with specific studies of Peru, Bolivia, Brazil, Guatemala, and Mexico. This work was commissioned by the Council on Foreign Relations.

3

Adie, Robert F., and Guy E. Poitras. *Latin America; the politics of immobility.* Englewood Cliffs, N.J., Prentice-Hall, 1974. x, 278 p. $3.95

> General study of a small number of basic topics in Latin American politics. The authors discuss key factors proving that Latin American politics will not change very rapidly because political groups block effective government. This is an important contribution. Includes bibliographies.

4

Aguilar, Alonso. *Pan-Americanism from Monroe to the present; a view from the other side.* Rev. ed. Translated by Asa Zatz. New York, Monthly Review Press, 1968. 192 p. $2.95

> An economist traces the history of U.S. relations with Latin America from Presidents Monroe to Johnson. The major part of the book analyzes the 20th century. For North American readers this work provides a radical view of what is defined as "U.S. imperialism." The original Spanish title is *El panamericanismo de la doctrina Monroe a la doctrina Johnson* (1965).

5

Aguilar, Luis E., ed. *Marxism in Latin America.* New York, Knopf, 1968. xii, 271 p. (Borzoi books on Latin America) $2.75

> Save for an excerpt from Marx' and Engels' own brief recognition of Latin America, the bulk of the material presented here is by Latin American authors. Prof. Aguilar's selection is very good, and he contributes an excellent introduction.

6

Alazraki, Jaime. *Jorge Luis Borges.* New York, Columbia University Press, 1971. 48 p. (Columbia essays on modern writers, 57) $1

This essay outlines Borges' place in Hispanic and world literature. One can state that Hispanic as well as contemporary western literature cannot be explained in its totality without keeping Borges in mind. Includes a brief bibliography of works by and about Borges.

7

Alba, Victor. *The Latin Americans.* New York, Praeger, 1970. 393 p. $4.95

Introduction to Latin America, its history, politics, social customs, cultural life, and aspirations for the future by a long-time student of Latin American problems.

8

Alba, Victor. *The Mexicans; the making of a nation.* New York, Pegasus, 1970. vii, 272 p. illus. $2.45

A perceptive history of Mexico after Porfirio Díaz. The author points out the relevance of Mexico's geography to the country's history. Regions and subregions have always played an important part in the diverse political and social history of that nation. This book captures the essence of Mexico.

9

Albaum, Charlet. *Ojo de Dios; eye of God.* Published in Association with Parade magazine. New York, Grosset & Dunlap, 1972. 87 p. illus. $1.50

Describes specific handweaving design techniques used by Indians in the U.S. Southwest and northern Mexico. Explains in some detail the religious and mythological foundations of the "ojo de Dios" motifs. Includes design patterns and instructions.

10

Alden, Peter. *Finding birds in western Mexico.* Tucson, University of Arizona Press, 1969. xiv, 138 p. illus., maps. $5.95

This is an interesting and scholarly description of birds in the western regions of Mexico.

11

Alegría, Ciro. *The golden serpent.* Translation and afterword by Harriet de Onís. New York, New American Library, 1963. 190 p. (Signet classics, CP-114) $.60

One of the greatest novels of Peru, this is the story about the remorseless Marañón country. The heroes are the outcast, the humble, the Indian. This excellent English translation of *La serpiente de oro* was first published in 1943.

12

Alegría, Fernando. *Instructions for undressing the human race.* Illustrated by Matta. Santa Cruz, Calif., Kayak, 1973. 78 p. illus. $1.50

New work of fiction by the Chilean novelist, literary critic, and biographer.

13

Alexander, Robert Jackson. *Agrarian reform in Latin America.* New York, Macmillan, 1974. 118 p. $5.95

Analyzes problems relating to land reform in Latin America in nontechnical language, from the economic and social viewpoints. Mexico, Cuba, Bolivia, and Venezuela are used as concrete examples of various forms of agrarian reform. Contains a bibliography.

14

Alexander, Robert Jackson. *The Communist party of Venezuela.* Edited by Jan F. Triska. Stanford, Calif., Hoover Institution Press, 1970. xxi, 246 p. $2.80

Analyzes the Communist Party of Venezuela as it seeks power through shifting national regimes and studies the party as party-out-of-power in a democratic nation-state. This book is one in a series which analyzes the state of the nonruling Communist Parties in the world.

15

Alexander, Robert Jackson. *Latin American politics and government.* New York, Harper & Row, 1966. 184 p. $4

A brief discussion of the historical background of politics and government structures in Latin America. Intended for use in college courses.

16

Alexander, Robert Jackson. *Today's Latin America.* 2d rev. ed. Garden City, N.Y., Doubleday, 1968. x, 261 p. (Anchor books) $1.95

Deals with contemporary Latin America, placing undue emphasis on similarities in culture, traditions, and society, and not enough on the basic ecological, historical, social, and cultural differences. Intended for the generalist.

17

Alford, Harold. *The proud peoples: the heritage and culture of Spanish-speaking peoples in the United States.* New York, McKay, 1973. ix, 325 p. $2.95

Describes the progress of Spanish-speaking peoples in the United States from the first landing to the present day. Alford has divided the work into five sections—the explorers, the settlers, the rancheros, the migrants, and the militants—and has included a collection of 60 biographical sketches of important Spanish-speaking people in the U.S.

18

Alisky, Marvin. *Government of the Mexican state of Nuevo Leon.* Tempe, Center for Latin American Studies, Arizona State University, 1971. 50 p. map. $1

This complete and lucid profile of Mexico's borderland state of Nuevo Leon emphasizes political, economic, and historical aspects of Mexican government vis-a-vis the northeast. Alisky offers a list of books in English on public life in Mexico at the end of the book.

19

Alisky, Marvin. *Guide to the government of the Mexican state of Sonora.* Tempe, Center for Latin American Studies, Arizona State University, 1971. 48 p. $1

Includes political, demographic, economic, biographical, and historical information on the state of Sonora. A concise bibliography and a glossary also enhance the value of this work.

20

Alisky, Marvin. *Who's who in Mexican government.* Tempe, Arizona State University Press, 1969. 64 p. $1

Not since 1946 when Stanford University Press brought one out, has any institution in the U.S. published a who's who for Mexico. Even textbooks on Mexican government do not include biographical data on the careers of Mexican government officials. This is a useful and welcome work.

21

Allen, Jack, and A. E. Howland. *Latin America.* Englewood Cliffs, N.J., Prentice-Hall, 1970. 190 p. illus. $1.60

A succinct overview of Latin America, intended for the nonspecialist.

22

Allison, Graham T. *Essence of decision; explaining the Cuban missile crisis.* Boston, Little, Brown, 1971. xii, 338 p. $4.70

> Originally a Harvard doctoral thesis, this became a Rand Corporation report, and is here published in book form. It analyzes the many logistic and technological facets of the Cuban missile crisis. Includes bibliographies.

23

Altbach, Philip G. *Higher education in developing countries,* by Philip G. Altbach, with the assistance of Bradley Nystrom. Cambridge, Center for International Affairs, Harvard University, 1970. 118 p. (Occasional papers in international affairs, no. 24) $3.75

> This bibliography is organized by country and geographical area. It covers Africa, Asia, and Latin America. Although much of the material listed is of recent origin, older titles have been included according to their relevance. The entries are not annotated.

24

Alvarado, Roger, and others. *Raza; why a Chicano party, why Chicano studies.* New York, Pathfinder Press, 1972. unpaged. $.30

> This is a brief, polemical presentation of the demands expressed by the Spanish-speaking minority in the U.S.

25

Alvarez, José H. *Return migration to Puerto Rico.* Introd. by K. Davis. Berkeley, Institute of International Studies, University of California, 1969. 101 p. $2

> This is a study of the people who return to Puerto Rico after having lived in the U.S. mainland. It provides interesting data and sociological insights.

26

Alvarez, Luisa M. *Good food from Mexico.* New rev. ed. New York, Macmillan, 1970. 253 p. $.95

> First published in 1950, this perennial favorite includes the better known dishes from Mexico, with very clear directions for their preparation.

27

Alves, Marcio Moreira. *A grain of mustard seed; the awakening of the Brazilian revolution.* Garden City, N.Y., Doubleday, 1973. 194 p. $1.95

> The author is a journalist, a former Brazilian congressman, and vocal opponent of the military regime currently ruling Brazil. This is his personal account of how he moved into the opposition, as well as an analysis of left-wing politics in Brazil.

28

Amado, Jorge. *Gabriela, clove and cinammon.* Translated from the Portuguese by James L. Taylor and William Grossman. New York, Dell/Bard, 1974. 312 p. $1.35

> The scene is the 1920's in a provincial Brazilian port city where gossip of love and politics is life's chief excitement. This is an important novel which strikingly depicts northeastern Brazil.

29

American Assembly. *United States and Latin America.* Edited by Herbert L. Matthews. 2d ed. Englewood Cliffs, N.J., Prentice-Hall, 1970. 179 p. illus. (A Spectrum book) $1.95

> Surveys U.S.-Latin American relations during the 20th century.

30

American Universities Field Staff. New York. *A select bibliography: Asia, Africa, Eastern Europe, Latin America.* Supplement 1971. New York, 1971. 89 p. $3.50

An annotated bibliography to assist college librarians in building their collections in area studies. Contains 212 English-language entries on Latin America prepared by Georgette M. Dorn. Complete bibliographic information is provided for each entry. The 1961, 1963, 1965, and 1969 supplements are also available from the publisher (Hanover, N.H., American Universities Field Staff).

31

Ancient Peruvian textiles from the collection of the Textile Museum, Washington, D. C.; The Museum of Primitive Art, New York. New York, Graphic Art Society, 1965. 48 p. illus., map. $3.75

Mary Elizabeth King provides the brief introduction and the notes that amplify the 44 illustrations of Peruvian textiles from the Paracas, Nazca, Tiahuanaco, Inca, and Central Coast cultures. A very attractive and informative volume.

32

Anderson, Charles W., Fred R. Van der Mehden, and Crawford Young. *Issues of political development.* Englewood Cliffs, N.J., Prentice-Hall, 1967. 284 p. maps. $5.90

This is a useful volume on comparative government dealing with political problems facing new nations.

33

Anderson, Charles W. *Politics and economic change in Latin America; the governing of restless nations.* New York, Van Nostrand, 1967. xii, 388 p. $4.95

Analyzes the political element in economic change in contemporary Latin America. Part I studies development policy-making; part II deals with the specific experience of 10 countries in formulating approaches to development; and part III outlines political change.

34

Anderson, Susan Heller, *see* Brunetti, Cosimo

35

Anderson-Imbert, Enrique. *Fuga.* Edited by J. V. Falconieri. New York, Macmillan, 1969. 110 p. $2.50

This is a short novel by a well-known contemporary Argentine novelist and literary critic celebrated for his avant-garde style.

36

Anderson-Imbert, Enrique, and Eugenio Florit, eds. *Literatura hispanoamericana; antología e introducción histórica.* Edición revisada. New York, Holt, Rinehart and Winston, 1970. 2 v. $7.95 each

Intended for U.S. students of Spanish-American literature, this anthology provides an excellent selection of works from the period of the conquest to the mid-1960's. All principal literary movements are represented.

37

Anderson-Imbert, Enrique. *Spanish-American literature; a history.* Detroit, Wayne State University Press, 1969. 2 v. $5.95 each

This comprehensive history of Spanish-American literature has become a major reference source since its first publication in 1963. It includes all major and a great many lesser figures of Spanish-American literature. This is a slightly updated edition. Indispensable for libraries and students of the hemisphere's literature.

38

Anderson-Imbert, Enrique, and Lawrence B. Kiddle, eds. *Veinte cuentos hispano-americanos del siglo veinte.* New York, Appleton-Century-Crofts, 1960. 242 p. $3.50

An anthology of Spanish-American short stories which includes many important Spanish-American literary figures of the 20th century, such as Leopoldo Lugones, Pedro Henríquez Ureña, Jorge Luis Borges, and Lino Novás Calvo, among others.

39

Andic, Fuat M., and Suphan Andic. *Fiscal survey of the French Caribbean.* Rio Piedras, Institute of Caribbean Studies, University of Puerto Rico, 1965. 107 p. tables. $3

Analyzes the revenue system of the French Caribbean and evaluates its importance within the general economic structure of the region. A section deals with economic relations between France and the French Caribbean.

40

Andic, Fuat M., and Suphan Andic. *Government finance and planned development.* Fiscal surveys of Surinam and the Netherlands Antilles. Rio Piedras, Institute of Caribbean Studies, University of Puerto Rico, 1968. 395 p. tables. $9

Studies the size and structure of the budgets of the Netherlands Caribbean countries in relation to the development objectives of these states.

41

Andreski, Stanislav. *Parasitism and subversion; the case of Latin America.* New York, Schocken Books, 1969. 310 p. tables. $2.45

The author presents a thoughtful analysis of contemporary social and political patterns in Latin America. Includes a bibliography.

42

Andrews, Charles J. *Economic performance of the Compañía de Acero del Pacífico, S.A.* Austin, Bureau of Business Research, Graduate School of Business, University of Texas, 1970. xi, 116 p. illus., maps. (University of Texas at Austin. Studies in Latin American business, no. 9) $3

Outlines in great detail the history of Chile's steel industry. The information is extensively supported by charts, maps, and comparative statistics. Includes a bibliography.

43

Antoine, Charles. *The Church and power in Brazil.* Translated by Peter Nelson. Maryknoll, N.Y., Orbis Books, 1973. 275 p. $4.95

A candid and insightful examination of the dilemma of the Catholic Church in the world's largest Catholic country: whether to take an active part toward helping the economic and social betterment of the disadvantaged or to defend the status quo.

44

Arce de Vázquez, Margot. *Gabriela Mistral; the poet and her work.* Translated from the Spanish by Helen Masslo Anderson. New York, New York University Press, 1964. 158 p. $1.75

A brief biography and critical study of the Chilean poet who was awarded the 1945 Nobel Prize in Literature. Mistral emerges as an exceptional educator and social philosopher as well as a first-rate poet. The greater part of this study deals with Mistral's poetry. The original Spanish edition is entitled *Gabriela Mistral, persona y poesía* (1957).

45

Arciniégas, Germán. *Temas de Arciniégas; invitación a conversar, leer y escribir.* Edited by Osvaldo N. Soto and Cecil D. McVicker. New York, Harcourt, Brace & World, 1967. 210 p. $4.50

This work is based on newspaper articles by the well-known Colombian writer and essayist. It is intended as a text for reading, composition, and conversation. Contains copious notes and a vocabulary.

46

Argentine-U.S. Commission on Foot-and-Mouth Disease. *Studies in foot and mouth disease.* Washington, National Academy of Sciences, 1969. 265 p. $5

Contains studies and reports by the Argentine-U.S. commission dealing with this dreaded cattle disease.

47

Arguedas, José María. *Los ríos profundos,* edited by W. Rowe. New York, Pergamon Press, 1973. 204 p. $6.25

First published in 1959, this novel deals with the Indian theme. The protagonist is a mestizo who was raised by the Indians and later lived in a small provincial town of Peru. Contains notes and vocabulary.

48

Aridjis, Homero, ed. *Seis poetas latinoamericanos de hoy.* Edited by Homero Aridjis, under the general editorship of Robert G. Mead, Jr. New York, Harcourt Brace Jovanovich, 1972. xii, 242 p. illus. $4.95

Aridjis has selected the most representative samples of poetry by the six giants of 20th-century Spanish-American poetry: Vicente Huidobro, César Vallejo, Jorge Luis Borges, Octavio Paz, Pablo Neruda, and Nicanor Parra. The poems presented here are generally acknowledged to be masterpieces of contemporary Spanish poetry.

49

Arnade, Charles W. *Siege of St. Augustine in 1702.* Gainesville, University of Florida Press, 1959. 67 p. illus. (University of Florida monographs. Social sciences, no. 3) $2

Presents a historical outline of St. Augustine during the early 18th century. The book is enhanced by attractive illustrations and a very good bibliography.

50

Arnold, Charles A. *Folklore, manners and customs of the Mexicans in San Antonio, Texas.* San Francisco, R. & E. Research Associates, 1971. 45 p. $7

Describes customs and folklore of the Mexicans living in San Antonio. Contains a good bibliography.

51

Arraes, Miguel. *Brazil: the people and the power.* Translated from the French by Lancelot Sheppard. Harmondsworth, England, Penguin Books, 1972. 232 p. (The Pelican Latin American library) $2.45

A political analysis of contemporary Brazil by a leftist Brazilian politician from the Northeast.

52

Arratia, Alejandro, and Carlos D. Hamilton, eds. *Diez cuentos hispanoamericanos;* with an introd., exercises, notes, and vocabulary. Illus. by Marjorie Auerbach. New York, Oxford University Press, 1958. 187 p. illus. (Oxford Spanish readers) $2.95

Includes short stories, arranged chronologically, by some of the greatest contemporary writers of Spanish America. An excellent introduction traces the history of the Spanish short story from the 1335 romance *Conde de Lucanor* to the present.

53

Arriaga, Eduardo E. *Mortality decline and its demographic effects in Latin America.* Foreword by Kingsley Davis. Berkeley, Institute of International Studies, University of California, 1970. xiv, 232 p. tables. (Population monograph series, no. 6) $3

New population data indicate that the mortality decline in Latin America has been the fastest ever experienced by a major world region. Includes a useful bibliography.

54

Arriaga, Eduardo E. *New life tables for Latin American populations in the nineteenth and twentieth centuries.* Berkeley, Institute of International Studies, University of California, 1968. 324 p. tables. (Population monograph series, no. 3) $2.75

The author has compiled a useful reference source containing numerous tables on vital statistics for the historian and the sociologist.

55

Ashcraft, Norman. *Colonialism and underdevelopment; processes of political economic change in British Honduras.* New York, Teachers College Press, 1973. 180 p. $3.95

Studies underdevelopment within its historical and institutional context, illustrating the concept that local behavior is a response to processes which occur at a wider institutional level. The author contends that dependency of underdeveloped countries frustrates attempts to reform national institutions.

56

Association for Latin American Studies. Midwest Council. *Human resources for Latin America; an interdisciplinary focus.* Frank T. Bachmura, editor. Bloomington, Bureau of Business Research, Indiana University, 1968. 214 p. (Indiana business paper, no. 16) $4.50

The papers included here were presented at the Midwest Conference of the Association for Latin American Studies, Indiana University, October 26-28, 1967, dealing with manpower policies, demography, and related topics. Includes bibliographies.

57

Astuto, Philip Louis, and R. A. Leal. *Latin American problems.* Jamaica, N.Y., St. John's University Press, 1970. 320 p. $3.50

A general study of contemporary Latin American problems intended for the nonspecialist.

58

Atwater, James D., and Ramón Eduardo Ruiz. *Out from under; Benito Juárez and Mexico's struggle for independence.* Illustrated by Paul Hogar. Garden City, N.Y., Doubleday, 1969. 118 p. illus. (Zenith books) $2.95

This book on Juárez and Mexican independence is intended for Chicano high school and junior college students. It is one in a series of books which aim to present the history of minority groups in the U.S. and their participation in the development of the country.

59

Aubey, Robert T. *Nacional Financiera and Mexican industry: a study of the financial relationship between the government and the private sector of Mexico.* Los Angeles,

Latin American Center, University of California, 1966. 205 p. illus. (Latin American Center, University of California, Los Angeles, Latin American Studies, v. 3) $5

This specialized study is useful for economics students and those interested in the technical and structural aspects of Mexican industry. Includes a bibliography.

60
Augier, F. R., and S. C. Gordon, eds. *Sources of West Indian history; a compilation of writings of historical events in the West Indies.* New York, Humanities Press, 1967. x, 308 p. $2

This selection of readings traces the history of the West Indies, particularly of those areas where English is spoken, from 1492 to the 1950's. Includes a bibliography.

60A
Autumn, Violeta. *A Russian Jew cooks in Peru.* Design, illus., and calligraphy by the author. San Francisco, 101 Productions; distributed by Scribner, New York, 1973. 119 p. illus. $3.95

An attractively illustrated and highly original cookbook which combines European Jewish cuisine with the sophisticated culinary wonders of Peru.

61
Avilez, Alexander. *Population increases into Alta California in the Spanish period, 1769-1821.* San Francisco, R. and E. Research Associates, 1974. 176 p. $8

A demographic study of early California during the Spanish period, with bibliographical references.

62
Azuela, Mariano. *Los de abajo; novela de la revolución mexicana.* Edited by John Englekirk and Lawrence B. Kiddle. New York, Appleton-Century-Crofts, 1971. xix, 175 p. fold. map. $2.75

Azuela's classic novel about the Mexican Revolution was first published in 1916. The editors have added a useful introduction to this edition, which also contains notes and a vocabulary.

63
Azuela, Mariano. *Two novels of Mexico: The flies; The bosses.* Translated from the Spanish by Lesley Byrd Simpson. Berkeley, University of California Press, 1956. 194 p. $1.95

Originally published in Spanish as *Las moscas* (1918) and *Los caciques* (1917), respectively, these are two remarkable vignettes of the Mexican Revolution. They describe the people caught in the great social upheaval which changed the course of Mexican history.

64
Azuela, Mariano. *The underdogs; a novel of the Mexican Revolution.* Translated by E. Munguía, Jr. Foreword by Harriet de Onís. New York, New American Library, 1963. 151 p. $.75

English translation of *Los de abajo* (1916), the great novel of the Mexican Revolution, which covers the period between Madero's assassination and the defeat of Pancho Villa's partisans in the battle of Celaya. Azuela presents people's lives with realism. His importance rests on being the founder of the novel of the Revolution, yet those who judge *Underdogs* from a political and not a literary point of view, consider it an antirevolutionary work.

65

Babín, María Teresa, and Stan Steiner, comps. *Borinquen; an anthology of Puerto Rican literature.* New York, Vintage Books, 1974. 544 p. $2.95

> Contains excerpts from short stories, poems, plays, novels, and essays by over 60 Puerto Rican authors of the past and the present. Their works mirror the island's varied cultural and ethnic background. Recommended for public and university libraries. Includes bibliographical notes.

66

Babín, María Teresa. *Puerto Rican spirit; their history, life and culture.* New York, Collier Books, 1971. xi, 180 p. $1.50

> Contains essays and sketches on Puerto Rican civilization and culture, intended to foster a better understanding of the island's past and its people. Includes bibliographical notes.

67

Bachmura, Frank T., ed. *Human resources in Latin America; an interdisciplinary focus.* Bloomington, Indiana University, Bureau of Business Research, 1968. 214 p. (Indiana business paper, no. 16) $4.50

> The 1967 meeting of the Midwest Council of the Association for Latin American Studies dealt with the human resources problem in Latin America. This volume contains the papers delivered at the conference.

68

Bakeless, John Edwin. *The eyes of discovery; the pageant of North America as seen by the first explorers.* New York, Dover Publications, 1968. 439 p. illus., maps. $3

> This is a popularized description of North America as the first white men saw it.

69

Bannon, John Francis, ed. *Indian labor in the Spanish Indies; was there another solution?* Boston, Heath, 1966. xii, 105 p. (Problems in Latin American civilization) $2.50

> Includes essays by Charles Gibson, Bartolomé de las Casas, Motolinia, Lewis Hanke, Lesley Byrd Simpson, and others, dealing with pre-Conquest labor practices, evolution of the post-Conquest labor system, and legislation to regulate Indian labor. The three interest groups studied are the Crown, the Indians, and the colonists.

70

Bannon, John Francis. *Spanish Borderlands frontier, 1513-1521.* New York, Holt, Rinehart and Winston, 1970. x, 308 p. illus., maps, ports. (Histories of the American frontier) $4.75

> This scholarly study of Spain's frontier movement in North America examines the Iberian brand of western civilization in considerable areas of the U.S. Prof. Bannon asserts that the Spaniard "proved to be a remarkable frontiersman . . . his story has an intrinsic interest as an example of human pioneering." Includes bibliographies.

71

Barager, Joseph, comp. *Why Peron came to power; the background to Peronism in Argentina.* New York, Knopf, 1968. xi, 274 p. (Borzoi books on Latin America) $2.75

> Includes a collection of essays on Argentine social and political history by Ricardo Levene, James Scobie, Gino Germani, and others. The first essay is taken from the writings of Domingo F. Sarmiento. The last essay, by British historian George Pendle, presents a retrospective view of the first Peron era.

72

Baring-Gould, Michael Darragh. *Agricultural and community development in Mexican ejidos: relatives in conflict.* Ithaca, N.Y., Cornell University, Latin American Studies Program, 1974. 239 p. (Latin American Studies Program, Dissertation series, no. 52) $4

Studies the tremendous increases in both agricultural production and technology that have occurred in Mexico during the last two decades. Includes tables and a bibliography.

72A

Barlow, Genevieve. *Leyendas latinoamericanas.* Illustrated by Robert Borja. Skokie, Ill., National Textbook Co., 1974. 129 p. illus. $4.50 single copy; 5 or more $3.60

The 16 legends included in this work hail from Argentina, Bolivia, Colombia, Guatemala, Honduras, Mexico, Paraguay, Peru, Puerto Rico, and Venezuela. They cover a span of over 2,000 years. The book contains exercises and a vocabulary.

72B

Barlow, Genevieve, and William N. Stivers, comps. *Leyendas mexicanas; a collection of Mexican legends.* Illus. by Phero Thomas. Skokie, Ill., National Textbook Co., 1974. 119 p. illus. $4.50 single copy; 5 or more $3.60 each

The 16 legends included in this brief anthology cover a time span of some 1,500 years. The legends include animals, people, and deities. Some are pre-Columbian and others are from the colonial period. Intended for early intermediate classes. Contains notes and vocabulary.

73

Barrenechea, Ana María. *Borges the labyrinth maker.* Edited and translated by Robert Lima. New York, New York University Press, 1965. x, 175 p. $1.95

The author has added new materials to *La expresión de la realidad en la obra de Jorge Luis Borges* (1957), co-authored with Borges. This work is a perceptive analysis of Argentina's most gifted writer with special emphasis on his approach to reality, symbolism, and transmutation of values. Includes a bibliography.

74

Barrios, Virginia B. de. *Guide to tequila, mezcal and pulque.* New York, International Publications Service, 1971. 64 p. illus. $1.20

Describes the history and manufacture of native Mexican beverages. It also contains information on pre-Columbian religions, Mexican folklore, and herbal medicine.

75

Bates, Henry W. *The naturalist on the river Amazon.* Foreword by Robert L. Usinger. Berkeley, University of California Press, 1962. 462 p. $2.45

First published in 1863 in London, this is a lucid and interesting account by an English naturalist of his 11 years of travel throughout the Amazon region.

76

Becco, Horacio Jorge, comp. *Bibliografía de bibliografías literarias argentinas.* Washington, Organization of American States, 1972. 100 p. (OAS, 109-S-8216) $1

A bibliography of Argentine bibliographies in the field of literature. This is of interest to librarians and to students of Argentine and comparative literature. Contains annotations.

77

Beck, Warren A., and Ynez D. Haase. *Historical atlas of New Mexico.* Norman,

University of Oklahoma Press, 1969. 152 p. 62 maps. $2.95

In 62 maps with an accompanying text, a cartographer and a historian trace the long history of New Mexico. The topics include Spanish and U.S. expeditions, stagecoach and railroad lines, state and national parks, as well as detailed geographical data. Includes bibliographies.

78
Béhague, Gérard. *The beginning of musical nationalism in Brazil.* Detroit, Information Coordinators, 1971. 43 p. music. (Detroit monographs in musicology, no. 1) $5

Explores the works of three key Brazilian composers of the 1880-1920 period: Brasilio Itibêre da Cunha, Alexandre Levy, and Alberto Nepomuceno. The composers of this transitional period continued to be largely geared to European romantic and postromantic music, although folk-popular themes were clearly emerging as a strong trend.

79
Béjar Rivera, Héctor. *Peru 1965; notes on a guerrilla experience.* Translated by William Rose. New York, Monthly Review Press, 1970. 142 p. maps. $1.95

English translation of *Peru 1965; apuntes sobre una experiencia guerrillera,* which in the author's words is a "frank and critical self-analysis of the origins of the guerrilla movement in Peru. . . and the immediate and less immediate causes of its initial failures."

80
Bell, Wendell, ed. *The democratic revolution in the West Indies; studies in nationalism, leadership, and the belief in progress.* With a foreword by Vernon L. Arnett. Cambridge, Mass., Schenkman Pub. Co., 1967. xxviii, 232 p. illus., tables. (International studies in political and social change) $3.95

The result of a large research project of the West Indies Studies Program, University of California, Los Angeles, this is the first of a projected four-volume set, dealing with the search for national identity as well as economic survival of the West Indian islands.

81
Bello, José María. *A history of modern Brazil, 1889-1964.* Translated from the Portuguese by James L. Taylor. With a new concluding chapter by Rollie W. Poppino. Stanford, Calif., Stanford University Press, 1966. xix, 362 p. maps. $5.75

Translation of the 4th edition of *História da República, 1889-1902* (1959), which became the basic political history of modern Brazil available in English. Professor Poppino's chapter entitled "Brazil since 1954" brings the book into the 1960's. Includes bibliographies.

82
Bemis, Samuel Flagg. *The Latin American policy of the United States; an historical interpretation.* New York, Norton, 1967. xiv, 470 p. illus., maps. $3.45

Traces the development of U.S.-Latin American relations from 1876 to the end of World War II. It was first published in 1943 and has been for many years the standard text of U.S. diplomacy in the hemisphere.

83
Bennett, Wendell Clark, and Junius B. Bird. *Andean culture history.* 2d rev. ed. Garden City, N.Y., Published by the Museum of Natural History [by] Natural History Press, 1964. xx, 257 p. illus., maps. (American museum science books, B9) $1.95

Originally published in 1947, this work reviews the archeology of the Central Andes from early man to the Incas. It begins with a general discussion of South

American archeology and ethnology followed by a chronological review of the known archeological cultures of Peru and northern Bolivia. Bird's contribution is an excellent exposition of the technology of Indian metallurgy, ceramics, and textiles. Includes a comprehensive bibliography.

84

Benrimo, Dorothy. *Camposantos; a photographic essay.* Photographs by Dorothy Benrimo, with a commentary by Rebecca Salisbury James, and historical notes by E. Boyd. Austin, University of Texas Press, 1966. 75 p. (chiefly illus.) $4

A beautiful photographic essay about New Mexico crosses and other folk art forms, accompanied by a succinct and informative historical essay.

85

Benson, Nettie Lee, comp. *Catalogue of Martin Fierro materials in the University of Texas Library.* Austin, Institute of Latin American Studies, University of Texas, 1972. 102 p. $4.50

Provides an invaluable guide to the University of Texas' rich and interesting collection of materials relating to the legendary Argentine folk hero.

86

Berle, Adolf Augustus, Jr. *Latin America: diplomacy and reality.* New York, Published for the Council on Foreign Relations by Harper & Row, 1962. 144 p. (Policy books) $1.95

In this brief book, a long-time officer of the Department of State and student of inter-American affairs discusses his understanding of Latin America's domestic and foreign policy problems.

87

Bernal, Ignacio, and others. *The iconography of Middle American sculpture.* Foreword by Dudley T. Easby, Jr. New York, Metropolitan Museum of Art, 1973. 167 p. illus. $4.50

Includes nine contributions on Middle American sculpture by noted scholars in the field. This is an important volume on the salient problems of Mesoamerican iconography. The illustrations are excellent.

88

Bernal, Ignacio, ed. *Mexican wall paintings of the Maya and Aztec periods.* New York, New American Library of World Literature by arrangement with UNESCO, 1963. 24 p. illus., 28 color plates. $.95

Bernal has assembled an attractive edition of Aztec and Maya mural paintings and has added an excellent explanatory text. The author is director of Mexico City's famed National Museum of Anthropology. Includes a bibliography.

89

Bernal, Ignacio. *Mexico before Cortez: art, history, and legend.* Translated by Willis Barnstone. Garden City, N.Y., Doubleday, 1963. 135 p. illus. (A Dolphin original, C-422) $1.45

This is a translation of *Tenochtitlán en una isla* (1959). The author focuses on the Toltec city of Tula and the Aztec city of Tenochtitlán, giving us a sharp insight into the spiritual and aesthetic qualities of Indian life before the arrival of the Spaniards.

90

Bernal, Ignacio. *Three thousand years of art and life in Mexico as seen in the National Museum of Anthropology of Mexico City.* Translated by Carolyn B. Czitrom. New York, New American Library, 1968. 216 p. illus. $3.95

An excellent guide and textual explanation of Mexico's extraordinary National Museum of Anthropology.

91

Bernard, Jean Pierre, and others. *Guide to the political parties of South America.* Translated by Michael Perl. Harmondsworth, England, Penguin Books, 1973. 574 p. maps. (Pelican Latin American library) $3.95

A comprehensive and informative guide to the most important political parties in South America, prepared by a number of historians and political scientists from Europe and Latin America.

92

Bernstein, Harry. *Venezuela and Colombia.* Englewood Cliffs, N.J., Prentice-Hall, 1964. 152 p. maps. (The modern nations in historical perspective) (A Spectrum book) $1.95

Owing to space limitations, the author compressed coverage of the colonial and national periods to some 80 pages per country, resulting in two compact essays. Includes a bibliography.

93

Bernstein, Marvin D., ed. *Foreign investment in Latin America: cases and attitudes.* Edited with an introd. by Marvin D. Bernstein. New York, Knopf, 1966. 256 p. (Borzoi books on Latin America) $2.50

A well-chosen collection of 19 essays which analyze foreign investment in Latin America during the last century and a half from the private-enterprise, nationalist, economic, as well as Marxist, point of view. Includes a bibliography.

94

Bianchi, Lois. *Chile in pictures.* Rev. ed. New York, Sterling Pub. Co., 1972. 64 p. illus., map. (Visual geography series) $1.50

An illustrated description of this narrow and fascinating Andean country, with information on the history, government, and culture of Chile.

95

Bingaman, Joseph W. *Latin America; a survey of holdings at the Hoover Institution on War, Revolution and Peace.* Stanford, Calif., Hoover Institution, 1972. 96 p. (Hoover Institution survey of holdings, 5) $3

Provides an introduction to the 13,400 volumes and 1,600 serial and newspaper titles on Latin America in the Hoover collection. This collection is especially strong on labor history and political organizations of the Left. A very important contribution.

96

Bingham, Hiram. *Lost city of the Incas: the story of Machu Picchu and its builders.* New York, Atheneum, 1963. 240 p. illus. $2.65

First published in 1948, this is a popularized restatement of Bingham's work on Machu Picchu and the neighboring sites during 1911-15, with excellent illustrations. The book contains no new archeological material.

97

Birkos, Alexander S., and Lewis A. Tambs, comps. *Academic writer's guide to periodicals.* v. l, Latin American studies. Compiled and edited by Alexander S. Birkos and Lewis A. Tambs. Kent, Ohio, Kent State University Press, 1971. 359 p. $7.50

Briefly describes journals and monographic series that have either a main or tangential interest in any facet of Latin American studies, the Spanish borderlands of North America, and other areas within the Luso-Hispanic cultural or political realm. The entries are arranged alphabetically, and each contains information on the address, price, type of articles, and other pertinent data. This is a welcome tool for researchers and librarians.

98

Birns, Laurence, ed. *The end of Chilean democracy; an IDOC dossier on the coup and its aftermath.* New York, Seabury Press, 1974. 219 p. $3.95

The editor has assembled articles, documents, and newspaper accounts, from both U.S. and Chilean sources, dealing with the coup that toppled Allende.

99

Bishop, Elizabeth, and Emanuel Brasil, comps. *An anthology of twentieth century Brazilian poetry.* Edited, with an introd. by Elizabeth Bishop and Emanuel Brasil. Middleton, Conn., Wesleyan University Press, 1972. xxi, 181 p. $3.35.

This bilingual anthology includes such major poets as Manuel Bandeira, Mano Andrade, Carlos Drummond de Andrade, and João Cabral de Melo Neto. The introduction provides a lucid analysis of contemporary Brazilian poetry. Includes a bibliography.

100

Blacker, Irwin R., ed. *The portable Hakluyt's voyages.* New York, Viking, 1967. 522 p. $1.85

Letters, reports, official correspondence, diaries, logs, and other first-hand accounts constitute *Hakluyt's Voyages.* Richard Hakluyt's 1,700,000-word compendium is basically an anthology written by eminent Elizabethans. The editor has chosen 49 selections and has added an introduction which places the original work in a historical perspective.

101

Blair, Calvin Patton, Richard P. Schaedel, and James H. Street. *Responsibilities of the foreign scholar to the local scholarly community: studies of U.S. research in Guatemala, Chile, and Paraguay.* Edited, with an introd. by Richard N. Adams. New York, Council on Educational Cooperation with Latin America, Education and World Affairs, 1969. 112 p. tables. $2.50

Report on the state and nature of social science research in three countries. The introduction outlines a set of recommendations that suggest the responsibilities of the individual investigator. [Charles Fleener]

102

Blakemore, Harold. *Latin America.* New York, Oxford University Press, 1973. 128 [12] p. illus., maps. (The modern world) $1.40

Reprints with corrections the 1966 edition of this useful introductory survey. The book describes the geographic, social, political, and historic characteristics of Latin America in terms of "the challenge of change." Includes a bibliography.

103

Blanksten, George I. *Argentina and Chile.* Consulting editor, Lindley J. Stiles. Boston, Ginn, 1969. 122 p. illus., maps, ports. (Today's world in focus) $1.60

A brief study of these two important countries of South America, contrasting the two societies and cultures. Includes bibliographies.

104

Bloch, Peter. *La-le-lo-lai; Puerto Rican music and its performers.* New York, Plus Ultra Educational Publications, 1973. 197 p. illus. (A Plus Ultra book) $1.95

Presents the music of Puerto Rico, with biographical and critical sketches about composers and performers.

105
Boatler, Robert Wayne. *Trade theory predictions in the growth of Mexico's manufactured exports.* Ithaca, N.Y., Cornell University, Latin American Studies Program, 1973. 158 p. (Latin American Studies Program, Dissertation series, no. 49) $4

Examines the pattern of growth of Mexico's manufactured goods and their export. Mexico's experience could serve as a model for developing countries. Includes tables and a bibliography.

106
Bock, Philip K., comp. *Peasants in the modern world.* Edited by Philip K. Bock. Albuquerque, University of New Mexico Press, 1969. 173 p. $2.45

Three of the essays included here deal exclusively with Hispanic topics. Eva and Robert Hunt explore the diverse use of rural Mexican courts by Indians and mestizos. Charles Erasmus studies the effects of land and agrarian reform in Mexico, Venezuela, and Bolivia. Edward Dozier analyzes the changes wrought in Mexican-American culture by the disappearance of the traditional village structure. [Charles Fleener]

107
Bodard, Lucien. *Green hell; massacre of the Brazilian Indians.* New York, Ballantine Books, 1974. 211 p. $1.65

A journalistic account describing the exploitation and murder of Brazilian Indians.

108
Boehm, David Alfred. *Peru in pictures,* [prepared] by Robert V. Masters. Rev. ed. New York, Sterling Pub. Co., 1972. 64 p. illus., maps. (Visual geography series) $1.50

This is a succinct, profusely illustrated description of Peru and its people. Intended for classroom use, as well as for the traveler.

109
Boehm, Lincoln A. *Venezuela in pictures.* New York, Sterling Pub. Co., 1973. 64 p. illus., maps. (Visual geography series) $1.50

Describes contemporary Venezuela with attractive illustrations and text. Intended for classroom use, as well as for the traveler.

110
Bolívar, Simón. *Escritos políticos.* Philadelphia, Center for Curriculum Development, 1970. n.p. $1.20

Political writings of the South American leader of the independence movement, presented in an annotated, textbook edition.

111
Bolton, Herbert Eugene. *Coronado on the Turquoise Trail; knight of pueblos and plains.* Drawing by Margaret Fearnside. Albuquerque, University of New Mexico Press, 1964. xvi, 494 p. illus. $3.45

First published in 1949, this is a reconstruction of the Coronado expedition of 1540, showing the hardships endured by the explorers and the discoveries they made.

112
Bolton, Herbert Eugene. *The Padre on horseback.* Chicago, Loyola University Press,

1963. xvi, 90 p. illus. (The American West, Loyola University reprint series) $2.25

Recounts the life and the 40 expeditions of Eusebio Kino, a Jesuit priest and apostle to the Indians of New Spain's northwest frontier. John F. Bannon provides a knowledgeable introduction to this edition. The monograph was first published in 1932.

113

Bolton, Herbert Eugene. *Wider horizons of American history.* Notre Dame, Ind., Notre Dame University Press, 1967. xiii, 191 p. $2.25

Contains four of Professor Bolton's most widely discussed essays: "The epic of greater America," his tentative, panoramic synthesis of Western Hemisphere history; "Defensive Spanish expansion and the significance of the borderlands," which sketches the meeting of two civilizations in the Southwest; "The mission as a frontier institution," which interprets the mission as an economic and socio-political institution, as well as a religious one; and "The Black robes of New Spain," which evaluates the work of the French and Spanish Jesuits in North America. Reprint of the 1939 edition.

114

Bonachea, Ramón, and Marta San Martín. *The Cuban insurrection, 1952-1959.* New Brunswick, N.J., Transaction Books, 1974. xxi, 451 p. illus., maps. $4.95

This is a serious analysis of the first stage of the Cuban Revolution, challenging the traditional premise that the insurrection began in the rural areas and only later expanded to the cities. It includes analyses of combat, strikes, and uprisings, as well as guerrilla political structures. Of great interest to academic libraries and students of contemporary Cuba. Includes a bibliography.

115

Bonachea, Rolando E., and Nelson P. Valdés, eds. *Cuba in revolution.* Garden City, N.Y., Doubleday, 1972. xii, 544 p. (Anchor books, A791) $2.95

The selections reflect a thorough review of the Cuban Revolution, treating such topics as the social origins of the rebellion, politics in Cuba, fighting economic underdevelopment, social development, and revolutionary ideology. This is an outstanding contribution of great interest to all Latin Americanists.

116

Bonilla, Heraclio. *Guano y burguesía en el Perú.* Lima, Instituto de Estudios Peruanos, 1974. 186 p. (Peru problema, 11) $3

Three studies by a Peruvian economic historian based on his doctoral dissertation at the University of Paris. The work uses European sources and examines the guano industry, which was the principal source of economic wealth in Peru from 1840 to 1880. Dr. Bonilla was a Woodrow Wilson Fellow at the Smithsonian Institution in 1974-75.

117

Bonilla, Heraclio. *El minero de los Andes; una aproximación a su estudio.* Lima, Instituto de Estudios Peruanos, 1974. 89 p. (Colección mínima, 4) $2

An economic and sociological essay focusing on the miners at the Morococha site of the big Cerro de Pasco mining center in Peru. It also analyzes patterns of migrant miners, productivity, and the economic and social setting.

118

Boorstein, Edward. *The economic transformation of Cuba; a first-hand account.* New York, Monthly Review Press, 1968. 303 p. illus., tables. $3.45

The author worked from 1960 to 1963 in the top planning agencies of revolutionary Cuba. Here he discusses the problems of running a socialist economy. The author's close association with Che Guevara gave him an inside view of the Castro regime.

119

Borah, Woodrow, and Sherburne Friend Cook. *The population of central Mexico in 1548. An analysis of the Suma de visitas de pueblos.* Berkeley, University of California Press, 1960. 215 p. maps, tables. (Ibero-Americana, 43) $3

Detailed population analysis of the Suma de visitas, presenting the thesis that the population figure of S. F. Cook and L. B. Simpson is too low. This conclusion is in part vitiated by an error in addition, but the study remains valuable, especially for its analysis of the relation between tributary and nontributary population. [HLAS 23:3148]

120

Borges, Jorge Luis. *The Aleph and other stories, 1933-1969.* Edited and translated by Norman Thomas di Giovanni in collaboration with the author. New York, Bantam Books, 1973. 286 p. $1.95

First published in 1970, the original Spanish version of *El* "Aleph" appeared in 1944. This outstanding selection includes "Streetcorner man," "The circular ruins," "Death and the compass," and several others. These short stories span three decades of an extraordinary Argentine writer's production.

121

Borges, Jorge Luis. *The book of imaginary beings,* by Jorge Luis Borges, with Margarita Guerrero; rev., enl., and translated by Norman Thomas di Giovanni in collaboration with the author. New York, Avon, 1971. 256 p. $1.45

The original edition, published in 1967, was entitled *El libro de los seres imaginarios.* Borges has collected here a wide array of material on imaginary beings from Spanish, medieval Latin, French, Eastern, and Western literature. This is a fascinating book for the specialist as well as for the aficionado of literature.

122

Borges, Jorge Luis. *Borges on writing.* Edited by Norman Thomas di Giovanni and others. New York, Dutton, 1973. 1973 p. $2.95

Provides interesting insights into translators' problems and a rich range of ancient and modern literary references. Borges also gives opinions on the writing of poetry and prose. Some of the material included has been published elsewhere in journals.

123

Borges, Jorge Luis. *Borges: sus mejores páginas.* Edited with an introd., notes and bibliography by Miguel Enguídanos. Englewood Cliffs, N.J., Prentice-Hall, 1970. 250 p. port. (Modern Spanish and Latin American authors series) $3.95

The editor has selected essays, short stories, and poems by this Argentine author.

124

Borges, Jorge Luis, and Richard Burgin. *Conversations with Jorge Luis Borges.* New York, Avon, 1970. xvi, 144 p. $1.65

Burgin is a young graduate student who taped an interview with the Argentine writer and philosopher. The dialog is warm, witty, and revealing of the writer and his art.

125

Borges, Jorge Luis. *Dreamtigers.* Translated by Mildred Vinson Boyer and Harold

Morland. Pref. by Victor Lange. Introd. by Miguel Enguídanos. New York, Dutton, 1970. 260 p. $1.95

The confrontation of the writer's inner life with reality is the theme of this fascinating book containing Borges' poems, stories, and sketches. The original Spanish edition is entitled *El Hacedor*.

126
Borges, Jorge Luis. *Ficciones*. Edited with an introd. by Anthony Kerrigan. New York, Grove Press, 1962. 174 p. $2.45

Includes "Tlön, Uqbar," "Orbis Tertius," "El jardín de los senderos que se bifurcan," "La muerte y la brújula," and other stories.

127
Borges, Jorge Luis. *Labyrinths: selected stories & other writings*. Edited by Donald A. Yates and James E. Irby. Pref. by André Maurois. Augmented ed., New York, New Directions Pub. Corp., 1964. xxiii, 260 p. bibl. (New Directions paperbook, 186) $1.95

Contains stories, sketches, and richly inquisitive essays by a powerful thinker endowed with a subtle sense of humor. Maurois' preface skillfully analyzes Borges' literary world.

128
Borges, Jorge Luis. *In praise of darkness*. Translated by Norman Thomas di Giovanni. New York, Dutton, 1974. 144 p. $3.95

This bilingual collection of poems, written between 1967 and 1969, deals with blindness, old age, ethics, love, places around the world, James Joyce, Ricardo Güiraldes, and other literary figures. The translations are pedestrian, but the edition will be of great interest to all those studying contemporary literature.

129
Borges, Jorge Luis. *Other inquisitions; 1937-1952*. Translated by Ruth L. C. Simms. Introd. by James E. Irby. New York, Washington Square Press, 1966. 205 p. $1.95

The first English translation of *Otras Inquisiciones* (1952), a collection of graceful and outstanding essays. They analyze such leading literary figures as Cervantes, Coleridge, Whitman, Hawthorne, and Shaw and probe the paradoxes and contradictions in their writings and actions.

130
Borges, Jorge Luis. *Other inquisitions: 1937-1952*. Translated by Ruth L. C. Simms. New York, Simon and Schuster, 1971. 205 p. $1.95

These outstanding essays range in time and place from Omar Khayyám to Joseph Conrad. Also see review above.

131
Borges, Jorge Luis. *A personal anthology*. Edited and with a foreword by Anthony Kerrigan. New York, Grove Press, 1969. x, 210 p. $2.45

Antología personal (1961) contains the author's own choice of his favorite stories, essays, poetry, and parables. Included are the following short stories: "The Aleph," "Death and the compass," "Funes, the Memorius," and "A new refutation of time." These stories by Borges have no equal in Spanish-American literature.

132
Boudreau, Eugene. *Trails of the Sierra Madre*. Santa Barbara, Calif., Capra Press, 1973. 77 p. illus., maps. $3.75

Introduces the reader to the relatively isolated region of northwest Mexico, where the author, a geologist, did extensive fieldwork. Lists esssential Spanish, Tarahumara, and English words, together with helpful maps for traveling through the region.

133

Bourne, Edward Gaylord. *Spain in America, 1450-1580.* With new introd. and supplementary bibliography by Benjamin Keen. New York, Barnes and Noble, 1962. 366 p. illus. (American nation series v. 3) $2.25

Published originally in 1904, this is an excellent source for the early colonial period. A detailed index and bibliography have been added to this edition.

134

Bourne, Richard. *Political leaders of Latin America: Che Guevara; Alfredo Stroessner; Eduardo Frei Montalva; Juscelino Kubitschek; Carlos Lacerda; Eva Perón.* Harmondsworth, England, Penguin, 1969. 306 p. (Political leaders of the twentieth century) $1.65

Analyzes the careers and personalities of leaders who have played major roles in shaping contemporary Latin American history. Includes a bibliography.

135

Boxer, Charles Ralph. *The golden age of Brazil: 1695-1750; growing pains of a colonial society.* Berkeley, University of California Press, 1962. 443 p. illus. $2.45

A highly literate and useful presentation of Brazil's most interesting colonial decades. Although not comprehensive, it is a thorough work by a well-known Brazilianist. Included are appendixes on economic, social, and political materials.

136

Boyd, Maurice. *Tarascan myths and legends; a rich and imaginative history of the Tarascans.* Fort Worth, Texas Christian University Press, 1969. xviii, 82 p. illus., maps. (Texas Christian University monographs in history and culture, no. 4) $3.50

Starts with the pre-Columbian period during which the Tarascans of western Mexico were building a powerful empire. The Spanish conquest provided a source for new legends, many of them based on the Tarascans' hatred of the Aztecs and Spaniards. The legends recorded provide a useful source of oral history. Tarascan design motifs illustrate the legends.

137

Brand, Donald Dilworth. *Mexico; land of sunshine and shadow.* Princeton, N.J., Van Nostrand, 1966. 159 p. illus., maps. (Van Nostrand searchlight books, 31) $2.95

This is an attractive book describing Mexico as an interesting place to visit.

138

Brand, Willem. *Impressions of Haiti.* New York, Humanities Press, 1968. 77 p. maps. $2.75

The author was a member of an OAS mission to Haiti concerned with demography in 1962. This essay deals with his major interest: the size, distribution, and economic activity of Haiti's population. Also touches on education, housing, and other social topics. [Charles Fleener]

139

Brau, Maria M. *Island in the crossroads; the history of Puerto Rico.* Illustrated by Herbert Steinberg. 1st ed. New York, Doubleday, 1968. 116 p. illus., map. (Zenith books) $1.45

A general history of Puerto Rico, with attractive illustrations.

140

Bravo, Douglas. *Douglas Bravo speaks; interview with the Venezuelan guerrilla leader.* New York, Pathfinder Press, 1973. 94 p. $.50

One of the most influential Venezuelan guerrilla leaders expounds on his theory of revolution.

141

Bravo, Enrique, comp. *An annotated, selected Puerto Rican bibliography,* compiled and annotated by Enrique Bravo. Translated by Marcial Cuevas. New York, The Urban Center, Columbia University, 1972. 114 p. $5

This useful bilingual bibliography contains 338 annotated entries of those works considered to be classics as well as those most relevant to the Puerto Rican experience. It is intended for Puerto Ricans, as well as for students seeking to work in the field of Puerto Rican studies. A very important contribution.

142

Briggs, Vernon M. *Chicanos and rural poverty.* Baltimore, Johns Hopkins University Press, 1973. 88 p. (Policy studies in employment and welfare, 16) $1.95

Analyzes the plight of rural Mexican-Americans in five southwestern states, many of whom migrated to the U.S. to perform in the agricultural sector. Their work has not improved their socioeconomic conditions. The author succinctly documents the main problems.

143

Brisk, William J. *The dilemma of a ministate: Anguilla.* Columbia, Institute of International Studies, University of South Carolina, 1969. x, 93 p. (Studies in international affairs, no. 7) $4

Anguilla in the British West Indies is three miles wide and 16 miles long, with a population of 5,500. Its thrust for independence is examined in this brief study. Includes bibliographical references.

144

Brotherston, Gordon, and Mario Vargas Llosa, comps. *Seven stories from Spanish-America.* Selected and introduced by Gordon Brotherston and Mario Vargas Llosa. New York, Pergamon Press, 1968. 98 p. (The commonwealth and international library) $2.50

The most influential contemporary writers have been included in this anthology, among them: Gabriel García Márquez, Julio Cortázar, Juan Rulfo, Mario Benedetti, Alejo Carpentier, and others. Excellent introductions precede each story.

145

Brotherston, Gordon, ed. *Spanish-American modernista poets; a critical anthology.* Selected, with an introd. by Gordon Brotherston. New York, Pergamon Press, 1968. xv, 171 p. (Pergamon Oxford Latin American series) $3

At the end of the 19th century modernismo initiated the contemporary period in Spanish-American literature, superseding romanticism. The most representative modernist poets have been included here.

146

Brower, Kenneth, ed. *Galápagos; the flow of wilderness.* Photos. by Eliot Porter. Introd. by Loren Eiseley. Foreword by David Brower. New York, Ballantine, 1971. 2 v. 138 illus., maps. (Sierra Club exhibit format series, 19-20) $3.95 each

The text includes excerpts from Charles Darwin, Herman Melville, and others. It also analyzes what the islands mean to the world's ecosystems and to the natural sciences. Beautiful illustrations enhance the text.

147

Brunetti, Cosimo. *Cosimo Brunetti: three relations of the West Indies, 1659-1660,* [edited by] Susan Heller Anderson. Philadelphia, American Philosophical Society, 1969. 49 p. maps. (Transactions of the American Philosophical Society, new ser., v. 59, pt. 6) $3

> The accounts presented here, in print for the first time, can be found in the Biblioteca Nazionale Centrale of Florence. Brunetti was a literate, well-traveled Sienese cleric, who was asked by the Duchesse de Chevreuse to explore the possibility of moving the convent of Port Royal, France, to the Caribbean, outside the legal jurisdiction of France.

148

Brunnschweiler, Tamar. *Current periodicals; a select bibliography in the area of Latin American studies.* East Lansing, Michigan State University Press, 1968. 100 p. $2

> Based on the Michigan State University Library's holdings, this bibliography includes agriculture, science and technology, applied sciences, as well as humanities and social sciences. Included are 740 unannotated entries and an index classifying materials by countries.

149

Brushwood, John S. *Mexico in its novel; a nation's search for identity.* Austin, University of Texas Press, 1970. xii, 292 p. (The Texas Pan American series) $2.45

> Analyzes Mexican reality as seen through the nation's novels. The author presents the Mexican novel as a cultural and historical phenomenon.

150

Bryant, Shasta M. *A selective bibliography of bibliographies of Hispanic American literature.* Washington, Organization of American States, 1966. 48 p. (OAS, 860-E-7253) $.75

> Lists bibliographies in the literary field. This is a useful acquisitions and research tool.

151

Bullock, Alice. *Living legends of the Santa Fe country.* Denver, Colo., Green Mountain Press, 1970. 144 p. illus., map. $2.45

> Outlines the history of folktales originating from Indian and Spanish American cultures. One map and 104 photographs supplement the text. Includes a select bibliography.

152

Bullrich, Francisco. *New directions in Latin American architecture.* New York, Braziller, 1969. 128 p. illus., plans. (New directions in architecture) $2.95

> A succinct study of new trends in Latin American architecture by a well-known Argentine architect. He describes the dynamic architectural milieu in Brazil, Mexico, and Argentina. Handsome black-and-white photographs enhance the text.

153

Burland, Cottie Arthur. *Gods of Mexico.* 1st American ed. New York, Putnam, 1967. xiii, 219 p. illus., maps. $1.85

> Describes the principal archeological sites which were used by the inhabitants of ancient Mexico for worship. Includes a bibliography.

154

Burma, John H., comp. *Mexican-Americans in the United States.* New York, Schenkman, 1970. xviii, 487 p. $5.95

Offers a detailed coverage of political, social, and behavioral patterns of Mexican-Americans. Several articles deal with the relations between the Mexican-Americans and other minority groups.

155
Burnett, Ben G., and Moisés Poblete Troncoso. *Rise of the Latin American labor movement.* New York, College and University Press, 1970. 179 p. $2.25

Provides a thorough review of the growth and development of labor movements in Latin America. Includes a bibliography.

156
Burns, E. Bradford, ed. *A documentary history of Brazil.* New York, Knopf, 1966. xii, 398 p. (Borzoi books on Latin America) $2.95

This is a useful collection of basic documents, sometimes marred by simplistic introductions. The documents on Dom Pedro II's "abdication" may astound many readers. Includes an excellent bibliography.

157
Burns, E. Bradford. *Latin America; a concise interpretive history.* Englewood Cliffs, N.J., Prentice-Hall, 1972. xv, 272 p. illus., maps. $4.95

This excellent survey covers the following topics: the origins of a multiracial society; the institutions of empire; independence; national consolidation; the emergence of the modern state; the past repudiated; and development, democracy, and disillusionment. Includes a bibliography on paperback literature.

157A
Burns, E. Bradford, ed. *Latin American cinema; film and history.* Los Angeles, University of California, Latin American Center, 1975. 137 p. illus. (UCLA Latin American studies, v. 26) $2.50

Three essays in this book present a methodological framework for the use of film for research and teaching. One of the essays analyzes how students regard the use of film for learning. It also includes a very useful bibliography on film sources and the Latin American cinema.

158
Burns, E. Bradford. *Nationalism in Brazil; a historical survey.* New York, Praeger, 1968. 158 p. $1.95

Defines the concept of nationalism and explains the formation of "19th century defensive nationalism." There is a good chapter on the bases of contemporary nationalism, another one entitled "Getúlio Vargas and economic nationalism," and a discussion of the impact literary figures have had on Brazilian nationalism.

159
Busey, James L. *Latin America: political institutions and processes.* New York, Random House, 1964. 184 p. map. (Studies in political science, PS-44) $2.95

A concise study of Latin American political institutions. Contains a bibliography.

160
Busey, James L. *Latin American political guide, 1972.* 14th ed. Manitou Springs, Colo., Juniper Editions, 1972. 40 p. maps. $1

This work is divided into three parts: Northern Latin America, South America, and Latin American International Relations.

161
Bush, John S. *The romantic novel in Mexico*. Columbia, The University of Missouri Studies, 1954. 98 p. illus., ports. $2.50

Examines the development of the Mexican novel from historical and literary points of view. The very complete annotated bibliography in the second part of the book contains handsome engravings of the authors.

162
Bushnell, David. *Eduardo Santos and the Good Neighbor; 1938-1942*. Gainesville, University of Florida Press, 1967. 128 p. tables. (Latin American monographs, second series, no. 4) $3.75

In-depth study of Colombian-U.S. relations during the administration of Eduardo Santos. It is largely a discussion of political, military, and economic contacts at the government level.

163
Bushnell, David, ed. *Liberator: Simon Bolivar; man and image*. Edited, with an introd. by David Bushnell. New York, Knopf, 1970. xxxiv, 218 p. map, port. (Borzoi books on Latin America) $2.95

Designed to serve as a ready reference and teaching aid, this work presents a selection from Bolívar's major writings and a sampling from the literature written about him. The selections offer a good range of interpretations.

164
Bushnell, Geoffrey H. S. *Ancient arts of the Americas*. New York, Praeger, 1965. 287 p. illus. (part col.), maps. (Praeger world of art series) $3.95

Presents a thorough outline of pre-Columbian art, enhanced by attractive illustrations. Includes a good bibliography. This is a basic course for art and ethnohistory.

165
Bushnell, Geoffrey H. S. *The first Americans; the pre-Columbian civilizations*. New York, McGraw-Hill, 1968. 144 p. illus. (part col.) (Library of the early civilizations) $2.95

This handsome volume on the pre-Columbian civilizations of America describes the significant stages of the beginning, growth, and apex of the different cultures. The illustrations are very good. Includes a bibliography.

166
Bushnell, Geoffrey H. S. *Peru*. Rev. ed. New York, Praeger, 1963. 246 p. illus., maps. (Ancient peoples and places) $3.95

The author intended this excellent and detailed summary of Peruvian archeology for the general reader as well as the scholar. Includes a good bibliography.

167
Butterfield, Marvin E. *Jerónimo de Aguilar, conquistador*. University, University of Alabama Press, 1969. 54 p. (University of Alabama studies, no. 10) $2.50

This is a brief biography of one of the conquistadors who accompanied Hernán Cortés in the conquest of Mexico. He served as a key figure on the interpreting and intelligence team composed of Doña Marina, Cortés, and Jerónimo. Includes a bibliography.

168
Caballero Calderón, Eduardo. *Ancha es Castilla*. Edited by Louis C. Perez and Leon F. Lyday. New York, Van Nostrand Reinhold, 1971. xiii, 323 p. illus. $4.95

First published in 1950, this is an interpretive essay on the significance of Castile as a cultural entity within Hispanic civilization by the noted Colombian novelist and essayist. This textbook edition is designed for more advanced Spanish courses.

169

Caballero Calderón, Eduardo. *El Cristo de espaldas*. Edited by Roberto Esquenazi-Mayo and Carmen Esquenazi-Mayo. New York, Macmillan, 1967. 153 p. (Macmillan modern Spanish-American literature series) $2.50

Written by the Colombian novelist Caballero Calderón in 1952, this is a powerful novel about a recently ordained young priest who begins to work in a small town parish in the Andes. He promptly realizes the infamy, injustice, and violence that the people suffer. Contains notes and vocabularies.

170

Cabrera, Ysidro Arturo. *Emerging faces; the Mexican-Americans*. Dubuque, Iowa, W. C. Brown Publishers, 1971. 99 p. $2.25

Presents a brief analysis of selected issues affecting Mexican Americans such as their treatment in literature, health, housing, political awareness, cultural identity, and religious crisis or the growing disenchantment of young militant Chicanos with the institutional church. Includes a bibliography.

171

Calderón de la Barca, Frances. *Life in Mexico; the letters of Fanny Calderón de la Barca*, with new material from the author's private journals. Edited and annotated by Howard T. Fisher and Marion Hall Fischer. Garden City, N.Y., Doubleday, 1969. xxix, 834 p. illus., maps., ports. $6.95

Contains letters written from 1838 to 1842 by the English wife of Angel Calderón de la Barca, Spanish ambassador to Havana and later to Mexico. This is a witty and delightful book by a keen observer, originally published in 1843.

172

California. University. Los Angeles. *Democratic revolution in the West Indies; studies in nationalism, leadership, and the belief in progress*. Edited by Wendell Bell and others. With a foreword by Vernon L. Arnett. Cambridge, Mass., Schenkman Pub. Co., 1969. xxiii, 232 p. (International studies in political and social change) $3.95

This is an incisive study of democratic movements in the West Indies. Contains bibliographic footnotes.

173

California. University. Los Angeles. *Statistical abstract of Latin America*. Los Angeles, University of California, Latin American Center, 1955- . (annual) tables. $10

This is an excellent source for comparative statistical data on Latin America. It also includes a good bibliography of statistical sources. As of 1975 the latest edition is 1970.

174

Calvert, Peter. *Latin America: internal conflict and international peace*. New York, St. Martin's Press, 1969. xvi, 231 p. maps. (The making of the twentieth century) $2.95

Presents a chronological outline of political and diplomatic developments in Latin America up to the mid 1960's. Contains a select bibliography. [Charles Fleener]

175

Campbell, Camilla. *Viva la patria*. Illustrated by Nilo Santiago. New York, Hill & Wang; distributed by Random House, 1970. 57 p. illus. (A challenger book. La Raza series) $1

Contains brief readings on the Chicano experience in the United States.

176

Cancian, Frank. *Economics and prestige in a Maya community; the religious cargo system in a Maya community; the religious cargo system in Zinacantán.* Stanford, Calif., Stanford University Press, 1969. xv, 238 p. illus., maps., ports. $2.95

Examines the religious hierarchy of an Indian municipio in the highland Maya area of southern Mexico. The cargo system provides one of the keys to the understanding of the social, religious, and economic systems of these communities. Includes a selective bibliography.

177

Cantón, Wilbert L. *Nosotros somos Dios: pieza en dos actos,* by William Cantón. Edited by Samuel Trifilo and Louis Soto-Ruiz. New York, Harper & Row, 1966. x, 158 p. $3.25

An annotated version of this outstanding Mexican playwright's drama. Contains notes and vocabularies.

178

Caracciolo-Trejo, Enrique, comp. *Penguin book of Latin American verse;* introduced by Henry Gifford; with plain prose translations by Tom Raworth and others. Harmondsworth, England, Penguin Books, 1971. xiv, 425 p. (The Penguin poets) $2.95

The introduction places Latin America in perspective. This anthology presents a representative selection of Latin American poetry, chiefly of the 19th and 20th centuries.

179

Carballido, Emilio. *Medusa; obra en cinco actos.* Edited by Jeanine Gaucher-Schultz, and Alfredo Morales. Englewood Cliffs, N.J., Prentice-Hall, 1972. 183 p. port. $3.95

This textbook edition of the modern Mexican play is intended for the intermediate Spanish student and is complete with questions, vocabulary, and a critical bibliography.

180

Cardenal, Ernesto. *Homage to the American Indians.* Translated by Monique and Carlos Altschul. Baltimore, John Hopkins Press, 1973. 116 p. illus. $2.50

This is an attractive presentation of the Nicaraguan Trappist monk's poems of lost Amerindian civilizations. Cardenal's lean, clear poetry is translated in free verse form and comes across as eloquent and rich.

181

Cardenal, Ernesto. *In Cuba.* Translated by Donald D. Walsh. Philadelphia, Lippincott, 1974. 300 p. $3.95

Contains impressions of Cuba by a noted contemporary Nicaraguan poet.

182

Cardenas, Leo. *Return to Ramos.* Illustrated by Nilo Santiago. New York, Hill and Wang, 1970. 54 p. illus. (A Challenger book. La raza series) $1

The Challenger Book Series contains original stories written with special sensitivity to the needs of Chicano or black groups in the U.S. This work deals with a western Texas farm laborer and his family.

183

The Cardinal points of Borges. Edited by Lowell Dunham and Ivar Ivask. Norman,

University of Oklahoma Press, 1971. 113 p. illus. $2.95

Contains scholarly papers presented by Borges specialists at the International Symposium on Borges held at the University of Oklahoma in 1969. Some of the contributors were among the earliest of the Borges scholars and others were close friends and associates. Includes bibliographies.

184
Carpentier, Alejo. *The kingdom of this world.* Translated by Harriet de Onís. New York, Macmillan, 1971. 150 p. $1.50

Describes Haiti through its time of revolt. Ti Noël, slave of a wealthy planter, is the central figure. Carpentier creates a brilliant world which has the stylized reality of the great myths. The original Spanish is entitled *El reino de este mundo* (1949), and the English translation was first published in 1975.

185
Carrillo-Beron, Carmen. *A comparison of Chicano and Anglo women.* San Francisco, R. and E. Research Associates, 1974. 121 p. $8

Deals with family structure, authoritarianism, achievement, alienation, socioeconomic background, and psychology. This pioneering comparative study also contains tables and bibliographical references. Originally presented as a thesis in 1971.

186
Carter, E. Dale, comp. *Anología del realismo mágico; ocho cuentos hispanoamericanos.* Edited by E. Dale Carter, Jr. New York, Odyssey Press, 1970. xv, 176 p. $2.50

This college textbook edition of short stories contains works by S. Ocampo, J. J. Arreola, J. Rulfo, A. Bioy Casares, J. Cortázar, J. L. Borges, E. Anderson-Imbert, and A. Carpentier. They represent the masters of the Spanish American short story. Includes notes and vocabulary.

187
Carter, E. Dale, and Joe Bas, comps. *Cuentos argentinos de misterio.* New York, Appleton-Century-Crofts, 1968. 112 p. $1.95

A textbook edition of Argentine mystery stories by Silvina Ocampo, Manuel Peyrou, W. I. Isen, Rodolfo Walsh, E. Anderson-Imbert, and J. L. Borges. Includes bio-bibliographic sketches of each author.

188
Carter, William E. *Aymara communities and the Bolivian agrarian reform.* Gainesville, University of Florida Press, 1964. 90 p. (University of Florida monographs. Social sciences, no. 24, fall 1964) $2

Examines Bolivia's agrarian reform program as it affects the Aymaras. The family and social structure of the Aymara communities receive special attention. This is a very useful analysis, enhanced by an excellent bibliography.

189
Carter, William E. *New lands and old traditions: Kekchi cultivators in the Guatemalan lowlands.* Gainesville, University of Florida Press, 1969. 153 p. illus., maps. (Center for Latin American Studies, University of Florida. Latin American monographs, 2d ser., no. 6) $3.75

Studies certain agricultural practices such as shifting cultivation in the lowlands of Guatemala. Includes a bibliography.

190
Carmichael, Elizabeth M. *Turquoise mosaics from Mexico.* New York, Columbia

University Press, 1973. 41 p. illus. (some col.), maps, port. $1.50

Examines and gives background information on the nine turquoise mosaics from Mexico in the British Museum, possibly the first examples of Mexican art seen in Europe. Includes bibliographies and numerous references to codices.

191
Carter, Hodding. *Doomed road of empire; the Spanish trail of conquest,* by Hodding Carter, with Betty W. Carter. Illus. by Don Almquist. New York, McGraw-Hill, 1963. 408 p. illus., map (on lining paper) (The American trails series) $3.50

This attractively illustrated book recounts the Spanish conquest and settlement in the southwestern part of the U.S. Based on primary and secondary sources, this work is of interest to libraries.

192
Cartey, Wilfred G. *Black images.* New York, Teachers College Press, 1970. xiv, 186 p. (Publications for the Center for Education in Latin America, Institute of International Studies) $3.95

Surveys black Antillean poetry through historical, cultural, and political discussions and by presenting numerous examples. Many of the pieces included here appear in English for the first time.

193
Carvalho Neto, Paulo de. *Diccionario del folklore ecuatoriano.* New York, Humanities Press, 1973. 488 p. illus., maps. *(His* Tratado del folklore ecuatoriano, 1) $14.50

This is a selective bibliography of Ecuadorian folklore, of great interest to people interested in this field. Includes a good bibliography.

193A
Casas, Bartolomé de las. *The devastation of the Indies.* Introd. by Hans Magnus Enzensberger. New York, Seabury Continuum Books, 1974. 128 p. illus., maps. $3.95

Presents a translation of *Destrucción de las Indias, o sea su conquista,* first published in 1552, accompanied by an introduction and notes which place this account of the Spanish conquest within historical perspective.

194
Casas, Bartolomé de las. *History of the Indies.* Translated and edited by André Collard. New York, Harper & Row, 1971. xxvi, 302 p. (European perspective. Harper Torchbooks, TB-1540) $3.25

This is based on the first edition, which in turn was based on the signed original manuscript. The translator has selected here those chapters most representative of the broad spectrum of the 16th-century friar's interests. This is an epoch-making and controversial work about the Spanish conquest of the Americas.

195
Casas, Bartolomé de las. *The tears of the Indians. The life of Las Casas,* by Sir Arthur Phelps. Introd. by Lewis Hanke. Williamstown, Mass., J. Lilburne, 1970. xviii, 292 p. $2

According to the author *The Tears of the Indians* was intended to shock his contemporaries. It is ironic that the writings of this Spanish friar were published in many lands to arouse hostility against Spain for many centuries.

196
Casaus, Víctor, and others. *Somos; We are.* Five contemporary Cuban poets. Edited by Anita Whitney. Washington, N.J., Times Change Press, 1974. 98 p. $2

Presents selections from the poetry of five new Cuban poets in a bilingual edition.

197

Castañeda, Carlos. *A separate reality; further conversations with Don Juan.* New York, Pocket Books, 1973. 312 p. $1.25

Describes the religion and mythology of the Yaqui Indians, based on conversations with Don Juan, the Yaqui sorcerer.

198

Castañeda, Carlos. *The teachings of Don Juan; a Yaqui way of knowledge.* New York, Ballantine Books, 1969. 195 p. $.95

An account and analysis of the author's apprenticeship to a Yaqui sorcerer in Arizona and Sonora (1961-65). Interesting points are the rigorous discipline during the preparation and use of hallucinogenic plants and the extraordinary force and leadership displayed by Don Juan. The author explains the cohesion and logic of the Yaquis' world view.

199

Castañeda Schular, Antonia, Tomás Ybarra Fausto, and Joseph Sommers, comps. *Literatura Chicana: texto y contexto. Chicano literature: text and context.* Compiled by Antonia Castañeda, Tomás Ybarra Fausto, and Joseph Sommers. Englewood Cliffs, N.J., Prentice-Hall, 1972. xvii, 368 p. illus. $3.95

These readings trace Chicano culture to its dual beginnings: Mexican and U.S. heritage and the Mexican-American War of 1846-48, which serves as a historical point of departure for Chicano literature. Many selections represent Chicano literature of the 1960's and 1970's.

200

Castedo, Leopoldo. *A history of Latin American art and architecture from pre-Columbian times to the present.* Translated and edited by Phyllis Freeman. New York, Praeger, 1969. 320 p. illus., maps, ports. (Praeger world of art series) $4.95

Traces over 3,000 years of Latin American art and architecture, emphasizing the fusion of Indian, African, and European elements which formed a unique style. Many illustrations enhance the text. Includes bibliographies.

201

Castillo, Homero, ed. *Antología de poetas modernistas hispanoamericanos.* Waltham, Mass., Blaisdell Pub. Co., 1966. xxi, 505 p. (A Blaisdell book in modern languages) $7.50

Each author studied in this anthology is introduced by several paragraphs of literary commentary, followed by a list of the author's principal works and studies about him. José Martí, Rubén Darío, Ricardo Jaime Freyre, and others are included. Contains a bibliography.

202

Castillo, Homero, and Audrey G. Castillo, eds. *3 [i.e., Tres] novelas cortas, 3 piezas teatrales.* New York, Holt, Rinehart and Winston, 1970. 243, xliv p. (Literatura hispanoamericana del siglo xx) $5.95

Includes short stories by Eduardo Barrios, Horacio Quiroga, and Carlos Fuentes. The playwrights represented are Florencio Sánchez, Emilio Carballido, Sergio Vodanović. Biographical sketches of the authors, notes, and vocabulary enhance this valuable work.

203

Castro, Fidel. *Castro speaks on unemployment.* New York, Pioneer Publications, 1967. 30 p. $.25

This is the text of Castro's speech on employment and working goals within a Socialist context.

204

Castro, Fidel. *Fidel Castro denounces bureaucracy and sectarianism; speech of March 26, 1962.* Pref. by H. Ring. New York, Pioneer Publications, 1967. 39 p. $.50

205

Castro, Fidel. *Fidel Castro speaks.* Edited by Martin Kenner and James Petras. New York, Grove Press, 1970. xvii, 299 p. $1.45

The editors have arranged Castro's speeches in a topical rather than a chronological sequence. They concentrate on the 1966-68 period when Castro became increasingly concerned with armed struggle, revolution, and the vision of a Communist society organized without a need for money. Includes a bibliography.

206

Castro, Fidel. *Fidel Castro's tribute to Che Guevara.* New York, Pioneer Publishers, 1969. 31 p. $.25

This is the text of Castro's speech eulogizing his old friend and corevolutionary.

207

Castro, Fidel. *Fidel in Chile; a symbolic meeting between two historical processes.* Selected speeches of Major Fidel Castro during his visit to Chile, November 1971. New York, International Publishers, 1972. 234 p. $2.65

Includes 15 speeches by Fidel Castro during his visit to Chile in 1971, as well as the Cuban-Chilean Joint Communiqué. The texts are based on the official Cuban transcripts, and not all the speeches are included.

208

Castro, Fidel. *History will absolve me.* Introduction by K.S. Karol. New York, Grossman, 1968. 109 p. $1.50

On October 16, 1953, Castro delivered this speech in "self defense and explanation" for his involvement in the July 26, 1953, attack on the Moncada Barracks of Santiago, Cuba. He presents a fiery indictment of Batista's regime and outlines a program for reforms in Cuba.

209

Castro, Fidel. *A new stage in the advance of Cuban socialism.* New York, Pioneer Publishers, 1968. 48 p. $.50

An official Cuban translation of a speech delivered by Castro on April 19, 1968, commemorating the seventh anniversary of the Bay of the Pigs (Playa Girón) invasion. [Charles Fleener]

210

Castro, Fidel. *Reform or revolution.* New York, Pioneer Publishers, 1970. 31 p. $.50

Castro talks about the issue of reform versus revolution as ways of changing existing social and political patterns in Latin America.

211

Castro, Fidel. *The revolution must be a school of unfettered thought.* New York, Pioneer Publishers, 1963. $.25

English translation of a speech given at the University of Havana, March 13, 1962.

212

Castro, Fidel. *Revolutionary struggle, 1947-1958.* Edited and with introd. by Rolando E. Bonachea and Nelson P. Valdés. Cambridge, Mass., MIT Press, 1972. xx, 471 p. illus. (Selected works of Fidel Castro, v. 1) $3.95

The editors have made a very good selection from Castro's vast writings before he took power. The introduction presents a succinct political history of that period. Contains a bibliography and an annotated bibliography of Castro's works. An important contribution.

213

Castro, Fidel. *Second declaration of Havana.* New York, Pioneer Publications, 1962. 33 p. $.35

English translation of a speech given on February 4, 1962, in reply to the Punta del Este decision to exclude the Castro regime from the Organization of American States.

214

Castro, Fidel. *Those who are not revolutionary fighters cannot be called Communists.* New York, Pioneer Publishers, 1968. 72 p. $.75

English translation of a speech delivered at the University of Havana, March 13, 1967. Among Castro's targets are the conventional Communist parties of Latin America and the "evolutionary" policies of the Soviet Union. [Charles Fleener]

215

Castro, Josué de. *The black book of hunger.* Translated by Charles Lam Markmann. Boston, Beacon Press, 1967. xiii, 161 p. illus. $1.95

Translation of *O livro negro de fome,* a thoughtful description of poverty and hunger in Brazil and in other underdeveloped areas of the world.

216

Castro, Josué de. *Death in the Northeast; poverty and revolution in the Northeast of Brazil.* New York, Random House, 1966. 206 p. $1.95

The problem of land use and land ownership is the focus of a short and powerful book. Dr. Castro, a leading Brazilian man of public affairs, does not pretend to be objective; as a nordestino he has a specific view to state. The original title is *Sete palmos de terra e un caixão* (1965). [HLAS 29:6413]

217

Catlin, Stanton Loomis, and Terence Grieder. *The art of Latin America since independence.* New York, October House, 1965. xiv, 246 p. illus., 118 plates (part col.) $8.50

The authors present an attractively illustrated history of Latin American art since independence.

218

Cesaire, Aimée. *The tragedy of King Christophe;* a play translated from the French by Ralph Manheim. New York, Grove Press, 1970. 96 p. (Evergreen original, E547) $1.95

Aimée Cesaire, the celebrated black poet from Martinique, wrote this epic of independence of a colony and psychological profile of Henri Christophe, the ex-slave and cook, who at the beginning of the 19th century became king of Haiti.

219

Céspedes, Guillermo. *Latin America; the early years.* New York, Knopf, 1974. 197 p. (Borzoi books on Latin America) $3.25

Contains essays on colonial and 19th-century Latin America by a well-known Spanish colonialist. Includes a bibliography.

220

Chafee, Wilber A., comp. *Dissertations on Latin America by U.S. historians, 1960-1970.* Austin, Institute of Latin American Studies, University of Texas, 1973. $2.50

Contains a listing of dissertations on Latin America prepared in the U.S.

221

Chase, Gilbert. *A guide to the music of Latin America.* 2d ed. rev. and enl. A joint publication of the Pan American Union and the Library of Congress. Washington, Pan American Union, 1962. 411 p. $1.50

This is a very useful bibliography, first published in 1945 under the title *Guide to Latin American music.* The present edition has been enlarged and brought up to date.

222

Chevalier, Francois. *Land and society in colonial Mexico; the great hacienda.* Translated by Alvin Eustis. Edited, with a foreword by Lesley Bird Simpson. Berkeley, University of California Press, 1970. 334 p. illus., maps (1 col.) $2.65

The central theme of this important work, which first appeared in 1952 as *La formation des grands domains au Méxique,* is the evolution of a landed aristocracy at a time when little progress was made in any other aspect of colonial life. Unfortunately, editing has deleted voluminous and relevant footnotes. Includes a bibliography.

223

Chilcote, Ronald H., and Joel C. Edelstein, eds. *Latin America: the struggle with dependency and beyond.* Cambridge, Mass., Schenkman Pub. Co., 1974. 781 p. maps. (A Halstead Press book) $4.95

Contains papers and essays on political and economic problems in Latin America, especially concerning the dependency of developing countries. Contains a significant bibliography.

224

Chiñas, Beverly. *The Isthmus Zapotecs; women's roles in cultural context.* New York, Holt, Rinehart and Winston, 1974. 122 p. illus. $3

A sociologist studies the role of Zapotec women in Mexico. Contains case studies and bibliographical footnotes. An important contribution.

225

Chommie, John, et al., eds. *El derecho de los Estados Unidos.* New York, Oceana Publications, 1963. 3 v. $15

This is a compendium of U.S. laws intended for Spanish speakers.

226

Cisneros, Antonio. *The spider hangs too far from the ground;* translated from the Spanish by Maureen Ahern, William Rowe, and David Tipton. New York, Grossman, 1973. 69 p. $2.95

The poems in this selection were taken from *Comentarios reales* and *Canto ceremonial contra un oso hormiguero.* The poems appear only in English translation.

227

Clark, Margaret. *Health in the Mexican-American culture; a community study.* 2d ed.

Berkeley, University of California Press, 1970. xiv, 253 p. illus., map. $2.45

The author describes every aspect of life in the Mexican-American community. The study is geared to those interested in community life, and the medical perspective is both enlightening and much needed. Includes bibliographies.

228
Cleaves, Peter S. *Developmental processes in Chilean local government*. Berkeley, Institute of International Studies, University of California, 1969. 63 p. (Politics of modern nations series, no. 8) $1.50

Studies the relationship between national and local government in Chile. The reform objectives of the Christian Democratic administration of President Eduardo Frei are also analyzed.

229
Cline, Howard Francis. *Mexico, revolution to evolution, 1940-1960*. New York, Oxford University Press, 1963. x, 374 p. maps, tables. $1.95

Describes the character, strength, and structure of the Mexican labor movement. It points out that the labor movement is a product of the revolution and is deeply interwoven with its goals. As a co-partner in the revolution, the labor movement must necessarily accept limitations upon its claims for increased benefits with the government acting as final arbiter between labor and management. Contains an excellent bibliography.

230
Cline, Howard Francis. *The United States and Mexico*. Rev. ed. enl. New York, Atheneum, 1963. 484 p. maps (part fold.) (Atheneum paperbacks, 40) $2.45

An especially important book on Mexico since 1910. Stresses the need to study Mexico from the point of view of the population, regionalism, and industrialization rather than the traditional national political interpretation. The chapters on the revolution and the period since 1934 are outstanding. Originally published in 1953, this edition includes a new preface, an epilogue entitled "A decade of developments, 1952-1962," and a bibliography brought up to date.

231
Clissold, Stephen. *Latin America; a cultural outline*. New York, Harper & Row, 1966. 160 p. (Harper colophon books, CN587H) $1.60

Interprets the literature and thought of Latin America from the colonial period to the present. Includes a bibliography.

232
Cochard, Charles E., and James W. Hardiman. *A Hammond guide to Mexico*. Maplewood, N.J., Hammond, 1971. 128 p. illus., maps. $1.95

An attractive, compact guide to Mexico, full of helpful hints for the traveler. Hotels, restaurants, and other facilities have been rated.

233
Cochran, Thomas Childs, and Ruben E. Reina. *Entrepreneurship in Argentine culture: Torcuato di Tella and S.I.A.M.* Research assistant Sue Nuttall. Philadelphia, University of Pennsylvania Press, 1962. xi, 338 p. illus. $3.95

This is a well-documented analysis of Torcuato di Tella's entrepreneurial career. The workings of the di Tella family are explored, and its pioneering spirit is put in perspective. Includes bibliographies and appendixes.

234
Cockroft, James D., and Andre G. Frank. *Dependence and development; Latin America's*

political economy. New York, Doubleday, 1973. 212 p. $2.50

>Discusses the many political facets of economic development in Latin America in light of the dependence theories.

235

Coe, Michael D. *The Maya.* New York, Praeger, 1966. 252 p. illus., maps. (Ancient peoples and places, v. 52) $3.95

>Surveys Mayan civilization, with emphasis on the achievements of the classic period. The rise, development, and fall of Mayan culture is integrated with a description of Mayan life and thought. Excellent plates and drawings illustrate the volume.

236

Coe, Michael D. *Mexico.* New York, Praeger, 1966. 245 p. illus., maps. (Ancient peoples and places, v. 29) $3.45

>Concise, well-illustrated general acount of pre-Hispanic culture history in central Mexico. Contains considerable material on late pre-Hispanic and Contact culture of the area, derived from standard primary and secondary sources. The hard cover edition was published in 1962. Includes a bibliography.

237

Cohen, John Michael, ed. *The four voyages of Christopher Columbus; being his own log-book, letters, and dispatchers with connecting narratives drawn from the life of the Admiral by his son Hernando Colón and other contemporary historians.* Edited and translated from manuscripts by J. M. Cohen. Baltimore, Penguin Books, 1969. 320 p. maps. (The Penguin classics, L-217) $1.75

>An important and fascinating account of Columbus' voyages.

238

Cohen, John Michael, ed. *Latin American writing today.* Baltimore, Penguin Books, 1967. 267 p. (The writing today series) $1.25

>A varied selection of the most outstanding contemporary Latin American writers such as Jorge Luis Borges, Alejo Carpentier, Gabriela Mistral, Julio Cortázar, Carlos Fuentes, Juan Rulfo, and others. The selection shows a vigorous, independent, and imaginative literature.

239

Cohen, John Michael, ed. *Writers in the new Cuba.* Baltimore, Penguin Books, 1967. 191 p. $1.25

>Includes 14 short stories, a short play, and 11 poems written in Cuba between 1959 and 1965. The editor has visited Cuba in 1965 and has taken part in awarding a literary prize of the Casa de las Américas.

240

Cohn, Arthur. *The collector's twentieth-century music in the Western Hemisphere.* Philadelphia, Lippincott, 1961. 256 p. (Keystone books in music, KB-23) $1.95

>Surveys contemporary music in the Americas, although a large part deals with the U.S. The works of Carlos Chávez, Alberto Ginastera, Silvestre Revueltas, and Heitor Villalobos are also included. Lists longplaying records of the composers' music.

241

Cole, Hubert. *Christophe, king of Haiti.* New York, Viking Press, 1969. 307 p. illus., maps. $2.45

A sympathetic study of the New World's first crowned king, Henry I of Haiti. The bloody wars of liberation, out of which rose an independent French-speaking black nation, serve as the backdrop for this well-researched book. It was first published in 1967.

242

Coleman, Alexander, ed. *Cinco maestros: cuentos modernos de Hispanoamérica.* Edited by Alexander Coleman, under the general editorship of Robert G. Mead, Jr. New York, Harcourt, Brace, & World, 1969. x, 318 p. $4.50

Includes short stories by Jorge Luis Borges, Julio Cortázar, Juan Rulfo, José Donoso, and Gabriel García Márquez. A very good selection.

243

Coleman, Kenneth M. *Public opinion in Mexico City about the electoral system.* Chapel Hill, University of North Carolina Press, 1972. 94 p. (James Sprunt studies in history and political science, v. 53) $4.50

This is a concise survey of public opinion based on personal interviews and questionnaires.

244

Coleman, William Jackson. *Latin American Catholicism. A self evaluation; a study of the Chimbote report.* Maryknoll, N.Y., Maryknoll Publications, 1958. 105 p. (World horizon reports, report no. 23) $1

In 1953 Inter-American Catholic Action Week was held in Chimbote, Peru, attended by representatives of most of the Catholic Action organizations of Latin America. The meeting produced a self-critique of Latin American Catholicism.

245

Colford, William Edward, ed. and tr. *Classic tales from Spanish America.* Great Neck, N.Y., Barron's Educational Series, 1962. 210 p. (Barron's library of literary masterpieces) $1.50

A collection of 21 Spanish American short stories in English translation. Selections include stories by Manuel Rojas, Ricardo Palma, Rubén Darío, Amado Nervo, Leopoldo Lugones, and others. Each story is preceded by a commentary on the author and his work.

246

Collier, John. *Indians of the Americas.* Abridged ed. New York, New American Library, 1968. 191 p. (Mentor, MP-496) $.95

The author spent 12 years as Commissioner of Indian Affairs for the U.S. Government. The history of the treatment of the American Indian is reviewed here, and a policy is outlined which is based on wide experience and a wealth of facts. The first half of the book deals with Indians of Latin America.

247

Collver, O. Andrew. *Birth rates in Latin America: new estimates of historical trends and fluctuations.* Berkeley, Institute of International Studies, University of California Press, 1969. 187 p. illus. (University of California, Berkeley. Institute of International Studies Research series, no. 7) $2.50

This is a very useful study of demographic trends in Latin America viewed from a historical perspective.

248

Colonnese, Louis M., ed. *Human rights and the liberation of man in the Americas.* Contributors: Victor Alba and others, Louis M. Colonnese, editor. Notre Dame, Ind., University of Notre Dame Press, 1970. xxvi, 278 p. illus. $3.95

LATIN AMERICA

The 21 papers included in this volume were presented at the 6th annual Catholic Inter-American Cooperation Program (CICOP) Conference held in New York, January 1969. The contributors range from Helder Pessoa Cámara, Archbishop of Recife, and Cardina Dearden of Detroit, to Robert J. Alexander and Victor Alba.

249

Columbus, Christopher. *Four voyages to the New World; letters and selected documents.* Translated and edited by R.H. Major; bilingual ed. Introd. by John E. Fagg. New York, Corinth Books, 1961. x, 240 p. (The American experience series, AE-5) $1.75

Originally published under the title *Select letters of Christopher Columbus, with other original documents relating to his four voyages to the New World* (1847). This edition contains seven new documents in English translation and in the original Spanish and Latin. There is a new introduction by John E. Fagg.

250

Comitas, Lambros, and David Lowenthal, comps. *Slaves, free men, citizens.* Garden City, N.Y., Anchor Books, 1973. xvii, 340 p. illus. (West Indian perspectives) $2.50

This collection of essays deals with Caribbean societies where class and status have been based on distinctions of color. The subjects cover the entire non-Hispanic Caribbean where societies with black majorities have emerged as free multiracial states. Almost two-thirds of the essays are by West Indians, ranging from 18th-century authors such as Edward Long and Médéric-Louis-Elie Moreau Saint-Méry to present-day analysts Orlando Patterson, Douglas Hall, Leo A. Despres, and others. An important contribution to the field of Caribbean studies.

251

Comitas, Lambros, and David Lowenthal, comps. *Work and family life.* Edited and introduced by Lambros Comitas and David Lowenthal. Garden City, N.Y., Anchor Press, 1973. xvii, 422 p. (West Indian perspectives) $2.95

Describes work and family life in the West Indies. The compilers have collected articles by outstanding West Indian and other authors and observers of Caribbean societal structure. A very important work, of interest to the specialist as well as the generalist.

252

Committee for Economic Development. *Economic development issues: Latin America,* by Roberto Alemann and others. New York, 1967. xii, 340 p. illus. (Committee for Economic Development. Supplementary paper no. 21) $4.25

Analyzes in a clear and factual style basic issues of economic development. Includes bibliographic notes.

253

Committee for Economic Development. *Economic development of Central America; a statement on national policy,* by the Research and Policy Committee of the Committee for Economic Development. New York, 1964. 123 p. $1.25

This is a bilingual study of economic development in the Central American countries.

254

Concheff, B., ed. *Pan-Americana: a pageant of the Americas.* Skokie, Ill., National Textbook Corp., 1969. 120 p. $2; 5 or more, $1.60 each

Descriptive essays on the countries of the Americas and their social customs.

255

Conrad, Robert. *The destruction of Brazilian slavery; 1850-1888.* Berkeley, University of

California Press, 1972. xviii, 344 p. illus. $4.25

The suppression of the African slave trade in the early 1850's and the emancipation of children born of slave women in 1871 had the effect of extinguishing slavery in Brazil. The author analyzes the abolitionist movement, the economic basis of slavery, and the political attitudes of abolitionists and slaveholders. An important contribution. Contains a bibliography.

256

Considine, John Joseph, ed. *The religious dimension in the new Latin America.* Notre Dame, Ind., Fides, 1967, c. 1966. xviii, 238 p. (A Fides paperback textbook) $2.95

The articles are divided into three sections, "contemporary religious challenges," "activation of religious personnel," and "the new pastoral apostolate." Clerics, both North and Latin Americans, delivered 16 of the 18 papers herein reproduced. Lady Barbara Ward, however, is probably the best known contributor; her essay is entitled "Haves and have-nots—the spiritual factor."

257

Considine, John Joseph, ed. *Social revolution in the new Latin America; a Catholic appraisal.* Notre Dame, Ind., Fides, 1965. xv, 245 p. (A Fides paperback textbook, PBT-2) $2.95

Nearly half of the 18 papers deal with social problems confronting the Catholic Church in Latin America. Dictatorship, Christian Democracy, capitalism, and social movements are among the topics discussed. [Charles Fleener]

258

Contreras de Darío, Rafaela. *Short stories.* Collected, with an introd., by Evelyn Uhrhan Irving. Coral Gables, Fla., University of Miami Press, 1965. 41 p. (University of Miami Hispanic American Studies, no. 20). $2

A collection of short stories by Rubén Darío's first wife, daughter of a distinguished Salvadorean, Ávaro Contreras. She was married to Darío from 1891 until she died in 1893. She is better known under her literary pseudonym Stella and was probably the great love in Darío's tormented life. Includes a bibliography.

259

Converse, Hyla Stuntz, comp. *Raise a signal: God's action and the church's task in Latin America today.* New York, Friendship Press, 1961. 126 p. $1.75

This is a survey of progress made by several Protestant denominations in Latin America.

260

Cook, Sherburne Friend. *Erosion morphology and occupation history in western Mexico.* New York, Impress House, 1963. iii, 53 p. maps, tables. (Anthropological records, v. 17, no. 3) $2.50

The author presents a thorough and highly specialized report on western Mexico from a geoanthropological point of view. Includes a bibliography.

261

Cook, Sherburne Friend, and Woodrow Borah. *The population of the Mixteca Alta, 1520-1610.* Berkeley, University of California Press, 1961. 89 p. illus., map. (Ibero-Americana, 50) $3

A detailed revision of the comprehensive work by Sherburne Cook and Lesley B. Simpson, analyzing the population of this central area of Mexico. Contains bibliographies.

262

Coombs, Orde, comp. *Is Massa Day dead? Black moods in the Caribbean.* Introd. by Orde

Coombs. Garden City, N.Y., Doubleday, 1974. 260 p. (Anchor books) $2.95

Contains contributions by 10 West Indian intellectuals on the black power movement in the Caribbean, among them: Edward Brathwaite, Locksley Edmondson, Derek Walcott, Gordon Rohler, and others. The contributors propose a return to African and Amerindian roots.

263
Cooper, John Montgomery. *Analytical and critical bibliography of the tribes of Tierra del Fuego and adjacent territory.* New York, Humanities Press, 1967. 233 p. maps. $8

This monograph is intended to be "a practical or working guide to the sources of Fuegian and Chonoan anthropology." The author has gathered, analyzed, and evaluated the written sources available as of 1916. The work is divided into three parts: The Introduction, the Bibliography of Authors, and the Bibliography of Subjects.

264
Copp, Nelson Gage. *"Wetbacks" and braceros; Mexican migrant laborers and American immigration policy 1930-1960.* San Francisco, R. and E. Research Association, 1971. xi, 123 p. $7

Offering a legal and socioeconomic perspective to the problem, this is an important study of the development of U.S. immigration policy. Originally presented as the author's thesis for Boston University.

265
Cordasco, Francesco. *Puerto Ricans on the United States mainland; a bibliography of reports, texts, critical studies, and related materials,* by Francesco Cordasco, with Eugene Bucchioni and Diego Castellanos. Totowa, N.J., Rowman and Littlefield, 1972. xiv, 146 p. $4.95

The author has collected a wide range of readings which focus on Puerto Rican culture, the Puerto Rican family, the Puerto Rican experience on the mainland, Puerto Rican education, and Puerto Rico from the historical perspective.

266
Cortázar, Julio. *Blow-up and other stories.* Translated from the Spanish by Paul Blackburn. New York, Macmillan, 1967. 248 p. $1.50

Contains well-known short stories by one of Argentina's most gifted writers.

267
Cortázar, Julio. *End of the game, and other stories.* Translated from the Spanish by Paul Blackburn. New York, Macmillan, 1974. 277 p. $1.50

The original Spanish edition, *Final de juego,* was published in 1956. The book deals with descriptions of animal-like people and several hallucinatory episodes. The English translation first appeared in 1967.

268
Cortázar, Julio. *Hopscotch.* Translated from the Spanish by Gregory Rabassa. New York, New American Library, 1969. 564 p. $.95

English translation of *Rayuela* (1963), an important and unusual novel which describes in minute detail the aimless wanderings of a brilliant but troubled man who enters into a series of tortured and bizarre relationships with a fascinating group of people in Paris and Buenos Aires. The writer uses a multiple point of view, presenting his protagonist in both the first and the third person.

269

Cortázar, Julio. *62: a model kit.* Translated from the Spanish by Gregory Rabassa. New York, Avon, 1974. 281 p. $1.50

This is one of the new books by Cortázar in which one finds experiments with syntax, spelling, and compositions within a timeless environment.

270

Cortés, Hernando. *Conquest: dispatches of Cortés from the New World.* Introductions and commentaries by Irwin R. Blacker. Texts edited by Harry M. Rosen. Maps by Hope Blacker. 1st ed. New York, Grosset & Dunlap, 1962. 269 p. illus., maps. (Grosset's Universal library, UL145) $1.95

A handy abridged edition of the famous dispatches from Cortés to Charles V concerning the conquest of Mexico and Guatemala. Intended for the general reader.

271

Cortés, Hernando. *Five letters, 1519-1562;* translated by J. Baynard Morris, with an introd. New York, W. W. Norton 1962, xlviii, 388 p. (The Norton library, N180) $1.95

This translation was originally published in 1928. The five letters of Cortés concern the conquest of Mexico and contain excellent descriptions of Mexico as seen by the conqueror.

272

Cortés Conde, Roberto. *First stages of modernization in Latin America.* New York, Harper & Row, 1974. $2.95

Analyzes industrial and economic growth in Latin America within a historical context. This scholarly work also contains an important bibliography.

273

Cosgrove, Isobel, and Richard Jackson. *The geography of recreation.* New York, Hutchinson University Library; Distributed by Humanities Press, New York, 1972. 168 p. illus., maps. $3.25

Analyzes various areas of the world from the point of view of tourism and recreation.

274

Cossa, Robert M. *Nuestro fin de semana.* Edited by Donald A. Yates. New York, Macmillan, 1966. 92 p. (Macmillan modern Spanish American literature series) $1.95

This is an annotated version of a contemporary Argentine play.

275

Cosío Villegas, Daniel. *American extremes (Extremos de América).* Translated by Américo Paredes. Introd. by John P. Harrison. Austin, University of Texas Press, 1964. xv, 227 p. (The Texas Pan American series) $2.25

Contains "policy-directed political essays" by a noted Mexican historian, which will aid North Americans in understanding complex Latin American problems. The original Spanish edition was entitled *Extremos de América.*

275A

Cotler, Julio, and Richard R. Fagen, eds. *Latin America and the United States; the changing political realities.* Stanford, Calif., Stanford University Press, 1974. 417 p. $4.95

The papers presented here pose many provocative questions and skillfully analyze hemispheric politics, markets, and other issues. Such prominent academicians as

Osvaldo Sunkel, Luigi Einaudi, Alfred Stepan, Octavio Ianni, and others contributed. Contains bibliographical references.

276
Courlander, Harold, and Rémy Bastien. *Religions and politics in Haiti;* two essays. Washington, Institute for Cross-Cultural Research, 1966. xvi, 81 p. illus., maps. $2.95

Includes two articles "Voudoun in Haitian culture" by Harold Courlander and "Voudoun and politics in Haiti" by Rémy Bastien. They seek to explain how folk religion influences are in turn influenced by the body politic. An important contribution. [Charles Fleener]

277
Cozean, Jon D. *Latin America: 1974.* Washington, Stryker-Post, 1974. 87 p. illus., maps. (The World today series) $1.50

Survey of Latin America offering all the basic geographic and demographic information, intended for high school and junior college students. The publication is revised annually.

278
Craig, Alan K. *Geography of fishing in British Honduras and adjacent coastal waters.* Baton Rouge, Louisiana State University Press, 1966. xv, 143 p. illus., maps. (Louisiana State University studies. Coastal studies series, no. 14) $4

Analyzes aspects of the cultural geography of fishing with emphasis on historical development and contemporary practices established on islands adjacent to an extensive barrier reef. Includes a bibliography.

279
Crawford, William Rex. *A century of Latin American thought.* Rev. ed. New York, Praeger, 1966. 322 p. $2.50

A selected group of essays on prominent Latin American thinkers from such 19th-century figures as Sarmiento and Alberdi to some 20th-century thinkers such as Gálvez, Ingenieros, Freyre, Caso, Vasconcelos, and Mariátegui. It was first published in 1944. Includes a bibliography.

280
Crist, Raymond E., and C. M. Nissly. *East from the Andes; pioneer settlements in the South American heartland.* Gainesville, University of Florida Press, 1974. 166 p. illus. (University of Florida monographs; Social sciences, no. 50) $4

Studies early and later European settlements in the eastern foothills of the Andes. Relies on primary sources and contains a good bibliography.

281
Cronos, Edmund David. *Josephus Daniels in Mexico.* Madison, University of Wisconsin Press, 1960. xiii, 369 p. illus., ports., facsims. $2.95

Surveys the diplomatic mission of Josephus Daniels in Mexico (1934-41), based on extensive use of manuscript materials including the Daniels, Roosevelt, and U.S. State Department papers, and interviews, contemporary press, and published sources. Daniels is portrayed as a consistent liberal and idealist, a warm friend of Mexican social reform.

282
Cross, Cliff. *Baja California, Mexico.* Photos and most maps by the author. 1970-71 ed. North Palm Springs, Calif., 1970. 170 p. illus., maps. $3.50

Contains much useful information on traveling through Baja California, which extends 800 miles south of the border below Tijuana.

283

Cross, Cliff. *Central America; travel guide.* Maps and photos by the author. 1968-69 ed. North Palm Springs, Calif., 1969. 170 p. illus., maps. $3.50

Offers detailed information on roads, accommodations and points of interest for the motorist traveling through Central America by car. This is a very useful guide with interesting illustrations and maps.

284

Cross, Wilbur, and Farrell Cross. *A guide to unusual vacations.* New York, Hart Pub. Co., 1973. 351 p. illus. $3.95

Describes 151 highly unusual trips such as schooner voyages to the Galapagos Islands, a canoe ride in the jungles of Ecuador and Brazil, hunting for game in Spain, Colombia, or Paraguay, just to name a few of the locales pertaining to the Hispanic world. Many other trips, of course, concern other areas.

285

Crow, John Armstrong, and G. D. Crow. *Panorama de las Américas.* 4th ed. New York, Holt, Rinehart and Winston, 1972. xxxiv, 235 p. illus. $3.50

This is a general work on the geography, economy, and national development of the Latin American countries, intended for high school and college use. Includes a vocabulary.

286

Crowley, Frances G. *Garcilaso de la Vega, el Inca and his sources in Comentarios reales de los Incas.* New York, Humanities Press, 1973. 167 p. (Studies in Spanish literature, 1) $8

Originally published in the Netherlands in 1971, this work examines Garcilaso as the historian of Incan culture. He advocated that the Incas be allowed to remain in their socioeconomic system. Garcilaso was able to understand both the Spanish and the Incan points of view. Includes bibliographies.

287

Crumrine, Lynne Scoggins. *Ceremonial exchange as a mechanism in tribal integration among the Mayos of Northwest Mexico.* Tucson, University of Arizona Press, 1969. xii, 52 p. illus., maps. (Anthropological papers of the University of Arizona, no. 14) $4

Analyzes a variety of exchange relationships between Mayo churches and households and between pueblos. Includes a bibliography.

288

Cruz Victor Hernandez. *Mainland; poems.* 1st ed. New York, Random House, 1973. 83 p. $195

This is the second book of poems published by a young Puerto Rican poet who now lives in New York. He deftly combines his two cultural worlds in a lyricism full of imagery. Especially recommended for students of Caribbean literature and for those specializing in literature produced by Spanish-speaking minorities in the U.S. It is of course a must for libraries in Puerto Rican neighborhoods.

289

Cruz, Victor Hernandez. *Snaps; poems.* New York, Random House, 1973. 135 p. $1.95

The author was born in Aguas Buenas, Puerto Rico, in 1949. His family moved to New York City in 1954. He is one of the new voices in street poetry. His poems have appeared in a number of magazines and two anthologies.

290

Cuban Economic Research Project (Grupo Cubano de Investigaciones Económicas). University of Miami. *Labor conditions in Communist Cuba.* English translations prepared by Raúl M. Shelton. Coral Gables, Fla., University of Miami, 1963. 149 p. maps. $2.95

This is a study of the worker's situation before and after the 1959 revolution, pointing out the radically altered role of the businessman vis-a-vis the state. It comments also on the new regime's method of imposing a Russian brand of communism upon the Cuban people and its political activities among other nations of the hemisphere.

291

Culp, Alice Bessie. *A case study of the living conditions of thirty-five Mexican families of Los Angeles with special references to Mexican children.* San Francisco, R. and E. Research Associates, 1971. 56 p. $7

Surveys the living conditions of Mexican families in the Los Angeles area. The author supports her conclusions with numerous statistics and tables and covers every aspect of the environment.

292

Cumberland, Charles. *The constitutionalist years.* With an introd. and additional material by David C. Bailey. Austin, University of Texas Press, 1974. xx, 450 p. $4.35

This is the second of Cumberland's works on the Mexican Revolution and covers the 1913-20 period during which a new constitution was formulated. This is a valuable reference tool for an important period of Mexican history.

293

Cumberland Charles C., comp. *The meaning of the Mexican Revolution.* Edited with an introduction by Charles C. Cumberland. Boston, Heath, 1967. xvi, 110 p. (Problems in Latin American civilization) $2.25

Treats the Mexican Revolution and its effect on the economic and political way of life in Mexico. Includes a bibliography.

294

Cumberland, Charles C. *The Mexican Revolution; genesis under Madero.* Austin, University of Texas Press, 1974. 298 p. $3.75

First published in 1952, this solid contribution is a study of the Mexican Revolution against Porfirio Díaz and the Madero administration. It emphasizes the political and military phases of the Madero revolution. Includes a bibliography.

295

Cumberland, Charles C. *Mexico; the struggle for modernity.* New York, Oxford University Press, 1968. 394 p. maps. $2.50

Describes the great changes occurring in Mexico between 1940 and 1960, the period in which the country achieved lasting political stability and saw phenomenal economic growth. These achievements were the result of the social revolution which destroyed the traditional alignments, ushered in agrarian reform, and saw the rise of the labor unions. Includes a bibliography.

296

Cunha, Euclydes da. *Rebellion in the backlands,* translated from *Os Sertoẽs* by Euclydes da Cunha, with an introduction and notes by Samuel Putnam. Chicago, University of Chicago Press, 1957. 536 p. illus., maps. $2.95

This English translation first appeared in 1944. It is commonly conceded to be Brazil's greatest and best loved classic. Writing in the *New York Times Book Review*, February 6, 1944, Erico Verissimo describes it as an "... admirable translation, in itself a literary landmark, for it is more difficult to translate da Cunha into English than to render into Portuguese, for example, the rich and untamed prose of Thomas Wolfe."

297

Curren, D. J., ed. *The Chicano Faculty Development Program: a report.* Edited by D. J. Curren in consultation with Manuel Fimbres. New York, Council on Social Work Education, 1973. 134 p. $2.95

Discusses the Chicano Faculty Development Program which was initiated to develop Chicano content in existing social work curricula and to devise alternative structures. Prominent educators contributed essays to this work, which also includes appendixes.

298

Curry, Mary Margaret. *The world of Mexican cooking.* Illustrated by Betty Stiff. Los Angeles, Nash Publishing, 1971. 101 p. illus. $2.95

This charmingly illustrated cookbook contains all the traditional recipes of Mexico and helpful hints along the way.

299

Curtin, Philip D. *The Atlantic slave trade: a census.* Madison, University of Wisconsin Press, 1969. xix, 358 p. maps. $2.50

This is the first book-length qualitative analysis of the Atlantic slave trade, with extensive historical re-interpretations. An important source for those studying the history of African slavery throughout the New World.

300

Curtin, Philip D. *Two Jamaicas; the role of ideas in a tropical colony, 1830-1865.* New York, Atheneum Pubs., 1968. xii, 270 p. illus., map, ports. $2.95

This is a very thorough, objective discussion of the problems besetting Jamaica in this 35-year period. Curtin stresses the lack of ideological unity between the "two Jamaicas" that caused discord and social upheaval.

301

Darío, Rubén. *Rubén Darío: sus mejores páginas.* Edited with an introd., notes, and bibliography by Ricardo Gullón. Englewood Cliffs, N.J., Prentice-Hall, 1972. 186 p. (Modern Spanish and Latin American literature series) $3.95

A representative selection of poems by Spanish America's great modernist poet of the turn of this century. It also includes short stories, Darío's comments about some of his works, articles, and an autobiography by the poet. The introduction deftly sketches the poet's work. Includes a selected bibliography.

302

Darwin, Charles Robert. *Voyage of the Beagle.* Annotated and with an introd. by Leonard Engel. Garden City, N.Y., Doubleday, 1962. xxxi, 524 p. illus., ports. (Anchor books) $1.95

New edition of *Journal of researches into the geology and natural history of the various countries visited by H.M.S. Beagle* (1839), an interesting account by the famous British naturalist of his travels in South America.

303

Dauster, Frank N., ed. *Teatro hispanoamericano; tres piezas.* New York, Harcourt, Brace and World, 1965. 272 p. $4.95

This annotated selection of plays includes *Rosalba y los llaveros* by Emilio Carballido, a comedy; Francisco Arriví's *Vejigantes,* a play about racial conscience; and *Collacocha* by Enrique Solari Swayne, which portrays the relationship between man and his natural surroundings. Includes vocabularies.

304
Davidson, Basil. *The African slave trade; precolonial history, 1450-1850.* Boston, Little, Brown, 1964. 311 p. maps. $2.45

Primarily a history of black Africa from 1450 to 1850, this work also treats Afro-American contacts through the slave trade. The original edition was entitled *Black Mother* (1961).

305
Davis, David Brion. *The problem of slavery in Western culture.* Ithaca, N.Y., Cornell University Press, 1966. xiv, 505 p. $2.95

Winner of the 1967 Pulitzer Prize in nonfiction, this is an important contribution to intellectual and social history. It is mainly concerned with the different ways in which men have responded to slavery and demonstrates that the institution has always been a source of social and psychological tension. Includes bibliographic notes.

306
Davis, Harold Eugene, and Larman C. Wilson. *Latin American foreign policies; an analysis.* Baltimore, Johns Hopkins Press, 1975. 496 p. tables. $5.95

Includes essays by well-known historians, economists, political scientists, and other specialists, analyzing Latin American foreign policy country by country. Also studies major international problems. Includes a bibliography.

307
Davis, Harold Eugene. *Latin American social thought; the history of its development since independence;* with selected readings. 2d ed. Washington, University Press of Washington, 1967. 560 p. $6

Presents valuable biographical and bibliographical information on 38 men who have influenced social thought in Latin America. Includes bibliographic references. Of interest to libraries.

308
Davis, Harold Eugene. *Social science trends in Latin America.* Issued in cooperation with the Inter-American Bibliography and Library Association. Washington, University Press of Washington, 1960. 136 p. $2.50

Professor Davis analyzes social science trends in Latin America through the 1950's. Includes a bibliography.

309
Davis, Ralph. *The rise of the Atlantic economies.* Ithaca, N.Y., Cornell University Press, 1973. xiv, 352 p. maps. (World economic history) $5.95

Presents a historical synthesis of the economic development of Portugal, Spain, France, England, and the Netherlands and their colonies from the 14th to the end of the 18th centuries. Includes bibliographical notes.

310
Day, Arthur Grove. *Coronado's quest; the history-making adventures of the first white man to invade the Southwest.* Berkeley, University of California Press, 1966. 419 p. $2.25

A careful study of Coronado (ca. 1510-54), the first explorer to reach the present southwestern part of the U.S. The book, semipopular in style, has a few debatable or erroneous statements but is based on a thorough examination of all known evidence. Includes an extensive bibliography.

311

Debray, Régis. *The Chilean revolution; conversations with Allende.* With a postscript by Salvador Allende. 1st American ed. New York, Vintage Books, 1972. 201 p. illus. $1.95

In 1970 Allende, leader of Chile's Socialist Party, became the world's first freely elected Marxist head of state. This work includes an introduction by Debray which is a brief capsule of Chilean politics, Debray's interview with Allende, and the latter's first message to the Chilean Congress in May of 1971. Translation of *La vía chilena.*

312

Debray, Régis. *Prison writings of Régis Debray;* translated from the French by Rosemary Sheed. New York, Random House, 1973. [6], 207 p. $1.95

These are the collected essays of a French Marxist, covering the 1967-70 period which he spent in a Bolivian prison following Che Guevara's revolutionary efforts in Bolivia.

313

Debray, Régis. *Révolution in the revolution? Armed struggle and political struggle in Latin America.* Translated from the Spanish and French by Bobbye Ortiz. New York, Grove Press, 1967. 126 p. $.95

Translation of *Révolution dans la révolution: lutte armée et lutte politique en Amérique Latine* (1967) in which a French philosopher and political activist describes the Cuban revolution as different from either the Russian or the Chinese revolutions.

314

Débray, Régis. *Strategy for revolution.* Edited with an introd. by Robin Blackburn. New York, Monthly Review Press, 1970. 255 p. $2.95

The author discusses revolutionary strategy for Latin America within a Marxist context. Che Guevara's failed Bolivian venture is also analyzed.

315

De Fleur, Lois B. *Delinquency in Argentina; a study of Córdoba's youth.* Pullman, Washington State University Press, 1971. 164 p. illus., maps. $4

A cross-cultural study of delinquency based on field work which was carried out in 1962. The conclusion reached is that the Argentine poor, responsible for a large percentage of delinquency, lack contact with major social institutions of their society: stable family, church, school, and steady jobs. Includes bibliographic notes.

316

Delaney, Patrick J. *Quaternary geologic history of the coastal plain of Rio Grande do Sul, Brazil.* Baton Rouge, Louisiana State University Press, 1971. xii, 63 p. illus., maps. (Louisiana State University Studies. Coastal studies, no. 7) $2.50

A concise, scholarly study of the geological history of the coastal plain of Rio Grande, which includes excellent maps and a bibliography.

317

Delpar, Helen, ed. *The Borzoi reader in Latin American history.* Edited, with introductions by Helen Delpar. New York, Knopf, 1972. 2 v. v. 1: $3.95; v. 2: $4.50

Intended to provide an introduction to Latin American civilization emphasizing the complexity of the area. The first volume covers the colonial period to independence and the second, the 19th and 20th centuries. The selections were written by outstanding scholars, politicians, and personalities. Includes bibliographies.

318
Denevi, Marco. *Ceremonia secreta y otros cuentos.* Edited by Donald A. Yates. New York, Macmillan, 1965. 117 p. (Macmillan modern Spanish American literature series) $2.95

An anthology of short stories and microcuentos by Denevi, Carlos Martínez Moreno, Alfonso Echevarría Yañez, and others.

319
Denevi, Marco. *Rosaura a la diez.* Edited, with an introd. by Donald A. Yates. New York, Scribner's, 1964. xix, 219 p. illus., map. (Scribner's Spanish series) $3.75

Published in 1955 as the winner of the first prize in the Guillermo Kraft literary competition, this was one of the most popular Latin American novels of the early 1960's. The setting is contemporary Buenos Aires. Includes notes and a vocabulary.

320
Denton, Charles F. *Patterns of Costa Rican politics.* Boston, Allyn & Bacon, 1971. x, 113 p. (The Allyn and Bacon series in Latin American politics) $2.50

Examines Costa Rican politics since 1946, especially the political process since the revolution of 1948 with the Partido de Liberación Nacional playing a central role. The author does not document his claim that Costa Rica is "an immobilist society." Includes a bibliography.

321
Descartes, Sol Luis. *Credit institutions for local authorities in Latin America.* Hato Rey, Puerto Rico, Inter-American University, 1073. 81 p. (Inter-American University of Puerto Rico. Occasional paper) $1.50

This work was prepared for use at the United Nations Seminar on Central Services to Local Authorities in Latin America, held in Rio de Janeiro, May 1972. Includes bibliographical references.

322
Desnoes, Edmundo. *Inconsolable memories.* New York, New American Library, 1974. 128 p. $1.95

A writer attempts to piece together an existence shattered by personal loss and the relentless forces of history in the early years of Castro's Cuba. Desnoes is a distinguished Cuban intellectual who chose to remain in Cuba.

323
Dewey, John. *John Dewey's impressions of Soviet Russia and the revolutionary world: Mexico, China, Turkey.* Edited by W. W. Brickman. New York, Teachers College Press, 1964. 178 p. $2.50

Dewey analyzes the principal revolutionary upheavals of the early part of the 20th century.

324
Díaz, May N. *Tonalá; conservatism, responsibility, and authority in a Mexican town.* Berkeley, University of California Press, 1966. 234 p. illus. $2.65

Examines the effect of industrialization of an urban center (Guadalajara) upon a nearby small community (Tonalá). The author maintains that all the changes are essentially matters of stylistic shifts rather than changes revolutionizing the traditional social system of Tonalá. Includes a bibliography.

325

Díaz del Castillo, Bernal. *The conquest of New Spain.* Translated, with an introd. by John Michael Cohen. Baltimore, Penguin Books, 1963. 412 p. map. (The Penguin classics, L-123) $1.75

This is an abridged edition of Díaz del Castillo's classic account. Mr. Cohen has omitted some repetitions, modernized punctuation, and abandoned the illogical chapter divisions of the original.

326

Díaz del Castillo, Bernal. *The discovery and conquest of Mexico; 1517-1521.* Edited from the only exact copy of the original ms (and published in Mexico) by Genaro García. Translated, with an introd. and notes by A.P. Maudslay. Introd. by Irving A. Leonard. New York, Noonday Press, 1965. xxxi, 478 p. $4.50

This is a re-edition of the 1956 abridged edition of Maudslay's English translation (1908-66), based on Genaro García's Mexican edition of 1904, of Díaz del Castillo's lively and entertaining eyewitness account of the conquest of Mexico.

327

Dibble, Charles E., ed. *Codex Hall: an ancient Mexican hieroglyphic picture manuscript;* with a silk screen facsimile reproduction of the codex by Louie H. Ewing. Albuquerque, University of New Mexico Press, 1971. 16 p. illus., facsims. (col.) $5

Includes a facsimile reproduction of Codex Hall, with some excellent notes by Professor Dibble.

328

Diederich, Bernard, and Al Burt. *Papa Doc: the truth about Haiti today.* Foreword by Graham Greene. New York, Avon Books, 1972. xii, 393 p. $1.25

In the words of the British novelist Graham Greene "this is a very full account of Duvalier's reign which will be indispensable to future historians." It gives a good synopsis of Haitian history and then proceeds to analyze Duvalier's life and regime.

329

Dinerstein, Herbert S. *Intervention against communism.* Baltimore, Johns Hopkins University Press, 1967. 53 p. (Washington Center of Foreign Policy Research. Studies in international affairs, no. 1) $1.45

Studies U.S. intervention against communism in Greece, Vietnam, Cuba, the Soviet Union, and the Dominican Republic. The author concludes that, with the exception of Greece, intervention against communism has tended not to inhibit the spread of communism but to increase it, largely because these interventions have been perceived as directed primarily against national aspirations rather than against communism.

330

Donoso, José, and William A. Henkin, comps. *The tri-quarterly anthology of contemporary Latin American literature.* New York Dutton, 1969. xi, 496 p. illus. $3.95

Poetry, fiction, and critical essays are presented in this collection of Latin American literature. More than 75 contributions are included, and special anthologies of Cuban, Peruvian, Argentine, Paraguayan, Mexican, and Chilean poetry survey national trends. The artwork throughout the book is also Latin American.

331

Dooley, Lester M. *That motherly Mother of Guadalupe.* Boston, St. Paul Editions, 1962. 74 p. illus. $1

Father Dooley has written a brief devotional account of the apparitions of the patroness of Mexico, Our Lady of Guadalupe, to Juan Diego in 1531. Hymns and prayers are also included.

332

Dorn, Edward, and Gordon Brotherston, comps. and trs. *Our word; guerrilla poems from Latin America. Poesía guerrillera de Latinoamérica.* New York, Grossman, 1968. 58 p. $2.95

Includes two dozen poems by revolutionary poets from Peru, Guatemala, and Nicaragua. Argentina is represented by Che Guevara's "Song to Fidel." This is a bilingual edition, the poems and the introduction appear in both English and Spanish.

333

Douglas, William Orville. *Holocaust or hemispheric cooperation; crosscurrents in Latin America.* New York, Random House, 1971. 216 p. $1.95

This is an interesting and topical work by a justice of the U.S. Supreme Court who is also an avid observer of Third World developments.

334

Dozer, Donald Marquand, ed. *The Monroe Doctrine; its modern significance.* New York, Knopf, 1968. xiv, 208 p. $2.75

The editor's thorough introduction traces the historical evolution of the Monroe Doctrine. The 26 selections which include articles, editorials, and official policy statements, illustrate the diverse interpretations of the doctrine. Includes bibliographic footnotes.

335

Draper, Theodore. *Castroism: theory and practice.* New York, Praeger, 1965. xiii, 263 p. $2.75

This is a summation and an updating of the author's conclusions of the topic, attempting to provide answers to two basic questions: what is the nature of the Castro regime and what is its relation to other Communist goverments? The books includes bibliographic footnotes.

336

Draper, Theodore. *Castro's revolution; myths and realities.* New York, Prager, 1962. 211 p. (Books that matter) $2.25

This is an authoritative and well-written study of Castro's first years. It is somewhat short, however, on historical perspective. Includes bibliographic footnotes.

337

Dulles, Foster Rhea. *The imperial years.* New York, Apollo, 1966. 340 p. $2.25

Studies the 1885-1908 period emphasizing U.S. emergence as a great power. Latin America becomes important in the narrative as the U.S. expands its influence in the Caribbean. [Charles Fleener]

338

Duncan, Walter Raymond, ed. *Soviet policy in developing countries.* Columbus, Ohio, *Latin America; sources for a twentieth-century analysis.* New York, Oxford University Press, 1970. xiv. 562 p. $4.95

The editors have selected writings, speeches, and documents of prominent Latin American leaders of the 20th century, reflecting divergent approaches to socioeconomic change. The leaders range from José Martí to Fidel Castro, Eduardo Frei, Rómulo Betancourt, and Che Guevara.

339
Duncan, Walter Raymond, ed. *Soviet policy in developing countries.* Columbus, Ohio, Xerox College, 1973. xvii, 350 p. $6.75

The readings included here review sensitive trouble zones in developing countries and analyze Soviet relationships with the Third World. Includes bibliographic references.

340
Durán, Juan Guillermo. *Literatura y utopia en Hispanoamérica.* Ithaca, N.Y., Cornell University Press, 1972. 346 p. (Latin American Studies Program Dissertation series, no. 53) $4

Analyzes one representative work from each of 10 Spanish-American authors, who present the New World as the land of Utopia. Among the authors studied: Christopher Columbus, Alonso de Ercilla, Bernardo de Balbuena, Garcilaso de la Vega, Domingo F. Sarmiento, José E. Rodó, Rubén Darío, José Vasconcelos, Alejo Carpentier, and Julio Cortázar. Includes a bibliography.

341
Dutton, Bertha Pauline, and Hulda R. Hobbs. *Excavations at Tajamulco, Guatemala.* Albuquerque, University of New Mexico Press, 1972. xii, 121 p. front., illus., maps. (Monographs of the School of American Research, Santa Fe, N.M., no. 9) $4

Based on field work conducted in 1938-39, the authors concentrated on a small ruin near the village of Tajamulco, in the western highlands, which seemed representative of the area. Includes appendixes and bibliographies. This thorough report was first published in 1943.

342
Earle, Peter G., ed. *Voces hispanoamericanas.* Under the general editorship of Robert G. Mead, Jr. New York, Harcourt, Brace and World, 1966. 303 p. $4.50

Included in this anthology are poems, short stories, and essays by such diverse Spanish American authors as José Martínez Estrada, Octavio Paz, Rubén Darío, Jorge Luis Borges, Julio Cortázar, and others. Includes vocabularies.

343
Easby, Elizabeth Kennedy, and John F. Scott. *Before Cortés: sculpture of Middle America;* a centennial exhibition at the Metropolitan Museum of Art from September 30, 1970, through January 3, 1971. Catalogue. Foreword by Thomas F.P. Hoving. Pref. by Dudley T. Easby, Jr. New York, Metropolitan Museum of Art, 1970. Distributed by the New York Graphic Arts Society. 324 p. illus. (part col.), maps. $6.95

This extensively annotated work reproduces 308 items in stone, pottery, and metal. It also contains a very useful "Relative Chronology of Middle America." It is a good outline to study the cultures of Middle America. The reproductions are excellent.

344
Edwards, Ernest Preston. *A field guide to the birds of Mexico; including all birds occurring from the northern border of Mexico to the southern border of Nicaragua.* Illustrated by Murrell Butler and others. Spanish descriptions by Miguel Alvarez del Toro and Ernest P. Edwards. Sweet Briar, Va., E.P. Edwards, 1972. 300 p. illus., 20 color plates. $8.50

Presents a comprehensive, attractively illustrated guide to birds found in Middle America. Includes a bibliography.

345

Edwards, Ernest Preston. *Finding birds in Mexico.* Illustrated by Edward Murrell Butler, Ernest P. Edwards, and Frederick K. Hilton. 2d ed., rev. and enl. Sweet Briar, Va., E.P. Edwards, 1968. xxi, 282 p. illus. (part col.), maps. $5.50

Includes a guide to birds in Mexico with handsome illustrations and a bibliography.

346

Edwards, Ernest Preston, and Horace Loftin. *Finding birds in Panama.* 2d ed., rev. and enl. Sweet Briar, Va., E.P. Edwards, 1971. ix, 97 p. illus., maps. $4

Contains a description of the bird life in Panama. Includes a bibliography.

347

Egan, E. W. *Argentina in pictures,* prepared by E. W. Egan. New York, Sterling Pub. Co., 1967. 64 p. illus., map, ports. (Visual geography series) $1.50

Presents an illustrated, descriptive geography of Argentina. The textual information is helpful and is intended for classroom use.

348

Egan, E. W. *Brazil in pictures,* prepared by E. W. Egan. New York, Sterling Pub. Co., 1967. 64 p. illus, map, ports. (Visual geography series) $1.50

This is an illustrated, succinct descriptive geography of this South American country. It points out the great variety of scenery and the mixture of cultures.

349

Egan, Ferol. *El Dorado trail; the story of the gold rush routes across Mexico.* New York, McGraw-Hill, 1970. xvi, 313 p. map. (American trails series) $3.50

Presents an interesting account of the trail that led through Mexico in search of gold.

350

Einaudi, Luigi R., ed. *Beyond Cuba; Latin America takes charge of its future.* New York, Crane, Russak, 1973. 232 p. $5.95

Contains 10 essays by scholars from various disciplines. The contributors challenge the view that Latin America is faced with a dilemma between fascism and socialism, pointing out several substantial institutional and economic changes which are paving the way towards development.

351

Einaudi, Luigi R. *Revolution from within? Military rule in Peru since 1968.* Santa Monica, Calif., Rand Corp., 1971. 15 p. (Rand Corporation paper, P-4676) $1

Succinctly analyzes Peru's present military government detailing its accomplishments as well as failures. Includes a short bibliography.

352

Eister, Allan W. *The United States and the ABC powers, 1889-1906.* Dallas, University Press in Dallas, 1971. 92 p. (Arnold Foundation studies, new series, v. 1) $1.50

Surveys the diplomatic and commerical relations between the U.S. and Argentina, Brazil, and Chile during the turn-of-the-century period. [Charles Fleener]

353

Eiteman, David K. *Stock exchanges in Latin America.* Ann Arbor, Bureau of Business Research, Graduate School of Business Administration, University of Michigan, 1966. 83 p. illus., facsims. (Michigan international business studies, no. 7) $3

Examines the operations and structure of stock exchanges in Latin America, providing some useful insights. Includes a bibliography.

354

Elder, Jacob D. *Song games from Trinidad and Tobago.* Austin, Published for the American Folklore Society by the University of Texas Press, 1962. 119 p. (Publications of the American Folklore Society. Bibliographical and special series, v. 16) $2

This handsome volume includes popular and many less well-known song games of Trinidadian folklore. Includes unaccompanied melodies.

355

Ellis, Joseph. *Latin America; its people and institutions.* New York, Bruce Pub. Co., 1971. 245 p. illus., maps. $3.50

This is a general outline of Latin American institutions, governments, and social dynamics aimed at college students. Includes a useful bibliography.

356

Embree, Edwin Rogers. *Indians of the Americas.* With a new introd. by Vine Deloria, Jr. New York, Macmillan, 1970. xv, 270 p. illus., maps. $1.50

Presents the ancient Americans in the full splendor of their civilizations.

357

Emmerich, André. *Art before Columbus: the art of ancient Mexico from the archaic villages of the second millenium B.C. to the splendors of the Aztecs.* With photos by Lee Boltin. New York, Simon and Schuster, 1963. 256 p. illus., maps. $4.95

This succinct discussion of the pre-classic, great classic, and historic periods in Middle American art, is relevant for the student as well as the collector of pre-Columbian artifacts. The photographs are excellent. Includes a short bibliography.

358

Ellis, John Tracy, ed. *Documents of American Catholic history.* Chicago, Regnery, 1967. 2 v. $2.25 each

Volume 1 deals with the Catholic Church in Spanish America up to the second plenary council of Baltimore.

359

Enciso, Jorge. *Design motifs of ancient Mexico.* New York, Dover Publications, 1959. 153 p. (chiefly illus.) $2.50

The author has assembled a catalog of designs from ancient Mexico, classified into categories, but lacking any integration.

360

Encisco, Jorge. *Designs from pre-Columbian Mexico.* New York, Dover Publications, 1971. 105 p. (chiefly illus.) (Dover pictorial archives) $1.50

All the designs in this book are from the surfaces of "malacates," spindle whorls like the one illustrated in the Mexican pictorial manuscript entitled Codex Vindobonensis. "Malacates" are made of baked clay, are circular, and have a hole through the center.

361
Engber, Marjorie, comp. *Caribbean fiction and poetry.* New York, Center for Inter-American Relations, 1970. 86 p. $1.25

Includes 427 entries of works by Caribbean authors published in the U.S. and England from 1900 to 1970. English translations of French, Spanish, and Dutch works have also been included in this useful reference work.

362
Enguídanos, Miguel, ed. *Borges: sus mejores páginas.* Edited with an introd., notes, and bibliography by Miguel Enguídanos. Englewood Cliffs, N.J., Prentice-Hall, 1970. 250 p. port. (Modern Spanish and Latin American author series) $4.25

The editor has assembled a good selection from the writings of Jorge Luis Borges. Includes an excellent bibliography. Of great interest to students of literature.

363
Engel, Frederic André. *A preceramic settlement on the central coast of Peru: Asia, unit 1.* Philadelphia, American Philosophical Society, 1963. 139 p. illus., maps. (Transactions of the American Philosophical Society. New series, v. 53, pt. 3) $4.50

In 1957 the author visited some mounds about 65 miles south of Lima, near the Indian community called Asia, which were to be flooded for farming purposes. He sifted the major part of the refuse before water inundated the site and discovered 52 funeral or cache pits.

364
Englekirk, John Eugene, and others, eds. *An anthology of Spanish American literature,* prepared under the auspices of the Instituto Internacional de Literatura Iberoamericana. New York, Appleton-Century-Crofts, 1968. xiv, 772 p. $4.50

This is a companion volume to the 3d edition of *Outline of Spanish American literature.* It offers a good sampling of contemporary writers and playwrights. Each selection is preceded by an introductory paragraph which evaluates the author and places him within his era. Includes a bibliography.

365
Englekirk, John Eugene, and others, eds. *An outline history of Spanish American literature.* 3d ed., prepared under the auspices of the Instituto Internacional de Literatura Iberoamericana. New York, Appleton-Century-Crofts, 1965. xiii, 252 p. maps (part fold. col.) $3.65

Outlines the development of Spanish American literature from the period of the discovery of America by the Spaniards to the middle of the 20th century. Each topic covered includes bibliographies.

366
English, Peter. *Panama and the Canal Zone in pictures.* New York, Sterling Pub. Co., 1973. 64 p. illus. map. (Visual geography series) $1.50

This is a profusely illustrated booklet describing Panama, the Canal Zone, its history, people, and culture.

367
Eoff, Sherman Hinkle, and Paul C. King, eds. *Spanish American short stories; graded for elementary students.* New York, Macmillan, 1964. xvii, 204 p. illus. (incl. maps), front. $2.95

A useful collection of short stories by contemporary Spanish-American authors, adapted for the intermediate level. Jesús, Millán, Horacio Quiroga, and Pablo Echagüe are among those represented. Includes notes and vocabulary.

368

Esquemeling, John. *The bucaneers of America.* Introd. by P.G. Adams. New York, Dover Publications, 1967. 506 p. illus., maps. $3

The original 1893 edition was subtitled "A true account of the most remarkable assaults committed of late years upon the coast of the West Indies . . . containing also Basil Rengrose's account of the dangerous voyage and bold assaults of Captain Bartholomew Sharp."

369

Evans, F.C. *A first geography of Trinidad and Tobago.* New York, Cambridge University Press, 1968. 56 p. illus., maps. $2

Surveys the geography, population, and economy of Trinidad and Tobago.

370

Evans, Les, ed. *Disaster in Chile; Allende's strategy and why it failed.* Edited with an introd. by Les Evans. New York, Pathfinder Press, 1974. 271 p. $2.95

This collection of articles was taken mainly from the international Trotskyite magazine *Intercontinental Press.* It records the three years of Allende's Popular Unity coalition from September 1970 to its overthrow in September 1973.

371

Ewing, Ethal. *Latin American society.* 2d ed. Chicago, Rand McNally, 1963. 78 p. illus., maps. $1.40

Outlines Latin American history from Columbus to Castro for the high school student.

372

Facts on File, Inc. New York. *Brazil 1954-1964; end of a civilian cycle.* Edited by Jordan M. Young. New York, 1972. 197 p. (Interim history) $2.95

Records important facts about Brazil during a decade that showed great promise and great disappointment. The following milestones are covered: the fall of Gétulio Vargas, the 1955 election of Juscelino Kubitschek and his administration, important economic trends in 1956-59, the elections of Janio Quadros and João Goulart, the political turmoil of 1961-63, and the fall of Goulart followed by the takeover by the military.

373

Fagan, Stuart I. *Central American economic integration; the politics of unequal benefits.* Berkeley, Institute of International Studies, University of California, 1971. xiv, 81 p. (University of California, Berkeley, Institute of International Studies. Research series no. 15) $1.75

Analyzes the problem facing the Central American Common Market. The member countries' unequal productivity and economic development present certain difficulties, as do occasional rivalry and nationalism. Includes a bibliography.

374

Fagen, Richard R., ed. *Cuba; the political content of adult education.* Edited and translated by Richard R. Fagen. Stanford, Calif., The Hoover Institution on War, Revolution, and Peace, Stanford University, 1964. 77 p. (Hoover Institution Studies, 4) $2

Castro declared that 1961 would be the "year of education." More than a million Cubans participated as either teachers or students. The first purpose of this movement was skill training but civic training was also an important element of the program. [Charles Fleener]

375
Fagen, Richard R., and Wayne A. Cornelius, Jr., eds. *Political power in Latin America: seven confrontations.* Englewood Cliffs, N.J., Prentice-Hall, 1970. xix, 419 p. $5.35

Includes essays on constitutional or electoral transfers (Chile, Venezuela); coups d'état (Argentina, Brazil, Dominican Republic); and confrontations which did change the form of government such as in Cuba and Mexico. Includes a bibliography.

376
Fagen, Richard R., and William S. Tuohy. *Politics and privilege in Mexico City.* Stanford, Calif., Stanford University Press, 1975. xiv, 210 p. $2.95

Studies local politics in one of the great Latin American capital cities, adding a new dimension to our understanding.

377
Fagen, Richard R. *The transformation of political culture in Cuba.* Stanford, Calif., Stanford University Press, 1969. 271 p. illus. (Stanford studies in comparative politics, 2) $2.95

Studies the new Socialist man that the Castro government has tried to fashion and the evolution of Cuban socialism. Includes bibliographical references.

378
Fagg, John Edwin. *Cuba, Haiti, and the Dominican Republic.* Englewood Cliffs, N.J., Prentice-Hall, 1965. 181 p. maps. (The Modern nations in historical perspective) $1.95

This is an excellent survey, half of which is devoted to Cuba. An extensive critical bibliography enhances the text.

379
Farabee, William Curtis. *The Central Arawaks.* New York, Humanities Press, 1967. 288 p. illus., maps. $15

Includes material dealing with Arawak tribes of northern Brazil and southern British Guiana (now Guyana), collected during a field trip sponsored by the University of Pennsylvania Museum's South American Expedition 1913-16. The somatic, ethnological and linguistic data are based on personal observation. Includes bibliography. [Charles Fleener]

380
Farabee, William Curtis. *The Central Caribs.* New York, Humanities Press, 1967. 299 p. illus., maps, $17

More than a dozen Carib tribes of southern Guyana and northern Brazil were studied by the University of Pennsylvania Museum's South American Expedition, 1913-16. This monograph presents a scientific account of the language, culture, and somatic characteristics for these isolated Amerindians. [Charles Fleener]

381
Faron, Louis C. *The Mapuche Indians of Chile.* New York, Holt, Rinehart and Winston, 1968. xiii, 113 p. illus. (Case studies in cultural anthropology) $2.75

A case study of a culture that has managed to retain significant traditional characteristics despite centuries of contact and conquest by westerners. The conflict between forces for change and those for stability is analyzed. Includes a bibliography. [Charles Fleener]

382

Faron, Louis C. *Mapuche social structure*. Urbana, University of Illinois Press, 1961. xvi, 247 p. illus. $5.95

A thorough analysis of Mapuche social relationships, including a study of the Mapuche belief in supernatural forces. Includes a bibliography.

383

Farr, Kenneth R. *The problem of institutionalization of a political party; the case of the Partido Popular Democrático of Puerto Rico*. Hato Rey, P.R., Interamerican University Press, 1973. 124 p. $5

Carefully documents the course of the Partido Popular Democrático during the 1960's. The party was founded earlier by Luis Muñoz Marín.

384

Feder, Ernest. *The rape of the peasantry; Latin America's landholding system*. Garden City, N.Y., Anchor Books, 1971. xiv, 304 p. $2.60

Analyzes land tenure systems and rural conditions in Latin America, providing some historical perspectives to current landholding patterns. It also touches on agrarian reform movements and other solutions. Includes bibliographies.

385

Feinberg, Richard E. *The triumph of Allende; Chile's legal revolution*. New York, New American Library, 1973. 276 p. (A Mentor book) $1.25

A former Peace Corps volunteer in Chile wrote this interesting account of Chile's 1970 election and Allende's first five months in office.

386

Fergusson, Erna. *Dancing gods; Indian ceremonials of New Mexico and Arizona*. Albuquerque, University of New Mexico Press, 1957. xxvi, 276 p. illus. $2.45

Describes native dances and rites in Arizona and New Mexico, which are very closely allied to practices in Mesoamerica. Handsome illustrations enhance the text.

387

Fergusson, Erna. *Mexican cookbook*. Albuquerque, University of New Mexico Press, 1970. 118 p. illus. $1.65

First published in 1934, this book contains the Mexican dishes in common use when New Mexico was part of Mexico. It points out the subtlety and delicacy in the use of spices and how the ingredients have to be well balanced and blended to form an authentic Mexican meal.

388

Fergusson, Harvey. *Rio Grande*. Drawings by Colden Whitman. New York, Apollo Publications, 1965. 296 p. illus. $1.95

Traces the history of the conquest of the Rio Grande valley from pre-Columbian days up to the early 20th century. The narrative focuses on individual histories which symbolize the area's development. [Charles Fleener]

389

Ferlinghetti, Lawrence. *The Mexican night; travel journal*. New York, New Directions, 1970. 58 p. illus. (A New Directions paperbook, NDP-300) $1.50

This is an impressionistic journal of an American poet who traveled through the Bohemian Quarters of Mexico.

390

Fernandes, Florestan. *The Negro in Brazilian society.* Translated by Jacqueline D. Skiles, A. Brunel, and Arthur Rothwell. Edited by Phyllis B. Eveleth. New York, Atheneum, 1972. xxv, 789 p. $4.50

The hard cover, English-language edition was first published in 1969. The author states his conclusion, reached after a sociological investigation into the contact between blacks and whites in the city of São Paulo, which is representative of an increasingly industrialized society.

391

Fernández, Justino. *A guide to Mexican art; from its beginnings to the present.* Translated by Joshua C. Taylor. Chicago, University of Chicago Press, 1969. xvii, 398 p. 183 illus. $3.95

This survey of more than 20 centuries of art provides a critical introduction to a great artistic heritage and serves as a guide to the masterpieces of Mexico. The 183 illustrations depict ceramics, sculpture, murals, buildings, and engravings. Translated from *Arte mexicano desde sus orígenes a nuestros días,* 2d ed. (1961).

392

Field, Arthur, ed. *City and country in the Third World; issues in the modernization of Latin America.* Cambridge, Mass., Schenkman, 1970. xi, 303 p. (A Schenkman paperback, SK-40) $4.95

These essays examine the growing trend towards urbanization in Latin America within the Third World context. The approach is interdisciplinary. Includes bibliographies.

393

Fieldhouse, David Kenneth. *The colonial empires; a comparative survey from the eighteenth century.* New York, Delacorte Press, 1967. xiii, 450 p. illus., maps. (Delacorte world history, v. 29) $2.95

An imaginative and thorough comparison of the European colonial empires during the 18th century. Although England, Holland, and France receive major emphasis, the parts pertaining to the Spanish Empire are interesting. Contains a good bibliography.

394

Fife, Austin E., ed. *Latin American interlude.* Logan, Utah State University Press, 1966. 86 p. (Utah State University. Monograph series, v. 13, no. 2) $1

Inclues "A quest for total culture," "Hispanic-American lyrics," and a bibliography entitled "Classical works on Latin American culture." These pieces present samples of the varied richness of Latin American life and literature.

395

Figueroa, John, comp. *Caribbean voices.* Washington, R. B. Luce; distributed by D. McKay, New York, 1973. 228 p. $6.95

Selections by leading poets from the West Indies. Reveals the uniqueness of West Indian poetic expression. A very good appendix discusses the complex language situation in the area.

396

Fitzgerald, Gerald E., comp. *The constitutions of Latin America.* Edited with an introd. by Gerald E. Fitzgerald. Chicago, Regnery, 1968. 242 p. $2.95

Six Latin American constitutions have been chosen as representative of the varieties of Latin American constitutionalism. The editor compares political reality with constitutional appearance and places the documents in their historical context. The constitutions of Chile, Colombia, Costa Rica, El Salvador, Mexico, and Venezuela are included.

397

Fitzgibbon, Russel Humke. *Latin America; a panorama of contemporary politics.* New York, Appleton-Century-Crofts, 1971. x, 546 p. maps. $4.50

This guide to contemporary Latin American politics is chiefly intended as a textbook. Contains an extensive bibliography.

398

Fitzpatrick, Joseph P. *Puerto Rican American; the meaning of migration to the mainland.* Englewood Cliffs, N.J., Prentice-Hall, 1971. xvi, 192 p. illus., maps. (Ethnic groups in American life series) $3.50

Surveys the economic and social adjustments that Puerto Rican migrants have to make when they decide to live in the U.S. mainland. Includes a bibliography.

399

Flandreau, Charles Macomb. *Viva Mexico.* Edited with an introd. by C. Harvey Gardiner. Urbana, University of Illinois Press, 1964. 302 p. $1.95

Fist published in 1908, this is a delightful description of rural Mexico under Díaz by an American humorist.

400

Foner, Nancy. *Status and power in rural Jamaica: a study of educational and political change.* New York, Teachers College Press, 1973. xx, 172 p. (Publications of the Center for Education in Latin America) $3.95

The author draws parallels between Jamaica's achievements, problems, and potentials and those of the other underdeveloped nations. Her study concentrates on the village of Coco Hill.

401

Foner, Philip Sheldon. *The Spanish-Cuban-American war and the birth of American imperialism: 1895-1902.* New York, Monthly Review Press, 1972. 2 v. (xxxiv, 716 p.) maps. (Modern reader) $8.75

Professor Foner presents the Cuban side of events between 1895 and 1902, basing his work on extensive research in several archives. Foner's central thesis is that the war and the Platt Amendment became foundations for American foreign policy in the Caribbean and in Latin America. Includes bibliographic notes.

402

Forbes, Jack D., ed. *The Indian in America's past.* Englewood Cliffs, N.J., Prentice-Hall, 1964. x, 181 p. (A Spectrum book) $1.95

Includes a collection of documents concerning Indians in the U.S. Some 10 percent of the documents selected are from Spanish and Mexican sources.

403

Ford, Norman D. *All of Mexico at low cost.* 4th rev. and expanded ed. Greenlawn, N.Y., Harian Publications; trade distributor: Grosset & Dunlap, New York, 1972. 188 p. $2.50

Fiesta lands (1965) is presented here in an enlarged edition with new illustrations.

404

Ford, Norman D. *Fabulous Mexico; where everything costs less.* 11th ed. New York, Crown Publishers, 1963. 82 p. illus. $2.50

A guide for the economy-minded tourist. Includes financial information about banks, real estate, and investments.

405

Foscue, Edwin J. *Taxco; Mexico's silver city.* Dallas, Texas, Southern Methodist University Press, 1960. 34 p. illus. $1.50

This is an attractive and knowledgeable introduction and guide to the geography and history of Taxco, "a resort town out of the colonial past." The author is a geographer at Southern Methodist University. This book was first published in 1947.

406

Foster, David William. *The myth of Paraguay in the fiction of Augusto Roa Bastos.* Chapel Hill, University of North Carolina Press, 1969. 88 p. (University of North Carolina. Studies in the Romance languages and literature, no. 80) $3.50

Roa Bastos is considered the most important figure in contemporary Paraguayan literature. Foster analyzes *El trueno entre las hojas* (1953) and *Hijo de hombre* (1959), both of which capture the spirit of Paraguayan social history and create a prophetic vision of mankind struggling towards self-liberation and a sensitive human fraternity. Includes bibliographical footnotes.

407

Foster, George McClelland. *Tzintzuntzan; Mexican peasants in a changing world.* Boston, Little, Brown, 1967. xii, 372 p. $4.50

This is an incisive monographic study about Mexican peasants and their adaptation to a rapidly changing social and economic environment. Includes a bibliography.

408

Francis, Michael J. *The Allende victory; an analysis of the 1970 presidential election.* Tucson, University of Arizona Press, 1973. 76 p. (The Institute of Government Research. Comparative studies, no. 4) $1.50

A brief but useful summary of the election that saw the first freely elected Marxist president come to power.

408A

Franco, Jean. *An introduction to Spanish-American literature.* New York, Cambridge University Press, 1975. 390 p. $4.95

The hard cover edition was first published in 1969. The period since then has been marked by the appearance of several important novelists and poets, such as Ernesto Cardenal, Gabriel García Márquez, and Mario Vargas Llosa. This is an important and scholarly work which will become a standard reference work.

409

Franco, Jean, ed. *Horacio Quiroga: cuentos escogidos.* New York, Pergamon Press, 1968. 198 p. (Pergamon Latin American series) $3

A textbook edition of short stories by the Uruguayan Horacio Quiroga, the great narrator of abnormal themes for whom nature became a literary topic.

410

Franco, Jean. *The modern culture of Latin America; society and the artists.* Rev. ed. Harmondsworth, England, Penguin Books, 1971. 381 p. illus., 32 plates. (A Pelican book) $2.95

Covers a large number of specialized topics concerning the contemporary Latin American artist and his relationship to the environment. The author points out that the Latin American writer, artist, and intellectual reflects his society and in many instances acts as its social conscience. Includes a lengthy bibliography.

411

Franco, Jean. *Spanish American literature since independence.* New York, Barnes & Noble; distributed by Harper, 1973. xiv, 306 p. (A literary history of Spain) $5.95

This is a clear and concise literary history of 19th- and 20th-century Latin America which will undoubtedly become a favorite reference work for scholars and librarians. The author points out that contemporary Latin American literature has asserted its individuality and is steadily gaining international stature. The hard-cover edition ($9.50) may be preferred for library use. Includes bibliographies.

412

Frank, André Gunder. *Capitalism and underdevelopment in Latin America; historical studies of Chile and Brazil.* Rev. and enl. ed. New York, Monthly Review Press, 1969. 343 p. $3.45

This economic history studies underdevelopment and agriculture in Brazil and Chile, the "Indian problem," and foreign investment in Latin America, as well as economic and social inequities.

413

Frank, André Gunder. *Latin America; underdevelopment or revolution;* essays on the development or underdevelopment and the immediate enemy. New York, Monthly Review Press, 1971. xviii, 409 p. $3.95

Focuses on underdevelopment and attempts to prove that foreign capital and social inequalities are the main causes for underdevelopment. The author foresees that change can only be brought about by revolution. Includes bibliographies.

414

Franz, Carl, and others. *The people's guide to Mexico.* Santa Fe, N. M., J. Muir; distributed by Book People, 1972. 380 p. illus. $3.95

A guide for travelers who want to spend well under $5 a day while traveling in Mexico, this is a clever, informative, and useful book. Drawings by Toby Williams.

415

Freyre, Gilberto. *The masters and the slaves; a study in the development of Brazilian civilization.* 2d ed. Translated by Samuel Putnam. New York, Knopf, 1964. 432 p. (Borzoi books on Latin America) $2.95

This is an abridged version of Samuel Putnam's 1948 English translation of *Casa grande e senzala* (1933), which is an outstanding work of social history on colonial Brazil. It examines Portuguese, black, and Indian contributions to Brazilian culture and life on the great plantations of the North.

416

Freyre, Gilberto. *The Portuguese and the tropics; suggestions inspired by the Portuguese methods of integrating autocthonous peoples and cultures differing from the European in a new, or Luso-tropical complex civilization.* Translated by Helen M. D'O. Matthew and F. de Mello Moser. New York, S.H. Service Agency, 1972. xi, 296 p. $8.50

Paperback edition of *O Luso e o tropico* (1961) published in Lisbon to commemorate the 5th centenary of the death of Prince Henry the Navigator.

417

Friedmann, John. *Venezuela from doctrine to dialogue.* Syracuse, N.Y., University of

LATIN AMERICA

Syracuse Press, 1969. xxiii, 87 p. (National planning series, 1) $2.95

Venezuela's national planning organization, the Oficina Central de Coordinación y Planificación (CORDIPLAN) is the subject of this study. Recognized as the outstanding example of democratic planning, CORDIPLAN is also one of the most effective economic organizations in Latin America.

418

Friedrich, Paul. *Agrarian revolt in a Mexican village.* Englewood Cliffs, N.J., Prentice-Hall, 1970. xvi, 158 p. illus., maps, ports. (Anthropology of modern societies series) $3.95

This is probably the first systematic ethnological history of the origins, development, and outcome of an agrarian revolt in a Tarascan village (Naranja). The author also analyzes community life. Includes bibliographies.

419

Fuentes, Carlos. *Change of skin.* Translated by Sam Hileman. New York, Noonday Press, 1971. 462 p. $3.25

English translation of *Cambio de piel* (1967) which is considered Fuentes' best novel to date and the winner of several literary awards. It is written with new literary techniques exposing the meaningless anguish of modern man. The translation is excellent.

420

Fuentes, Carlos. *The death of Artemio Cruz.* Translated from the Spanish by Sam Hileman. New York, Noonday Press, 1966. 306 p. $1.95

English translation of *La muerte de Artemio Cruz* (1962), the panoramic novel about the life and death of a rich and powerful landowner. It covers the last half century of Mexican history.

421

Fuentes, Carlos. *Good conscience.* New York, Noonday Press, 1961. 148 p. $1.95

The original Spanish edition, *Las buenas conciencias,* was published in 1959. It describes the life of a bourgeois Catholic family in Guanajuato around the time when Porfirio Díaz was president of Mexico. The plot concerns an adolescent's rebellion and his intellectual friendship with an Indian.

422

Fuentes, Carlos. *Where the air is clear; a novel.* Translated by Sam Hileman. New York, Noonday Press, 1971. 346 p. $2.95

The original Spanish edition is entitled *La región transparente* (1958); in it Fuentes interweaves the mental processes of various characters with events. The setting is Mexico City. An ambitious early undertaking by one of Latin America's best known novelists.

423

Fuller, John Frederick Charles. *Military history of the western world.* New York, Funk & Wagnalls, 1954-56. 3 v. illus., maps. $3.95 each

Volume 1 is entitled *Earliest Times to the Battle of Lepanto,* the second volume is *From the Defeat of the Spanish Armada, 1588, to the Battle of Waterloo,* and volume 3 bears the title *From the Seven Day Battle to the Battle of Leyte Gulf, 1944.* Spain's role is prominent in the first two volumes. Includes bibliographies.

424

Furtado, Celso. *Development and underdevelopment.* Translated by Ricardo W. de

60

Aguiar and Eric Drysdale. Berkeley, University of California Press, 1963. 285 p. $2.85

This is a translation of *Formação econômica do Brasil* (1959), in which a well-known Brazilian economist sketches his country's economic history and analyzes the many factors that have affected its development. Includes a section on inflation and coffee production.

425
Furtado, Celso. *Obstacles to development in Latin America.* Translated by Charles Ecker. Garden City, N.Y., Anchor Books, 1970. xxvi, 204 p. $1.45

Emphasizes external factors which tend to aggravate and perpetuate underdevelopment in Latin America. Also discusses underdevelopment and its relation to industrial capitalism. The author is a noted economist of Latin America. Includes bibliographies.

426
Galarza, Ernesto. *Merchants of labor; the Mexican bracero story.* Santa Barbara, Calif., McNally and Loftin, 1964. 284 p. illus., tables. $2.95

Describes in detail the managed migration of Mexican farm workers to California from 1942 to 1960. It is an important social document of interest to those studying migrating farm labor.

427
Galarza, Ernesto, Herman Gallegos, and Julian Samora. *Mexican-Americans in the Southwest.* Santa Barbara, Calif., McNally and Loftin, 1969. xi, 90 p. illus., tables. $2.50

The result of a two-year survey, this study assesses the current economic, political, and educational status of the Mexican Americans in the Southwest.

428
Galarza, Ernesto. *Zoo-risa; rimas y fotografías de Ernesto Galarza.* Santa Barbara, Calif., McNally and Loftin, 1968. 48 p. illus. $1.25

A humorous book in Spanish about people and animals by a prominent Chicano scholar and writer.

429
Galeano, Eduardo. *Guatemala; occupied country.* Translated by Cedric Belfrage. New York, Monthly Review Press, 1969. 159 p. map. $2.25

English translation of *Guatemala; país ocupado* (1967), presenting the view of the Guatemalan guerrilla fighters and stating that they have settled for a long-term revolution. Relies on some old clichés, but it is well written and should be read to understand the strife and violence in contemporary Guatemala.

430
Galet, Paul, pseud. *Freedom to starve.* With an introd. by Michel Quoist and Rosemary Sheed. Translated by Rosemary Sheed. Baltimore, Pelican Books, 1973. 249 p. (The Pelican Latin American library) $2.45

Consists of excerpts from the diary and letters of a French priest who works with the urban poor of Brazil. It describes thoughtfully and with deep compassion the frustrations of a demoralized community that the author served as pastor.

431
Galíndez Suárez, Jesús. *The era of Trujillo, Dominican dictator.* Edited by Russell H. Fitzgibbon. Tucson, University of Arizona Press, 1973. xxvii, 298 p. illus. $4.50

Galíndez was a Basque lawyer who lived in the Dominican Republic in the 1940's where he observed first-hand Trujillo's regime. Ten years later he wrote a doctoral thesis at Columbia University on Trujillo's rule. Galíndez disappeared at that time, and it is believed that he was assassinated. First published in 1956 as *La era de Trujillo.*

432

Gallagher, David P. *Modern Latin American literature.* New York, Oxford University Press, 1973. 197 p. $1.95

This critical guide to Latin American literature from the 19th century to the present by a Fellow at Oxford, focuses on the major figures such as César Vallejo, Pablo Neruda, Octavio Paz, Jorge Luis Borges, Mario Vargas Llosa, Gabriel García Márquez, and Guillermo Cabrera Infante. Also includes chapters on poetry, the regional novel, and fiction since 1940.

433

Gallegos, Rómulo. *Doña Barbara.* Edited by Lowell Dunham. New York, Appleton-Century-Crofts, 1962. xx, 280 p. $2.65

When it first appeared in 1929, this work was hailed as one of the best novels of South America. Gallegos describes the tremendous power and beauty of the Venezuelan landscape. He is a master of spontaneous and authentic dialog. His main character, Doña Barbara, constitutes a skillful study of a ruthless devourer of men. Includes vocabularies.

434

Gamio, Manuel. *The life story of the Mexican immigrant; autobiographic documents.* With a new introd. by Paul S. Taylor. New York, Dover Publications, 1971. xix, 288 p. map. $3

This is an unabridged publication of a work first published in 1931, which studies the effects of Mexican immigration to the U.S. Dr. Gamio, a noted anthropologist, interviewed 76 Mexicans who talked to him freely about their reasons for leaving Mexico. Gives an insight into the social and cultural adjustment of migrants. An important and lasting contribution.

435

Gamio Manuel. *Mexican immigration to the United States.* New York, Dover Publications, 1972. xviii, 262 p. maps. (The American immigration collection) $3

This is a reprint of the 1930 edition of a work which studied the patterns and economic variables of the migration of Mexican workers to the U.S.

436

Garbacz, Christopher. *Industrial polarization under economic integration in Latin America.* Austin, Bureau of Business Research, Graduate School of Business, University of Texas at Austin, 1971. xvii, 101 p. maps. (Studies in Latin American business, no. 11) $3

Analyzes the tendency of an economic union of countries with divergent levels of development to result in further extreme concentration of economic activity at a few industrial poles. Suggests solutions such as the projected Latin American Common Market.

437

García Márquez, Gabriel. *Leaf storm and other short stories.* Translated from the Spanish by Gregory Rabassa. New York, Avon, 1973. 146 p. $1.65

In addition to *Hojarasca,* this work includes *The handsomest drowned man in the world; A very old man with enormous wings; Blacamán the Good, vendor of miracles; The last voyage of the ghost ship; Monologue of Isabel watching it rain in Macondo;* and *Nabo.* All are masterful short stories centering around the town of Macondo, wrapped in mystery and fantasy.

438

García Márquez, Gabriel. *No one writes to the colonel, and other stories.* Translated from the Spanish by J. S. Bernstein. New York, Avon, 1969. 170 p. $1.50

Translation of *El coronel no tiene quién le escriba* and other outstanding short stories by this Colombian writer. Included are *Big Mama's funeral; Tuesday siesta; One of these days; There are no thieves in this town; Balthazar's marvelous afternoon; Montiel's widow; One day after Saturday;* and *Artificial roses.*

439

García Márquez, Gabriel. *One hundred years of solitude.* Translated from the Spanish by Gregory Rabassa. New York, Avon, 1972. 422 p. $1.50

This is an excellent translation of *Cien años de soledad* (1967), one of the most important Latin American novels of this century. It is a witty combination of fantasy and reality about a mythical town on the Caribbean founded by Col. Aureliano Buendía. The town of Macondo emerges as a microcosmic South America, portraying the very essence of Spanish America.

440

García Robles, Alfonso. *The denuclearization of Latin America.* Translated by Marjorie Urquidi. Washington, Carnegie Endowment for International Peace, 1967. xx, 167 p. $1.95

Contains 11 speeches delivered by García Robles, Mexico's under secretary for foreign affairs, at various international meetings related to the denuclearization of Latin America. Also included are official documents on the subject.

441

Garcilaso de la Vega, El Inca. *The Incas; the royal commentaries of the Inca Garcilaso de la Vega.* Translated by Maria Jolas from the critical, annotated French ed. of Alain Gheerbrant. Introd. by Alain Gheerbrant. New York, Avon Books, 1961. xlviii, 447 p. illus. $1

This edition of the classic *Royal commentaries of the Inca* was translated from the annotated French edition. The narrative runs from the origins of the Incas to Atahualpa's death. Contemporary illustrations are included.

442

Gardner, Mary A., ed. *The press of Latin America; a tentative and selective bibliography in Spanish and Portuguese.* Austin, Institute of Latin American Studies, University of Texas, 1973. 34 p. (Guides and bibliographies, 4) $2

Includes titles by Latin American writers available at the libraries of Michigan State University, University of Minnesota, and the University of Texas at Austin. Newspapers are also listed. A very informative and useful guide.

443

Garrett, Naomi Mills. *The renaissance of Haitian poetry.* New York, University Place Book Shop, 1973. 257 p. $7.50

Examines the historical background and predominant qualities of early Haitian poetry, the internal and external causes of the renaissance, as well as the works of representative poets. It also traces the influence of French poetry. An extensive bibliography enhances the importance of this excellent critical work. First published in 1963. [HLAS 26:2133]

444

Gasparini, Graziano. *Arquitectura colonial en Venezuela.* Fotografías del autor. New

York, Wittenborn, 1965. 379 p. illus. (part col.) $30

Describes colonial architecture in Venezuela. The text is enhanced by attractive illustrations and photographs.

445

Gasparini, Graziano. *La casa colonial venezolana.* New York, Wittenborn, 1962. 187 p. illus. $7.50

This is a visually beautiful and very informative study of colonial architecture and interior decoration in Venezuela. Of great interest to all who study colonial art and architecture.

446

Gastmann, Albert L. *The politics of Surinam and the Netherlands Antilles.* Rio Piedras, Institute of Caribbean Studies, University of Puerto Rico, 1968. x, 185 p. (Caribbean monograph series, no. 3) $4

A scholarly survey of the political and constitutional questions that currently face the Netherlands Caribbean. Contains a select bibliography. [Charles Fleener]

447

Gaucher-Shultz, Jeanine, and Alfredo Morales, comps. *1, 2, 3 [i.e. Uno, dos, tres]; tres dramas mexicanos en un acto.* New York, Odyssey Press, 1971. xvi, 88 p. $1.95

A fine introductory essay in Spanish analyzes contemporary Mexican theater. The three short plays included are *Los fantoches,* by Carlos Solórzano; *Un hogar sólido,* by Elena Garro; and *El suplicante,* by Sergio Magaña. Contains a lengthy vocabulary.

448

Gaulert, Earl T., and Lester D. Langley, eds. *The United States and Latin America.* Reading, Mass., Addison-Wesley Pub. Co., 1971. 240 p. $2.95

The editors have selected interpretive essays by historians which attempt to illustrate the ideas that shaped the U.S. role in the hemisphere. Useful as supplementary reading in courses on U.S. diplomatic history.

449

Gaxiola, Manuel J. *La serpiente y la paloma; análisis del crecimiento de la Iglesia Apostólica de la Fé en Cristo Jesús de México.* South Pasadena, Calif., W. Carey Library, 1970. xiv, 177 p. illus., maps. $2.95

A minister of Apostolic Faith, a Pentecostal denomination, analyzes the development of his faith in Mexico. Includes maps and a bibliography.

450

Gay, Carlo T. E. *Xochipala; the beginnings of Olmec art.* Princeton, N.J., Distributed by Princeton University Press, 1972. 61 [2] p. illus. $3.95

Describes material shown in an exhibition at the Art Museum, Princeton University. Xochipala is a newly discovered complex which has opened an entirely new chapter in the history of Olmec art.

451

Geiger, Theodore. *The conflicted relationship: the West and the transformation of Asia, Africa & Latin America.* New York, Published for the Council on Foreign Relations by McGraw-Hill, 1967. xiv, 303 p. (The Atlantic policy series) $4

Surveys western attitudes towards what is known as the Third World. Contains bibliographies.

452

Genovese, Eugene, and Laura Foner, comps. *Slavery in the New World; a reader in comparative history,* edited by Eugene Genovese and Laura Foner. Englewood Cliffs, N.J., Prentice-Hall, 1970. xii, 268 p. $3.95

> The first part deals with general views on slavery in the Americas, including articles by Frank Tannenbaum, Sidney Mintz, etc. The second covers comparative viewpoints by Herbert Klein, Genovese, and others. The third part raises issues in the debate over differences among slave societies in the Americas.

453

Genovese, Eugene D. *The world the slaveholders made; two essays in interpretation.* New York, Vintage Books, 1971. x, 274 p. (A Vintage book, V-676) $1.95

> The first essay compares the different slave systems in the New World, and the second deals with the theories of George Fitzhugh. Includes bibliographical notes. Of interest to historians, economists, and sociologists.

454

George, Alexander L., David K. Hall, and William E. Simons. *The limits of coercive diplomacy: Laos, Cuba, Vietnam.* Boston, Little, Brown, 1971. xviii, 268 p. $3.50

> Analyzes U.S. diplomatic approaches to Cuba, Vietnam, and Laos in a systematic manner. Includes bibliographies.

455

Gerassi, John. *The great fear in Latin America.* New rev. ed. New York, Collier Books, 1965. 478 p. illus. $1.50

> A new and revised edition of the one that appeared in 1964. The first part contains a country-by-country report on political, social, and economic trends, and the second part examines problems in U.S.-Latin American relations. The author advocates some radical changes in U.S. hemispheric policies. Contains a bibliography.

456

Gerber, Stanford N., ed. *The family in the Caribbean; proceedings of the first Conference on the Family in the Caribbean.* Rio Piedras, Institute of Caribbean Studies, University of Puerto Rico, 1968. 147 p. $3

> Contains papers presented at the conference mentioned in the title, which was held in 1967 in St. Thomas, Virgin Islands. The objective of the conference was to present "the widest possible range of topics," from anthropological, sociologic, economic, and other viewpoints. [Charles Fleener]

457

Gibson, Charles, ed. *The Black Legend; anti-Spanish attitudes in the Old World and the New.* New York, Knopf, 1971. 222 p. (Borzoi books on Latin America) $4.50

> The Black Legend considered the Spaniards guilty of excesses and cruelties in the American conquests and was essentially anti-Hispanic propaganda. The editor assembled different views on Spain's role in the New World, of historical figures from the 16th through the 19th centuries, such as William of Orange, Oliver Cromwell, Bartolomé de las Casas, Julián Juderías, Ramón Menéndez Pidal, and others.

458

Gibson, Charles. *Spain in America.* New York, Harper & Row, 1967. xiv, 239 p. maps, ports., plates. (New American nation series, TB-3077) $2.45

> This excellent study is an overall summary of colonial Spanish-American history. It covers the conquest, the encomienda, Church and state relations, social

stratification, and the problem of empire. There is a special chapter on the Spanish borderlands of North America. Includes a good bibliography.

459
Gibson, Charles, ed. *The Spanish tradition in America.* New York, Harper & Row, 1968. 257 p. (Harper Torchbooks, TB-1351) $2.45

Contains documentary selections extending from the late 15th century when Spain began to conquer the New World, to the beginnings of the 19th century when most of Spanish America overthrew Spanish rule. The documents are well chosen and will provide the reader with a glimpse of treaties, laws, and accounts by conquistadors and other political figures. Contains bibliographical footnotes.

460
Gil, Federico Guillermo. *Latin-American—United States relations.* New York, Harcourt, Brace, Jovanovich, 1971. x, 339 p. illus., map (on lining papers) $3.95

Contains enough factual information to serve as a text in courses on hemispheric diplomacy. Professor Gil presents objectively both the Latin American and the U.S. points of view on the issues he discusses. The traditional chronological framework includes such excellent chapters as "Social Revolution in the 1960's" and "The Latin American Scene." Includes bibliography.

461
Gilmore, Betty, and Don Gilmore. *A guide to living in Mexico.* New York, G.P. Putnam's Sons, 1971. 233 p. map. $7

This is a useful book, intended for those who wish to live in Mexico. The suggestions offered are practical and present a wide range of possibilities.

462
Girard, Rafael. *Les Indiens de l'Amazonie peruvienne.* Traduit de l'espagnol par R. Siret. Port Washington, N.Y., Paris Publications, 1970. 321 p. $4.25

From field work in 1957 and from informants, the author has collected data on 13 tribes of Tropical Forest Peruvian Indians. Although data on material culture and social structure are included, the author is most interested in myths, cosmology, magic, religion, etc. Compares these tribes with other cultures of South America and the Caribbean. Translation of *Indios del Amazonas peruano.* [HLAS 29:1740]

463
Girard, Rafael. *Popul Vuh; histoire culturelle des Maya-Quichés.* Port Washington, N.Y., Paris Publications, 1962. 351 p. illus. $4.25

Analysis and historical interpretation of the Popol Vuh, the sacred book of the ancient Mayas. Proposes three epochs—primitive, formative, and advanced horticultural—to study the cultural evolution of the Mayas. A stimulating but controversial book. Translation of *El Popol Vuh, fuente histórica* (1952). [HLAS 18:108]

464
Gittler, Joseph Bertram, ed. *Understanding minority groups.* Contributors: John Collier, and others. New York, Wiley, 1970. xii, 139 p. $2.45

Studies minority groups and their integration, or lack of it, into the mainstream of social and economic life.

465
Gjelsness, Rudolph Hjalmar. *American books in Mexico; a bibliography of books by authors of the United States of America, published in Mexico, 1952-55.* Ann Arbor,

University of Michigan, Dept. of Library Science, 1957. xii, 92 p. illus. (University of Michigan, Dept. of Library Science Studies, 4) $2

Lists books by North American authors published in Mexico during the early 1950's.

466

Gjerde, Mary. *Off the beaten track in Mexico City.* Los Angeles, Nash Pub. Co., 1972. 110 p. maps. (A Nash travel guide) $2.50

Presents Mexico City as the unique and dramatic city which blends together the old and the new. The work aids the traveler to select the most comfortable and suitable way to visit Mexico City.

467

Glade, William P., and Charles Anderson. *The political economy of Mexico: two studies.* Madison, University of Wisconsin Press, 1969. 242 p. $2.95

By analyzing political situations as they affect credit institutions, Anderson offers a good study of mechanisms operating in the development of a national economy. Glade devotes his study to the clarification of the economic, political, and social factors affecting development and the changes that have taken place since 1910. Includes a bibliography.

468

Glazer, Nathan, and Daniel Patrick Moynihan. *Beyond the melting pot: the Negroes, Puerto Ricans, Jews, Italians, and Irish of New York City.* Cambridge, Massachusetts Institute of Technology Press, 1970. 363 p. map. $1.95

This is an examination of cultural patterns assumed by diverse ethnic groups in the U.S. An interesting and important study.

469

Goldbaum, D. *Towns of Baja California.* Translated by W. B. Hendricks. Glendale, Calif., La Siesta, 1970. 210 p. illus. $2.75

This is an attractive description of and a helpful guide to towns in Baja, Calif.

470

Goldberg, Isaac, ed. and tr. *Brazilian tales.* Translated from the Portuguese with an introd. by Isaac Goldberg. Boston, International Pocket Library, 1965. 96 p. (International Pocket Library, 29) $.85

First published in 1921, it presents a selection of short stories by Machado de Assis, José de Medeiros e Albuquerque, Coelho Netto, and Carmen Dolores. Goldberg's introduction provides insight into the change in literary taste that has come about in 40 years. Includes a bibliography.

471

Golding, Morton J. *A short history of Puerto Rico.* With an introd. by Luis Quero-Chiesa. New York, New American Library, 1973. 174 p. illus. (A Mentor book) $1.25

Succinctly describes the history of Puerto Rico from the colonial period to the present. This will be a valuable addition to the collections of either public or college libraries because it serves as an introduction to the history and culture of the island. Not intended for the specialist.

472

Goldman, Irving. *Cubeo: Indians of the Northwest Amazon.* Urbana, University of Illinois Press, 1969. 305 p. illus., maps. (Illinois studies in anthropology, no. 2) $5.95

Based on 10 months of field work during 1938-40, this work describes a Tucanoan-speaking, relatively unacculturated tribe of the Uapés River near the Brazilian border. This work is important because the Cubeo sociocultural system was recorded before appreciable disorganization, due to contact, had significantly altered its aboriginal ways. Includes a bibliography.

473
Goldrich, Daniel. *Sons of the establishment; elite youth in Panama and Costa Rica.* Chicago, Rand-McNally, 1966. 139 p. maps. (Studies in political change) $3.95

An interesting parallel study of the young men who will dominate the political establishments of their respective nations and their views about the existing systems.

474
Goldwin, Robert A., comp. *Readings in American foreign policy.* 2d ed. rev. by Harry M. Clor. New York, Oxford University Press, 1971. xii, 721 p. $4.95

Intended as a supplementary text for university students. The readings are grouped in 10 sections, each considered a unit, as opposing views of certain questions are often juxtaposed. Luis Quintanilla, Germán Arciniegas, and Walter Lippmann, among others, write on Latin American-U.S. relations. Includes bibliographical references.

475
Gómara, Francisco López de. *Cortés; the life of the conqueror of Mexico, by his secretary.* Translated and edited by Lesley Bird Simpson. Berkeley, University of California Press, 1966. xxvi, 425 p. illus., map (on lining papers) $2.45

Translation of *Istoria de la conquista de Mexico,* the second part of Gómara's *Historia general de las Indias* (1578), this book is a vivid account of the exploits of Hernan Cortés and the conquest of Mexico.

476
Gómez, Rosendo Adolfo. *Government and politics in Latin America.* Rev. ed. New York, Random House, 1963. 128 p. (Studies in political science, PS-32) $1.95

A short, general but very useful introduction to the subject, intended for textbook use. Its brevity prevents it from being more than a suggestion of themes, although it is based on well-defined patterns. [HLAS 24:3421]

477
Gómez, Rosendo Adolfo. *Intergovernmental relations in highways.* Minneapolis, University of Minnesota Press, 1960. 123 p. $2.50

Examines international cooperation between governments concerning highway construction and traffic. Also deals with the Pan American highway which at the time the book was written was far from complete. Contains appendixes.

478
Gómez, Rosendo Adolfo. *The study of Latin American politics in university programs in the United States.* Tucson, University of Arizona Press, 1967. 75 p. (Comparative government studies, no. 2) $1.50

A thorough survey of university programs dealing with Latin American politics in the U.S., especially valid for the 1960's. Our present decade has seen a certain amount of curtailment in area studies programs. Includes a good bibliography.

479
Gómez, Rudolph, comp. *The changing Mexican-American; a reader.* Boulder, Colo., Pruett Pub. Co., 1972. 321 p. $4.95

Provides essays dealing with historical perspectives, social, economic, and cultural problems, as well as more recent Chicano political activity. The articles should serve to inform the reader of the complexity of the Chicano experience in the U.S. Includes a bibliography.

480
Gómez-Gil, Orlando, comp. *Literatura hispanoamericana; antología crítica.* New York, Holt, Rinehart and Winston, 1972. 2 v. $9.95 each

The first volume contains representative selections of Mayan, Aztec, and Incan literature, as well as early accounts of the discovery and conquest, examples of colonial and baroque writings, through neoclassicism and romanticism. The second volume presents modernism and contemporary literature. The selections consist of poetry and prose.

481
Gonzalas, Kathleen M. *The Mexican family in San Antonio, Texas.* San Francisco, R. and E. Research Associates, 1971. 40 p. $7

Originally presented as a doctoral thesis in 1928, this is an interesting sociological case study of Mexican families in San Antonio. Contains appendixes and a bibliography.

482
Gonzalez, Edward. *Cuba under Castro: the troubled revolution.* Boston, Houghton, Mifflin, 1974. xii, 241 p. $3.95

A scholarly analysis of Castro's rule. The author objectively examines some economic and political difficulties encountered by Cuba in the last few years. He also maintains that the time is right for the U.S. to take the initiative in ending the boycott of Cuba.

483
González, Justo J. *The development of Christianity in the Latin Caribbean.* Grand Rapids, Mich., W.B. Eerdmans Pub. Co., 1969. 136 p. $2.65

A professor at the Union Evangelical Seminary of Puerto Rico briefly describes the development of Christianity in the Latin Caribbean, from the Spanish and French missions established by Catholic friars to the Protestant churches which appeared under changing political and social circumstances.

484
González, Luis J., and Gustavo A. Sánchez Salazar. *The great rebel: Che Guevara in Bolivia.* Translated from the Spanish by Helen R. Lane. New York, Grove Press, 1969. 254 p. illus., maps, ports. $1.45

The authors present an interesting and thorough account of Che Guevara's trying Bolivian compaign. Includes bibliographical footnotes.

485
González, Nancie L. *The Spanish-Americans of New Mexico; a heritage of pride.* Rev. and enl. ed. Albuquerque, University of New Mexico Press, 1969. xv, 246 p. illus., maps, tables. $3.95

Traces the heritage of Spanish-speaking people in New Mexico from 1598 to the present, describing the mounting tensions between their traditional culture and the Anglo society that surrounds them, with particular emphasis on problems of urbanization. A concluding chapter covers recent growth of political activism.

486
González Peña, Carlos. *History of Mexican literature.* Translated by Gusta Barfield

Nance and Florence Johnson Dunstan. 3d ed. rev. and enl. Dallas, Southern Methodist University Press, 1968. xii, 540 p. $3.45

This is the most authoritative single volume in its field. It provides a clear interpretation of Mexican literature for English-speaking readers. Previous editions have been brought up to date with the addition of appendixes.

487
Goodman, Marian. *Missions of California.* Text and illus. by Marian Goodman. Redwood City, Calif., Redwood City Tribune, 1962. 47 p. illus. $1.50

Presents brief histories of 21 California missions founded between 1769 and 1823.

487A
Gorden, Raymond L. *Living in Latin America; a case study in cross-cultural communication.* Edited by H. Ned Seelye. Skokie, Ill., National Textbook Co., 1974. xiv, 117 p. $5.75 single copy; 5 or more $4.60 each

Surveys routine interpersonal relations in Latin America, by using the experiences of North American students in Colombia. This is an important contribution to cross-cultural communications.

488
Gordon, Wendell C. *The political economy of Latin America.* New York, Columbia University Press, 1965. 401 p. tables. $2.95

This is a substantially rewritten version of the *The economy of Latin America* (1950). The new title is more appropriate since major emphasis has been placed on institutional factors, utilizing the theoretical framework of Veblen and Ayres. Includes a brief selective bibliography.

489
Gorostiza, Celestino. *El color de nuestra piel.* Edited by Luis Soto-Ruiz and S. Samuel Trifilo. New York, Macmillan, 1966. 119 p. (Macmillan modern Spanish American literature series) $2.25

Textbook edition of the Mexican novelist's most celebrated work which was first published in 1952. It deals with the skin color as a social problem. Includes notes and vocabulary.

490
Goslinga, Cornelius Christian. *Venezuelan painting in the nineteenth century.* New York, Wittenborn, 1967. xvi, 128 p. illus. $6.75

Surveys Venezuelan painting during the Independence period. It contains biographical information on some artists.

491
Gott, Richard. *Guerilla movements in Latin America.* Garden City, N.Y., Doubleday, 1971. xvi, 626 p. illus., maps, ports. $4.95

Extraordinary work based on personal experience, reporting, and on research available. Deals largely with Guatemala, Venezuela, Colombia, Peru, and Bolivia. Valuable appendixes, a bibliography, and exceptional photographs enhance the work. [HLAS 33:7408]

492
Graff, Henry Franklin, ed. *American imperialism and the Philippine insurrection; testimony taken from hearings on affairs in the Philippine Islands before the Senate Committee on the Philippines, 1902.* Boston, Little, Brown, 1969. xx, 172 p. (Testimony of the times: selections from Congressional hearings) $2.95

Studies U.S. policy during the period of the insurrection in the Philippines. A valuable work.

493

Graham, Lawrence. *Politics in a Mexican community.* Gainesville, University of Florida Press, 1968. 73 p. (University of Florida monographs. Social sciences, 35) $2

Examines the political life of a city in the central highlands plateau of Mexico. A city of 125,000 inhabitants has been chosen to study local politics, the tension between political groups, and the degree of elitism to be found in the city. Culturally, the municipality is predominantly Spanish American with Roman Catholic values. Includes a bibliography.

494

Graham, Richard W. *Britain and the onset of modernization in Brazil, 1850-1914.* New York, Cambridge University Press, 1968. xvi, 385 p. 6 illus., 6 plates, 3 maps. (Cambridge Latin American Studies, no. 4) $3.95

This is a very sophisticated analysis of Brazilian modernization vis-a-vis British industrial and social advancement of the last century. Professor Graham concludes that both internal and external forces contributed to the change in Brazil's socioeconomic structure. The book is well indexed and includes an exhaustive list of sources.

495

Graham, Richard. *A century of Brazilian history since 1865; issues and problems.* New York, Knopf, 1969. 233 p. (Borzoi books on Latin America) $2.75

An excellent study of Brazilian history in which the author points out the social, economic, and cultural factors which influenced its political history. Includes a bibliography.

496

Graham, Richard. *Independence in Latin America.* New York, Knopf, 1972. xiii, 140 p. (Studies in world civilization) $2.50

Professor Graham gives a critical and comparative look at Latin American revolutions and on how the regions of the hemisphere won their political independence. This book is a good introduction to a dramatic period in Latin American history. Includes a bibliography.

497

Grauer, Benjamin Franklin. *How Bernal Díaz's "True history" was reborn.* New York, Between-Hours Press, 1960. 229, 248 p. $5

This is an unusual account of a collector's successful attempt to restore the original manuscript of Bernal Díaz del Castillo's *True history of the conquest of New Spain.* Mr. Grauer reproduced this volume on his own press. The narrative is very interesting.

498

Gray, Richard Butler, comp. *Latin America and the United States in the 1970's.* Edited by Richard B. Gray. Itasca, Ill., F.E. Peacock, 1971. xi, 370 p. $5.95

The readings presented here illustrate the dynamics of change in inter-American relations. There are several pieces on the Alliance for Progess, the common markets, and forces operating upon the OAS. The selections about the OAS perceptively point out why and how that international organization has changed. Also included are selections on the policies of President Nixon as well as a bibliography.

499
Green, Dana S., ed. *Chasms in the Americas.* New York, Friendship Press, 1970. 127 p. illus., ports. $1.95

Reviews social and economic inequalities in the Americas.

500
Green, Gilbert. *Revolution, Cuban style; impressions on a recent visit,* by Gil Green. New York, International Pub. Co., 1970. 125 p. illus. (Little New World paperback, LW-21) $1.25

The author describes his visit to Cuba and outlines his impressions on the role of work incentives, the goal of the sugar harvest, and the transformation of man under a Socialist system.

501
Greenberg, Arnold, and Harriet Greenberg. *South America on five and ten dollars a day.* New York, Frommer-Pasmantier Pub. Corp., 1972. 192 p. $2.95

This perennial favorite is useful for travelers who visit South America.

502
Greene, Graham. *Another Mexico.* New York, Viking Press, 1964. 279 p. illus., map. (Compass books, C-154) $1.45

First published in England under the title *The lawless roads* (1939), this is the English novelist's personal impression of a small part of Mexico and its religious problems and conflicts in 1938.

503
Greene, Graham. *The honorary consul. The third man.* New York, Pocket Books, 1974. 452 p. $1.25

The first title is Greene's newest novel. It centers around the political kidnapping of an Englishman in South America. It contains several deft characterizations and the usual insight into people's psychological traits. Issued together with an older Graham Greene classic.

504
Greene, Graham. *The power and the glory.* Text and criticism edited by R.W.B. Lewis and Peter J. Conn. New York, Viking Press, 1970. xix, 552 p. facsim., map. (The Viking library) $2.25

Greene's powerful novel about a Catholic priest caught in the Mexican Revolution is presented here in a new edition. The novel has high literary value with good descriptions of the Mexican people and the countryside. Includes a bibliography.

505
Greene, Graham. *The power and the glory.* New York, Bantam Books, 1969. 301 p. $1.25

Another edition of entry 504.

506
Greene, Theodore P., ed. *American imperialism in 1898.* Boston, Heath, 1955. 105 p. $2.25

Papers by Samuel F. Bemis, Charles A. Beard, Richard Hofstadter, and others analyze the background of the Spanish-American War, as well as other issues arising from the conflict.

507
Greenleaf, Richard E., and Michael C. Meyer, eds. *Research in Mexican history; topics, methodology, sources, and a practical guide to field research.* Lincoln, University of Nebraska Press, 1973. xiii, 226 p. illus., map. (A Bison book) $3.75

This is a guide by 35 U.S. scholars to aid the graduate student researcher. It suggests topics needing study, discusses various historical approaches, and includes much practical advice on how to do research in Mexico. A very valuable and important work. Includes bibliographies.

508
Greenleaf, Richard E., ed. *The Roman Catholic church in colonial Latin America.* Edited with an introd. by Richard Greenleaf. New York, Knopf, 1971. xi, 272 p. (Borzoi books on Latin America) $4.50

Includes essays on a broad range of Catholic church activities in colonial Latin America in an effort to present a balanced picture. Church history is one of the most difficult aspects of Latin American colonial history. The essays were prepared by some of the most prominent colonialists in the field.

509
Gregersen, Hans M., and Arnold Contreras. *U.S. investment in the forest-based sector in Latin America.* Baltimore, Johns Hopkins Press, 1974. 128 p. illus. $4.50

Offers an overall view of present forest conditions and the production, trade, and consumption of forest products. Based on information obtained from personal interviews with investors and host country officials.

510
Gregg, Andrew K. *Drums of yesterday; the forts of New Mexico,* by Andy Gregg. Santa Fe, N.M., Press of the Territories, 1968. 40 p. illus. (Series of Western Americana, no. 17) $1.50

Describes and illustrates old forts of New Mexico, many of them dating from the Spanish colonial period.

511
Gregory, Peter. *Industrial wages in Chile.* Ithaca, N.Y., State School of Industrial and Labor Relations, Cornell University, 1967. xii, 113 p. (Cornell international industrial and labor relations report, no. 8) $2.65

Examines the wages, productivity, and industrialization in Chile. This is a thorough, well-written work with extensive bibliographical footnotes.

512
Griffen, William B. *Cultural change and shifting populations in central northern Mexico.* Tucson, University of Arizona Press, 1969. xii, 196 p. maps. (Anthropological papers of the University of Arizona, no. 13) $6

Studies demographic and cultural changes in the central northern regions of Mexico. Includes a thorough bibliography.

513
Grove, David C. *The Olmec paintings of Oxtotitlán Cave, Guerrero, Mexico.* Washington, Dumbarton Oaks, 1970. 36 p. illus., plates. (Studies pre-Columbian art and archaeology, 6) $2.50

An attractive survey of the paintings of the Oxtotitlán Cave with excellent illustrations and handsome color plates.

514
Guevara, Ernesto. *Che Guevara speaks.* Edited by G. Lavan and J. Hansen. New York,

Grove Press, 1967. 159 p. $.95

Includes a selection of Guevara's writings, concentrating on his earlier period as well as on the Cuban period.

515
Guevara, Ernesto *Che Guevara's Bolivian diaries.* New York, Bantam Books, 1973. 212 p. $1.45

Contains the Bolivian diaries of Che Guevara in an abridged edition.

516
Guevara, Ernesto. *Che: selected works of Ernesto Guevara.* Edited, with an introd. by Rolando E. Bonachea and Nelson P. Valdés. Cambridge, Massachusetts Institute of Technology Press, 1970. 512 p. $3.95

This is the best and most complete selection of Che's essays, speeches, interviews, and letters for the 1958-67 period. The editors chose those that most clearly illustrate Guevara's development as a political thinker. Contains a bibliography.

517
Guevara, Ernesto. *The complete Bolivian diaries of Che Guevara and other captured documents.* Edited and with an introd. by James Daniel. Translated from the Spanish. New York, Stein and Day, 1969. 330 p. illus., facsims., maps, ports. $2.95

The editor's 70-page introduction serves as a useful guide to Guevara's diary of the Bolivian campaign that ended with the leader's death in October 1967. Three additional diaries offer a counterpoint to Guevara. [Charles Fleener]

518
Guevara, Ernesto. *Episodes of the revolutionary war.* New York, International Publishers, 1968. 114 p. illus., maps. $1.65

English translation of *Pasajes de la guerra revolucionaria* (1963), in which Guevara describes how his small band of followers was transformed into a rebel army, starting with the first battle of December 1956 in which Che was wounded and then covers the eight months during which the army was formed in Sierra Maestra.

519
Guevara, Ernesto. *Guerrilla warfare.* New York, Random House, 1969. 387 p. $1.65

Guevara expounds his views on guerrilla warfare and on how to organize the population for revolution.

520
Guevara, Ernesto. *Reminiscences of the Cuban revolutionary war.* Translated by Victoria Ortiz. New York, Grove Press, 1968. 287 p. illus., maps. $1.25

Personal reminiscences of attacks, battles, and skirmishes in which the author participated in his effort to overthrow President Fulgencio Batista. The memoirs were written several years later, based on hasty notes taken on the battlefield. An important book, written by one of most influential revolutionaries of Latin America.

521
Guevara, Ernesto. *Socialism and man.* New York, Pathfinder Press, 1965. 18 p. $.35

In this pamphlet Guevara explains his theory about man in a Socialist system.

522
Guevara, Ernesto. *Venceremos: the speeches and writings of Che Guevara.* Edited,

annotated, and with an introd. by John Gerassi. New York, Simon and Schuster, 1969. xxi, 442 p. $2.95

Includes selected writings of Guevara. The editor neglects to inform the reader when he leaves out parts of the text. Nonetheless, this is a useful edition, of interest to those who study revolutionary Cuba.

523
Guillén, Nicolás. *Man-making words; selected poems of Nicolás Guillén.* Translated, annotated, with an introd. by Robert Márquez and David Arthur McMurray. Amherst, University of Massachusetts Press, 1972. xx, 214 p. $2.50

The poems collected in this brief anthology contain "the full ideological thrust of the poet's writings," opposing capitalism and praising the Cuban revolution. Spanish and English texts appear on opposite pages. Includes bibliographical references.

524
Guillén, Nicolás. *Patria o muerte! The great zoo and other poems.* Translated from the Spanish, annotated, and with an introd. by Robert Márquez. New York, Monthly Review Press, 1972. 223 p. $3.25

Includes Spanish and English poems from *El gran zoo* (1967) and other poems (1925-69). The translator has selected primarily Guillén's poetry of social protest. Guillén has been regarded as the major exponent of black poetry in the Spanish-speaking world. The introduction highlights the poet's life and work.

525
Güiraldes, Ricardo. *Don Segundo Sombra.* Edited by Angela B. Dellepiane. Englewood Cliffs, N.J., Prentice-Hall, 1971. 265 p. port. $4.95

This classic from Argentina was first published in 1926. Don Segundo is a shadow, an idea, emerging from an Argentina that is passing away. Scenes of country life are knitted into poetic prose about regional customs and folktales.

526
Güiraldes, Ricardo. *Don Segundo Sombra, shadows on the Pampas.* Translated and with an afterword by Harriet de Onís. Illustrated by Alberto Güiraldes. New York, New American Library, 1966. 222 p. illus. (A Signet classic, CT-317) $.75

This is an excellent English translation of the Argentine classic about gaucho life on the Pampas.

527
Gunther, John. *Inside South America.* New York, Pocket Books, 1970. 386 p. $1.25

A general book on South America aimed at the lay reader and traveler.

528
Gutierrez, Gustavo. *A theology of liberation: history, politics, and salvation.* Translated and edited by Sister Caridad Inda and John Eagleson. Maryknoll, N.Y., Orbis Books, 1973. xi, 323 p. $4.95

Outlines the beliefs and views of the reform-minded Catholic church in Latin America. Social, economic, and political reforms are seen as an attainable goal. This is an important and provocative book. Includes bibliographical references.

529
Guzmán, Martín Luis. *El águila y la serpiente.* Edited by E.R. Moore. New York, Norton, 1969. 289 p. $2.50

This novel was first published in 1928. It is a collection of episodes drawn from

Guzmán's own experiences during the Mexican Revolution. The style is vigorous and colorful. Contains notes and vocabularies.

530

Guzmán Campos, Germán. *Camilo Torres, le cure guerrillero.* Port Washington, N.Y., Paris Publications, 1970. 315 p. $4.30

This is a French translation of *El padre Camilo Torres,* a sympathetic biography of the Colombian guerrilla priest. Includes bibliographical notes.

531

Hageman, Alice, and Philip Wheaton, eds. *Revolution and religion in Cuba.* New York, Association Press, 1971. 357 p. $2

Prepared under the sponsorship of the Movimiento Estudiantil Cristiano, a member of the World Council of Churches. Contributors include Sergio Arce, Germán Renés, and statements by various Cuban religious leaders. It deals more with protestantism than with other religions.

532

Haigh, Roger M. *Martin Güemes; tyrant or tool? A study of the sources of power of an Argentine caudillo.* Fort Worth, Texas Christian University Press, 1968. 77 p. (Texas Christian University monographs in history and culture, no. 3) $3.50

Studies a powerful provincial caudillo of Argentina, who with his gauchos of Salta made an important contribution to the cause of independence by holding off the Royalists in 1915. The intricate patterns of the ruling provincial oligarchy, to which Güemes was related, are analyzed deftly. When Güemes set out to oppose the establishment he was destroyed. Includes a bibliography.

533

Hall, Barbara J. *Mexico in pictures.* Prepared by Barbara J. Hall. New York, Sterling Pub. Co., 1970. 64 p. illus., maps. (Visual geography series) $1.50

Describes contemporary Mexico with attractive illustrations and text. Intended for the high school and freshman college student as well as the traveler.

534

Halmos, Paul, ed. *Latin American sociological studies.* New York, Humanities Press, 1967. 179 p. (The sociological review. Monograph 11) $5.25

Contains essays ranging from K.H. Silvert's "The politics of social and economic change in Latin America," to Stanislav Andreski's "Genealogy of public vices in Latin America." Charles Wagley provided the introduciton. Includes bibliographic references.

535

Halperín-Donghi, Tulio. *The aftermath of revolution in Latin America.* Translated by Josephine de Bunsen. New York, Harper & Row, 1973. 149 p. $2.95

An excellent study of the early independence era (1820-50) in Latin America. The author analyzes the relations among urban and rural elites and national armies and militias in each country. It also deals with foreign economic interests, particularly the role played by British merchants. Includes a bibliography.

536

Hamill, Hugh M., ed. *Dictatorship in Spanish America.* New York, Knopf, 1965. x, 242 p. (Borzoi books on Latin America) $2.50

Presents papers by prominent U.S. and Latin American historians which trace the development of caudillismo and personalismo through the 19th century to such contemporary figures as Trujillo and Juan and Eva Perón. Includes a bibliography.

537

Hamilton, Daniel Lee, and Ned Carey Fahs, eds. *Contos do Brasil.* New York, Appleton-Century-Crofts, 1965. xiii, 332 p. $3.95

Presents short stories by prominent Brazilian authors such as Machado de Assis, Monteiro Lobato, Mario de Andrade, and others, written in various levels of language ranging from the classical style of Machado de Assis to the colloquial idiom of Andrade. Includes bibliographies and vocabularies.

538

Hammel, Eugene A. *Power in Ica; the structural history of a Peruvian community.* Boston, Little, Brown, 1969. xvi, 142 p. illus., maps. (Latin American case study, 1) $2.95

An abridged version of *Wealth, authority, and prestige in the Ica Valley,* which describes agriculture, industry, and transportation as these have influenced the distribution of power in the valley. Modern families are used to illustrate the values and organization patterns found in five social classes. Originally presented as a doctoral dissertation.

539

Hammel, Eugene A. *Wealth, authority, and prestige in the Ica Valley, Peru.* Albuquerque, University of New Mexico Press, 1962. 110 p. maps, plates. (University of New Mexico publications in anthropology, no. 10) $2

A thorough case study of the distribution of wealth and power from the socioeconomic viewpoint. The author also examines social mobility and cultural change as related to wealth, authority, and prestige.

540

Hammond, Inc. *Atlas moderno universal.* Maplewood, N.J., 1972. 1 v. col. maps. $1.25

This is an excellent Spanish-language world atlas of great interest to public and college libraries.

541

Hanke, Lewis U. *Aristotle and the American Indians; a study in race prejudice in the modern world.* Bloomington, Indiana University Press, 1970. 164 p. illus. (A Midland book, MB-132) $1.95

This is an account of the debates between Juan Ginés de Sepúlveda and Bartolomé de las Casas held in Valladolid 1550-51. Sepúlveda bases his defense of Cortés' method of conquest on Aristotle's *Politics;* Las Casas declared these arguments contradictory to the Gospels and to the laws of the Church. [Charles Fleener]

542

Hanke, Lewis U. *Do the Americans have a common history? A critique of the Bolton theory.* New York, Knopf, 1964. x, 269 p. (Borzoi books on Latin America) $2.75

Professor Hanke compiles and analyzes a wealth of material which brings to life the most fascinating debate on the unity of the Western Hemisphere. Includes a bibliography.

543

Hanke, Lewis, U., ed. *History of Latin American civilization; sources and interpretations.* v. 1, *The colonial experience.* 2d ed. Boston, Little, Brown, 1973. xiv, 555 p. $5.95

Thoroughly revised edition which presents a good selection of sources and interpretations of some important events and topics in Latin American colonial history. The volume includes sections on the influence of the Iberian civilization, Inca rule, relations between Indians and Spaniards, population studies, race relations, and many other interesting facets of the colonial experience.

544

Hanke, Lewis U., ed. *History of Latin American civilization; sources and interpretations.* v. 2. *The modern age.* 2d ed. Boston, Little, Brown, 1973. xvi, 672 p. illus. $5.95

Revised edition presenting new selections of important sources and views on events of 19th- and 20th-century Latin America. Deals with key problems such as dictatorship, revolutions, economic change, intellectual trends, slavery and social history, agrarian problems, and the role of the military in politics. An excellent and highly recommended compilation, with bibliographies.

545

Hanke, Lewis U., ed. *Latin America; a historical reader.* Boston, Little, Brown, 1974. xvi, 671 p. illus., map. $5.95

Designed particularly for one-semester courses, this work is intended to provide students with a representative collection of historical documents on the civilization of Latin America from the colonial experience to the present 20th-century revolutionary changes. This is a very useful compilation.

546

Hanke, Lewis U., ed. *Mexico and the Caribbean.* 2d ed. Princeton, N.J., Van Nostrand, 1967. 192 p. $1.95

Consists of a general historical introduction comprising about half the book. Over 30 readings are appended, some consisting of documents, others of secondary sources.

547

Hanke, Lewis U., ed. *Readings in Latin American history; selected articles from the Hispanic American Historical Review.* New York, Crowell, 1966. 2 v. $3.95 each

Volume 1 covers the colonial period from the time of contact to 1810 and volume 2 brings the readings up to the present. The contributors include Lyle McAlister, Woodrow Borah, Robert Potash, Stanley R. Ross, Richard Morse, and many other prominent specialists in their fields.

548

Hanke, Lewis U., ed. *South America.* 2d ed. Princeton, N.J., Van Nostrand, 1967. 191 p. $1.95

This handy volume sets forth the nature of the fundamental problems of South America. The editor has selected appropriate readings and contributes a long historical introduction.

549

Hanke, Lewis U. *The Spanish struggle for justice in the conquest of America.* Boston, Little, Brown, 1967. xi, 217 p. illus. $3.25

First published in 1949, this is a definitive study of the Spaniards who fought for justice in the colonies. It centers around Bartolomé de las Cases, a strong advocate of the application of Christian ethics to the administration of the Spanish empire. Includes bibliographical notes.

550

Hanson, Earl Parker. *Puerto Rico; ally for progress.* Princeton, N.J., Van Nostrand, 1962. 136 p. (Van Nostrand Searchlight books, no. 7) $1.45

Describes the developments which have taken place in Puerto Rico during the past decade and suggests that the relationship between the U.S. and Puerto Rico is an example of what the Alliance for Progress can accomplish. Includes bibliographies.

551

Harblin, Thomas Devaney. *Urbanization, industrialization, and low-income family organization in São Paulo, Brazil.* Ithaca, N.Y., Cornell University, Latin American Studies Program, 1971. 287 p. (Latin American Studies Program, Dissertation series, no. 48) $3

> Analyzes the impact of urbanization and industrialization upon low-income family organization. This is a very important study, with an excellent bibliography.

552

Harding, Timothy F. *The university, politics, and development in contemporary Latin America.* Riverside, University of California, Latin American Research Program, 1968. 32 p. $1

> Maintains that there exists a gap between the Latin American university's self-image of innovation and freedom of action and its behavior which actually perpetuates the elitist social structure. The university in Latin America is bound by its antecedent, and it rarely promotes social change. [Charles Fleener]

553

Hardoy, Jorge Enrique. *Urban planning in pre-Columbian America.* New York, G. Braziller, 1968. 128 p. illus., map. (Planning and cities) $2.95

> Surveys the process of urbanization in pre-Columbian America. Attractive photographs, plans, and drawings illustrate the text, which analyzes the designs and forms of urban areas in Central Mexico and South America. Includes a bibliography. [Charles Fleener]

554

Hardoy, Jorge Enrique, and Richard P. Schaedel, eds. *The urbanization process in America from its origins to the present day.* Buenos Aires, Editorial del Instituto Torcuato Di Tella, 1969. 364 p. illus., maps, tables. $2.50

> These papers were originally presented at the 37th International Congress of Americanists, Mar del Plata, 1966. The 24 articles appear in their original language. The contributors include Charles Gibson, Richard Morse, Richard Schaedel, George Kubler, and many others prominent in their field. [Charles Fleener]

555

Hargrave, Lyndon Lane. *Mexican Macaws; comparative osteology and survey of remains from the Southwest.* Tucson, Arizona, University of Arizona Press, 1970. 67 p. (Anthropological papers of the University of Arizona, no. 20) $5

> A very detailed and scientific study of Mexican Macaws, intended for the specialist.

556

Hargreaves, Dorothy, and Bob Hargreaves. *Tropical trees: found in the Caribbean, South America, Central America, Mexico.* Text and color photography by Dorothy and Bob Hargreaves. Portland, Oregon, Hargreaves Industrial, 1965. 64 p. col. illus. $2

> This handsomely illustrated book describes in great detail the exotic trees of the Caribbean, the Americas, and other tropical zones, citing at the end of each section the location and common names of each tree. The bibliography and glossary at the end of the volume are most useful.

557

Haring, Clarence H. *Empire in Brazil; a New World experiment with monarchy.* New York, Norton, 1968. 182 p. maps. $1.75

This is a reissue of the same title published in 1958. It is a general survey, and the first in English, of the Brazilian monarchy. Useful for college and graduate courses, it presents an able interpretation and analysis of the Brazilian empire. Includes a bibliography.

558
Haring, Clarence H. *The Spanish empire in America.* New York, Walker, 1966. 371 p. $3.95

A thorough and amply documented history of the colonial period with emphasis on political and economic administration. Originally published in 1947, this is an indispensable volume for the student of Spanish colonial institutions and imperial politics. Includes a bibliography.

559
Harmon, Mary. *Efrén Hernández: A Mexican writer and philosopher.* Hattiesburg, University and College Press of Mississippi, 1972. xi, 115 p. (The University and College Press of Mississippi series. Humanities) $2.95

Discusses the philosophical and poetic work of a distinguished Mexican writer whose work combines the profound, the humorous, and the light. Includes a thorough bibliography.

560
Harris, Louis K., and Victor Alba. *The political culture and behavior of Latin America.* Kent, Ohio, Kent State University Press, 1974. 232 p. illus. $4.50

Presents a geographical overview and a recounting of the shared history of colonialism, independence struggles, economic domination, proceeding then to examine contemporary Latin American politics. A very lucid introductory text.

561
Harris, Marvin. *Town and country in Brazil.* New York, Norton, 1971. 302 p. illus. $2.95

This is a reprint of the 1956 edition, which was issued as no. 37 of the Columbia University Contributions to Anthropology. The monograph studies social patterns and economic interaction in rural and urban Brazil. Includes a bibliography.

562
Harss, Luis, and Barbara Dohmann. *Into the mainstream; conversations with Latin American writers.* New York, Harper & Row, 1969. 385 p. $2.95

These essays are based on interviews with the following Latin American writers: Alejo Carpentier, Miguel Ángel Asturias, Jorge Luis Borges, João Guimarãs Rosa, Juan Carlos Onetti, Julio Cortázar, Carlos Fuentes, Juan Rulfo, Gabriel García Márquez, and Mario Vargas Llosa. The writers talk about their work and their opinions about literature.

563
Hartz, Louis. *The founding of new societies; studies in the history of the United States, Latin America, South Africa, Canada, and Australia.* With contributions by Kenneth D. McRae and others. New York, Harcourt Brace Jovanovich, 1964. xi, 336 p. $2.45

In the first section, Professor Hartz develops a theory of the development of new societies. In the second portion, five case studies are reviewed. Richard Morse presents a provocative analysis of "The Heritage of Latin America." [Charles Fleener]

564
Haverstock, Nathan A., and John P. Hoover. *Cuba in pictures.* New York, Sterling Pub. Co., 1974. 64 p. illus., maps. (Visual geography series) $2.25

An attractively illustrated introduction to modern day Cuba, with a brief history of the island and with a clear explanation of the new Cuba.

565
Havighurst, Robert J., and J. Roberto Moreira. *Society and education in Brazil.* Pittsburgh, University of Pittsburgh Press, 1965. xviii, 263 p. illus. (Pittsburgh. University. Studies in comparative education, no. 4) $2.50

Analyzes Brazilian education within the social and cultural context of the country.

566
Hayner, Norman S. *New patterns in old Mexico; a study of town and metropolis.* Includes bibliographical references by Norman S. Hayner in collaboration with Una Middleton Hayner. New Haven, Conn., College and University Press, 1966. 316 p. illus., map, tables. $2.45

Emphasizes selected social institutions in Mexico during the dynamic 1941-61 period, by comparing the Spanish-Indian town of Oaxaca with Mexico City.

567
Hays, Hoffman Reynolds, ed. *12 [i.e. Twelve] Spanish American poets; an anthology.* English translations, notes, and introd. by the editor. Boston, Beacon Press, 1972. 336 p. $3.95

Originally published in 1943, this anthology includes a representative selection of works by Latin American poets, such as Vicente Huidobro, Eugenio Florit, Jorge Luis Borges, Jorge Carrera Andrade, Pablo de Rokha, Nicolás Guillén, César Vallejo, Pablo Neruda, and others. The author states that through poetry we may become familiar with Latin America and its people. Includes bibliographies.

568
Healy, Gary W. *Self-concept; a comparison of Negro, Anglo, and Spanish-American students across ethnic, sex, and socioeconomic variables.* San Francisco, R. and E. Research Associates, 1974. 188 p. $8

An influential study which surveys ethnic youth comparatively. Includes a bibliography.

569
Hegen, Edmund Eduard. *Highways into the Upper Amazon Basin; pioneer lands in southern Colombia, Ecuador, and northern Peru.* Gainesville, University of Florida Press, 1966. 168 p. illus., maps, tables. (Latin American monographs, 2d series, no. 2) $3.75

Studies the role of roads, rivers, and runways in penetrating the vast tropical lowlands of Colombia, Ecuador, and Peru. These nations have developed considerably, and Bogotá, Quito, and Lima have become dynamic foci from which elements of commerce and culture radiate. Includes bibliographies.

570
Helfritz, Hans. *Mexican cities of the gods; and archaeological guide.* New York, Praeger, 1970. 180 p. illus., maps. $3.50

Describes pre-Hispanic religious monuments of the Plateau, Gulf Coast, and southern areas of Mexico. Attractive black-and-white illustrations enhance the text. The author has added information on archeological details and also on travel.

571
Heller, Celia Stopnicka. *Mexican-American youth; forgotten youth at the crossroads.* New York, Random House, 1966. 113 p. $2.25

Studies trends among Mexican American youth suggesting that they do no
constitute an exception to the characteristic historical pattern of minority ethni
groups in the U.S.

572
Heller, Celia Stopnicka. *New converts to the American dream? Mobility aspirations o
young Mexican-Americans.* New Haven, Conn., College and University Press, 1972
287 p. $2.95

Sociological study of educational and occupational goals of Mexican-Americans i
the U.S. based on field work in the Los Angeles area in 1957-58. It seems that th
data on which the study was based are somewhat outdated, but it nonetheless is
worthwhile and pioneering effort. Includes bibliographical references.

573
Helm, J. *Spanish-speaking people in the United States.* Seattle, University of Washingtor
Press, 1971. 369 p. $4

Surveys Spanish-speaking populations in the U.S. in a methodic and orderly
manner. Includes a bibliography.

574
Helm, MacKinley. *Modern Mexican painters.* New York, Dover Publishers, 1968. xxi
205 p. illus. (Essay index reprint series) $3.50

This history of modern Mexican painters from Dr. Alt, precursor of Diego Rivera
to present-day artists, is told with a perspective of artistic criticism and persona
anecdote. The black-and-white reproductions illustrate the author's points and
make the book worthwhile.

575
Hemingway, Ernest. *The old man and the sea.* New York, Scribner, 1961. 159 p. illus
$1.20

This is a textbook edition of what many critics consider Hemingway's best work
Set in Cuba, it deals with the struggle of an old Cuban fisherman who wants t
catch a large fish. The descriptions of Cuba and the sea are hauntingly beautiful

576
Henríquez Ureña, Pedro. *A concise history of Latin American culture.* Translated and
with a supplementary chapter by Gilbert Chase. New York, Praeger, 1967. 214 p
$2.50

Translation of *Historia de la cultura en la América hispánica* (1947), by one o
Latin America's foremost literary historians. It describes the development o
Latin American art and culture, tracing its civilization from the interaction of th
Indian and Spanish cultures to European and North American influences. Include
select bibliography.

577
Henry, Jules. *Jungle people; a Kaingáng tribe of the highlands of Brazil.* New York
Vintage Books, 1964. xxv, 215 p. illus. (A Caravelle edition) $1.95

This classic work by a noted anthropologist was first published in 1941. It is ar
excellent study on the Kaingáng Indians of Brazil. Includes informative
appendixes and bibliographical footnotes.

578
Hepburn, Andrew. *Rand McNally guide to Mexico.* Chicago, Rand McNally, 1968. 149
p. illus., maps. (Rand McNally guides) $2.95

A thorough guide to Mexico with several helpful maps and directions to special points of interest.

579

Merschel, Manuel T. *Spanish-speaking children of the Southwest; their education and the public welfare.* Austin, University of Texas Press, 1970. 222 p. $2.50

Examines educational training centers and indicates that special instruction must be designed and implemented to overcome language barriers and cultural gaps. Includes bibliographic notes.

580

Heyerdahl, Thor. *Kon-Tiki.* New York, Random House, 1965. 281 p. illus. $2.95

English version of the famous Norwegian explorer's epic voyage with five companions on a raft built of balsa wood, to prove that the Peruvian Indians traveled to Polynesia carried by ocean currents.

581

Heyerdahl, Thor. *Kon-Tiki; across the Pacific by raft.* Translated by F.H. Lyon. Illustrated with 80 photographs. New York, Pocket Books, 1973. 240 p. illus. (Washington Square Press enriched classics) $.95

English translation of *Kon-Tiki ekspedisjonen* (1947), in which the author describes his epic voyage.

582

Hills, Elijah Clarence. *Odes of Bello, Olmedo, and Heredia,* with an introduction by Elijah Clarence Hills. New York, Hispanic Society, 1973. 153 p. $2

In this collection of odes, Hills brings together three distinguished Latin American poets, Andrés Bello from Venezuela, José Joaquín de Olmedo from Ecuador, and José María Heredia from Cuba. Hills' introduction contains a brief but insightful biographical sketch of each poet. All the odes are written in the free metrical style of the silva, whose lines are seven to eleven syllables in length and are often unrhymed.

583

Hine, Robert V. *Bartlett's West: drawing the Mexican boundary.* New Haven, Published for the Amon Carter Museum, Fort Worth, by Yale University Press, 1968. xv, 155 p. illus. (part col.), map, col. port. (Yale Western Americana series, 19) $4.95

Artist and scientist of the 1850's, John Russell Bartlett was in charge of the Mexican Boundary Survey of that period. Hine's text is informative and easily read, and the 48 illustrations are drawn chiefly from the John Russell Bartlett papers in the John Carter Brown Library.

584

Hirschman, Albert O. *Bias for hope; essay on development and Latin America.* New Haven, Yale University Press, 1973. $3.45

Explores development in Latin America, analyzing many positive factors. The essays are lucid and informative. Contains bibliographical notes.

585

Hirschman, Albert O. *Exit, voice, and loyalty; response to decline in firms, organizations, and states.* Cambridge, Mass., Harvard University Press, 1970. 162 p. $1.95

A noted economist and theoretician on Latin American problems discusses certain aspects of organization decline in the hemisphere. Includes bibliographical references.

586

Hirschman, Albert O., comp. *Latin American issues; essays and comments.* New York, Twentieth Century Fund, 1973. 201 p. tables. $3

This is a reprint of the 1961 edition, containing a series of essays by Victor Alba, David Felix, Victor Urquidi, Thomas F. Carroll, and others, on political ideology, inter-American relations, economic problems and agrarian reform. Editor analyzes basic trends. Includes a bibliography.

587

Hirschman, Albert O. *The strategy of economic development.* New Haven, Conn., Yale University Press, 1961. xii, 217 p. (Yale studies in economics, 10) $1.95

The author's concepts were inspired by his experience in Colombia and other Latin American countries. He puts considerable emphasis on complementary and "linkage" effects which some industries use to a better effect than others. Includes bibliographical footnotes. [HLAS 23:1671]

588

Hirschhorn, Howard H. *Technical reader in English for Spanish speaking students.* New York, Regents Pub. Co., 1973. 199 p. $1.75

Useful compilation for Spanish-speaking persons.

589

Hodder, B.W. *Economic development in the tropics.* 2d ed. London, Methuen, 1973. xii, 258 p. map. £2.40

In an interdisciplinary manner, the author examines the major problems of development confronting tropical countries today. Venezuela and Trinidad and Tobago are used as case studies in a work that is basically a microcosm for the American tropics. Includes a bibliography. [Charles Fleener]

590

Hoetink, Harry. *Caribbean race relations; a study of two variants.* Translated from the Dutch by Eva M. Hooykaas. New York, Oxford University Press, 1971. xii, 207 p. (A Galaxy book, 337) $1.95

This is an abridged English version of *De gespleten samenleving in het Caribisch gebied* (1962). The author studies and compares race relations in the Caribbean countries of West European and Latin American provenience. [HLAS 27:1055a]

591

Hoetink, Harry. *Slavery and racism in the Americas.* New York, Harper & Row, 1973. 295 p. $2.95

Analyzes slavery and racism in the Americas from the sociological, demographic, and economic viewpoints. The author is a well-known sociologist who specializes in Caribbean problems. Includes a bibliography.

592

Holiday magazine editors. *Travel guide to Mexico.* Rev. ed. New York, Random House, 1971. 278 p. illus. (col.), map. (A Holiday magazine travel guide, v. 11) $1.95

This is a very useful guide for travel through Mexico.

593

Holiday magazine editors. *Travel guide to the Caribbean and the Bahamas.* Rev. ed. New

York, Random House, 1971. 259 p. illus. (col.), map. (A Holiday magazine travel guide, v. 12) $1.95

Introduces the traveler to most Caribbean islands and the Bahamas. Contains beautiful photographs.

594

Holmberg, Allan R. *Nomads of the long now; the Siriono of eastern Bolivia.* New York, Doubleday, 1960. 104 p. $1.95

Prepared in cooperation with the U.S. Dept. of State as a project of the Interdepartmental Committee on Scientific and Cultural Cooperation, this important study, first published in 1950, examines the Siriono Indians. The author is a noted anthropologist. Includes a bibliography.

595

Hopkins, Jack W. *The government executive of modern Peru.* Gainesville, University of Florida Press, 1967. 141 p. map, tables. (Latin American monographs; 2d series, no. 3) $1.95

This case study examines the senior civil servants in the Peruvian government. The origins, family education, and attitudes are investigated empirically. An introductory study of the role and nature of the Latin American government executive has been added. [Charles Fleener]

596

Hopper, Janice H., ed. *Indians of Brazil in the twentieth century.* Edited and translated by Janice H. Hopper. Washington, Institute of Cross-Cultural Research, 1967. 256 p. illus., map. (Institute of Cross-Cultural Research studies, 2) $6.95

Provides the most accurate information available in English on indigenous Brazilian tribes. Includes contributions by Gertrude Dole, Dale Kietzman, Darcy Ribeiro, Eduardo Galvão, and Herbert Baldus. Also includes a tribal catalog, a glossary of terms, and a critical report of research completed between 1953 and 1960, with a bibliography.

597

Horgan, Paul. *The centuries of Santa Fe.* New York, Dutton, 1960. 363 p. illus. $1.75

This is a popular history of Santa Fe under Spanish rule (1610-1821), under Mexico (1821-46), and as part of the U.S. from 1848 to the present. It highlights the long Hispanic tradition of this old capital of Spain in America. Includes a select bibliography.

598

Horgan, Paul. *Conquistadors in North American history.* Greenwich, Conn., Fawcett Publications, 1965. 303 p. $.95

Popular treatment of the Spanish conquerors in what is today Mexico and the U.S. Southwest. This interesting narrative includes a select bibliography.

599

Horgan, Paul. *Great river; the Rio Grande in North American history.* New York, Funk & Wagnalls, 1973. 2 v. maps (fold.) $2.95 each

Volume I deals with the Indians and Spain and their use of the Rio Grande, and volume II covers the Mexican and U.S. periods. Attractively written popular history, which includes a bibliography.

600

Horowitz, Irving Louis, ed. *The anarchists.* Edited, with an introd. by Irving Louis Horowitz. New York, Dell Pub. Co., 1964. 640 p. (A Laurel original) $.95

Contains a collection of essays on anarchism by leading political scientists, historians, and journalists. Includes bibliographical notes.

601

Horowitz, Irving Louis, ed. *Cuban communism*. Chicago, Aldine Pub. Co., 1970. 143 p. (Trans-action books, TA-2) $2.45

These essays originally appeared in the April 1969 issue of *Trans-action*. The essay titles include "Cuban communism," "Revolution for internal consumption only," "Student power in action," "The moral economy of a revolutionary society," "Cuba–Revolution without blueprint," and "Military dimensions of the Cuban revolution," among others. Includes bibliographies.

602

Horowitz, Irving Louis, Josué de Castro, and John Gerassi, eds. *Latin American radicalism; a documentary report on Left and National movements*. New York, Random House, 1970. xiii, 653 p. illus. $2.45

The contributors include politicians, economists, sociologists, and other professionals. The essays deal with socioeconomic, political, and international problems. Interesting selection of great value to students of contemporary Latin America.

603

Horowitz, Irving Louis, ed. *Masses in Latin America*. New York, Oxford University Press, 1970. 608 p. tables. $3.95

The essays seek to define social sectors, interest groups, and ethnic as well as national elements existing in Latin America and to place these in historical perspective. Includes bibliographies.

604

Horowitz, Irving Louis, ed. *The rise and fall of Project Camelot;* studies in the relationship between social science and practical politics. Cambridge, M.I.T. Press, 1967. xi, 385 p. $3.95

Presents viewpoints of social scientists and officials who were involved in Project Camelot, "a study whose objective was to determine the feasibility of developing a general social systems model which would make it possible to predict and influence politically significant aspects of social change in the developing countries." [Charles Fleener]

605

Horowitz, Michael M., comp. *Peoples and cultures of the Caribbean; an anthropological reader*, edited with an introd. by Michael M. Horowitz. Garden City, N.Y., Published for the American Museum of Natural History by the Natural History Press, 1971. 606 p. illus., maps. $4.50

This is a wide-ranging selection of readings concerning the anthropology of the Caribbean, by some of the top specialists in their fields. Includes bibliographies.

606

Howard, John R., comp. *Awakening minorities; American Indians, Mexican Americans, Puerto Ricans*. Edited by John R. Howard. Chicago, Aldine Pub. Co., 1970. 189 p. (Trans-action books, TA-18) $2.95

Contains essays dealing with special problems facing certain minorities in the U.S. Emphasizes political action rather than cultural trends. Includes bibliographical references.

607

Hoyos, Arturo de. *Occupational and educational levels of Mexican-American youth.* San Francisco, R. & E. Research Associates, 1973. 91 p. $7

Interesting analyses of the educational levels of certain groups of Mexican-American young people, based mainly on California samples. Includes tables and bibliographies.

608

Huberman, Leo, and Paul M. Sweezy. *Cuba: anatomy of a revolution.* 2d ed. with new material added. New York, Monthly Review Press, 1961. 208 p. $2.95

A very broadly conceived study of the Castro revolution based on a slim base of objective evidence. The authors, who have written previously on U.S. labor unions and socialism, appear to have sought evidence to support their theories. [HLAS 24:3538]

609

Huberman, Leo, and Paul M. Sweezy, eds. *Régis Debray and the Latin American revolution; a collection of essays.* New York, Monthly Review Press, 1969. 138 p. $1.95

Several commentators review Régis Debray's 1967 book *Revolution in the revolution?* Most of the reviewers are critical of Debray's severe judgment handed down against all the existing political parties in a letter from his Bolivian jail cell. [Charles Fleener]

610

Huberman, Leo, and Paul M. Sweezy. *Socialism in Cuba.* New York, Monthly Review Press, 1969. 221 p. $2.95

Socialist report on how the revolutionary government solves the basic economic problems by two authors who visited Cuba four times during the 1960's. The book was largely completed before Huberman's death in 1968. Of interest to sociologists and political scientists. [HLAS 33:2822]

611

Hudson, William Henry. *Green mansions.* New York, AMSCO Music Book Pub. Co., 1965. 234 p. $.95

A haunting novel revealing a passionate love of nature by the famous Anglo-Argentine novelist and writer. By sheer glow of beauty it is a prose poem in a South American jungle setting.

612

Hudson, William Henry. *Green mansions.* Introd. by N.R. Teitel. Airmont, 1970. 254 p. $.95

The introduction analyzes Hudson's life and work. See above comment.

613

Hudson, William Henry. *Green mansions.* New York, Bantam Books, 1963. 269 p. $.75

See above comment.

614

Hudson, William Henry. *Green mansions.* New York, Dell Pub. Co., 1968. 255 p. $.60

Another edition of the perennial favorite. See above comment.

615

Hufford, Charles H. *The social and economic effects of the Mexican migration into*

Texas. San Francisco, R. & E. Research Associates, 1971. 70 p. $7

This thorough monograph closely examines the impact of Mexican migration into Texas. Includes bibliographies. Of interest to libraries and students of borderlands sociology. Originally written as the author's thesis in 1929.

616

Hughes, Helen (MacGill), comp. *Population growth and the complex society.* Compiled and edited by Helen MacGill Hughes. Boston, Allyn and Bacon, 1972. xii, 211 p. (Readings in sociology series) $2.25

Several prominent specialists in demography and sociology examine issues and problems related to population growth and society. Contains bibliographical notes.

617

Huizer, Gerrit. *Peasant rebellion in Latin America; the origins, forms of expresssion, and potential of Latin American peasant unrest.* Harmondsworth, England, Penguin Books, 1973. 183 p. (The Pelican Latin American library) $1.95

A succinct analysis of peasant rebellions in Latin America. Of interest to sociologists and political scientists. Includes a bibliography.

618

Hulet, Claude L., comp. *Latin American poetry in English translation; a bibliography.* Washington, Pan American Union, 1965. 192 p. (PAU 860-E-7157; Basic bibliographies, 2) $.75

This is a very useful bibliography of anthologies, books, and individual poems by Latin Americans which have appeared in English translation.

619

Hulet, Claude L., comp. *Latin American prose in English translation; a bibliography.* Washington, Pan American Union, 1964. 191 p. (PAU-E-6939; Basic bibliograhpies, 1) $.75

Attempts to cover all English translations of Latin American novels, short stories, and literary essays published through August 1962. A very useful reference work.

620

Humboldt, Alexander Freiherr von. *Political essay on the kingdom of New Spain.* Edited by Mary M. Dunn. New York, Knopf, 1974. 311 p. $3.10

This is a translation of *Essai politique sur le royaume de la Nouvelle Espagne* which is part 3 of *Voyage de Humboldt et Bonpland.* The famed German naturalist was born in 1769 and died in 1859. His massive writings on Middle and South America became a lasting scholarly contribution.

621

Humphreys, Robert Arthur, and John Lynch, eds. *The origins of the Latin American revolutions, 1808-1826.* Edited, with an introd. by R.A. Humphreys and John Lynch. New York, Knopf, 1965. 308 p. (A Borzoi book on Latin America) $2.50

A collection of scholarly essays on such topics as the enlightenment in Spanish America, the exiled Jesuits, the role of Britain, France, and the U.S., and the decline of the Spanish empire. Includes a bibliography.

622

Hunter, Frederick James, ed. *A guide to the theater and drama collection of the University of Texas.* Austin, University of Texas Press, 1967. 64 p. illus. $2

This is a welcome guide to the University of Texas Library's collection of theatrical works.

623

Hutchinson, William Henry. *Pasó por aquí.* Norman, University of Oklahoma Press, 1973. 213 p. illus. (The Western frontier library) $2.95

Contains information on Spanish influence in the U.S. Southwest.

624

Huxley, Francis. *Affable savages; an anthropologist among the Urubu Indians of Brazil.* New York, Putnam, 1966. 285 p. illus., maps. $1.75

Contains considerable data on the Urubu Indians of north-central Maranhão State but difficult to desengage from the travel-account aspect because most of the data occur in the form of dialogues between Huxley and his Indian friends. First published in 1956. [HLAS 20:560]

625

Im Thurn, Everard F. *Among the Indians of Guiana.* New York, Dover Publications, 1967. 445 p. illus., maps. $3.50

Originally published in 1883, this work presents the first extensive observations of the culture of the Indians of the forest and remote interior Savannah country of present-day Guyana. This edition is an unabridged version of the first one.

626

Imaz, José Luis de. *Los que mandan [Those who rule].* Translated from the Spanish by Carlos A. Astiz, with Mary F. McCarthy. Albany, State University of New York Press, 1970. 279 p. $2.45

English translation of an important sociological study first published in 1964, which utilizes social backgrounds of political leaders, landowners, industrialists, military officers, and labor union leaders in examining the power structure of modern Argentina. [HLAS 35:8436]

627

Indian Mexico: past and present. Symposium papers 1965. Betty Bell, editor. Los Angeles, Latin American Center, University of California, 1967. 109 p. illus. (University of California, Los Angeles, Latin American studies, 7) $3

These papers were presented at a symposium held under the joint sponsorship of the Dept. of Anthropology and the Latin American Center of the University of California at Los Angeles. The contributions present a systematic picture of the Indians of Mexico through a long time span. Includes bibliographies.

628

Inman, Samuel Guy. *Inter-American conferences, 1826-1954; history and problems.* Edited by Harold Eugene Davis. Washington, University Press of Washington, 1966. 282 p. $5

The author traces the development of the inter-American system through the hemispheric conferences. This is a very valuable survey for the student of international relations.

629

Instituto Internacional de Literatura Iberoamericana. *An outline history of Spanish American literature.* 3d ed. John E. Englekirk, editor. New York, Appleton-Century-Crofts, 1965. xiii, 252 p. maps (part fold. col.) $3.45

This revised edition, published in 1941, is a continuous outline of the development of Spanish-American literature arranged into three periods: from discovery to Independence, from Independence to the Mexican Revolution, and from the Mexican Revolution to the present. Each topic has references to the leading handbooks and works of criticism and sound evaluations of the writers. An excellent compilation which will be very useful in literature courses.

630

Inter-American Port and Harbor Conference, 2d, Mar del Plata, Argentine Republic, 1963. *Cargo loss preservation; papers prepared for the Second Inter-American Port and Harbor Conference.* Sponsored by the Organization of American States. Foreword by Fred Weissman. New York, International Insurance Monitor, 1963. 39, 41 p. $1.50

The papers are presented here in Spanish and English.

631

International Bank for Reconstruction and Development. *Economic growth of Colombia; problems and prospects.* Baltimore, Johns Hopkins Press, 1972. 2 v. $8.50

This comprehensive analysis of the Colombian economy was compiled by a World Bank mission under the leadership of Dragoslaw Avramovic. A very important study. Contains a useful bibliography.

632

International Bank for Reconstruction and Development. *Economic development of Nicaragua.* Baltimore, Johns Hopkins University Press, 1970. 57 p. tables. $1

Outlines briefly the principal aspects of economic development in Nicaragua.

633

International Music Council. *Folk songs of the Americas.* Edited by A. L. Lloyd and Isabel Aretz de Ramón y Rivera. New York, Oak Publications, 1970. 285 p. $3.95

This edition includes the music and words of 150 popular folksongs of this hemisphere. Those in Spanish and French Creole are accompanied by English translations.

634

Irving, Brian, and others. *Guyana; a composite monograph.* Hato Rey, P.R., Inter-American University Press, 1973. 292 p. $5

The contributors include Brian Irving, Harold Lutchman, Brian Wearing, Yereth Knowles, Ved Duggal, Della Walker, and Alexander Acholonu. The topics deal with politics, history, socioeconomic problems, Amerindian acculturation, and ecological problems of Guyana. Includes bibliographies.

635

Ivask, Ivar, ed. *The perpetual present; the poetry and prose of Octavio Paz.* Norman, University of Oklahoma Press, 1973. xiv, 160 p. illus. $5.95

Includes papers originally presented at a Paz conference sponsored by the Department of Modern Languages of the University of Oklahoma, together with *Books Abroad.* The papers contain criticism and commentary on the works of the noted Mexican writer. Contains a bibliography.

636

Jackson, D. Bruce. *Castro, the Kremlin, and communism in Latin America.* Baltimore, Johns Hopkins Press, 1969. 163 p. (Washington, Center of Foreign Policy Research, Studies in international affairs series, 9) $2.45

Surveys Soviet-Cuban relations, from 1964 to 1967, concentrating on Cuban radicalism, Castro's feud with Mao Tse-Tung, the 1965 Dominican crisis, the 1966 Tricontinental Conference, the withdrawal of the Venezuelan Communist Party from guerilla warfare, and the replacement of Che Guevara by Régis Debray as chief Cuban ideologist. Includes bibliographical references.

637

Jacobs, Charles Richmond, and Babette M. Jacobs. *Mexico travel digest.* 3d rev. ed. Los Angeles, Paul, Richmond, 1969. 169 p. illus. $3.95

Unusual points of interest are presented in this travel guide to Mexico.

638

Jacobs, Charles Richmond, and Babette M. Jacobs. *South America travel digest.* 6th ed. Los Angeles, Paul, Richmond, 1970. 159 p. illus. $3.50

The authors present an attractive and informative guide to travel throughout South America.

639

Jacobs, Wilbur R., John W. Caughey, and Joe B. Frantz. *Turner, Bolton, and Webb: three historians of the American frontier.* Seattle, University of Washington Press, 1956. xii, 113 p. facsims., illus., ports. $1.95

Bolton chiefly studies the Spanish borderlands and Spain's influence in North America. Turner and Webb deal with the cultural clash between Anglo-American and Spanish-Mexican traditions on the American frontier. Includes a bibliography.

640

Jahn, Ernst A. *Latin American travel and Pan American highway guide.* New York, Compaco Pub. Co., 1969. 421 p. illus., maps. $4.95

The author has compiled current information on train, bus, and freighter fares and schedules of both the popular and remote areas of Mexico and Central and South America.

641

James, Cyril Lionel Robert. *The Black Jacobins: Toussaint l'Ouverture and the San Domingo Revolution.* 2d ed. rev. New York, Random House, 1963. xi, 426 p. map. $1.95

First published in 1938, this book traces the career of Toussaint L'Ouverture and the history of the San Domingo Revolution. The appendix entitled "From Toussaint L'Ouverture to Fidel Castro" deals with Haiti and the West Indian quest for national identity during the last century and a half. Includes a bibliography.

642

James, Daniel. *Che Guevara.* New York, Stein and Day, 1970. 256 p. $3.95

The author has assembled a thorough biography of Ernesto (Che) Guevara.

643

James, Daniel, comp. *The complete Bolivian diaries of Che Guevara and other captured documents.* Edited and with an introd. by Daniel James. New York, Stein and Day, 1968. 330 p. illus., facsims., maps, ports. $2.95

The compiler presents the diaries and other documents connected with Che Guevara's Bolivian campaign. Includes bibliographical footnotes and photographs.

644

James, Thomas. *Three years among the Indians and Mexicans.* Introd. by A.P. Nasatir. Philadelphia, Lippincott, 1962. 173 p. illus. (Keystone Western Americana series, KB51) $1.25

This is an abridged version of the original 1846 edition of the author's experiences as a fur trader among the Comanches and Mexicans along the Santa Fe trail, 1809-10 and 1821-25. It also discusses U.S. expansion in Mexico.

645

Jaquiera, Joaquim, and Manoel B. Mansa. *The warriors; peleja between Joaquim Jaquiera and Manoel Barra Mansa.* Translated by Ernest J. Barge and Jan Feidel, with illus. by Donald Canzana. New York, Grossman, 1972. 131 p. illus. $3.95

646

Jekyll, Walter, ed. *Jamaican song and story; Annancy stories, digging tunes, ring tunes, and dancing,* with new introductory essays by Philip Sherlock, Louise Bennett, and Rex Nettleford. New York, Dover, 1966. xv, 288 p. $2.50

Fifty-one stories and 145 songs collected by the editor are presented with their music. Of great interest to folklorists and ethnologists, this is an unabridged new edition of the original published in 1907. [Charles Fleener]

647

Jesús, Carolina María de. *Child of the dark; the diary of Carolina María de Jesús.* Translated from the Portuguese by David St. Clair. New York, New American Library, 1969. 159 p. $.95

English translation of the award-winning Brazilian novel *Quarto de despejo; diário de una favelada* (1960), written by a woman who was unemployed, uneducated, and burdened with three illegitimate children. A moving account of life in a São Paulo slum as it could be described only be one who has lived there many years.

648

Jodorowsky, Alejandro. *El topo; a book of the film.* Edited by Ross Firestone. Translations by Joanne Pottlitzer. New York, Douglas Book Corp., Distributed by World Book Pub. Co., 1972. 173 p. illus. $2.95

Brings to the public an annotated script of the controversial Mexican film and includes conversations with the director, Alejandro Jodorowsky.

649

Joffroy, Pierre. *Brazil.* Translated by Douglas Garman. New York, Viking Press, 1965. 192 p. illus., col. map. (Vista travel, W-27) $1.65

Translated from the French original *Le Brésil* (1963), this is an attractive book devoted to the description of Brazil.

650

Johnson, Dale L., ed. *The Chilean road to socialism.* Introd. by Dale L. Johnson. Garden City, N.Y., Doubleday, 1973. xiv, 546 p. (Anchor books) $2.95

Brings important Unidad Popular documents into English for the first time. Nearly all the documents and writings have been drawn from U.S. New Left sources. Includes a select bibliography.

651

Johnson, Dale L. *The sociology of change and reaction in Latin America.* Indianapolis, Bobbs-Merrill, 1973. 56 p. (The Bobbs-Merrill studies in sociology) $2.45

Deals with economic development and social change in contemporary Latin America. Includes a succinct bibliography.

652

Johnson, Henry Sioux, and William J. Hernández M., eds. *Educating the Mexican-American.* Valley Forge, Pa., Judson Press, 1970. 384 p. $6.95

Contains essays on various programs and studies on educating Mexican Americans in the U.S. Includes bibliographical references. An important contribution of interest to colleges with Chicano programs and to public libraries.

653

Johnson, John J., ed. *Continuity and change in Latin America.* Edited by John J. Johnson. Contributors: Richard N. Adams and others. Stanford, Calif., Stanford University Press, 1967. xiii, 282 p. $2.95

Nine papers prepared for a conference held at Scottsdale, Ariz., in 1963. The authors are academic specialists in the several disciplines of the social sciences and humanities. Although the central theme is of change and continuity, each has its political connotations. This is a distinguished collection, worthy of attention. [HLAS 27:3038b]

654

Johnson, John J. *The military and society in Latin America.* Stanford, Calif., Stanford University Press, 1964. 308 p. $2.95

A good interpretation of military and civilian relations in the Latin American republics during the 19th and 20th centuries. The chapter on Brazil is especially good. The Cuban military under Castro is also covered. Contains a bibliography.

655

Johnson, John J. *Political change in Latin America; the emergence of the middle sectors.* Stanford, Calif., Stanford University Press, 1961. xiii, 272 p. (Stanford studies in history, economics and political science, 15) $2.95

First published in 1958. The author states that political change occurs when the middle sectors (not middle classes) of society become aware of their interests and demand power. Argentina, Brazil, Chile, Mexico, and Uruguay are covered. Includes a bibliography.

656

Johnson, John J., ed. *The role of the military in underdeveloped countries.* Princeton, N.J., Princeton University Press, 1962. 427 p. $2.95

Presents papers read at a 1959 Rand Corporation conference designed to provide a forum for the exchange of information and ideas on militarism. The editor, Edwin Lieuwen, and Víctor Alba participated with papers on the military in Latin America. [Charles Fleener]

657

Johnson, John J. *Simon Bolivar and Spanish American independence; 1783-1830,* by John J. Johnson, with the collaboration of Doris M. Ladd. Princeton, N.J., Van Nostrand, 1968. 223 p. (An Anvil original, 95) $1.95

A factual biography of Simón Bolívar, the most influential figure in Spanish American independence. Bolívar was in favor of strong government as the only workable system to ward off anarchy. He also wanted a large federated state for South America. Includes a bibliography.

658

Johnson, Kenneth F. *Mexican democracy; a critical view.* Boston, Allyn and Bacon, 1971. xiii, 190 p. (The Allyn and Bacon series in Latin American politics) $1.95

The author relies on clandestine literature of protest as well as on the more traditional sources and on many interviews. Analyzes the PRI (Partido Revolucionario Institucional), the opposition groups, and outlines the political dilemmas among voters. Includes bibliographical footnotes.

659

Johnson, Mildred Edith, ed. and tr. *Swan, cygnets, and owl; an ant anthology of modernist poetry in Spanish-America,* with an introductory essay by J. S. Brushwood. Columbia, University of Missouri Press, 1971. 199 p. (The University of Missouri studies, v. 29) $4.95

Modernismo is a literary movement which, at the end of the 19th century, initiated the contemporary period in Spanish literature. This bilingual anthology includes biographic sketches and selections from the works of Gutiérrez Nájera, Martí, Silva, Darío, Jaime Freyre, Nervo, Lugones, Santos Chocano, Herrera y Reissig, Agustini, Storni, Ibarbourou, Banchs, Torres Bodet, Neruda, and several others. This is an important contribution, first published in 1956.

660
Johnson, Paul Willard. *Field guide to the gems and minerals of Mexico, exclusive of Baja California; a guide to the most productive and interesting minerals and gem collecting localities with Spanish-English, English-Spanish glossary of gem, mineral and mining terms.* Mentone, Calif., Gembooks, 1965. 96 p. illus., map. $2

This is a compact and interesting compilation which will be of great interest to collectors of minerals. The glossary enhances the value of this work.

661
Jones, Anita Edgar. *Conditions surrounding Mexicans in Chicago.* San Francisco, R. & E. Research Associates, 1971. 124 p. $7

Originally presented as the author's thesis in 1928, this study focuses on the Mexican migrants in Chicago. Contains a bibliography.

662
Jones, Fayette Alexander. *Old mines and ghost camps of New Mexico.* Edited by E. E. Bartholomew. 2d ed. Fort Davis, Texas, Frontier Book Co., 1964. 92 p. illus. $4

The original title was *New Mexico mines and minerals.* It describes mining in New Mexico, with attractive illustrations.

663
Jones, Joseph, and Johanna Jones. *Authors and areas of the West Indies.* Austin, Tex., Steck-Vaughn, 1974. 89 p. $2

Outlines West Indian society and its most representative writers in a very readable book.

664
Jones, Julie. *The art of the empire; the Inca of Peru.* New York, Museum of Primitive Art, Distributed by the New York Graphic Arts Society, 1964. 56 p. illus., map. $3.95

This is a beautifully illustrated guide to the art of the Inca empire, reproducing works in gold, silver, and also textiles, all of which were shown in an exhibition held November 20, 1963, to February 2, 1964, at the Museum of Primitive Art. Includes a good select bibliography.

665
Jones, Julie. *A bibliography of Olmec sculpture. No. 2.* New York, Museum of Primitive Art, distributed by the New York Graphic Arts Society, 1969. 31 p. illus. $.95

This useful bibliography of Olmec sculpture is a welcome addition for the collector's and the student's library of pre-Columbian art.

666
Jones, Julie. *Sculpture from Peru.* New York, Museum of Primitive Art, Distributed by the New York Graphic Arts Society, 1963. 8 p. illus. $.75

A catalog of an exhibit of Peruvian sculpture which bridges several periods.

667
Jones, Tom B., Elizabeth Ann Warburton, and Anne Kingsley, comps. *A bibliography of*

South American affairs; articles in 19th century periodicals. Minneapolis, University of Minnesota Press, 1955. xv, 146 p. $5.50

An unusual compilation of great interest to economic historians as well as to historians and political scientists. Includes good indexes to aid the user.

668

Jong, Gerrit de. *Four hundred years of Brazilian literature; outline and anthology.* Provo, Utah, Brigham Young University Press, 1973. 311 p. $5.95

Provides a literary history and brief anthology of Brazilian literature. Includes bibliographies.

669

Joralemon, Peter David. *A study of Olmec iconography.* Washington, Dumbarton Oaks Museum, 1971. 40 p. illus. (Studies in pre-Columbian art and archaeology, 7) $2.50

An analytical study of diverse elements of Olmec sculpture. It is attractively illustrated.

670

Jordan, June, and Terri Bush, comps. *The voice of the children;* writings by black and Puerto Rican young people. New York, Washington Square Press, 1974. 101 p. $.95

Twenty black and Puerto Rican children write their poetic impressions of growing up in the ghettos of America. This work will be of interest to urban public libraries as well as high school libraries.

671

Judge, William James. *The Paleo Indians of the central Rio Grande Valley in New Mexico.* Albuquerque, University of New Mexico Press, 1973. x, 361 p. illus. $8.95

Originally presented as the author's thesis, this is a scholarly study of a group of Indians of the central Rio Grande Valley. Contains a very significant bibliography.

672

Kahl, Joseph Alan, ed. *Comparative perspectives of stratification: Mexico, Great Britain, Japan.* Edited and with introd., by Joseph A. Kahl. Boston, Little, Brown, 1968. xvii, 235 p. illus. $3.95

Compares levels of economic development and social stratification in three countries which are at different stages of industrialization. Includes bibliographical references.

673

Kahn, Michael. *Ancient sculpture of ancient West Mexico: Nayarit, Jalisco, Colima; the Proctor Stafford Collection.* Articles by Michael Kahn, Clement Meighan and H. B. Nicholson. Los Angeles, County Museum of Art, 1971. 116 p. illus. (part col.), col. map. $2.45

The text is enhanced by 74 illustrations depicting clay sculptures from the graves and tombs of Nayarit, Jalisco, and Colima.

674

Kantor, Harry. *Bibliography of José Figueres.* Tempe, Center for Latin American Studies, Arizona State University, 1972. 50 p. $1

Includes books, articles, and other materials on José Figueres.

675

Kantor, Harry. *Ideology and program of the Peruvian Aprista party.* Rev. ed. Washington, Savile Book Store, 1966. 175 p. $4.95

An authoritative essay on Aprismo, its development, policies, and programs. The first edition (1952) also appeared in Spanish under the title *Ideología y programa del movimiento Aprista*. The present edition has been revised and brought up to date with an epilog to 1965.

676

Kantor, Harry, ed. *Latin American political parties; a bibliography.* Compiled by Harry Kantor and the staff of the University of Florida Program in the Comparative Study of Latin American Political Parties. Gainesville, University of Florida Press, 1968. 113 p. (Florida. University. Gainesville. Libraries. Bibliographic series, no. 6) $2.50

A specialized bibliography of the most important political parties of Latin America. More than 2,200 items are included. This is an important guide for researchers in the field, as well as for libraries with an interest in Latin American studies. Contains a good index.

677

Karner, Frances P. *The Sephardics of Curaçao; a short story of socioculture patterns in flux.* Foreword by H. Hoetink. New York, Humanities Press, 1971. 94 p. $3.50

Studies the social acculturation of Sephardic Jews in Curaçao. This is an important and thoughtful contribution with an excellent foreword by Harry Hoetink, leading sociologist in Caribbean studies.

678

Karnes, Thomas L., comp. *Readings in the Latin American policy of the United States.* Edited and with narrative by Thomas L. Karnes. Tucson, University of Arizona Press, 1972. xii, 302 p. $4.95

Presents a balanced selection of essays dealing with U.S. foreign policy in Latin America. Includes a select bibliography.

679

Karol, K. S. *Guerrillas in power; the course of the Cuban revolution.* Translated from the French by Arnold Pomerans. New York, Hill and Wang, 1970. x, 624 p. $4.50

Translation of *Les guérilleros au pouvoir,* a major work based on a number of periods of study in Cuba. Karol states he writes in a sense of solidarity with the Cuban revolution but that his obligation is to critical truth rather than to unjustified praise. [HLAS 33:7817]

680

Katz, Friedrich. *The ancient American civilizations.* Translated by K. M. Lois Simpson. New York, Praeger, 1974. xii, 386 p. maps. $5.95

First published in German under the title *Vorkolumbische Kulturen* (1969), this is a major attempt to compare Meso-American and Andean civilations. Addressed to the general public, it is remarkably current and is based on sound ethnohistorical research. Recommended for public and academic libraries. [HLAS 31:1061]

681

Kaufman, Robert R. *The Chilean political right and agrarian reform; resistance and moderation.* Washington, Institute for the Comparative Study of Political Systems, 1967. 48 p. tables. (Operations and Policy Research, Inc., Washington, D.C., Institute for the Comparative Study of Political Systems. Policy study, no. 2) $2

Argues that rightist political groups in Chile have shown a disposition towards bargaining on the issue of agrarian reform. [Charles Fleener]

682

Kaufman, William Irving. *Recipes from the Caribbean and Latin America.* New York, Dell Pub. Co., 1974. 201 p. $.75

Many Caribbean and Latin American favorites are presented here with good directions for preparation.

683

Kazami, Takehide. *The Andes; mountain empire of the Incas.* Tokyo, Palo Alto, Calif., Kodansha International, 1972. 118 p. col. illus., map. (This beautiful world, v. 33) $2.75

Describes the Andean region for the traveler with succinct texts and attractive photographs. This would be a welcome addition for high school and public libraries.

684

Kebschull, Harvey G., comp. *Politics in transitional societies; the challenge of change in Asia, Africa, and Latin America.* New York, Appleton-Century-Crofts, 1968. xv, 435 p. illus. $4.95

Analyzes political problems faced by the Third World countries. The essays included here are by prominent specialists in their fields. Includes bibliographical references.

685

Keen, Benjamin, ed. *Americans all; the story of our Latin American neighbors.* New York, Dell Pub. Co., 1966. 254 p. (Laurel leaf library) $.50

A simplified history of Latin America from the conquest to the present, by various authors. Includes a chapter on the history of U.S.-Latin American relations.

686

Keen, Benjamin, ed. *Latin American civilization.* 3d ed. Boston, Houghton, Mifflin, 1973. 2 v. illus. $6.50 each

The first volume is entitled *The colonial origins,* and the second *The national era.* The section on the 20th century has been thoroughly reorganized, with new materials and introductions, and a chapter on the Cuban revolution. This is a useful book of readings for background courses.

687

Kelemen, Pál. *Art of the Americas; ancient and Hispanic, with a comparative chapter on the Philippines.* New York, Crowell, 1970. xiii, 402 p. illus., maps. $4.95

The archeological sections on ancient American art include new data gathered at new sites. This is a valuable book showing the transition from pre-Hispanic to colonial art, pointing out trends, and including a section on colonial art in the Philippines. 338 well-chosen, black-and-white illustrations enhance the text.

688

Keleman, Pál. *Baroque and rococo in Latin America.* Rev. ed. New York, Dover Publications, 1967. 2 v. illus $3 each

First published in 1951, this handsome work contains a comprehensive study of colonial art in Latin America. Of special interest is the method of presenting works in iconographic groups, so that a given theme may be seen as interpreted in different countries throughout the New World. A major contribution with good illustrations.

689

Keleman, Pál. *Medieval American art; masterpieces of the New World before Columbus.* Rev. ed. New York, Dover Publications, 1970. 2 v. illus., map. $4.50 each

One of the foremost authorities on American art proves that the great art period of pre-Columbian America coincides in time and quality with those of medieval Asia and Europe. Describes the art history of native Americans from the U.S. Southwest through the Andean regions. Almost 1,000 photographs illustrate art and architectural works.

690

Kelly, Isabel Truesdell. *The archaeology of the Autlán-Tuxcacuesco area of Jalisco.* Berkeley, University of California Press, 1972. 2 v. illus., maps (part fold.), tables. (Ibero-Americana 26-27) $5

First published in 1945-49. Volume 1 deals with the Autlán zone, and volume 2 covers the Tuxcacuesco-Zapotitlán zone. Considerable emphasis has been placed on early historical accounts. The probable location of 16th-century villages is discussed in detail. Intended for the specialist. Includes bibliographies.

691

Kelsey, Vera, and Lilly de Jongh Osborne. *Four keys to Guatemala.* Rev. ed. New York, Funk and Wagnalls, 1961. 332 p. illus. $.95

Provides a good general treatment of Guatemala, with new information since the 1952 edition. Includes a bibliography. Of interest to all those studying Guatemala.

692

Kendall, Aubyn. *The art of pre-Columbian Mexico; an annotated bibliography of works in English.* Austin, Institute of Latin American Studies, University of Texas, 1973. 115 p. illus. (Guides and bibliographies series, 5) $4

This is a very useful, exhaustive, annotated bibliography of pre-Columbian art, of great interest to the specialist and to college and public libraries.

693

Kender, Martin, and James Petras, eds. *Fidel Castro speaks.* New York, Grove Press, 1969. xvii, 332 p. $1.95

The editors have selected a broad topical sampling of speeches by Fidel Castro. Includes a select bibliography.

694

Kennedy, Robert F. *Thirteen days; a memoir of the Cuban missile crisis,* with introductions by Robert S. McNamara and Harold Macmillan. New York, Norton, 1971. 184 p. illus. $2.25

One of the principal protagonists of the momentous confrontation between the U.S. and the Soviet Union over the Cuban missiles presents his memoirs of those fateful days. It is an important document.

695

Kendrick, Edith Johnston. *Regional dances of Mexico.* Illus. by Rose Remund. Lincolnwood, Ill., B. Upshaw, 1966. 58 p. maps. (Dollar language series) $1

Describes folk music and dances from various regions of Mexico. Aimed at providing audiovisual aids for Spanish programs. [Charles Fleener]

696

Kenworthy, Leonard Stout. *Studying South America in elementary and secondary schools.* Rev. ed. New York, Bureau of Publications, Teachers College, Columbia

University, 1967. 54 p. map. (*His* World affairs guides) $1.95

Contains curriculum materials for elementary and secondary school teachers who are planning units on South America. Also included are lists of a wide variety of teaching aids on the subject, such as film strips, booklets, etc. [Charles Fleener]

697

Kepple, Ella Huff. *Fun and festival from Latin America.* New York, Friendship Press, 1961. 48 p. (Fun and festival series) $.95

Describes a variety of celebrations and fiestas in Latin America. Includes music, principally unaccompanied melodies.

698

Kidder, Alfred Vincent. *An introduction to the study of Southwestern archaeology,* with a preliminary account of the excavations at Pecos, and a summary of Southwestern archaeology today, by Irving Rouse. New Haven, Conn., Yale University Press, 1962. 377 p. (A Yale paperbound, YW-5) $2.95

Describes archeological sites and materials in the Southwest. Includes a bibliography.

699

Kiev, Ari. *Curanderismo; Mexican-American folk psychiatry.* New York, Free Press, 1968. xiii, 207 p. $2.45

An interesting study of forms of psychotherapy employed by practitioners of folk medicine among the Mexican Americans. Includes a bibliography.

700

King, Mary Elizabeth. *Ancient Peruvian textiles from the collection of the Textile Museum, Washington, D.C.* Catalog of an exhibition at the Museum of Primitive Art, New York. Introd. and notes by Mary Elizabeth King. New York, Museum of Primitive Art; distributed by the New York Graphic Arts Society, Greenwich, Conn., 1965. 45 p. (chiefly illus., map) $3.75

Presents items from Washington's Textile Museum. The illustrations are excellent.

701

Kingsbury, Robert C., and Ronald M. Schneider. *An atlas of Latin American affairs.* Text by Ronald M. Schneider; maps by Robert C. Kingsbury. New York, Praeger, 1965. 136 p. maps. (Praeger series of world affairs atlases) $1.95

Sixty excellent maps by Kingsbury and accompanying text by Schneider present a sound picture of the historical background and the contemporary political, economic, and social reality of Latin America.

702

Knox, William J. *The economic status of the Mexican immigrant in San Antonio, Texas.* San Francisco, R. & E. Research Association, 1971. 39 p. $7

Originally presented as the author's thesis at the University of Texas in 1927, this work studies the economic conditions faced by Mexican immigrants in the U.S. during the first part of this century. Includes a select bibliography.

703

Korngold, Ralph. *Citizen Toussaint.* New York, Hill and Wang, 1965. xvii, 338 p. $2.95

Biography of the Haitian slave who became the leader of his country's independence movement which was first published in 1944. It is a balanced study, part personal biography and part a general history of the struggle for independence from France. [Charles Fleener]

704
Kraft, Walter C. *Codices Vindobonenses Hispanici. A catalog of the Spanish, Portuguese, and Catalan manuscripts in the Austrian National Library in Vienna.* Corvallis, Oregon State University Press, 1957. 64 p. illus. (Oregon State College, Corvallis. Bibliographic series, no. 4) $1

Presents facsimile reproductions from and an annotated listing of the codices in the collections of the Austrian National Library, with bibliographical references.

705
Kramer, P., and Robert E. McNicoll, eds. *Latin America panorama.* New York, Putnam, 1971. 321 p. illus. $2.75

This is a general description of Latin America aimed at the generalist.

706
Krause, Walter, and others. *International tourism and Latin American development.* Foreword by C. P. Blair. Austin, University of Texas Press, 1974. 174 p. $2

Analyzes tourism in Latin America, its economic impact, and suggests possible improvements to encourage travelers to the area. Includes a select bibliography.

707
Kriesberg, Martin, ed. *Public administration in developing countries.* Conference on Public Administration in Developing Countries, 1st, Bogotá, 1963. Washington, Brookings Institution, 1965. 168 p. $2.95

Presents the papers which were delivered at the 1963 conference in Bogotá. The articles analyze factors affecting public administration in developing countries; the establishment of civil services; and training and research in public administration. Includes bibliographical notes.

708
Krutch, Joseph Wood. *The forgotton peninsula; a naturalist in Baja California.* New York, Apollo Editions, 1961. 277 p. illus. $2.25

Describes "this long, ruggedly beautiful peninsula called Baja California," which after more than four centuries of stubborn resistance has successfully resisted progress.

709
Kurland, Gerald. *Fidel Castro; Communist dictator of Cuba.* Charlottesville, N.Y., Sam Har Press, 1972. 32 p. $.98

A brief biography of the man who has been the leader of Cuba's government since 1959. Includes a select bibliography.

710
Kwon, H. J. *Barrier islands of the northern Gulf of Mexico coast: sediment sources and development.* Baton Rouge, Louisiana State University Press, 1969. 51 p. illus., maps. (Louisiana State University studies. Coastal studies series, no. 25) $2

This is a scholarly study of the geological development of certain islands off the coast of the Gulf of Mexico, based on meticulous field work. Contains an extensive and thorough bibliography. Of great interest to the specialist.

711
La Barre, Weston. *The peyote cult.* Rev. ed. New York, Schocken Books, 1969. xvii, 260 p. illus. $2.45

This scholarly anthropological study was published in 1938. The author has added a new preface, as well as a survey of recent studies about the Amerindian ritual based on the peyote plant. Contains a bibliography.

712

La Belle, Thomas J., comp. *Education and development; Latin America and the Caribbean.* Los Angeles, Latin American Center, University of California, 1972. xiv, 732 p. (Latin American studies series, v. 18) $6.50

A thorough survey of education and development, as well as national planning in Latin America and the Caribbean, which will be of great interest to sociologists, educators, political scientists, and librarians. Includes bibliographical references.

713

Lamb, Ruth Stanton. *Antología del cuento guatemalteco.* Selección, prólogo y biografías de Ruth S. Lamb. Claremont, Calif., Claremont College, 1973; distributed by Ocelot Press, Claremont, Calif. 141 p. (Antologías studium, 7) $4

Presents a very useful anthology of Guatemalan short stories, concentrating on the 19th and 20th centuries. Includes bibliographical references.

714

Lamb, Ruth Stanton. *Bibliografía del teatro mexicano del siglo veinte.* Claremont, Calif., Ocelot Press, 1972. 98 p. $4

This is a comprehensive bibliography of the Mexican theater during the 20th century. Of interest to librarians, theater classes, and to those teaching modern Latin American literature.

715

Lamb, Ruth Stanton. *Latin America; sites and insights.* Claremont, Calif., Creative Press, 1963. 67 p. $4

Vignettes about people, places, and ideas in Latin America from the period of the conquest to the present. The style is readable and interesting. Includes a select bibliography.

716

Lamb, Ruth Stanton. *Mexican Americans; sons of the Southwest.* Claremont, Calif., Ocelot Press, 1970. 198 p. maps. $5.95

Presents succinctly key essays on the cultural, historical, and ethnic heritage of Mexican Americans in the Southwest. The author also discusses the political and social awakening of Mexican Americans to the need to insist upon fulfillment of their civil rights. Includes a good bibliography.

717

Lamb, Ruth Stanton, ed. *Three contemporary Latin American plays: René Marqués, Egon Wolff, Emilio Carballido.* Waltham, Mass., Xerox College, 1971. xii, 203 p. ports. $4.50

Designed for second- and third-year Spanish students, this work includes Marqués' *El apartamiento;* Wolff's *Los invasores;* and Carballido's *Yo también hablo de la rosa.* Each play is representative of contemporary Latin American theater. Includes notes, vocabularies, and bibliographies.

718

Lambert, Jacques. *Latin America; social structure and political institutions.* Translated by Helen Katel. Berkeley, University of California Press, 1967. 413 p. $3.25

Analyzes Latin American political institutions in relation to the different social structures. Includes bibliographic references.

719

Langley, Lester D. *The Cuban policy of the United States; a brief history.* New York, Wiley, 1968. xi, 203 p. maps. (America and the world) $4.75

A brief historical outline of the Cuban policy of the U.S. from the early part of the 20th century to the Cuban missile crisis of 1962. Points out the self-interest mixed with idealism that has characterized U.S. foreign policy towards Cuba. Includes bibliographic notes.

720

Langley, Lester D., comp. *The United States, Cuba, and the Cold War: American failure or Communist conspiracy.* Edited with an introd. by Lester D. Langley. Lexington, Mass., Heath, 1971. xi, 285 p. (Problems in American civilization) $2.25

Analyzes U.S.-Cuban relations within the context of the 1960's. The contributions were preared by well-known specialists in the field of international politics.

721

Lanning, Edward P. *Peru before the Incas.* Englewood Cliffs, N.J., Prentice-Hall, 1967. 216 p. illus., tables. (A Spectrum book) $2.95

A survey of Peruvian prehistory beginning about 12,000 years ago. Peruvian cultural history is divided into preceramic and ceramic stages and then further into periods. This work is a major contribution to the study of Andean prehistory, updating with new research Bennett and Bird's *Andean culture history* and Mason's *Ancient civilizations of Peru.* Includes a bibliography.

722

Lara-Braud, Jorge, ed. *Our claim on the future; a controversial collection from Latin America.* Illus. by K. Tureck. New York, Friendship Press, 1971. 135 p. $1.95

Studies Protestantism in Latin America from an area and topical point of view. Includes bibliographical references.

723

Lara-Braud, Jorge, ed. and trans. *Social justice and the Latin churches.* Richmond, Va., John Knox Press, 1969. 137 p. $2.95

Contains papers presented at the Latin American Conference on Church and Society which met in El Tabo, Chile, in January 1966. They conclude that the hope for justice in Latin America lies in self-determination and that this cannot be achieved without a radical transformation of society.

724

Larreta, Enrique Rodríguez. *La gloria de don Ramiro; una vida en tiempos de Felipe Segundo.* Edited by Frank Sedwick and Robert Matton. Boston, Heath, 1966. xx, 256 p. illus., map. $3.95

First published in 1908, this is a historical novel set in Philip II's reign and cleverly linking the old world and the new. Larreta is considered one of the best modernist novelists of South America. He evokes the past in a vivid and impressionistic style. Contains notes and vocabulary.

725

Larson, Magali Sarfatti, and Arlene Eisen Bergman. *Social stratification in Peru.* Berkeley, University of California Press, 1970. 341 p. $2.50

According to the authors, this monograph attempts to present an image of the structure of social stratification in Peru. They outline processes that may represent important conditions in the evolution or stagnation of the Peruvian social system. [Charles Fleener]

726

Latin American research and publications at the University of Texas at Austin, 1893-1969. Austin, Institute of Latin American Studies, University of Texas, 1971. 187 p. (Guides and bibliographies series, 3) $3.75

Issued to commemorate the 30th anniversary of the establishment of the Institute of Latin American Studies, this book lists the appropriate publications. An important contribution to the field of bibliography.

727

Lawrence, David Herbert. *Morning in Mexico and Etruscan places.* New York, Viking, 1966. 214 p. $1.95

Written by a very important figure in 20-century English literature, this work contains penetrating glimpses and beautiful imagery of Mexico in the 1920's.

728

Lawrence, David Herbert. *The Plumed Serpent; Quetzalcoatl.* Introd. by William York Tindall. New York, Random House, 1955. 487 p. $2.20

A splendid novel set in Mexico and New Mexico, full of symbols and superb descriptions of dancing Indians and other colorful rituals.

729

Lazo, Mario. *Dagger in the heart: American policy failures in Cuba.* New York, Funk and Wagnalls, 1968. xviii, 426 p. $1.95

Finds the "soft" and misinformed liberal responsible for Castro's rise to power. Includes bibliographical footnotes. [HLAS 31:7405]

730

Leal, Luis, ed. *Cuentistas hispanoamericanos del siglo veinte.* Introd., notas y vocabulario por Luis Leal. New York, Random House, 1972. xi, 243 p. $3.95

Includes short stories by such 20th-century Latin American writers as Jorge Luis Borges, Alejo Carpentier, Juan Rulfo, Nicolás Nováš Calvo, Alfonso Reyes, Gabriel García Márquez, and others. The introduction traces the history of the Latin American short story. Contains notes and vocabulary.

731

Leal, Luis. *México; civilizaciones y culturas.* Boston, Houghton, Mifflin, 1955. 205 p. illus. $4.50

Outlines the rich mosaic of Mexican culture and civilization, tracing it back to the ancient pre-Columbian cultures. The preface is in English. Includes a bibliography.

732

Leff, Nathaniel M. *Economic policy-making and development in Brazil, 1947-1964.* New York, J. Wiley, 1968. xiv, 201 p. $9.25

This is a study of economic policymaking in Brazil from the standpoints of economics, sociology, and politics. Although interesting, the study has some overlapping in its parts. Includes bibliographical footnotes. [HLAS 31:3949]

733

Leiden, Carl, and Karl M. Schmitt, eds. *The politics of violence; revolution in the modern world.* Englewood Cliffs, N.J., Prentice-Hall, 1968. 244 p. (A Spectrum book) $2.95

Explores the meaning of revolution in the 20th century. The essays presented seek the connection between violence and the political process. Cuba and Mexico (along with Turkey and Egypt) are studied to ascertain the role of ideology and the relationship of violence to revolutionary action. [Charles Fleener]

LATIN AMERICA

734

León-Portilla, Miguel. *The broken spears; the Aztec account of the conquest of Mexico.* Translated by Angel Marf Garibay and Lysander Kemp. Boston, Beacon Press, 1966. xxxi, 168 p. illus., map. $2.95

Assembled from native accounts, this is largely the story of the defeat and subsequent chaos and grief of the fallen Aztecs, written by men who wanted to remind Spain of her debt to them. The introduction summarizes the Aztec way of life. First published in 1962, it contains a bibliography.

735

Leonard, Irving Albert. *Baroque times in old Mexico; seventeenth-century persons, places, and practices.* Ann Arbor, University of Michigan Press, 1966. xi, 260 p. illus., maps. $2.25

Analyzes the characteristics of the Baroque period in Mexico. Emphasis is on literary manifestations, but the Baroque is seen also as the pattern in which "the frustrated dynamism of old and New Spain alike found its most enduring expression." Includes a good bibliography.

736

Leonard, Irving Albert, ed. *Colonial travelers in Latin America.* Edited with an introd. by Irving A. Leonard. New York, Knopf, 1972. x, 235 p. (Borzoi books on Latin America) $2.95

This is an interesting anthology of selections from travel accounts in the colonial period. The author's introductory essay is an enlightening discussion of general problems of travel to and within the Spanish colonies. [HLAS 34:1360]

737

Leonard, Olin E., and Charles P. Loomis, eds. *Readings in Latin American social organization and institutions.* East Lansing, Michigan State University Press, 1963. 320 p. maps, tables. $5

Contains 36 articles with a social science orientation designed to acquaint students with Latin American social issues. Includes bibliographies.

738

Lévi-Strauss, Claude. *Tristes tropiques; an anthropological study of primitive societies in Brazil.* Translated from the French by John and Doreen Wightman. New York, Atheneum, 1974. 432 p. $3.95

A noted French cultural anthropologist describes his field work among the Bororo, Caduveo, Tupi-Kawahib, and Nambikwara of the Brazilian Amazon. He relates behavior patterns, beliefs, tribal life, etc., to the cultural life and physical environment. This is the first unabridged English edition of this work.

739

Levine, Suzanne Jill, comp. *Latin America; fiction and poetry in translation.* New York, Center for Inter-American Relations, 1971. 70 p. $1.25

Includes books by authors from Spanish- and Portuguese-speaking countries of the Americas through the end of 1961. This is a welcome and important contribution.

740

Levinson, Jerome, and Juan de Onís. *The Alliance that lost its way; a critical report on the Alliance for Progress.* Chicago, Quadrangle Books, 1970. xi, 381 p. $2.95

This study was undertaken on behalf of the Twentieth Century Fund. The authors believe that "Latin America is on the threshold of a new decade in which pressures for economic growth and social change will . . . test the political strength of inter-American relations." Includes bibliographic references.

741
Levinson, Sandra, and Carol Brightman, eds. *Venceremos Brigade; young Americans sharing the life and work of revolutionary Cuba; diaries, letters, interviews, tapes, essays, poetry* by the Venceremos Brigade. New York, Simon and Schuster, 1971. 412 p. illus. $3.95

Contains the collected reminiscences of a total of two months' stay in Cuba by many members of the Venceremos Brigade in late 1969 to January 1970.

742
Lewald, Harold Ernest, comp. *Buenos Aires; retrato de una sociedad hispánica a través de su literatura.* Boston, Houghton, Mifflin, 1968. xiv, 234 p. illus., facsims, maps. $3.95

Illustrates the cultural and social aspects of Buenos Aires through rich and varied literary presentations by its authors.

743
Lewald, Herold Ernest, and George E. Smith, comps. *Escritores platenses del siglo veinte,* por H. Ernest Lewald y George E. Smith. Boston, Houghton, Mifflin, 1971. xi, 241 p. $3.30

A collection of 12 short stories by representative authors from Argentina and Uruguay, ranging from Jorge Luis Borges to Dalmiro J. Saénz. The stories have been arranged in an order of increasing linguistic difficulty. It includes bibliographies, notes, and vocabularies.

744
Lewis, Gordon K. *The growth of the modern West Indies.* New York, Monthly Review Press, 1968. 506 p. map (on lining papers) $4.50

This is an important book dealing with the contemporary history of the English-speaking West Indies. Chapters on British colonialism delineate factors which contributed to shape the national societies and trace their evolution to the 1960's. Highly recommended. Includes bibliographical references. [HLAS 31:2029]

745
Lewis, Gordon K. *Puerto Rico; freedom and power in the Caribbean.* New York, Harper & Row, 1974. xii, 626 p. $3.45

First published in 1963, this is a formidable study, employing social science data from all fields, to present an historical and socio-cultural interpretation of Puerto Rican society. Bibliographical references included. [HLAS 27:1070]

746
Lewis, Oscar. *The children of Sánchez; autobiography of a Mexican family.* New York, Random House, 1963. 499 p. $2.95

Taped interviews with members of a poor urban family in Mexico City give a unique inside view of lower class family life. Dr. Lewis' work constitutes an important contribution to the study of social dynamics.

747
Lewis, Oscar. *Death in the Sánchez family.* New York, Random House, 1970. xxvii, 160 p. $1.65

The author allows the members of the Sánchez family to tell their own stories of how the poor die. This is the story of the death of Aunt Guadalupe and of her funeral. A good case study of social anthropology.

748

Lewis, Oscar. *Five families; Mexican studies in the culture of poverty.* Foreword b Oliver La Farge. New York, New American Library, 1959. 351 p. illus. $.95

The author presents one day in the life of five urban Mexican families. It compellingly written and of considerable interest to the specialist as well as th lay public.

749

Lewis, Oscar. *Life in a Mexican village; Tepoztlán restudied.* Illus. by Alberto Beltrár Urbana, University of Illinois Press, 1963. xxvii, 512 p. illus., maps. $3.95

A new study of the Mexican village where Robert Redfield spent eight months i 1926 and 1927, with special reference to methodological and theoretical aspec of the study of social change. Includes a bibliography.

750

Lewis, Oscar. *Pedro Martínez; a Mexican peasant and his family.* Drawings by Albert Beltrán. New York, Random House, 1964. 507 p. illus. $3.45

A detailed account of a Mexican peasant's life from his birth in 1889 to th present. The book consists of taped materials, interviews, and conversations, a well as some projective data. This is the best available account of domesti relations in a Meso-American family. Data supplied by the mother add son ar also included. [HLAS 29:1379]

751

Lewis, Oscar. *Tepoztlán; village in Mexico.* New York, Holt, Rinehart and Winston 1960. 104 p. (Case studies in anthropology) $2.75

This is an abridged version of Lewis' *Life in a Mexican Village,* a book of broad scope about a single village. Includes a bibliography.

752

Lewis, Oscar. *La vida; a Puerto Rican family in the culture of poverty—San Juan and New York.* New York, Random House, 1967. 669 p. $2.95

An important but controversial study utilizing the life-history techniques developed by the author in his Mexican research. Methodological refinements include intensification of the technique by which informants and events are seen from multiple perspectives, the inclusion of observed typical days in the life of the family, and the study of the family in two urban settings—San Juan and New York. [HLAS 29:1507]

753

Lieuwen, Edwin. *The United States and the challenge to security in Latin America.* Columbus, Ohio State University Press, 1966. 98 p. map. (Social science program of the Mershon Center for Education in National Security, Ohio State University. Pamphlet series, no. 4) $1.50

Professor Lieuwen sees the challenge in terms of Communist effectiveness in the area. This single issue is discussed extensively but with little more detail than is generally known. [HLAS 29:6140]

754

Lieuwen, Edwin. *U.S. policy in Latin America; a short history.* New York, Praeger, 1965. x, 150 p. $1.95

Traces the history of U.S. policy from the Monroe Doctrine to the Good Neighbor Policy. It also offers a view of mid-1960's policy in Latin America. Includes a select bibliography.

755

Liggett, Thomas J. *Where tomorrow struggles to be born; the Americas in transition.* New York, Friendship Press, 1970. 160 p. illus. $1.75

Deals with current social, political, and economic problems of Latin America. Intended for the generalist or for survey courses.

756

Linn, George Byron. *A study of several linguistic functions of Mexican-American children in a two-language environment.* San Francisco, R. & E. Research Association, 1971. 120 p. $7

Originally presented as the author's thesis at the University of Southern California in 1965, it examines linguistic variables that can be found in bilingual children. An important study which includes a good select bibliography in the field.

757

Lindquist, Sven. *The shadow: Latin America faces the seventies.* Translated by Keith Bradfield, with an editorial foreword by Richard Gott. Harmondsworth, Middlesex, England, Penguin Books, 1972. 311 p. illus. (The Pelican Latin American library) $2.45

Skillfully analyzes social problems facing most Latin American countries in the 1970's. The author draws on recorded conversations and personal observations. This is an English translation of the original Swedish edition, *Slagskuggan: Latin Amerika inför 70-talet,* which appeared in 1969.

758

Lipp, Solomon, and Sylvia Lipp, eds. *Hispanoamérica vista por sus ensayistas.* New York, Scribner's, 1969. xx, 283 p. $3.25

Intended to bring to the college student of intermediate Spanish a representative sampling of essays dealing with philosophy, history, sociology, and physchology. The authors include such major figures as Alfonso Reyes, Domingo F. Sarmiento, Juan Montalvo, Germán Arciniégas, José Martí, Antonio Caso, and others. Includes notes, vocabularies, and biographical sketches of each writer represented.

759

Lipset, Seymour M., and Aldo Solari, eds. *Elites in Latin America.* New York, Oxford University Press, 1967. xii, 531 p. $3.50

A collection of monographs on various elite groups (labor, military, business, intellectuals, church, etc.). Many were originally presented as papers at the June 1965 Montevideo Seminar on Elites and Development in Latin America. Includes bibliographies.

760

Liscano, Juan. *Panorama de la literatura venezolana actual.* Washington, Organization of American States, 1973. 414 p. (OAS, 868,4-S-8141) $5

A well-known Venezuelan poet and folklorist presents here an excellent analysis of contemporary Venezuelan literature. This is a welcome and important contribution. Contains bibliographical notes.

761

Liss, Sheldon B. *The Canal: aspects of United States-Panamanian relations.* Notre Dame, Ind., University of Notre Dame Press, 1967. xii, 310 p. maps. $2.25

Studies relations between the U.S. and Panama from 1903 to 1966, centering around the Panama Canal. The author emphasizes the socioeconomic factors which contributed to the turbulent relationship between the two countries, culminating in the 1964 crisis. Contains a bibliography.

762
Liss, Sheldon B. *A century of disagreement; the Chamizal conflict, 1864-1964.* Washington, University Press, 1965. 167 p. maps, tables. $4

Documented history of the controversy between Mexico and the U.S. over the Chamizal tract between Cuidad Juárez and El Paso, with texts of the relevant treaties, including the settlement of 1963. Includes a bibliography.

763
Liss, Sheldon B., and Peggy K. Liss, comps. *Man, state, and society in Latin American history.* Edited by Sheldon B. Liss and Peggy K. Liss. New York, Praeger, 1972. xvi, 456 p. maps. (Man, state and society) $5.95

This anthology contains valuable paperback bibliographies, glossary, and maps, in addition to a short introduction to each selection. It covers the area from pre-Columbian societies through World War II, emphasizing postindependence history. [HLAS 35:1275]

764
List, George, and Juan Orrego Salas, eds. *Music in the Americas.* Bloomington, Indiana University Research Center in Anthropology, Folklore, and Linguistics, 1971. 257 p. illus. (Inter-American music monographs series, 1) $10

Includes papers read at the 2d Inter-American Conference on Ethnomusicology and the 1st Inter-American Seminar of Composers, held at Indiana University, April 24-28, 1965. A variety of topics were covered. Among these: "Raíces europeas de la música folklórica," by Isabel Aretz; Lauro Ayestarán's "El tamboril afro-uruguayo"; Luis Felipe Ramón y Rivera's "El mestizaje de la música afro-venezolana"; and several others. Includes bibliographies.

765
Livingston, James T., ed. *Caribbean rhythms; the emerging English literature of the West Indies.* Edited, with an introd. by James T. Livingston. New York, Washington Square Press, 1974. 379 p. illus. $1.95

The introduction offers a succinct literary history of the area. This is a representative anthology of poems, short stories, and two one-act plays. Includes biographies of the authors and a bibliography. Of great interest to most libraries.

766
Lockwood, Lee. *Castro's Cuba, Cuba's Fidel: an American journalist's inside look at today's Cuba.* With a new afterword by the author. New York, Random House, 1969. xvii, 363 p. illus. $2.95

Presents an unusual view of Fidel Castro and Cuba based on personal interviews with the Premier and many members of his government. The text is accompanied by numerous photographs depicting everyday life. This book should be of great interest to those studying contemporary Cuba.

767
Loomie, Albert Joseph. *Toleration and diplomacy; the religious issue in Anglo-Spanish relations, 1603-1605.* Philadelphia, American Philosophical Society, 1963. 60 p. port. (Transactions of the American Philosophical Society, new series, v. 53, pt. 6) $1.75

Surveys the reasons which prompted Philip III to intervene on behalf of his coreligionists in England in 1603. It also explores Spain's quest for toleration which formed a part of secret discussions between the two courts for two years.

768
López-Lavalle, María Esther, comp. *Bilateral treaty development in Latin America, 1953-1955.* Washington, Pan American Union, Legal Division, Dept. of International Law, 1956. 158 p. (Treaty series, 2; PAU 327-E-5504) $1

Lists bilateral treaties, conventions, and agreements entered into by the Latin American republics from 1953 through 1955.

769

López y Fuentes, Gregorio. *El indio.* Edited by E.H. Hespelt. New York, Norton, 1970. 271 p. $3.25

This is an annotated textbook edition of a Mexican classic containing notes and a vocabulary.

770

López y Fuentes, Gregorio. *El indio.* Translated by Anita Brenner. New York, Ungar, 1961. 256 p. illus. $1.45

First published in 1935, this novel epitomizes the essence of Mexico from pre-conquest days to the present. Attractive drawings by Diego Rivera illustrate this prize-winning novel.

771

Lott, Leo B. *Venezuela and Paraguay; political modernity and tradition in conflict.* New York, Holt, Rinehart, and Winston, 1972. 395 p. illus. (Modern comparative politics series) $3.45

This important college text makes use of nearly all contemporary tools for examination of political systems and retains awareness that it should inform students and other readers. [HLAS 35:7810]

772

Lowenfels, Lillian, and Nan Braymer, eds. and trans. *Modern poetry from Spain and Latin America,* by César Vallejo and others. New York, Corinth Books; distributed by Citadel Press, 1964. 63 p. $1.45

Includes translations of poems by César Vallejo, Nicolás Guillén, Salomón de la Selva, Victoriano Crémer, Blas de Otero, Agustín Millares, Rafael Alberti, Enoch Cancino Casahonda, Juan Oliver, José Agustín Goytisolo, Nuria Sales de Bohigas, and Francisco Valverde. The poems are linked by an essential unity and emotional texture.

773

Lowenthal, David, and Lambros Comitas, comps. *The aftermath of sovereignty.* Garden City, N.Y., Anchor Books, 1973. xvii, 422 p. $2.50

Articles included in this compilation examine the political problems encountered by newly independent West Indian countries. Eric Williams, Prime Minister of Trinidad and Tobago, is one of the contributors. Most of the authors included are from the West Indies. Contains a bibliography.

774

Lowenthal, David, and Lambros Comitas, comps. *Consequences of class and color; West Indian perspectives.* Garden City, N.Y., Anchor Books, 1973. xx, 334 p. (West Indies perspectives) $2.50

Pan Africanism has enjoyed a recent revival owing to the efforts of African and Afro-Latin scholars. This collection presents important articles on race and class in the black Caribbean.

775

Loy, Jane M., comp. *Latin America: sights and sounds; a guide to motion pictures and music for college courses.* Gainesville, Consortium of Latin American Studies Programs, University of Florida, 1973. 243 p. (Consortium of Latin American Studies Programs, publication, 5) $2.50; $1.50 to LASA members.

Prepared under the auspices of the U.S. Office of Education's Regional Research Program in Boston, this guide lists information about 16 mm education films and feature films suitable for classroom use. The core of the work consists of the subject heading index and the title description index. Appended is a list of distributors, explanations on how to order and how to use films, and a bibliography. This compilation will doubtless help to enrich many courses on Latin America.

776
Lucena, Vinicius G. de. *Why to invest in Pernambuco; the booming state in Brazil's Northeast.* Recife, Brazil, Distritos Industriais de Pernambuco, 1970. 68 p. illus. $2

Contains information on investments in Pernambuco, a rapidly growing area of Brazil.

777
Ludwig, Edward, and James Santibañez, comps. *The Chicanos: Mexican American voices.* Baltimore, Penguin Books, 1971. 286 p. $1.50

A collection of very personal essays on the lifestyles and events in the history of Mexican Americans. Includes biographical notes on each writer as well as a complete bibliography. Worthwhile and timely.

778
Lummis, Charles Fletcher. *Land of poco tiempo.* Foreword by P.A. Walter. Albuquerque, University of New Mexico Press, 1962. 236 p. $2.25

This is a facsimile edition of the 1928 classic which deals with New Mexico's Spanish heritage, the Pueblo Indians, and the role of the Franciscans in the Spanish Southwest. It also includes texts of Spanish folksongs.

778A
Luzuriaga, Gerardo, and Robert S. Rudder, eds. *The orgy; modern one-act plays from Latin America.* Edited and translated by Gerardo Luzuriaga and Robert S. Rudder. Los Angeles, Latin American Center, University of California, 1974. 180 p. illus. (UCLA Latin American studies, v. 25) $2.50

Includes 11 one-act plays by contemporary Latin American playwrights, making available to English-speaking readers examples of modern Latin American theater. There are brief biographical notes about each author.

779
Lynch, John. *The Spanish American revolutions, 1808-1826.* New York, Norton, 1973. 433 p. maps. (Revolutions in the modern world series) $3.95

First comprehensive synthesis in English of the revolutions for independence in Spanish Latin America. Lynch views positively the revolutions as creators of new nations, rather than as the dissolution of the Spanish Empire, but he notes that separation from Spain did not change the social and economic structure of Latin America, nor has it basically changed to this day. This is a well-written, superbly researched book and a major contribution. [HLAS 36:1656]

780
Macaulay, Neill. *The Prestes column.* New York, F. Watts, 1974. 175 p. $4.95

Surveys Brazilian politics in the 1930's, especially the influence of the revolutionary leader Carlos Prestes.

781
McCarty, Fred M. *Chihuahua al Pacífico; a dream come true,* by F.M. McCarty. Amarillo, Tex., 1968. 63 p. col. illus., map. $1.50

Towards the end of the 19th century Arthur E. Stilwell planned to organize a railway which would run through Kansas, Oklahoma, and Texas to Presidio and cross the desert to Chihuahua and Creel. The road would then cross the Sierra Madre to Los Mochis and Topolobampo. The total distance was over 1,600 miles. Díaz was granted a charter to build the railroad. Stilwell did not live to see the project completed. Includes a bibliography and attractive illustrations.

782
McClung, Ahlean Masters. *Mexican mystique.* New York, International Publications Service, 1968. 96 p. (Minutiae Mexicana series) $2

Contains essays and descriptions of Mexican civilization and mores, aimed at the traveler or the student of Latin American society.

783
McDonald, Archie P., comp. *Mexican war; crisis for American democracy.* Lexington, Mass., Heath, 1969. 112 p. (Problems in American civilization) $2.25

Selected essays on the Mexican-American War by analysts who have specialized in that particular historical period. Contains bibliographical footnotes.

784
McDonald, Ronald H. *Party systems and elections in Latin America.* Chicago, Markham Pub. Co., 1971. 324 p. (Markham political science series) $4.50

Analyzes political parties and election procedures in Latin America. This is a very useful book for political scientists with many bibliographical footnotes.

785
MacEoin, Gary. *Revolution next door; Latin America in the 1970's.* New York, Holt, Rinehart and Winston, 1971. 243 p. $2.95

Presents a readable, journalistic analysis of revolutionary potentials in Latin America during the 1970's. Includes a bibliography.

786
McGann, Thomas F. *Argentina: the divided land.* Princeton, N.J., Van Nostrand, 1966. 127 p. (Van Nostrand searchlight book 28). $1.95

A thoughtful and compact study of contemporary Argentina analyzing the country's national and international situation in light of its geography, history, and cultural background. A good bibliography is included.

787
Machado, Manuel A. *An industry in crisis: Mexican-United States cooperation in the control of foot-and-mouth disease,* by Manuel A. Machado, Jr. Berkeley, University of California Press, 1968. 99 p. (University of California publications in history, v. 80) $3.50

A detailed account of the foot-and-mouth disease (*fiebre aftosa*) epidemic introduced into Mexico through Brazilian bulls in 1946 and not totally eradicated until 1954. Based on primary sources, this is an important study of Mexican agriculture and of international agricultural cooperation. A bibliography is included.

788
Machado de Assis, Joaquim Maria. *Dom Casmurro, a novel;* translated by Helen Caldwell with an introd. by Waldo Frank. Berkeley, University of California Press, 1966. 269 p. $1.50

First published in 1900, *Dom Casmurro* did not become available in English until

1953. It is an enchanting, lucid, and humorous love story set in 19th-century Rio de Janeiro.

789

Machado de Assis, Joaquim Maria. *Epitaph of a small winner*. Translated from the Portuguese by William L. Grossman. Drawings by Shari Frisch. New York, Noonday Press, 1955. 223 p. $1.95

English translation of *Memórias póstumas de Brás Cubas* (1881), first published in 1952, in which Machado de Assis initiated his technique of short chapters and brief sentences of a fanciful and humoristic tone with emphasis on psychological analysis. It is one of his great novels.

790

Machado de Assis, Joaquim Maria. *The psychiatrist and other stories*. Translated by William L. Grossman & Helen Caldwell. Berkeley, University of California Press, 1963. 147 p. $1.95

These 12 selections should serve to explain to the English-reading public why many critics rate Machado de Assis higher as a short story writer than as a novelist. The four translations by Grossman are excellent, and the others are somewhat literal.

791

McHenry, John Patrick. *Short history of Mexico* by J. Patrick McHenry. Rev. ed. Garden City, N.Y., Doubleday, 1970. xii, 240 p. (Dolphin books, C363) $1.45

McHenry gives an encyclopaedic treatment of Mexican history which is well organized and very readable. The work is divided chronologically from the year 10,000 B.C. to the present day, and although the scope of the book does not permit lengthy discussion of the facts, McHenry is able to give a representative historical view. A useful reference tool.

792

McIntyre, Alister. *CARIFTA; a step toward a Caribbean economic community*. New York, Taplinger, 1971. 88 p. $.60

Outlines the aims and accomplishments of the Caribbean Free Trade Association and its economic implications for the area it covers. Contains bibliographical notes.

793

MacLeod, Murdo J. *Spanish Central America; a socioeconomic history, 1520-1720*. Berkeley, University of California Press, 1974. xvi, 554 p. maps. $4.95

This scholarly work examines Central America's first great economic, demographic, and social cycle. The study deals with what was then known as the Audiencia of Guatemala, a fairly populous and prosperous area of Middle America. Includes a bibliography. Highly recommended.

794

McNeill, Malvina Rosat, comp. *Guidelines to problems in education in Brazil; a review and selected bibliography*. New York, Teachers College Press, 1970. 66 p. (Center for Education in Latin America) $3.95

Part I concentrates on the development of Brazilian education from the colonial beginnings to contemporary phases. Part II consists of an annotated bibliography of publications and laws pertaining to education.

795

McVicker, Cecil D., and Osvaldo N. Soto, eds. *Temas de Arciniégas; invitación a conversar, leer y escribir*. New York, Harcourt, Brace and World, 1971. 421 p. $3.95

Essays on Arciniégas are presented here in a book of readings witn good vocabularies.

796

McWhiney, Grady, and Sue McWhiney, comps. *To Mexico with Taylor and Scott, 1845-1847.* Waltham, Mass., Blaisdell, 1969. 214 p. (Primary sources in American history) $3.50

Presents nearly 30 eyewitness accounts by American soldiers of the Mexican War. These primary sources, in the form of letters, diaries, reports, and memoirs, describe and analyze the major campaigns and reveal the actions of the participants in the war. Includes bibliographical references.

797

McWilliams, Carey. *Brothers under the skin.* Rev. ed. Boston, Little, Brown, 1964. xix, 364 p. $1.95

Examines the integration of Mexican-Americans in U.S. society. Includes bibliographical references.

798

McWilliams, Carey. *Factories in the field; the story of migration and farm labor in California.* Santa Barbara, Peregrine Publishers, 1971. xxiii, 335 p. illus. $2.95

The author has written a thorough socioeconomic study of migrant farm labor in California. This major contribution, with an excellent bibliography, will be an important work for libraries as well as for teachers dealing with Chicanos and the history of the U.S. Southwest.

799

McWilliams, Carey. *The Mexicans in America; a student's guide to localized history.* Edited by C. Lord. New York, Columbia University Teachers College, 1968. 32 p. (Localized history series) $1.50

Presents sources for the study of Mexican Americans in the U.S. Includes a bibliography, as well as several topical essays on Mexican culture.

800

Madariaga, Salvador de. *Bolívar.* New York, Schocken Books, 1969. xix, 711 p. illus., ports., map (on lining papers) $4.50

This is an English translation of the challenging and provocative biography of South America's hero of the wars for independence published in 1952.

801

Maddison, Angus. *Economic policy and progress in developing countries.* New York, W.W. Norton Books, 1970. 313 p. $3.25

Latin America is included in this general analysis of economic policy in developing countries.

802

Maddron, William F., and Edith Maddron. *Vacation air Mexico: guide to pleasure flying in Mexico.* 2d ed. Glendale, Calif., Aviation Book Co., 1973. 301 p. illus., maps. $10

Contains much helpful information and guidance for pilots wishing to fly in Mexico.

803

Madsen, William, and Claudia Madsen. *A guide to Mexican witchcraft.* New York, International Publications Service, 1969. 96 p. illus. (Minutiae Mexicana series) $2

Journalistic description of the occult and other practices in Mexico.

804

Madsen, William. *Mexican-Americans of South Texas.* New York, Holt, Rinehart and Winston, 1965. xii, 112 p. illus., map. (Case studies in cultural anthropology) $2.75

A careful study of the Mexican American way of life, sponsored by the Hidalgo Project on Differential Culture Change and Mental Health, which examines the difficulty Mexican Americans experience in the process of Anglicization.

805

Maddox, Robert Casey. *Wage differences between United States and Guatemalan industrial firms in Guatemala.* Austin, Bureau of Business Research, University of Texas at Austin, 1971. xi, 57 p. (Studies in Latin American business, no. 10) $2

"The purpose of this study is to develop some systematic evidence for a specific setting by analyzing wage levels of U.S. . . . and Guatemalan firms operating in Guatemala, in terms of selected factors which should be relevant in wage-level determination." Although this comparative statistical study draws the expected conclusion that foreign firms pay higher wages than national firms, the author is quick to point out that other assumed conclusions do not bear out and thus opens new questions in this field. Includes bibliographical references.

806

Magdoff, Harry. *The age of imperialism; the economics of U.S. foreign policy.* New York, Monthly Review Press, 1969. 315 p. illus. $1.95

The author argues that capitalism is by its nature expansionist, and the U.S. as the leader of the capitalist world is the most expansionist of all and emphasizes what he calls the era of "new imperialism" of the last two decades. Also studied are international financial problems and multinational corporations.

807

Maldonado-Denis, Manuel. *Puerto Rico; a socio-historic interpretation.* Translated by Elena Vialo. New York, Random House, 1972. xiv, 336 p. $2.45

English translation of *Puerto Rico: una interpretación histórico-social* (1972) which is in the author's words "a dissenting view of Puerto Rican history and society," concentrating on Spanish colonialism (1493-1898) and on subsequent U.S. domination. Includes a bibliography.

808

Mallea, Eduardo. *Chaves.* Edited by Bernardo Gicovate and Alicia Gicovate. Englewood Cliffs, N.J., Prentice-Hall, 1971. 94 p. $2.50

This novel, by one of the most admired Argentine writers of the last 30 years, was first published in 1953. The protagonist, a worker in a sawmill, is surrounded by hostility and gains superiority from surviving many tragedies. This is a masterful and important work. Includes notes and bibliography.

809

Mallin, Jay. *Fortress Cuba: Russia's American base.* Chicago, H. Regnery, 1965. 192 p. illus. $.75

Written by a correspondent who covered Havana for *Time* magazine from 1952 until 1962, this is a journalistic account of Castro's Cuba.

810

Mancini, Pat McNees, comp. *Contemporary Latin American short stories.* Greenwich, Conn., Fawcett Publications, 1974. 344 p. $1.75

Contains selections from the works of 34 major contemporary Latin America writers. Included are Darío, Lugones, Gallegos, Asturias, Borges, Carpentier, Paz, Cortázar, Fuentes, García Márquez, Donoso, Benedetti, Cabrera Infante, Vargas Llosa, Puig, and others. Contains a bibliography.

811

Mandar, John. *Unrevolutionary society; the power of Latin American conservatism in a changing world.* New York, Harper & Row, 1974. xii, 270 p. $2.75

Analyzes the power of conservative political and economic forces in Latin America. This is an important and thoughtful work, which also contains a bibliography.

812

Mandel, Ernest, ed. *Fifty years of world revolution, 1917-1967; an international symposium.* Translations by Gerald Pane. New York, Merit Publishers, 1968. 366 p. $2.45

A Trotskyite view of communism over the last 50 years. The Latin American contributors include Luis Vitale (Chile), Nahuel Moreno (Argentina), and Hugo González Moscoso (Bolivia). The Bolivian is represented by an essay on "The Cuban Revolution and its lessions." Includes bibliographical references. [Charles Fleener]

813

Mannix, Daniel Pratt, and Malcolm Cowley. *Black cargoes; a history of the Atlantic slave trade, 1518-1865.* New York, Viking Press, 1965. 306 p. illus., map, tables. $1.85

First published in 1962, this is a description of the Atlantic slave trade based on contemporary sources. Includes a very good bibliography.

814

Manucy, Albert, and Ricardo Torres-Reyes. *Puerto Rico and the forts of Old San Juan.* New York, Viking Press, 1974. 94 p. illus. $3.95

An attractive military history of San Juan and its forts throughout more than four centuries of Spanish domination. The photographs, diagrams, reproductions of early prints, and other illustrations are excellent. Intended for collectors and libraries, as well as for Caribbean historians.

815

Marbán Escobar, Edilberto. *El mundo iberoamericano: sus pueblos y sus tierras.* New York, Regents Pub. Co., 1968. 192 p. $2.95

A description of the Spanish-American countries and their cultures. This is a general treatment for use in survey courses and by the general public.

816

Marighella, Carlos. *For the liberation of Brazil.* Translated by John Butt and Rosemary Sheed, with an introd. by Richard Gott. Harmondsworth, England, Penguin Books, 1971. 191 p. (The Pelican Latin American library, A-1341) $1.45

Contains a collection of writings by a Brazilian Communist leader who drew up blueprints for urban guerrilla warfare. [HLAS 35:7859]

817

Marshall, Andrew. *Brazil.* New York, Walker, 1966. 231 p., illus., maps, ports. (New nations and peoples) $3.50

Although the author has a tendency to generalize somewhat about Brazilians and their way of living, he presents an informative overview of the country's historic, economic, and social aspects. The photographs are very good, and the short biographical sketches and select bibliography enhance the text.

818
Martinez, Manuel Guillermo. *Don Joaquín García Icazbalceta: his place in Mexican historiography.* Washington, D.C., McGrath, 1973. 127 p. $12

Describes the life and work of this famous Mexican historiographer by means of anecdotes and personal narrative. Each of his works is discussed in detail, and the text is embellished with portraits, photographs, and reproductions of manuscrip material.

819
Martínez, Rafael V. *My house is your house.* New York, Friendship Press, 1964. 127 p illus., ports. $1.95

This is a popularized study of the background and influence on U.S. culture of the five million North Americans of Hispanic descent.

820
Martins, Wilson, and Seymour Menton, eds. *Teatro brasileiro contemporaneo.* New York Appleton-Century-Crofts, 1966. 405 p. $5.50

Includes unabridged texts of five plays that illustrate various aspects of the contemporary theater: Raimundo Magalhães Júnior, "O homem que fica"; Pedre Bloch, "As Mãos de Eurídice"; Jorge Andrade, "A moratória"; Guilherm Figueiredo, "A rapôsa e as uvas"; and Ariano Suassuna, "Auto da compadecida. A general introduction and a prefatory note to each play give this school edition unusual distinction. [HLAS 28:2654]

821
Martz, John D., ed. *The dynamics of change in Latin American politics.* 2d ed Englewood Cliffs, N.J., Prentice-Hall, 1971. 395 p. illus. $6.50

Several prominent U.S. scholars give their views on the political settings and the rapidity of current political changes in Latin America. The first edition appeared in 1965. Includes bibliographical references.

822
Mason, John Alden. *The ancient civilizations of Peru.* Rev. ed. Baltimore, Penguin Books, 1957. 330 p. plates. $2.95

Written for the layman and full of up-to-date information, this is a well organized and readable book with excellent plates. It is divided into background, history of Peruvian culture, the Inca, arts and crafts, appendix, and a bibliography.

823
Mathews, Thomas G. *Luis Muñoz Marín; a concise biography.* New York, American RDM Corp., 1967. 61 p. group ports., illus. (A study master publication 909) $1

This is a clear, concise biography of Puerto Rico's creative ex-governor, Luis Muñoz Marín, the architect of the island's current prosperity. Includes a good bibliography.

824
Mathis, Ferdinand John. *Economic integration in Latin America; the progress and problems of LAFTA,* by F. John Mathis. Austin, University of Texas Press, 1969. xv 112 p. illus. (Studies in Latin American business series, no. 8) $3

A brief discussion of economic integration in Latin America in which the author analyzes the success and prospects of regional common markets.

825
Matilla, Alfredo, and Iván Silén, eds. *The Puerto Rican poets.* New York, Bantam Books 1973. xiii, 238 p. $1.45

This work is divided into "Most Important Poets Before 1955," "Major Poets," and "Latest Poets." Poetry of exile occupies half the volume, presenting the work of young Puerto Rican poets in New York who write poetry of the street in Spanish or English, with a claustrophobic quality about it. Afro-Antillean poetry is also well represented, especially through poems of Luis Palés Matos. English translations of contemporary poems are better and more readable than the translations of the earlier and more formal poems. The editors consider Palés Matos, Julia de Burgos, and Hugo Margenat the most important figures in Puerto Rican poetry. The introduction describes briefly the development of the island's poetry. This is an excellent anthology, with a bibliography, which will be a welcome addition to libraries, public and academic alike.

826
Matthews, Herbert Lionel. *Fidel Castro.* New York, Clarion Press, 1970. 382 p. $2.95

This book is the result of long conversations that took place in Havana in 1967 between *New York Times* reporter Matthews and Fidel Castro. This political biography sheds new light on Castro and his government. Includes a useful bibliography.

827
Matthews, Herbert Lionel, ed. *The United States and Latin America.* 2d ed. Englewood Cliffs, N.J., Prentice-Hall, 1963. 179 p. illus., maps, tables. (A Spectrum book) $1.95

Contains the text of the final report of the 16th American Assembly, October 15-18, 1959, at Columbia University and background papers for the meeting, prepared by Edward W. Barrett and Penn T. Kimball (press and communications), Reynold E. Carlson (economic relations), Herbert L. Matthews (diplomatic relations), K.H. Silvert (political change in Latin America), and Frank Tannenbaum (on understanding Latin America). [HLAS 23:2759]

828
Matthiessen, Peter. *The cloud forest: a chronicle of the South American wilderness.* New York, Pyramid Publications, 1966. 280 p. illus., maps. $.75

A U.S. naturalist describes his travels through the jungles and mountains of South America.

829
Mecham, John Lloyd. *Church and state in Latin America: a history of politico-ecclesiastical relations.* Rev. ed. Chapel Hill, University of North Carolina Press, 1966. 465 p. $3.45

First published in 1934, this is a revised edition of the best survey of church-state relations in the national period of Latin American history. The emphasis in this scholarly and readable book is on the political significance of church-state relations. Contains a bibliography.

830
Meggers, Betty Jane. *Amazonia: man and culture in a counterfeit paradise.* Chicago, Aldine Atherton, 1971. 182 p. illus., maps. (World of man) $2.95

This is an excellent in-depth study of the Amazonia region, which explores all pertinent aspects of anthropology and ecology. Dr. Meggers expertly traces the evolution and process of adaptation to the environment of the various Indian tribes. An essential and most valuable work. Includes a glossary and a select bibliography.

831
Meggers, Betty Jane. *Prehistoric America.* Chicago, Aldine Pub. Co., 1972. 200 p. illus. $3.95

Brief introduction to New World archeology organized by pairs of environment areas in North and South America. After describing the peopling of the hemisphere and the transition to agriculture, cultural evolution in these areas traced to the time of European contact. Important contribution, with a thorough bibliography. [HLAS 35:517]

832
Meier, Matt S., and Feliciano Rivera. *The Chicanos; a history of Mexican American* New York, Hill and Wang, 1972. xviii, 302 p. maps. (American century series) $2.

Analyzes the historical and cultural background of Mexican Americans in the U. It also describes the evolution of Chicano identity during the last decade, and the emergence of this minority as a distinct political entity. Includes a bibliograph and a glossary of Chicano terminology.

833
Meighan, Clement E., and Leonard J. Foote. *Excavations at Tizapán El Alto, Jalisco.* L Angeles, Latin American Center, University of California, 1973. 299 p. illus. $5

Based on field studies, it describes recent excavations at Tizapán. Includes bibliography and illustrations.

834
Merk, Frederick. *Manifest destiny and mission in American history: a re-interpretatio* With the collaboration of Lois Bannister Merk. New York, Random House, 196 265 p. $1.95

The author analyzes Mexican and Caribbean examples of "manifest destiny" an presents an appraisal of varying North American opinions regarding U. expansionism in the 19th century. Includes a useful bibliography.

835
Mesa-Lago, Carmelo. *Cuba in the 1970's; pragmatism and institutionalizatio* Albuquerque, University of New Mexico Press, 1974. 296 p. $3.95

A major study of contemporary Cuba by a noted scholar who specializes in Cuba problems. Includes a thorough bibliography. This important contribution shoul be acquired by all Latin American collections.

836
Mesquita Filho, Julio de. *Citadels, ramparts, and censors; freedom and dictatorship* *Brazil.* Translated by Mark Curran, Carmelo Virgillo, and David W. Foster. Temp Arizona State University, Center for Latin American Studies, 1974. 106 p. $2

Criticizes some practices of the current Brazilian government. Contains bibliography.

837
Métraux, Alfred. *History of the Incas.* Translated from the French by George Ordish New York, Schocken Books, 1970. 221 p. illus., map. $2.45

A comprehensive survey of the Incas from the cultures of the Mochica and Chim through the empire and Spanish rule to the 20th century. The original Frenc edition is entitled *Les Incas* (1961). Contains a chronology and a bibliography.

838
Métraux, Alfred. *Voodoo in Haiti.* Translated by Hugo Charteris. New introd. by Sidne W. Mintz. New York, Schocken Books, 1972. 400 p. illus. $3.95

Paperback edition of the 1959 English translation of *Le voudou haïtien* (1958) b one of the most important anthropologists of this century. Métraux becam interested in Haiti in 1941. After steeping himself in the island's folk religion h wrote this definitive work. Voodoo "has blended together not only different African cults but also certain beliefs from European folklore." According to the author, voodoo as a religious system has lost none of its creative force. Of great interest to anthropologists and sociologists.

839

Mezerik, Avrahm G. *Cuba.* New York, International Review Service, 1973. 2 v. $5 each

A general description of Cuba from colonial times to the present. Contains bibliographical references.

840

Mezerik, Avrahm G. *Cuba, U.S., and U.S.S.R. relations.* New York, Internaional Review Service, 1969. 92 p. maps. $5

Chronological review of U.S. diplomacy towards Cuba and the U.S.S.R. since the Cuban revolution.

841

Milla, José. *Cuadros Guatemaltecos.* Edited by G.J. Edberg. New York, Macmillan, 1965. 115 p. (Macmillan modern Spanish American literature series) $2.50

Contains Guatemalan plays, intended for students of Latin American literature. Contains bibliographical references and vocabularies.

842

Millares Carlo, Agustín. *Ensayo de una bibliografía de la imprenta y el periodismo en Venezuela.* Washington, Organization of American States, 1968. 91 p. (OAS, 109-S-8057) $1

A distinguished Venezuelan historian has compiled an important annotated bibliography on the history of printing and the press in Venezuela.

843

Millen, Nina. *Children of South America.* New York, Friendship Press, 1972. 55 p. illus. $1.50

A book written for young people about the children of South America in their setting.

844

Miller, Theodore R. *Graphic history of the Americas.* New York, J. Wiley, 1969. 61 p. of maps, illus., tables. $4.25

Although the U.S. is the principal subject of this volume, 16 large maps of the Western Hemisphere depict the flow of history from Cape Horn to Baffin Bay. This is a convenient, graphic source for students of the Americas. [Charles Fleener]

845

Miller, Wayne Charles, ed. *A gathering of ghetto writers; Irish, Italian, Jewish, black, and Puerto Rican.* Edited, with an introd., by Wayne Charles Miller. New York, New York University Press, 1972. xiii, 442 p. $2.15

Presents samplings from the works of ethnic minority members. Includes bibliographical references.

846

Millon, René Francis, Bruce Drewitt, and James A. Bennyhoff. *Pyramid of the Sun at Teotihuacán, 1959 investigations.* Philadelphia, American Philosophical Society, 1965. 93 p. illus., plans. (American Philosophical Society Philadelphia Transactions, new ser., v. 55, pt. 6) $3

The fascinating story of the Pyramid of the Sun is told from the first excavations to the time of publication in 1964, and although the study is intended for the specialist, the language is not overly technical. The list of references, illustrations, diagrams and drawings complement the text and are themselves very valuable. Includes a bibliography.

847
Millon, Robert Paul. *Zapata: the ideology of a peasant revolutionary*. New York, International Publishers, 1969. 159 p. $2.25

Emiliano Zapata and land reform symbolized the essence of the Mexican Revolution of 1910. Although agrarian reform was their main objective, the Zapatistas also had a program of social and political reforms. The author presents a rather superficial study of the Zapatista movement against the background of political ideologies. Contains a good bibliography.

848
Milne, Jean. *Fiesta time in Latin America*. Los Angeles, Ritchie Press, 1968. xii, 236 p. illus. $2.95

"Fiestas (Spanish America), *festas* (Brazil), or *fêtes* (Haiti) are given for just about every reason that one might think of...," and they can be divided into three groups: religious, civil, and tribal. This book describes a great number of celebrations in a general way. A useful appendix outlines the fiestas by countries.

849
Mistral, Gabriela [pseud.]. *Selected poems of Gabriela Mistral*. Translated and edited by Doris Dana. Introd. by Francisco Aguilera. Woodcuts by Antonio Frasconi. Baltimore, Published for the Library of Congress by the Johns Hopkins University Press, 1971. xxix, 235 p. illus. (Hispanic Foundation publications) $2.95

Bilingual edition of the most representative poems by the Chilean Nobel Prize winner. The Library of Congress has simultaneously issued a recording by Gabriela Mistral reading her poetry. It may be obtained from the Music Division, Library of Congress, Washington, D.C. 20540; $5.50 postpaid.

850
Mistral, Gabriela [pseud.]. *Selected poems of Gabriela Mistral*. Translated by Langston Hughes. Bloomington, Indiana University Press, 1966. 119 p. (Indiana University poetry series) $1.75

This translation is the product of one poet's liking for another. The clear simplicity of Hughes' own style is a perfect medium to allow Gabriela Mistral's own to come through with a minimum of distortion. The work contains an introduction by Hughes and the citation by the Nobel Prize Committee. Mistral was awarded the Nobel Prize for Literature in 1945.

851
Mitchell, James Erskine. *Emergence of a Mexican church; the Associate Reformed Presbyterian Church of Mexico*. South Pasadena, Calif., William Carey Library, 1970. 183 p. illus. $2.95

This description of the establishment of a Presbyterian church in Mexico was originally presented as the author's thesis at the Fuller Theological Seminary. Includes a bibliography.

852
Moerner, Magnus, ed. *Expulsion of the Jesuits from Latin America*. New York, Knopf, 1965. 207 p. (Borzio books on Latin America) $2.95

A collection of 18 essays on the expulsion of the Jesuits from Spanish (1767) and Portuguese (1759) America. The editor's introduction and bibliographical notes are excellent.

853

Moerner, Magnus, ed. *Race mixture in the history of Latin America.* Boston, Little, Brown, 1967. xii, 178 p. illus., maps. $3.40

This selection of scholarly monographs contains sections on historical demography concerning ethnic groups in Latin America, mestizaje in the legislation, and social stratification in colonial Spanish America. Black slavery and its abolition are also covered. Contains bibliographical footnotes.

854

Momsen, Richard P. *Brazil: a giant stirs,* by Richard P. Momsen, Jr. Princeton, N.J., Van Nostrand, 1968., 144 p. (Van Nostrand searchlight book, 38) $2.95

Momsen presents a well-organized and detailed survey of the social and economic picture of Brazil, concentrating on the country's future vis-a-vis the world community. Although the scope of the book does not permit in-depth discussions, Momsen draws conclusions which are well documented by means of maps and tables. Includes a bibliography and index.

855

Montejo, Esteban. *Autobiography of a runaway slave.* Edited by Miguel Barnet; translated from the Spanish by Jocasta Innes. New York, World Pub. Co., 1969. 223 p. $2.25

Translation of *Biografía de un cimarrón* (1966), it deals with the personal impressions of a perceptive man who observed the impact of the abolition of slavery in Cuba, his thoughts on the independence movement (1895-98), its various leaders, and their efforts to form a government after 1901. Includes his views on 20th-century Cuba and insightful remarks on the Cuban Revolution of 1959. Montejo lived to be over 100 years old, and the translation compassionately portrays his humanity and political commitments. For graduate students as well as undergraduates, this is a valuable document for understanding the perspectives of the lower class swept up in major events. [Vincent C. Peloso]

856

Moore, G. Alexander. *Life cycles in Atchalán; the diverse careers of certain Guatemalans.* New York, Teachers College Press, 1973. x, 220 p. illus. (Anthropology and education series) $4.95

Examines problems and realities of schooling in Guatemala as it affects various social groups. Formal and informal learning processes are studied. The author skillfully compares Ladino and Indian careers and adds a chapter on modernization of life. Includes a bibliography.

857

Moore, Joan W., and Alfredo Cuellar. *Mexican Americans.* Englewood Cliffs, N.J., Prentice-Hall, 1970. xii, 172 p. illus. (Ethnic groups in American life series) $3.50

Briefly traces the social and cultural history of Mexican Americans within the broader context of U.S. society. Includes a bibliography.

858

Moquin, Wayne, and Charles Van Doren, comps. *A documentary history of Mexican Americans.* Introd. by Feliciano Rivera. New York, Bantam Books, 1973. xiv, 399 p. illus., facsims., ports. $1.25

This is a comprehensive documentary history of the second oldest component of American society—the Mexican Americans. The selections cover material from 1536 to the present. Includes a bibliography. This is a major contribution, and an important addition for library collections. Also available in hard cover.

859
Moreno, Francisco José, and Barbara Mitrani, eds. *Conflict and violence in Latin American politics: a book of readings*. New York, Crowell, 1971. 452 p. $2.95

Includes essays and short studies on the role of violence in the political processes of various Latin American countries. Includes bibliographical references.

860
Morison, Samuel Eliot. *Christopher Columbus, mariner*. New York, New American Library, 1956. 160 p. $.60

This is a condensation and rewriting of the well-known biography entitled *Admiral of the ocean sea* (1942), written after the author, for many years a yachtsman, had made four sailing voyages in which he went over much of Columbus' route, traveling, as far as possible, at the same time of the year.

861
Morley, Sylvanus Griswold. *The ancient Maya*. Rev. by George W. Brainerd. 3d ed. rev. Stanford, Calif., Stanford University Press, 1969. 507 p. illus., maps, tables. $4.95

This is a classic work on the Mayas for the nonspecialist. The author presents the magnificent world of the Mayas, and includes material on the wall paintings of Bonampak and the Palenque tomb. The text is enhanced with beautiful illustrations. Includes a good bibliography.

862
Morris, David J. *We must make haste slowly; process of revolution in Chile*. New York, Vintage Books, 1973. 307 p. $2.45

This work by a teacher and free-lance journalist examines Chilean political problems of the 1970's. He concentrates on economics, land reform, bureaucracy, and the polemics among rival leftist parties. Does not cover the events in Chile of September 1973.

863
Morris, Raymond P. *A theological book list*. Produced by the Theological Education Fund of the International Missionary Council for Theological Seminaries and Colleges in Africa, Asia, Latin America, and the Southwest Pacific. Oxford, Blackwell; Naperville, Ill., Allenson, distributors, 1960. xiv, 242 p. $3.95

Includes books dealing with Christianity and other religions. Titles dealing with ethnology, anthropology, economics, politics, and sociology have also been added.

864
Morse, Richard McGee, ed. *The bandeirantes: the historical role of the Brazilian pathfinders*. Edited with an introd. by Richard M. Morse. 1st ed. New York, Knopf, 1965. 215 p. (Borzoi books on Latin America) $2.95

A useful compilation of documents and essays on the bandeirantes and on the Brazilian frontier expansion, preceded by a fine essay on the phenomenon.

864A
Muckley, Robert L., and Eduardo E. Vargas, comps. *Cuentos puertorriqueños*. Introd. by Hernán LaFontaine and Marco A. Hernández. Skokie, Ill., National Textbook Co., 1975. 119 p. illus. $4. single copy; 5 or more $3.60 each

Includes outstanding Puerto Rican short stories by Pedro Juan Soto, Wilfredo Braschi, Jaime Carrero, Tomás Blanco, and José Luis González. This representative selection is intended for intermediate students. Contains a vocabulary.

865
Mulford, John W. *Volcano watcher's guide to the Caribbean.* Bloomfield Hills, Mich., Cranbook Institute of Science, 1969. 29 p. illus. (Cranbook Institute of Science. Bulletin, 54) $1

Presents a listing of past and present volcanic activity in the Caribbean area. Includes a bibliography.

866
Nach, James. *Guatemala in pictures.* New York, Sterling Pub. Co., 1970. 64 p. illus. (Visual geography series) $1.50

The author presents the land, history, government, people, and culture of Guatemala in an illustrated booklet. This is a convenient aid for high school and freshman college classes.

867
Namikawa, Banri. *Mexico; realm of the sun.* Tokyo, Palo Alto, Calif., Kodansha International, 1971. 130 p. illus. (part col.), map. (This beautiful world, v. 20) $2.75

A Japanese journalist presents a description of Mexico with beautiful illustrations, many of them in color.

868
Nance, Afton Dill. *A study of Mexico and Central America.* Menlo Park, Calif., Pacific Coast Publications, 1971. 250 p. illus. $1.85

A general description of Mexico and Central America, intended for the traveler and nonspecialist.

869
Nance, James. *Pre-Spanish trade in the Bay Islands.* Birmingham, Ala., Southern University Press, 1969. 218 p. illus., maps. $1

Studies trading patterns in the Bay Islands based on evidence which survived conquest, colonization, pirates, and independence. Includes a bibliography.

870
Nash, Manning. *Machine age Maya; the industrialization of a Guatemala community.* Chicago, University of Chicago Press, 1967. xv, 155 p. illus., maps. $1.95

Describes an Indian mountain community, which has successfully adapted to the establishment of Central America's largest textile mill in its midst. This is a scholarly well-organized study with notes and bibliography. [Charles Fleener]

871
Nash, Manning. *Primitive and peasant economic systems.* San Francisco, Chandler Pub. Co., 1970. xiii, 166 p. (Chandler publications in anthropology and sociology) $2.75

Studies primitive, peasant, and rural systems and their adaptation into industrialized 20th-century society. Includes a good bibliography.

872
National Education Association. Washington, D.C. *Education for the Spanish speaking.* Washington, 1972. 98 p. $2

Outlines educational theory and practical methods for teaching Spanish-speaking children on the elementary school level.

873
Neale-Silva, Eduardo. *Horizonte humano; vida de José Eustasio Rivera.* Madison, University of Wisconsin Press, 1960. 506 p. illus. $2.25

A biography of the Colombian poet and novelist, exhaustively documented and executed by a professor who specializes in studying the man and his period. It would be difficult to find another Spanish American writer who has been favored with a biography comparable to this one in scope and quality. Includes a bibliography.

874

Nearing, Scott, and Joseph Freeman. *Dollar diplomacy; a study in American imperialism.* New York, Monthly Review Press, 1969. xv, 353 p. maps. (Socialist classics series, no. 1) $3.95

More than 50 years ago when this work first appeared the authors coined the phrase that has been used subsequently to describe the first decades of U.S. expansion in Latin America. They analyze cases in which the U.S. economic and business interests have intervened in the Caribbean area. [Charles Fleener]

875

Needler, Martin Cyril. *Anatomy of a coup d'état: Ecuador 1963.* Washington, Institute for the Comparative Study of Political Systems, 1964. 54 p. $2.50

With firsthand knowledge of many personalities, the author has written an accurate analysis of the 1963 coup in Ecuador which deposed Carlos Julio Arosemena as President. Includes a select bibliography.

876

Needler, Martin Cyril. *Latin American politics in perspective.* Rev. ed. Princeton, N.J., Van Nostrand, 1970. 200 p. (New perspectives in political science, 3) $2.95

A good general study by an experienced Latin Americanist, describing Latin American politics. Includes a bibliography.

877

Needler, Martin Cyril. *Political development in Latin America; instability, violence, and evolutionary change.* New York, Random House, 1968. 210 p. $3.50

Analyzes political development, institutions, and specific processes in contemporary Latin America. Includes bibliographies.

878

Needler, Martin Cyril. *Politics and society in Mexico.* Albuquerque, University of New Mexico Press, 1971. xii, 143 p. $2.45

Chapters on the PRI, elections, presidency, economic policy, military, and political culture are integrated by the theme that Mexican politics have evolved from open conflict to constitutional procedures. [HLAS 35:7528]

879

Nehemkis, Peter Raymond. *Latin America; myth and reality.* Rev. ed. New York, New American Library, 1966. 317 p. (A Mentor book MQ-685) $1.25

In a general treatment, written for the nonspecialist, the author points out the fascinating diversity of Latin America and attempts to unmask the mythology that blocks understanding of Latin Americans by North Americans.

880

Neistein, José, and Manoel Cardozo, comps. *Poesia brasileira moderna; a bilingual anthology.* Edited, with introd. and notes by José Neistein. Translations by Manoel Cardozo. Washington, Brazilian-American Cultural Institute, 1972. xxii, 207 p. $4.50

Selected verses by 19 poets representative of the best Brazilian poetry in the last 50 years. Verse-by-verse English translations are printed on facing pages. Mario de Andrade, Manuel Bandeira, Jorge de Lima, Cecilia Meireles, Vinicius de Moreis are among those included. Highly recommended for literature courses and students of Portuguese.

881

Neruda, Pablo. *The captain's verses (Los versos del capitán). Love poems.* Translated by Donald D. Walsh. New York, New Directions Books, 1972. 151 p. $1.95

This is a bilingual edition of the original which appeared in 1954. There are lyrical love poems, with some surrealistic and political poems added. The translations are very good.

882

Neruda, Pablo. *Extravagaria.* Translated from the Spanish by Alistair Reid. New York, Noonday Press, 1973. 303 p. $2.95

According to Anderson-Imbert, in *Estravagaria* (1958) "there is a gross and noisy superficiality: nevertheless, his creative force is always impressive." This edition presents Spanish text parallel with the English translation.

883

Neruda, Pablo. *Five decades; poems, 1925-1970.* Translated by Ben Belitt. New York, Grove Press; distributed by Random House, 1974. 240 p. $3.95

This is a bilingual selection of 130 poems published between 1925 and 1970. It presents an important cross-section of Neruda's work.

884

Neruda, Pablo. *The heights of Macchu Picchu.* Translated by Nathaniel Tarn. New York, Noonday Press, 1969. 75 p. $1.95

An excellent translation of one of Neruda's longer poems (*Las alturas de Macchu Picchu*) presented here in a bilingual edition. The poem is a song of praise to indigenous America.

885

Neruda, Pablo. *A new decade, poems 1958-1968.* Translations by Ben Belitt and Alistair Reid. New York, Grove Press, 1971. xlvi, 274 p. $2.95

Professor Belitt states that this edition was culled from six volumes of poetry and that the selections recall "the true measure of Neruda's long traffic with the democracy of letters."

886

Neruda, Pablo. *New poems (1968-1970).* Edited, translated and with an introd. by Ben Belitt. New York, Grove Press; distributed by Random House, 1972. xxxii, 153 p. $1.95

Translation of recent poems by Neruda, with English and Spanish text on opposite pages. Includes bibliographical references.

887

Neruda, Pablo. *Pablo Neruda: the early poems.* Translated by David Ossman and Carlos B. Hagen. Drawings by Lucas Johnson. New York, New Rivers Press, 1969. 100 p. illus. $3.75

Includes some early uncollected poems written in the 1920's, along with selections from *Crepusculario* (1923), *El hondero entusiasta* (1933), *Veinte poemas de amor y una canción desesperada* (1924), and *Anillos* (1926).

888

Neruda, Pablo. *Residence on earth. Residencia en la tierra.* Translated by Donald D. Walsh. New York, New Directions Pub. Corp., 1973. 359 p. (A New Directions book) $3.75

This is the first English edition of the complete three volumes of *Residencia en la tierra* (1933, 1935, 1947), considered to be the major work of the Nobel Prize-winning poet. It presents the best of Neruda, lyrical, vibrant, and politically committed. It is after *Residencia III* that he steers away from personal lyricism into dogmatism. Here we see a many-faceted poet with his intensely personal poetry, as well as his surrealism. According to the critic Anderson-Imbert, "to read Neruda is to penetrate within the creative process of a poet."

889

Neruda, Pablo. *Selected poems of Pablo Neruda.* Edited and translated by Ben Belitt. Introd. by Luis Monguió. New York, Grove Press, 1963. 319 p. $2.95

These translations by Ben Belitt and the excellent study by Luis Monguió constitute much more than just an introduction of Pablo Neruda to the North American public. For the student of Hispanic poetry, however, they prove how difficult it is to translate Neruda. The selection is very representative.

889A

Neruda, Pablo, and César Valejo. *Selected poems.* Edited by R. Bly. Boston, Beacon, 1971. 198 p. $2.95

Contains selections of poems by two leading Latin American poets of the 20th century.

890

Neruda Pablo. *Selected poems of Pablo Neruda.* Translated by Angel Flores. New York, Dell Pub. Co., 1970. 289 p. $2.95

Presents a representative selection of poems by Neruda. This edition was originally published in 1944. New translations have been added here.

891

Neruda, Pablo. *Splendor and death of Joaquín Murieta.* Translated by Ben Belitt. New York, Farrar, Strauss, and Giroux, 1972. xvii, 182 p. $2.95

This play is a translation of *Fulgor y muerte de Joaquín Murieta,* with the original Spanish text on facing pages. The translation is excellent.

892

Neruda, Pablo. *Twenty love poems and a song of despair.* New York, Grossman Publications, 1971. 150 p. $1.95

First published in 1924 as *Veinte poemas de amor y una canción desesperada,* this is a collection of lyric poems by the most inspired Latin American poet of the contemporary period.

893

Neruda, Pablo. *We are many.* Translated by Alistair Reid. Illustrated by Hans Ehrmann. New York, Grossman Publications, 1967. 32 p. 2 plates, illus. $2.95

Contains several recent poems by Neruda in a bilingual edition.

894

Nettl, Bruno. *Folk and traditional music of the western continents.* With chapters on Latin America by Gérard Béhague. 2d ed. Englewood Cliffs, N.J., Prentice-Hall, 1973. xiii, 258 p. (Prentice-Hall history of music series) $2.95

The first two chapters introduce the subject. Others deal with the traditional music of the American Indians, the Afro-Latins, and western and western-descended folk music in the Americas. The chapters on Latin America by Béhague are excellent. Contains bibliographies and discographies.

895
Newcomb, William Wilmon. *The Indians of Texas; from prehistoric to modern times.* With drawings by Hal M. Story. Austin, University of Texas Press, 1961. 404 p. illus. $2.95

Traces many tribes who have lived in what today is Texas from the pre-Columbian period to the present. Contains an extensive bibliography.

896
Newlon, Clarke. *The men who made Mexico.* New York, Dodd, Mead, 1973. 273 p. illus., map. $4.95

Describes the rise and fall of the Aztec and Maya civilizations and then analyzes the conquest of Mexico by Spain. The lives of national heroes Hidalgo, Morelos, Iturbide, Santa Anna, Juárez, Díaz, Zapata, and others are sketched, as well as contemporary figures in the arts and literature. Intended for a background on Mexico.

897
Noble, Enrique, comp. *Literatura afro-hispanoamericana; poesía y prosa de ficción.* Lexington, Mass., Xerox College Publishing, 1973. 200 p. $4.95

This is an anthology of Afro-Latin poetry and prose fiction in Spanish, which will be of great interest to university and public libraries as well as to graduate programs specializing in Afro-Latin literature.

898
Nicholson, Irene. *A guide to Mexican poetry; ancient and modern.* New York, International Publications Service, 1968. 96 p. illus., ports. (Minutiae mexicana series) $2

This guide to Mexican poetry starts with pre-Columbian works by Aztecs and others and extends up to the present.

899
Nicholson, Norman L. *Canada in the American community.* Princeton, N.J., Van Nostrand, 1963. 128 p. (Van Nostrand searchlight book, 19) $2.95

Canada is part of the British Commonwealth by tradition yet is American by location and sentiment. This book explores to what extent Canada forms part of the Western-Hemisphere economic, cultural, and social life. Includes a bibliography.

900
Niemeier, Jean Gilbreath. *The Panama story.* Portland, Ore., Metropolitan Press, 1968. xi, 303 p. illus. $2.95

Consists of extracts chiefly from the *Panama Star and Herald,* and *La Estrella de Panamá,* with extensive commentaries by the author. Includes a bibliography.

901
Niggli, Josephina. *Mexican village.* Chapel Hill, University of North Carolina Press, 1970. xiv, 491 p. illus. $2.95

The author artfully depicts and analyzes life in Hidalgo, Nuevo León.

902
Niggli, Josephina. *Un pueblo mexicano; selections from Mexican Village.* Translated and edited by Justina Ruiz de Cone. Designs by Marion Fitz-Simmons. New York, Norton, 1969. 267 p. illus. $4.25

The stories center in the village of Hidalgo, one of the five towns in the Sabinas Valley in northern Mexico, and the same characters appear and reappear. Christian and pagan elements mix to form a unique cultural picture.

903
Nisbet, Charles T. *Latin America; problems in economic development.* New York, Free Press, 1969. x, 357 p. $5.50

Presents a systematic outline of Latin American economic development and the lack of it within the social and cultural context of the hemisphere. Includes a bibliography.

904
North, Lisa. *Civil-military relations in Argentina, Chile, and Peru.* Foreword by David E. Apter. Berkeley, Institute of International Studies, University of California, 1966. 86 p. (Politics of modernization series, no. 2) $1.75

Analyzes civilian political communities through an examination of the patterns of military organizations in Peru, Chile, and Argentina. The second two are often compared and contrasted. Peru is treated separately. The appendixes list the military revolts in each nation chronologically from 1900 through 1963. [Charles Fleener]

905
North American Congress on Latin America. *NACLA's bibliography on Latin America.* New York, 1973. 48 p. illus. $1

Contains a briefly annotated list of NACLA publications on Latin America.

906
North American Congress on Latin America. *New Chile.* New York, 1972. 176 p. illus. $2.50

NACLA compiled its Chile reports from 1969 to the present, including charts on foreign investment in Chile, copper economics, and a list of nationalizations. These valuable radical reports do not pretend to be objective. Includes bibliographical references.

907
Nun, José. *Latin America: the hegemonic crisis and the military coup.* Berkeley, Institute of International Studies, University of California, 1969. xii, 73 p. (Politics of modernization series, no. 7) $1.50

Analyzes the frequent military coups in Latin America in connection with the rapid changes experienced by the middle sectors. Argentina, Uruguay, Chile, Brazil, and Mexico receive special attention. [Charles Fleener]

908
Nuñez, Carlos. *Tupamaros; urban guerrillas of Uruguay.* Introd. by T. Wodetzki. New York, Times Change Press, 1972. 32 p. $1

Brief description of Tupamaro activities and goals in Uruguay during the last five years.

909
Nye, Joseph S. *Central American regional integration.* New York, Carnegie Endowment of International Peace, 1967. 66 p. map. (International conciliation, no. 572) $.60

Surveys the accomplishments of Central America's economic integration. Trade has quadrupled during the first five years of the Common Market's existence. The author warns the reader that "a political upheaval in one member country could swamp the fragile bark." Contains bibliographical footnotes.

910

Nystrom, J. Warren, and Nathan A. Haverstock. *The Alliance for Progress: key to Latin America's development.* Princeton, N.J., Van Nostrand, 1966. 126 p. maps. $1.95

This is a perceptive and somewhat optimistic analysis of the Alliance for Progress.

911

Oakes, Maud Van Courtland. *Two crosses to Todos Santos; survivals of Mayan religious rituals.* Princeton, N.J., Princeton University Press, 1969. xiii, 274 p. illus., maps. $2.95

First published in 1951, this is a scholarly study of the religious customs of the Mayans in the Cuchumantes Mountains. The author has uncovered much data on the Mayans of Guatemala and presents them in an interesting style. Includes bibliographies. [Charles Fleener]

912

O'Donnell, Guillermo A. *Modernization and bureaucratic authoritarianism; studies in South American politics.* Berkeley, Institute of International Studies, University of California, 1973. xv, 219 p. illus. (Politics of modernization series, no. 9) $4.50

Presents a detailed examination of bureaucratic authoritarianism within the general social context. This is an important study with a good bibliography.

913

O'Leary, Timothy J. *Ethnographic bibliography of South America.* New Haven, Human Relations Area Files, 1963. xxiv, 387 p. maps. (Behavior science bibliographies) $11

This is an impressive compilation of over 24,000 entries, including articles from some 650 serials. The most complete coverage is of ethnography and social anthropology, but archeology, physical anthropology, and related fields are also included. This work should be acquired by most academic and large public libraries. [HLAS 27:164a]

914

Ordish, George. *Man, crops, and pests in Central America,* by G. Ordish. New York, Pergamon Press, 1966. 119 p. illus., plates. (The Commonwealth and international library. Biology division. Biology in action series, v. 3) $2.95

The general problems of losses of agricultural products owing to the attacks of pests are the main concern of this book. It is very interesting and helpful for economists and sociologists.

915

Organization of American States. Division of Philosophy and Letters. *Fuentes de la filosofía Latinoamericana; bibliografía recopilada por la División de la Filosofía y Letras con la colaboración y el asesoramiento de distinguidos especialistas de América.* Washington, 1967. 100 p. (OAS, 199.8-S-7471) $2

Many noted specialists have contributed to this bibliography of sources of Latin American philosophy. This is a very important contribution.

915A

Organization of American States. Division of Philosophy and Letters. *Los "fundadores" en la filosofía de América Latina.* Washington, 1970. 199 p. (PAU-S-7895) $1

Includes 20 philosophers from different countries who are considered the founding fathers of philosophy in Latin America. The thinkers are presented in chronological order. Includes bibliographical notes.

916

Organization of American States. General Secretariat. *A bibliographical guide to the*

Spanish American theatre. Washington, 1969. 84 p. (OAS, 016-E-7732) $2

Presents a bibliography on various aspects of the theater in Spanish America. This is a very important contribution.

917
Organization of American States. General Secretariat. *Bibliography of statistical textbooks and other teaching material.* 2d ed. Washington, 1960. 120 p. (OAS, 016-SE-6090) $.75

Contains listings of Spanish and English titles of statistical textbooks.

918
Organization of American States. General Secretariat. *Motoring in Central America and Panama.* Washington, 1969. 37 p. map. $.25

A useful booklet which contains information for the motorist who wishes to travel to Central America.

919
Organization of American States. General Secretariat. *National anthems of the American nations.* Washington, 1972. 134 p. illus., facsims., music. (OAS, 783-ESPF-6152) $5

Contains facsimile editions of official versions for voice and piano of the national anthems of the American republics.

920
Organization of American States. General Secretariat. *Planeamiento nacional de servicios bibliotecarios.* Washington, Organization of American States, 1972. 2 v. (Estudios bibliotecarios, no. 8; OAS, 027-S-8226) $1 each

Surveys national library planning in the Americas, with individual studies and statistical data.

921
Ortego, Philip D., ed. *We are Chicanos; an anthology of Mexican-American literature.* New York, Washington Square Press, 1973. xxi, 330 p. illus. $1.25

The editor presents writings by and about Chicano authors, with introductions and commentaries on each writer. The first part is devoted to material concerning cultural background, folklore, and ethnic awareness. The larger part of the book presents poetry, short stories, a play, and excerpts from a book by Raymond Barrio. Contains a good bibliography.

922
Ortiz, Elisabeth Lambert. *Complete book of Mexican cooking.* Drawings by Roger Chapin. New York, Bantam Books, 1969. 161 p. illus. $.95

Compiles and describes recipes and instructions for the preparation of well-known Mexican main courses and desserts.

923
Ortiz Fernández, Fernando. *Cuban counterpoint; tobacco and sugar,* by Fernando Ortiz. Translated from the Spanish by Harriet de Onís. Introd. by Bronsilaw Malinowski. Prologue by Herminio Portell Vilá. New York, Random House, 1970. xxi, 352 p. $1.95

Maintains that Cuba's main crops, tobacco and sugar, have shaped Cuban society and together have formed the backbone of the Cuban economy. This important study was first published in 1940 under the title *Contrapunto cubano del tabaco y del azúcar.*

924

Ossa, Fernando José. *Payments problems in the economic integration of Latin America.* Ithaca, N.Y., Cornell University, Latin American Studies Program, 1973. 257 p. (Latin American Studies Program, Dissertation series, 51) $4

Analyzes balance of payments problems of a free trade area, describes institutional developments in international payments, and suggests new approaches to the economic integration of Latin America. This thesis includes tables and a bibliography.

925

Otero, Lisandro. *Cultural policy in Cuba.* New York, UNIPUB, 1973. 184 p. $2

Published under the auspices of UNESCO, this is a study of Cuban cultural policy since the ascent of Fidel Castro to the seat of power. Includes bibliographical notes.

926

Ovchynnk, Michael. *Freshwater fishes of Ecuador and perspective for development of fish cultivation.* East Lansing, Latin American Studies Center, Michigan State University, 1967. 44 p. illus., map. $1

The first part of this study is devoted to describing Ecuadorean fish. The final section studies the lack of protein in the diet of most Ecuadoreans and suggests how this might be improved through the introduction of modern techniques of fish cultivation. [Charles Fleener]

927

Oviedo y Valdés, Gonzalo Fernández de. *De la natural historia de las Indias.* Chapel Hill, University of North Carolina Press, 1970. 116 p. $5

An early eyewitness description of the Caribbean and Middle America, first published in 1526. This is a valuable historical document for the conquest period.

928

Oxaal, Ivar. *Black intellectuals come to power; the rise of creole nationalism in Trinidad and Tobago.* 2d ed. Cambridge, Mass., Schenkman Pub. Co., 1968. xiii, 194 p. illus., maps, ports. (International studies in political and social change, 3) $3.95

Analyzes the rise of black intellectuals to power in Trinidad and Tobago. This is a careful study with bibliographical references. Recommended for academic and public libraries.

929

Oxaal, Ivar. *Race and revolutionary consciousness; a documentary interpretation of the 1970 black power revolt in Trinidad.* Cambridge, Mass., Schenkman Pub. Co., 1971. 96 p. (A Schenkman paperback) $2.95

This is a well-documented analysis of the 1970 black power revolt in the Caribbean republic, with bibliographical references.

930

Pachter, Henry Maximilian. *Collision course; the Cuban missile crisis and co-existence.* New York, Praeger, 1963. 261 p. $2.50

This is a detailed account of the Cuban missile crisis of October 1962. Contains a thoughtful analysis of implications of U.S.-Soviet coexistence. The last part of the book has a concise chronology of the crisis and a collection of documents, as well as bibliographies. [HLAS 27:3429]

931

Padden, Robert C. *The hummingbird and the hawk; conquest and sovereignty in the*

Valley of Mexico, 1503-1541. New York, Harper & Row, 1973. xvi, 319 p. maps. $1.95

First published in 1967, this is a reexamination from the sources of late Aztec history and Spanish-Indian contacts to about 1540. Contains original interpretations of Aztec religion and Spanish conquest, with new data on Indian social adjustment in the early colony. An important achievement.[HLAS 30:1236]

932
Paddock, William, and Elizabeth Paddock. *We don't know how; an independent audit of what they call success in foreign assistance.* Ames, Iowa State University Press, 1973; distributed by The Latin American Service, Washington, D.C. xv, 331 p. $5

The Paddocks have traveled extensively in the developing nations. They lived in Latin America for 10 years, where William Paddock was head of Guatemala's corn improvement program with the U.S. aid mission. He has also written several prophetic works on world hunger.

933
Padgett, Leon Vincent. *The Mexican political system,* by L. Vincent Padgett. Boston, Houghton, Mifflin, 1966. 244 p. map. $4

A good analysis of Mexico's political system and political parties by a professor of political science at the University of California at San Diego. Contains a bibliography. [HLAS 29:6774]

934
Painter, Muriel Thayer. *Easter at Pascua Village.* Tucson, University of Arizona Press, 1960. 35 p. illus. $1

Describes traditional Easter celebrations in an Arizona village. Many of the traditions are of Spanish and Indian origin.

935
Painter, Muriel Thayer. *Faith, flowers, and fiestas.* Tucson, University of Arizona Press, 1970. 250 p. illus. $2

Includes descriptions of traditional Arizona folk festivals and folk art practices. Attractive illustrations enhance the text.

936
Palma, Ricardo, and Darryl Hunt. *Revolution or routine; the future of the Latin American church.* Maryknoll, N.Y., Orbis Books, 1973. 192 p. $2.95

Contains essays analyzing the position the Catholic church will occupy in the social and intellectual mainstream of Latin America during the next decades.

937
Palma, Ricardo. *Tradiciones peruanas.* Selected and annotated by Pamela Francis. New York, Pergamon Press, 1973. 108 p. (Pergamon Oxford Latin American series) $2.40

Palma (1833-1919) was a born narrator. He began *Tradiciones* in 1852 and completed the cycle in 1883. The editor has selected very representative sections which reflect the social, intellectual, and political history of Peru.

938
Palmatary, Helen Constance. *The archaeology of the lower Tapajós Valley, Brazil.* Philadelphia, American Philosophical Society, 1960. 243 p. illus., maps (1 fold.) (Transactions of the American Philosophical Society. New series, v. 50, pt. 3) $5

This is a thorough and scholarly study of the lower Tapajós region in Brazil, based on an extensive field study, as well as other evidence. Contains an important bibliography on this specialized subject.

939

Pan American associations in the United States, with supplementary lists of other inter-American and general associations. 8th ed. rev. Washington, General Secretariat, Organization of American States, 1974. 96 p. illus. $.75

Lists Pan American associations in the U.S. by states, as well as associations in other American republics, binational centers in OAS member states, and other inter-American associations.

940

Pan American Union. *Bilateral treaty developments in Latin America, 1953-1955.* Washington, 1956. 158 p. (Law and treaty series, 2; PAU 327-E-5504) $1

Includes bilateral treaties, agreements, and conventions for the 1953-55 period.

941

Pan American Union. *Bilateral treaty developments in Latin America, 1938-1948.* Washington, 1950. 154 p. (Law and treaty series, 32; PAU 341-E-4483) $1.50

Includes bilateral treaties, agreements, and conventions for the period mentioned in the title, which were entered into by the Latin American republics.

942

Pan American Union. *Copyright protection in the Americas; under national legislation and inter-American treaties.* 3d ed. rev. and enl. Washington, 1968. 301 p. $2.45

Outlines copyright legislation in the Latin American republics and contains the texts of relevant inter-American treaties.

943

Pan American Union. *Supplement to the third edition [of] Copyright Protection in the Americas.* Washington, 1969. 80 p. $1

Provides supplementary material not included in the previous 1968 edition.

944

Papadake, S. *Oscar Niemeyer.* New York, Braziller, 1970. 149 p. illus. $2.95

Studies the famed Brazilian architect who is the most influential trend setter of contemporary Latin America.

945

Paredes, Américo, ed. *Folktales of Mexico.* Edited and translated by Américo Paredes. Foreword by Richard M. Dorson. Chicago, University of Chicago Press, 1970. lxxxiii, 282 p. (Folktales of the world) $3.95

The editor has assembled 80 samples of Mexican oral tradition ranging from legends of pre-Columbian origin to contemporary stories and anecdotes. Contains a bibliography.

946

Paredes, Américo, and Raymund Paredes, comps. *Mexican-American authors.* Boston, Houghton, Mifflin, 1972. 152 p. illus. (Multi-ethnic literature) $2

Mexican-Americans are heirs to the culture of Spain as well as to the Indian civilizations of Mexico, in addition to having been in contact for over 100 years with U.S. cultural forces. This English-language compilation of samples from the writings of Mexican Americans includes Jovita González, Josephina Niggli, Arnulfo Trejo, and several others.

947

Pariseau, Earl J., ed. *Cuban acquisitions and bibliography; proceedings and working papers of an international conference held at the Library of Congress, April 13-15, 1970.* Washington, Library of Congress, Hispanic Foundation, 1971. 164 p. Free upon request.

Surveys Cuban holdings of the Library of Congress, including newspapers, periodicals, and manuscripts. It also contains articles on Cuban sources available in England, Spain, Germany, and other countries. The conference was sponsored jointly by the Hispanic Foundation [now Latin American, Portuguese, and Spanish Division] of the Library of Congress and Yale University.

948

Parkes, Henry Bamford. *A history of Mexico.* Rev. ed. Boston, Houghton, Mifflin, 1969. 460 p. illus. $3.45

Since 1938, Parkes' work has been the standard one-volume survey in English. This revised edition in paperback will be useful to students of Mexico. It covers the history of Mexico from pre-Columbian times to the presidency of Díaz Ordaz. [Charles Fleener]

949

Parra, Nicanor. *Emergency poems.* Translated by Miller Williams. New York, New Directions; distributed by Lippincott, 1972. 154 p. (A New Directions book) $2.75

Parra continues to write poetry in the vein of his earlier antipoems describing his highly personal and iconoclastic interpretation of reality. The vigorous translations reflect accurately the verse of this major Chilean poet. This bilingual edition is a welcome contribution to the growing collection of English translations of Latin American poetry.

950

Parra, Nicanor. *Poems and antipoems.* Edited by Miller Williams. Translators: Fernando Alegría and others. New York, New Directions, 1967. 149 p. (A New Directions paperback, ND-242) $1.95

Bilingual edition of poems taken from *Poemas y antipoemas* (1938-53), *Versos de salón* (1953-1962), and *Canciones rusas* (1963-64). Parra is a poet and professor of theoretical physics who has shaken the rigid structure of poetic theory with his antipoems. He is one of the most original and audacious contemporary poets and is widely read in the U.S. and in Europe. One of the most outstanding poems included here is "Soliloquy of the Individual" in which the poet concludes that "life has no meaning."

951

Parra, Teresa de la. *Mama Blanca's souvenirs.* Translated by Harriet de Onís. Washington, Pan American Union, 1959. 129 p. $1.50

The Venezuelan novelist Teresa de la Parra (1891-1936) describes beautifully rural life in an old society. *Las memorias de Mamá Blanca* (1929) are reminiscences of a life on a sugarcane plantation near Caracas.

952

Parry, John Horace, and P. M. Sherlock. *A short history of the West Indies.* 3d ed. New York, St. Martin's Press, 1971. xii, 337 p. illus., maps. $3.95

This is a scholarly history of the islands in the Caribbean sea from 1492 to 1966. While treating the history of these islands as a connected whole, it is addressed to readers in the British Caribbean. Includes a bibliography. [Charles Fleener]

953

Parson, Francis. *Early 17th century Spanish missions of the Southwest.* Tucson, Ariz., Dale Stuart King, 1968. 120 p. illus. $2.45

Describes the early missions of west Texas, New Mexico, and northern Arizona with attractive drawings, photos, as well as textual information.

954

Pasadena Art Museum. Pasadena, California. *Santos; New Mexican folk art.* Introd. by L. P. Frank. Foreword by T. W. Leavitt. La Jolla, Calif., McGilvery, 1970. 192 p. illus. $1.50

An illustrated guide to New Mexican folk art which can be found at the Pasadena Art Museum.

955

Patterson, Thomas C. *Pattern and process in the early intermediate period pottery of the central coast of Peru.* Berkeley, University of California Press, 1966. 180 p. illus., map. (University of California publications in anthropology, v. 3) $3.50

Based on field work in 1962-63 on the central coast and comparative collections of the intermediate period of sites from the Chancay Valley to Lurin Valley. Describes in detail, with illustrations, Miramar and Lima pottery styles. Also reviews and interprets earlier work on the central coast region. An important contribution to Andean archeology. [HLAS 29:1272]

956

Pauline, Lawrence J. *Latin America; history, culture, people.* Bronxville, N.Y., Cambridge Book Co., 1969. 250 p. illus., maps. $.95

This survey is designed for high school use. The author aims to "provide background for the understanding of important concepts concerning Latin America." Questions for the classroom and activities are suggested at the end of each chapter. [Charles Fleener]

957

Payne, Arnold. *The Peruvian coup d'etat of 1962; the overthrow of Manuel Prado.* Washington, Institute for the Comparative Study of Political Systems, 1968. 85 p. $2

Places the 1962 coup d'etat in perspective as it describes other coups which may be considered turning points in Peruvian history. It then analyzes the coup of July 8, 1962, and suggests its political significance.

958

Paz, Elena, comp. *Favorite Spanish folksongs; traditional songs from Spain and Latin America.* Foreword by Pru Devon. Music autography by Carl Rosenthal. Illus. selected and positioned by Moses Asch. Cover: woodcut by Mariana Yampolski. Cover design by Ronald Clyne. New York, Oak Publications, 1971. 96 p. illus. $3.95

Most of the songs are from Latin America. The melodies are unaccompanied and unharmonized except when meant to be sung in parallel thirds or simple chords, and few have instrumental introductions. There is a brief descriptive note about each song. This is a welcome addition to most library shelves. [HLAS 30:4519]

959

Paz, Elena, ed. *Spanish and Latin American guitar.* New York, Macmillan, 1971. 89 p. $3.95

Contains songs and scores of Spanish and Latin American songs for guitar.

960

Paz, Octavio. *¿Aguila o sol? Eagle or sun?* Translated by Eliot Weinberger. Bilingual ed. New York, October House, 1970. 125 p. $2.95

Contains essays by one of Mexico's outstanding poets and essayists. It includes *Trabajos del poeta* (1949), *Arenas movedizas* (1949), and *¿Aguila o sol?* (1950). The essays explore Mexico, the relations between language and poetry, and the poet and history.

961

Paz, Octavio, comp. *An anthology of Mexican poetry*. Translated by Samuel Beckett. Pref. by C. M. Bowra. Bloomington, Indiana University Press, 1971. 213 p. (UNESCO collection of representative works: Latin American series) $2.45

Includes selected poems translated into English from the works of 34 Mexican poets from Francisco Terrazas of the 16th century to Alfonso Reyes of the 20th. The selections are representative of the various periods covered. The compiler added succinct biographic notes on each poet.

962

Paz, Octavio. *Configurations;* translated from the Spanish by G. Aroul and others. New York, New Directions, 1971. 198 p. (A New Directions book) $2.75

Contains *Sun stone* and *Blanco* in their entireties. The former is Paz' most ambitious poem synthesizing his lyricism; *Blanco* is his important experimental work. This is an important bilingual edition, which in addition also contains selections from *Salamandra* and *Ladera este*. Most libraries will wish to acquire this anthology for their collections.

963

Paz, Octavio. *Early poems, 1935-1955*. Translated from the Spanish by Muriel Rukeyser, and others. New York, New Directions, 1973. 145 p. (A New Directions paperbook, NDP-354) $3.75

In this selection Paz collected what he liked best from his early poetry. These are excellent English translations, presented on facing pages with the original Spanish text.

964

Paz, Octavio. *The labyrinth of solitude; life and thought in Mexico*. Translated by Lysander Kemp. New York, Grove Press, 1963. 212 p. $1.95

In this penetrating examination of the nature of Mexico and Mexicans by a distinguished poet and intellectual, the basic theme is the universal alienation of all mankind. The author studies the Mexican manifestation of this condition in a series of nine essays.

965

Paz, Octavio. *Marcel Duchamp; or the castle of purity*. Translated from the Spanish by Donald Gardner. New York, Grossman, 1972. 50 p. col. illus., plate, port. $2.95

Contains illustrations and plates depicting Marcel Duchamp's work, with interpretive comments by Octavio Paz. This is a handsome edition with attractive illustrations from the work of the great French avant garde painter.

966

Paz, Octavio. *The other Mexico; critique of the pyramid*. Translated by Lysander Kemp. New York, Grove Press, 1972. xii, 148 p. (An Evergreen black cat book, B-359) $1.65

A continuous river of images flows through these essays about the essence of Mexico. This is a good translation of *Postdata.*

967

Paz, Octavio, and others. *Renga; a chain of poems,* by Octavio Paz, and others. With a foreword by Claude Roy. Translated by Charles Tomlinson. New York, G. Braziller, 1972. 95 p. $2.95

This is an original, polyglot poem in English, French, Italian, and Spanish with English translations on facing pages.

968

Pearcy, George Etzel. *The West Indian scene.* Princeton, N.J., Van Nostrand, 1968. 136 p. maps. $2.25

Presents brief, timely sketches of each political entity in the West Indies. The emphasis is on the political, economic, and social aspects, as well as on the islands' relations with the U.S.

969

Pendle, George. *A history of Latin America.* Baltimore, Penguin Books, 1963. 249 p. maps. (Pelican Books) $1.25

General treatment of Latin America, useful for review purposes. Includes a bibliography.

970

Perkins, Dexter. *History of the Monroe Doctrine.* Rev. ed. Boston, Little, Brown, 1968. 462 p. $2.95

First published in 1941 as *Hands off: a History of the Monroe Doctrine,* this is a historical analysis of the famous doctrine. Includes a good bibliography.

971

Pesman, Michiel Walter. *Meet flora Mexicana: an easy way to recognize some of the more frequently met plants of Mexico as seen from the main highways.* Globe, Ariz., Dale Stuart King, 1962. illus., map. $5

The author describes and catalogs the numerous plants and flowers that one is apt to see in Mexico. This is a helpful guide, complete with good illustrations.

972

Peterson, Frederick. *Ancient Mexico: an introduction to the pre-Hispanic cultures.* Maps and drawings by José Luis Franco. New York, Putnam, 1962. 313 p. illus., maps. $2.45

This is a popularized general account of the pre-Hispanic Mesoamerican culture, with special emphasis on Mexico during the last few centuries before the conquest. Includes a useful bibliography.

973

Petras, James. *Chilean Christian Democracy: politics and social forces.* Berkeley, Institute of International Studies, University of California, 1967. 61 p. (Politics of modernization series, no. 4) $1.50

Deals with Christian Democracy as a contemporary political movement in Latin America. The author analyzes Frei's government with its heterogeneous backing and examines the behavioral characteristics of the party and its role in government.

974
Petras, James, and Maurice Zeitlin, eds. *Latin America: reform or revolution? A reader.* Greenwich, Conn., Fawcett Publications, 1968. 511 p. (The political perspective series) $1.95

Includes an introduction by the editors and 23 papers of varying views, premises, and quality. The authors include both Latin Americans and North Americans. An important book for college courses on contemporary Latin American problems. A Fawcett Premier book.

975
Petras, James F., and Hugo Zemelman Merino, comps. *Peasants in revolt; a Chilean case study, 1965-1971.* Translated by Thomas Flory. Austin, Published for the Institute of Latin American Studies by the University of Texas Press, 1973. xiii, 154 p. (Latin American monographs, no. 28) $6.50

Translated from the authors' unpublished manuscript, this work consists of interviews of peasant leaders and other agricultural workers, and their views of Chilean politics and society.

976
Petras, James F. *Politics and social structure in Latin America.* New York, Monthly Review Press, 1970. 382 p. $3.95

Contains 24 papers, some coauthored with others, analyzing Latin American politics and their relationship to various social structures that can be found in the hemisphere. Includes bibliographical references.

977
Petrunkevitch, Alexander Ivanovitch, and others. *Studies of fossiliferous amber arthropods of Chiapas, Mexico.* Berkeley, University of California Press, 1963. 59 p. illus. (University of California publications in entomology, v. 31, no. 1) $4.50

This scholarly entomological study of insects, crustaceans, and other arthopods of Chiapas is an important contribution. Includes a bibliography.

978
Picón-Salas, Mariano. *A cultural history of Spanish America: from conquest to independence.* Translated by Irving A. Leonard. Berkeley, University of California Press, 1962. 192 p. $195.

This is a well-known work on Spanish colonial culture, skillfully translated by Irving A. Leonard.

979
Piedra, Alberto Martinez, ed. *Socio-economic change in Latin America.* Washington, Catholic University of America Press, 1970. xiii, 271 p. $12

Contains a collection of essays originally presented in July of 1967 and 1968 at a series of seminars sponsored by the Latin American Institute of Catholic University in Washington and expanded to include articles by various other scholars. Includes bibliographical references.

980
Pike, Fredrick B., ed. *Conflict between church and state in Latin America.* New York, Knopf, 1964. 239 p. (Borzoi books on Latin America) $2.50

A short compilation of 20 previously published papers on the topic in question, divided chronologically into the colonial, 19th-century, and modern periods. Includes a bibliography.

981

Pike, Fredrick B., ed. *Freedom and reform in Latin America.* Notre Dame, Ind., University of Notre Dame Press, 1967. 308 p. (International studies of the Committee on International Relations, University of Notre Dame) $3.25

The 11 papers included in this work deal with both freedom and reform in Latin America as a whole and in relation to specific nations. Professor Pike provides a new introduction to this book which was first published in 1959. Includes bibliographical footnotes.

982

Pike, Fredrick B., ed. *Latin American history: select problems, identity, integration, and nationhood.* New York, Harcourt, Brace and World, 1969. xxi, 482 p. illus., maps. $6.95

Contains readings on the discovery of the New World, the problem of conflicting Spanish imperial ideologies, the impact of Iberic culture on the indigenous populations, the roots of revolution, slavery, questions of national identity, current social problems, etc. The selection of materials, some from primary sources, is excellent. Includes bibliographical references.

983

Pike, Fredrick B. *The modern history of Peru.* New York, Praeger, 1973. xix, 386 p. illus., maps, ports. (Praeger histories of Latin America) $4.95

By far the best treatment in a single volume in English of the national period of Peruvian history. Emphasizes intellectual currents and their impact on political events. [HLAS 30:2026]

984

Pike, Fredrick B. *Spanish-America, 1900-1970; tradition and social innovation.* New York, Norton, 1974. 445 p. illus., maps, ports. (Library of world civilization) $3.45

An insightful survey of Latin America civilization within the appropriate social context in 20th-century Latin America. This important contribution should be noted by generalists and specialists alike. Contains bibliographies.

985

Piña Chán, Román. *A guide to Mexican archaeology.* Translator: Virginia B. de Barrios. New York, International Publications Service, 1972. 128 p. illus., maps (both part col.). (Minutiae mexicana series) $2.40

First published in 1969, this is a reissue of an excellent archeological guidebook to Mexico's famed pre-Columbian past. The author is a well-known archeologist, and the book is enhanced with excellent illustrations and a bibliography.

986

Pino, Frank. *Mexican-Americans; a research bibliography.* East Lansing, Latin American Studies Center, Michigan State University, 1974. 2 v. $10

An interdisciplinary guide to the study of Mexican-Americans, with some entries on other Spanish-speaking groups such as the Puerto Ricans and Cubans. The bibliography is divided into 35 general areas, and there are numerous cross references. The entries appear without annotations. Of great interest to academic and research libraries.

987

Pitt, Leonard. *The decline of the Californios: a social history of the Spanish-speaking Californians, 1846-1890.* Berkeley, University of California Press, 1966. x, 324 p. illus., ports. $2.85

A thoughtful, exhaustively documented social history of Spanish Americans in California from 1846 through 1890. Contains a useful bibliography.

988

Pohl, Irmgard, Joseph Zepp, and Kempton E. Webb. *Latin America: a geographical commentary.* Edited by Kempton Webb. New York, Dutton, 1967. x, 315 p. maps, plates, tables. $2.35

The present edition has been adapted for English-speaking readers from the German work *Amerika* (1955). The book provides a geographical and sociological analysis of all the countries of Latin America. Includes a bibliography.

989

Pomeroy, William J., comp. *Guerilla warfare and Marxism: a collection of writings from Karl Marx to the present on armed struggles for liberation and for socialism.* New York, International Pub. Co., 1969. 336 p. $2.50

Several authors discuss current controversies over the strategy and tactics of guerilla warfare. Also published in hard cover. Includes bibliographical footnotes.

990

Pontiero, Giovanni, comp. *An anthology of Brazilian Modernist poetry,* with notes and introd. by Giovanni Pontiero. Oxford; New York, Pergamon Press, 1969. xiii, 245 p. (Pergamon Oxford Latin American series) $4.75

Contains a very good selection of Brazilian modernist poetry in English translation, with an excellent introduction by the compiler. Also includes biographical and critical notes on the poets whose works are presented.

991

Poppino, Rollie E. *Brazil: the land and the people.* Illus. by Carybé and Poty. New York, Oxford University Press, 1968. 370 p. illus., maps, tables. (Latin American histories) $2.50

A concise study of Brazil from the Portuguese conquest to modern times. Social and economic history receive special emphasis, a fact which makes this book more valuable than the standard accounts of successions of political events. Includes a good general bibliography.

992

Posada, José Guadalupe. *Posada's popular Mexican prints; 237 cuts.* Selected and edited, with an introd. and commentary by Roberto Berdecio and Stanley Applebaum. New York, Dover Publications, 1972. xxi, 156 p. illus. $3.50

José Guadalupe Posada (1852-1913) was one of the finest printmakers in Mexico. Almost all the illustrations in this book have been reproduced in their original size directly from the artist's original blocks and plates.

993

Pozas Arciniega, Ricardo. *Juan the Chamula: an ethnological recreation of the life of a Mexican Indian.* Translated from the Spanish by Lysander Kemp. Berkeley, University of California Press, 1962. 115 p. illus. $1.95

Translation of *Juan Pérez Jolete: biografía de un tzotzil* (1952), by a prominent Mexican anthropologist. It is a thorough biographical study of a Tzotzil Indian in the 20th century, full of informative passages.

994

Prado, Caio. *The colonial background of modern Brazil.* Translated from the Portuguese by Suzette Macedo. Berkeley, University of California Press, 1969. 439 p. $3.45

This is an important book about colonial Brazil which will be very useful in college-level courses. The translation is excellent and close to the original entitled: *Formação do Brasil contemporâneo*. Includes a bibliography.

995

Pratt, Julius William. *Expansionists of 1898; the acquisition of Hawaii and the Spanish Islands*. Chicago, Quadrangle Books, 1964. $2.95

A study of United States expansion in the Pacific and Caribbean areas, emphasizing the influence of business interests on diplomacy. It is based on primary sources and contains a useful bibliography.

996

Prescott, William Hickling. *The conquest of Mexico, The conquest of Peru, and other selections*. Edited and abridged, with an introd. by Roger Howell. New York, Washington Square Press, 1966. xxxvi, 406 p. (The Great histories, W-1414) $1.45

Consists of excerpts from the author's *History of the Reign of Ferdinand and Isabella, The Conquest of Mexico, The Conquest of Peru*, and *The History of the Reign of Philip II*.

997

Prescott, William Hickling. *The conquest of Peru*. Abridged and edited by Victor W. Von Hagen. New York, New American Library, 1961. 416 p. $.75

Abridged version of the well-written and well-researched account of the conquest of Peru by the famous 19th-century historian.

998

Prescott, William Hickling. *Portable Prescott. The rise and decline of the Spanish empire*. Edited by Irwin R. Blacker. New York, Viking Press, 1966. 568 p. maps. $1.85

This volume offers selections from Prescott's four histories, *The conquest of Mexico; Ferdinand and Isabella; The conquest of Peru;* and *Philip II*.

999

Price, Richard, ed. *Maroon societies; rebel slave communities in the Americas*. Garden City, N.Y., Anchor Books, 1973. 429 p. $2.95

Presents a comprehensive anthology on runaway-slave communities in the hemisphere. The selections concentrate on Brazil, Peru, Jamaica, and the U.S. Southeast, as well as Surinam. The editor assembled sources in five languages spanning four centuries. Includes a bibliography.

1000

Puig, Manuel. *Betrayed by Rita Hayworth*. Translated by Suzanne Jill Levine. New York, Avon-Bard, 1973. 222 p. $1.65

First published in 1968, *La traición de Rita Hayworth* became a bestseller in Latin America, Spain, and France. The novel could have been subtitled "growing up at the movies." It describes the life of an adolescent and his family on the Argentine pampa. He escapes bleak reality by taking refuge in the world of celluloid. The novel presents mediocre lives in brilliant fashion.

1001

Quijano, Aníbal. *Nationalism and capitalism in Peru; a study in neo-imperialism*. Translated by Helen R. Lane. New York, Monthly Review Press, 1971. 122 p. $2.25

Highly tentative, critical essay on the actions of the military junta from its coup in 1968 through early 1971. The junta has gone further than Quijano predicted in some areas, and the final page presents a vision of a socialist uprising. Includes bibliographical references. [HLAS 35:2297]

1002

Quintana, Bertha B., and Lois Gray Floyd. *¡Qué gitano! Gypsies of southern Spain.* New York, Holt, Rinehart and Winston, 1971. xviii, 126 p. illus. (Case studies in cultural anthropology) $2.25

This monograph presents a study in cultural anthropology of the gypsies of southern Spain, based on field research. This important contribution contains attractive illustrations and bibliographies.

1003

Quirk, Robert E. *An affair of honor: Woodrow Wilson and the occupation of Veracruz.* New York, Norton, 1967. 184 p. $2.95

First published in 1962, this is a well-documented account of the American occupation of Veracruz in 1914, which received deserved recognition from the Mississippi Valley Historical Association. Mexicans may object to the title but will have no quarrel with the author's conclusion that the Wilson policy, however admirable in theory, was impossible in practice. Includes bibliographies. [HLAS 26:655]

1004

Quirk, Robert E. *The Mexican Revolution, 1914-1915; the Convention of Aguascalientes.* New York, Norton, 1969. 325 p. maps (on lining papers) $1.95

Significant, well-written volume describing the origin, development, program, and collapse (owing to dissension and defeat) of the revolutionary convention of Aguascalientes. The work is based on primary sources, including the private papers of convention leader Roque González Garza. It was first published in 1960 and includes bibliographical references.

1005

Rabinovitz, Francine F., Felicity M. Trueblood, and Charles J. Savio. *Latin American political systems in an urban setting; a preliminary bibliography.* Gainesville, University of Florida Press, 1967. 42 p. Free of charge

A bibliography to aid scholars interested in the study of the political systems of Latin America and students of the field of comparative urban development. 434 items are listed. [Charles Fleener]

1006

Randall, Margaret. *Cuban women now: interviews with Cuban women.* Toronto, The Women's Press, 1974. 375 p. illus., maps. $5.50

The interviews of Cuban women presented here, describe the changing role of women in revolutionary Cuba. The author lives in Cuba.

1007

Ramos, Samuel. *Profile of man and culture in Mexico.* Translated by Peter G. Earle. Introd. by Thomas B. Irving. Austin, University of Texas Press, 1970. 198 p. (The Texas Pan American series) $1.95

First published in 1934, this evaluation of Mexican character by a philosopher has both literary merit and psychological insight. It should be required reading for understanding modern Mexico.

1008

Rappaport, Armin, ed. *The Monroe Doctrine.* New York, Holt, Rinehart and Winston, 1964. 122 p. (American problem studies) $2.60

Presents divergent opinions on the historical impact of the Monroe Doctrine. Raúl Díaz de Medina and Luis Quintanilla present Latin American perspectives. Includes a bibliography.

1009

Rappaport, Armin, ed. *The War with Mexico: why did it happen?* Chicago, Rand, McNally, 1964. 60 p. (The Berkeley series in American history) $1

Includes a selection of contemporary documents presenting the advocates of "manifest destiny," slave interest, and President Polk as the chief culprits. Includes a bibliography.

1010

Rascoe, Jesse, ed. *The treasure album of Pancho Villa.* Toyahvale, Tex., Frontier Book Co., 1962. 127 p. illus. $3

This is a profusely illustrated book about Pancho Villa who fought in the Mexican Revolution under Madero. His cavalry became the most famous force in the revolutionary armies. In 1916 he attacked Columbus, N.M., and Gen. John Pershing was sent to capture Villa. This is an interesting pictorial history of the bandit-rebel.

1011

Ratliff, William E. *Yearbook on Latin American Communist affairs.* Stanford, Calif., Hoover Institution Press, 1973. xi, 194 p. $4.50

Provides a concise country-by-country description of the Marxist-Leninist parties and movements in Latin America. Contains a comprehensive bibliography.

1012

Ray, Philip Alexander. *South wind red; our hemispheric crisis.* Chicago, H. Regnery, 1962. 242 p. $2

The author argues for a U.S. foreign economic policy toward Latin America based upon enlightened private entrepreneurship in place of massive government-to-government aid which is said to place the U.S. in alignment with the Left in most parts of Latin America. [HLAS 25:5348]

1013

Read, R. B. *Gastronomic tour of Mexico.* New ed. New York, Doubleday, 1972. xi, 299 p. (A Doubleday Dolphin book) $2.50

Contains a guided tour to the unusual as well as typical cuisine of Mexico. A traveler should read this work before embarking on a trip to Mexico.

1014

Read, William R. *New patterns of church growth in Brazil.* Grand Rapids, Mich., Eerdmans Pub. Co., 1965. 240 p. illus., maps. (Church growth series) $2.45

This statistical and descriptive work provides a comparative analysis of the rapid growth of several Protestant denominations in Brazil. Includes a bibliography.

1015

Redfield, Robert, and Alfonso Villa Rojas. *Chan Kom; a Maya village.* Abr. ed. Chicago, University of Chicago Press, 1962. 236 p. $1.95

Originally published in 1934, this is the abridged edition of a scholarly anthropolitical study of a Mayan village in Yucatán. The classic contribution contains a bibliography.

1016,

Redfield, Robert. *The little community and Peasant society and culture.* Chicago, University of Chicago Press, 1962. 177, 88 p. $2.45

This is a reissue of two studies, *The little community; viewpoints for the study of a human whole* (1955) and *Peasant society and culture; an anthropological approach to civilization* (1956). Both are important works studying the ethnology and culture of Yucatán. Includes bibliographies.

1017

Redfield, Robert. *The primitive world and its transformation.* Ithaca, N.Y., Cornell University Press, 1957. 198 p. $1.95

First published in 1953, this is a general study of the people who lived before the rise of the first cities, the ones the author refers to as "precivilized" or folk societies and their subsequent transformation. Includes a bibliography.

1018

Redfield, Robert. *The village that chose progress: Chan Kom revisited.* Chicago, University of Chicago Press, 1962. xiv, 187 p. illus., maps. (The University of Chicago publications in anthropology. Social anthropological series) $1.50

First published in 1950, this is a description of socioeconomic development of a village in Yucatán from 1930 through 1948, by a well-known anthropologist.

1019

Reed, Irving B., Jaime Suchlicki, and Dodd L. Harvey. *The Latin American scene of the seventies; a basic fact book.* Washington, Center for Advanced International Studies, University of Miami, 1972. xxvii, 220 p. (Monographs in international affairs) $4.95

Intended for the generalist and the student beginning to study Latin America, this book presents factual and up-to-date information on the hemisphere.

1020

Reed, John. *Insurgent Mexico.* New York, International Publishers, 1969. xxvi, 325 p. $2.65

John Reed was sent to cover the Mexican Revolution for the *New York World.* He joined the Revolution and fought with the guerrillas, earning the confidence and trust of many of the participants, and wrote this account about the Revolution in 1914. He later became internationally famous for his book about the Soviet Revolution, *Ten days that shook the world,* and is buried in the Kremlin.

1021

Reed, John. *Insurgent Mexico.* Edited, with an introd. and notes by Albert L. Michaels and James W. Wilkie. New York, Simon and Schuster, 1969. 252 p. maps. $2.95

This is a scholarly annotated edition of Reed's reports from the scene of the early period of the Mexican Revolution, with an insightful introduction and good notes.

1022

Reed, Nelson. *The Caste War of Yucatán.* Stanford, Calif., Stanford University Press, 1967. x, 308 p. illus., maps, plan. $2.95

The author describes in detail the Caste War which lasted from 1847 to 1855. He also analyzes the social and economic systems of Yucatán in the 19th and 20th centuries. The work is based on solid documentary evidence and includes a good bibliography. It was originally published in 1964.

1023

Reedy, Daniel R. *The poetic art of Juan del Valle Caviedes.* Chapel Hill, University of North Carolina Press, 1964. 152 p. (University of North Carolina. Studies in the Romance languages and literatures, no. 46) $5

This is a study of the life and times of the satirical poet of colonial Peru (1652?-97?), together with a discussion of critical commentaries on his work since 1791 and an analysis of his collected writings. Includes a bibliography.

1024

Reeve, Frank Drive. *New Mexico; a short history.* Denver, A. Swallow, 1966. 112 p. $2

This is an illustrated history of New Mexico and its mixture of Indian, Hispanic, and Anglo-Saxon heritage.

1025

Reever, Frank Driver, and Alice Ann Cleveland. *New Mexico, land of many cultures.* Maps and illus. by Harold F. Lee. Boulder, Colo., Pruett Pub. Co., 1969. 231, 25 p. illus., maps (fold. col.), port. $3.50

An attractively illustrated description of the many-faceted cultural background of New Mexico. Includes a good bibliography.

1026

Reina, Rubén E. *The law of the saints; a Pokoman pueblo and its community culture.* Indianapolis, Bobbs-Merrill, 1966. xx, 338 p. illus., maps. $3.25

This book is the result of a prolonged study of the descendants of a group of Maya Indians called Pokoman. The author concentrates on the pueblo of Chinautla, 16 miles north of Guatemala City, and stresses the economic activities and cofradía customs of the Chinautlans. Includes a bibliography. [Charles Fleener]

1027

Remmling, Günter W. *South American sociologists; a directory.* Austin, University of Texas Press, 1970. 59 p. $1

This reference work will constitute a welcome addition to library collections as well as to all those interested in the social sciences.

1027A

Rendón, Armando B. *Chicano manifesto.* New York, Macmillan, 1971. 337 p. $1.95

An important synthesis of the Chicano experience in the U.S. It describes historically and culturally the fusion of two revolutionary wellsprings (the U.S. and Mexico), both in rebellion against Old World colonialism.

1028

Research Institute for the Study of Man, New York, N.Y. *Papers of the Conference on Research and Resources of Haiti.* New York, 1969. 624 p. tables. $3

Includes papers presented at a conference held November 1-4, 1967, in New York. The topics covered include demography, human resources, language and literacy, health, and public and private institutions of Haiti. Many of the participants were Haitian. This is a very important contribution to the study of Haiti.

1029

Revueltas, José. *From a Mexican prison; the youth movement and the alienation of society.* New York, Merit Publishers, 1969. 34 p. $.35

In 1968 Revueltas was accused of being the intellectual leader of the student revolts that broke out in Mexico. He was arrested and subsequently wrote this eassay which represents his interpretation of the student rebellion and its implications from a Marxist point of view. [Charles Fleener]

1030

iesenberg, Felix. *The golden road; the story of California's Spanish mission trail.* New York, McGraw-Hill, 1962. 315 p. illus. (The Americans trails series) $3.50

Traces the history and development of missions established during the Spanish colonial period to the present. Includes a bibliography. Recommended for public and college libraries.

1031

Ring, Henry. *How Cuba uprooted racial discrimination.* New York, Merit Publishers, 1961. 15 p. $.25

A report on Cuba's attempt to abolish racial discrimination.

1032

Río. Eduardo del. *Cuba for beginners an illustrated guide for Americans.* Translated by Robert Pearlman. New York, Pathfinder Press, 1969. 145 p. illus. $1.95

This is a translation of *Cuba para principiantes* which describes the new Cuba.

1033

Rivera, Feliciano. *A Mexican American source book.* Menlo Park, Calif., Educational Consulting Associates, 1970. xi, 196 p. illus., facsims., ports. $6

Includes biographical sketches of outstanding Americans of Mexican descent in English and Spanish, in addition to documents and sources on the history of Chicanos in the U.S. A thorough bibliography has been appended.

1034

Rivera, Julius. *Latin America; a sociocultural interpretation.* New York, Appleton--Century-Crofts, 1971. xvi, 204 p. illus., maps. $4.70

An imaginative and objective analysis of a complex continent. The emphasis is on society and norms governing social relationships, as well as on the multiple cultures of Latin America. Includes bibliographies.

1035

Robb, John Donald. *Hispanic folk songs of New Mexico; with selected songs collected, transcribed, and arranged for voice and piano.* Albuquerque, University of New Mexico Press, 1954. 83 p. (University of New Mexico publications in the fine arts, no. 1) $2

Includes folksongs with English translations. It also contains a general discussion of Hispanic folksongs and a detailed examination of a few specific tunes.

1036

Roberts, C. Paul, and Mukhtar Hamour, eds. *Cuba 1968; supplement to the Statistical abstract of Latin America.* Los Angeles, Latin American Center, University of California, 1970. 213 p. (The Statistical abstract of Latin America; supplement series, 1) $12

Presents in a concise manner relevant statistical data from Cuba. Chiefly U.N. sources were used. The compilation of this work was made difficult by the inaccessibility of much of the data.

1037

Roberts, C. Paul, and Takako Kohda, eds. *Statistical abstract of Latin America: 1966.* Los Angeles, Latin American Center, University of California, 1967. 194 p. (The Statistical abstract of Latin America series, 1) $46,

This is the first number of an important series which presents all available statistical information in a concise manner. The center does not assume responsibility for the limitation or for the accuracy of the data although it does assume responsibility for the selection and presentation of the material.

1038

Roberts, C. Paul, and Takako Kohda, eds. *Statistical abstract of Latin America: 1967.* Los Angeles, Latin American Center, University of California, 1968. 218 p. (The Statistical abstract of Latin America series, 2) $7

A compilation of Latin American statistical data for the year 1967.

1039

Roberts, C. Paul, and Takako Kohda Karplus, eds. *Statistical abstract of Latin America: 1968.* Los Angeles, Latin American Center, University of California, 1969. 276 p. (Statistical abstract of Latin America series, 3) $8

Contains concise statistical data for Latin America for the year 1968, covering the 24 independent nations.

1040

Roberts, W. Dayton. *Strachan of Costa Rica; missionary insights and strategies.* Grand Rapids, Mich., Eerdmans, 1971. 187 p. (Christian world mission books) $2.95

Contains information of the administrations and management of missions in Costa Rica, as well as information on the role of the Protestant missionary in Central America.

1041

Robertson, Donald. *Pre-Columbian architecture.* New York, Braziller, 1963. 128 p. illus., maps, plans. (The great ages of world architecture) $2.95

This is a succinct and lucid discussion of characteristics and differences of architecture in Middle America and the Andean region. Public and college libraries should consider the acquisition of this work. Includes a bibliography.

1042

Robertson, William Spence. *The rise of the Spanish-American republics as told in the lives of their liberators.* New York, Free Press, 1965. 348 p. maps. (A Free Press paperback) $2.95

Paperback edition of a book first published in 1918. It has been superseded in some respects by more recent scholarship, but is still a good survey of its subject in English.

1043

Robinson, Cecil. *With the ears of strangers; the Mexican in American literature.* Drawings by H. Beaumont Williams. Tucson, University of Arizona Press, 1972. 338 p. illus. $4.95

Traces references to Mexicans and their culture from the earliest time of contact of Anglo-Saxon America with Mexico. The author wrote an interesting chapter on the Southwest as a literary region, describing how the vitality of Mexico extends culturally into America. Includes a bibliography.

1044

Robinson, Harvey. *Latin America; a geographical survey.* New York, Praeger, 1967. 499 p. illus., maps. $4.95

This contemporary survey describes both the geographical unity and diversity of Latin America. The introductory section deals with the physical and cultural background of the hemisphere. In the second, larger section, each nation is described in terms of its geographic, human, and economic resources. [Charles Fleener]

1045

Robock, Stefan Hyman. *Brazil's developing northeast; a study of regional planning and foreign aid.* Washington, Brookings Institution, 1962. xv, 213 p. maps, tables. $2

This is an important study of the economic problems of Brazil's northeast. Robock's work had great impact on the Development Bank of the Northeast and later upon the Superintência do Desenvolvimento de Nordeste (SUDENE). Includes bibliographical references.

1046

Rocca, Marie L., comp. *Opportunities for study in Latin America; a guide to group programs.* Prepared under the direction of Kempton Webb. Gainesville. Consortium of Latin America Studies Programs, University of Florida, 1972. 120 p. (Consortium of Latin American Studies Programs, publication, 4) $1.57

Describes opportunities for study in Latin America for U.S. undergraduate students. Only academic sessions sponsored by North and Latin American institutions are listed. Each entry describes the scope of the program as completely as possible. The work is divided into two sections, one dealing with programs sponsored by U.S. universities and the other with foreign-sponsored programs. The various programs offer the chance of first-hand experience in living in a Latin American country, as well as opportunities to earn credits. An excellent compilation.

1047

Rockefeller, Nelson Aldrich. *The Rockefeller report on the Americas. The official report of a United States Presidential Mission for the Western Hemisphere.* With an introd. by Tad Szulc. New York Times ed. Chicago, Quadrangle Books, 1969. x, 144 p. maps. $1.95

New York State's Governor Rockefeller warned President Nixon in this report that the hemisphere is again in the throes of violent political, economic, and social upheaval. He emphasizes the importance of Latin America to the U.S.

1048

Rodman, Selden. *Mexican journal; the conquerors conquered.* Carbondale, Southern Illinois University Press, 1965. xvi, 298 p. illus., maps, ports. $2.45

First published in 1958, this account of a trip to Mexico (1956-57) describes ancient ruins and records interviews with José Vasconcelos, Diego Rivera, Clemente Orozco, Carlos Fuentes, and David Siqueiros.

1049

Rodman, Selden. *Tongues of fallen angels; conversations with Jorge Luis Borges and others.* New York, New Directions, 1974, 271 p. illus. $3.75

A critic, poet, and prolific writer offers portraits of such Latin American writers as Borges, Neruda, García Márquez, Paz, Vinícius de Moraes, and João Cabral de Melo Neto, along with Hemingway, Mailer, Ginsberg, and others. This is an important book on many key literary figures.

1050

Rodriguez, Mario. *Central America.* Englewood Cliffs, N.J., Prentice-Hall, 1965. xi, 178 p. maps. (The Modern nations in historical perspective series. A Spectrum book) $1.95

This excellent survey of Central American history in the 19th and 20th centuries provides a thorough background for an understanding of the region and its complex politics. This work can be used as a textbook or as supplemental reading in the classroom. It should also be acquired by academic and large public libraries. Includes bibliographies.

1051

Rodriguez, Mario, and Vincent C. Peloso, comps. *A guide for the study and culture in Central America; humanities and social sciences.* Washington, Pan American Union, 1968. 88 p. (Basic bibliographies, 5) $2

This bibliography is a thorough compilation of works on Central America. The 934 entries have been selected carefully. Outstanding works have been evaluated with succinct annotations. This is an especially useful reference aid for scholars, libraries, researchers, and others.

1052

Rodriguez-Alcalá, Hugo, and Sally Rodriguez-Alcalá, comps. *Cuentos nuevos del sur: Argentina, Chile, Uruguay, Paraguay.* Englewood Cliffs, N.J., Prentice-Hall, 1967. 234 p. $3.95

Contains a selection of outstanding short stories from South America by Jorge Luis Borges, Juan Carlos Onetti, and others.

1053

Roett, Riordan J. *Brazil; politics in a patrimonial society.* Boston, Allyn and Bacon, 1972. x, 197 p. (The Allyn and Bacon series in Latin American politics) $3.50

Analyzes the principal political developments in Brazil since 1946, within the context of the paternal state and the continuing involvement of the military in national affairs. This is an important contribution, with a good bibliography.

1054

Roett, Riordan J. *Latin America; the emerging lands.* Columbus, Ohio, C. E. Merrill Pub. Co., 1974. $1.50

This is a succinct textbook on contemporary political problems facing the nations of Latin America. Includes a bibliography.

1055

Rogers, Francis Millet, and David T. Haberly, comps. *Brazil, Portugal, and other Portuguese-speaking lands; a list of books primarily in English.* Cambridge, Mass., Harvard University Press, 1968. 73 p. $1

Contains over 800 entries of books in English published since World War II. No books in Portuguese are included, but a few of the most important works in Catalan, Dutch, French, German, Italian, Latin, Russian, and Spanish are present. Of interest to scholars and research libraries.

1056

Rojo, Ricardo. *Che Guevara; vie et mort d'un ami.* Port Washington, N.Y., Paris Publications, 1969. 209 p. illus. $1.20

French translation of *Mi amigo el Che* by an Argentine fellow-revolutionary of Guevara. It includes much information on the history of the Cuban revolution.

1057

Rojo, Ricardo. *My friend Che.* Translated from the Spanish by Julian Casart. New York, Grove Press, 1970. 220 p. facsims., ports. $1.25

A fellow political activist of Guevara from Argentina discusses his friend with whom he was closely associated through the 1950's and especially through the Cuban Revolution. Translation of *Mi amigo el Che.*

1058

Romanell, Patrick. *The making of the Mexican mind; a study in recent Mexican thought.* Foreword by Edward Brighman. Notre Dame, Ind., University of Notre Dame Press, 1967. 213 p. (Essay index reprint series) $2.75

First published in 1952, this work rapidly traces the development of Mexican philosophy from colonial times to the present, concentrating on the thought of Alfonso Caso and José Vasconcelos, and the new trends such as perspectivism and existentialism. Includes a thorough bibliography.

1059

Romanucci-Ross, Lola. *Violence, conflict, and morality in a Mexican village.* Palo Alto, Calif., National Press Books, 1973. 203 p. illus. $2.75

Based on three years of field work, this work analyzes social stratification which followed land reform after the revolution, kinship and patronage, violence and conflict, social behavior, and the concept of machismo. The village studied is located in the state of Morelos. Includes a bibliography.

1060

Romero, José Luis. *A history of Argentine political thought.* Introd. and translation of the 3d ed. by Thomas McGann. Stanford, Calif., Stanford University Press, 1968. 270 p. maps. $2.95

A study of Argentine political thought from colonial times to the present. The author synthesizes social and economic perceptions into political trends. Professor McGann's introduction stresses the comparative studies that may be made with the U.S. translation of *Las ideas políticas en Argentina* (1963). Contains a bibliography.

1061

Romero, José Rubén. *La vida inútil de Pito Pérez.* Edited by William O. Cord. Englewood Cliffs, N.J., Prentice-Hall, 1972. xxv, 198 p. $3.95

First published in 1938, this is one of the novels which belongs to the cycle of the Mexican Revolution. The protagonist is a rogue from the lower classes. The novel reflects deftly the social dissolution which followed the upheaval. Contains notes and vocabulary.

1062

Romney, Antone Kimball, and Romaine Romney. *The Mixtecans of Juxtlahuaca, Mexico.* New York, J. Wiley, 1966. xxxv, 150 p. illus. maps. (Six cultures series, v) $2.95

Explores patterns of child rearing and subsequent effects on the personality in a small barrio of Oaxaca. Authors study the ethnographic background of the people and their present-day customs. Includes bibliographies and attractive illustrations.

1063

Ronning, C. Neale, comp. *Intervention in Latin America.* New York, Knopf, 1970. 220 p. (Borzoi books on Latin America) $2.95

The editor selected 23 essays which trace various aspects of U.S. intervention in the Caribbean and Latin America. The book has been divided into: "Intervention: motives, methods, and consequences" and "Non-intervention: the evolution of a doctrine." Includes a thorough introduction and a chronology of U.S. armed intervention in Latin America from 1798 to 1945.

1064

Roosevelt, Theodore. *The Rough Riders.* New York, New American Library, 1961. 215 p. illus. $.95

This is Theodore Roosevelt's own account of the Rough Riders' participation in the Spanish American War. Includes attractive illustrations.

1065

Ross, Stanley Robert, ed. *Is the Mexican Revolution dead?* New York, Knopf, 1966. 255 p. (Borzoi books on Latin America) $3.10

Without settling the title's issue, the editor's introduction is a thoughtful analysis, providing a general framework for 22 selections, emphasizing various aspects of the Revolution. A good selective bibliography enhances this teaching aid. [Howard F. Cline]

1066

Rothchild, John, ed. *Latin America, yesterday and today.* New York, Bantam Books, 1974. xiii, 462 p. maps. $1.25

Describes concisely Latin America's social and economic past within its cultural context, contrasting it with the contemporary period. This will be very useful for survey courses. Contains bibliographical references.

1067

Rotschild, Mario Francisco. *Regional development and sectoral specialization: the Chilean case.* Ithaca, N.Y., Cornell University, Latin American Studies Program, Dissertation series, no. 50) $4

The author conducted a case study for his doctoral thesis, using 70 economic regions of Chile as units of analysis. This is an important study with tables and a bibliography.

1068

Rout, Leslie B., Jr., *Which way out? A study of the Guayana-Venezuela boundary dispute.* East Lansing, Latin American Studies Center, Michigan State University, 1971. x, 130 p. maps. (Michigan State University. Latin American Studies Center, Monograph, no. 4) $3.95

The area between the Orinoco and Essequibo rivers, known as the "wild coast," has been the basis of a centuries old dispute. The author traces the complicated controversy and negotiations, based on solid documentation. Includes a bibliography.

1069

Rubin, Vera, and Marisa Zavalloni. *We wish to be looked upon; a study of the aspirations of youth in a developing society.* New York, Teachers College Press, 1969. xi, 257 p. (Center for Education in Latin America) $5.95

An anthropologist and a social psychologist analyze ethnic and social class differences and the impact of economic and social change on the youth of Trinidad. They used questionnaires and interviews of secondary school students. Includes a bibliography.

1070

Ruddle, Kenneth, and Philip D. Gillette, eds. *Latin American political statistics; Supplement to the Statistical abstract of Latin America.* Introd. by Luigi Einaudi. Los Angeles, Latin American Center, University of California, 1972. 128 p. (The Statistical abstract of Latin America; supplement series, 2) $4.50

Contains all of the election and registration statistics available to the editors for all presidential congressional elections for the 1940-71 period. The task of compiling this work was hampered by the difficulty or even impossibility of obtaining primary data in many cases. This is a very useful reference source.

1071

Ruddle, Kenneth, and Mukhtar Hamour, eds. *Statistical abstract of Latin America: 1969.* Los Angeles, Latin American Center, University of California, 1970. 332 p. (The Statistical abstract of Latin America series, 4) $8

All available statistical data for Latin America for the year 1969 is abstracted in this compilation.

1072

Ruddle, Kenneth, and Mukhtar Hamour, eds. *Statistical abstract of Latin America: 1970.* Los Angeles, Latin American Center, University of California, 1971. 450 p. (The Statistical abstract of Latin America series, 5) $9.50

Includes statistical data for 1970.

1073

Ruddle, Kenneth, and Mukhtar Hamour, eds. *Statistical abstract of Latin America: 1971.* Los Angeles, Latin American Center, University of California, 1972. 462 p. (The Statistical abstract of Latin America series, 6) $9.50

Presents 1971 statistical data for Latin America.

1074

Ruddle, Kenneth. *The Yukpa cultivation system: a study of shifting cultivation in Colombia and Venezuela.* Los Angeles, Latin American Center, University of California, 1974. 119 p. $2.50

Studies the cultivation of the yukpa plant in Colombia and Venezuela.

1075

Ruiz, Ramón Eduardo. *Cuba: the making of a revolution.* New York, Norton, 1970. 190 p. $1.85

Contends that the Cuban Revolution does not represent a sharp break with the island's past but that it grew out of events and circumstances that had been developing for well over half a century. This is a well-documented analysis of the background of Castro's revolution. Includes a bibliography. [Charles Fleener]

1076

Ruiz, Ramón Eduardo, ed. *Interpreting Latin American history; from Independence to today.* New York, Holt, Rinehart and Winston, 1970. ix, 453 p. $2.95

The first section covers the histories of Argentina, Brazil, Mexico, and Cuba. The second part includes readings on Chile, Peru, Bolivia, and Venezuela. Section three contains topical issues that cut across national boundaries. The readings were contributed by prominent specialists in each field. Includes bibliographic references.

1077

Ruiz, Ramón Eduardo, ed. *The Mexican War; was it manifest destiny?* New York, Holt, Rinehart and Winston, 1963. 118 p. (American problem studies) $2.25

Hubert Bancroft and Justo Sierra present Mexican viewpoints, but they are outnumbered in these selections by U.S. historians discussing national problems. The editor ably directs questions.

1078

Rulfo, Juan. *Burning plain and other stories.* Translated with an introd. by George D. Schade. Illustrated by Kermit Oliver. Austin, University of Texas Press, 1967. xv, 175 p. illus. (Texas Pan American series) $2.25

Translation of *El llano en llamas* (1953), by one of Mexico's most gifted writers who present rural themes. His characters are anachronistic creatures, some of whom have already passed from the world of the living. The interior monologs are starkly regionalistic.

1079

Rulfo, Juan. *El llano en llamas.* Edited by Hugo Rodríguez Alcalá and Ray A. Verzasconi. Englewood Cliffs, N.J., Prentice-Hall, 1973. x, 160 p. $3.95

This is a Spanish version of one of the most important prose writings of contemporary Mexico, exuding a tragic quality of life on the dry and parched landscape. This edition contains notes and vocabulary, as well as a valuable bibliography of critical works on Rulfo.

1080

Rulfo, Juan. *Pedro Páramo.* Edited by Luis Leal. New York, Appleton-Century-Crofts, 1970. 178 p. $2.95

First published in 1955, this work depicts the life of a Mexican peasant from infancy to death. It is a violent, brutal, vengeful, and sensual life, dignified by his love for Susana. This annotated textbook edition also includes a critical bibliography.

1081

Rulfo, Juan. *Pedro Páramo.* Translated by Lysander Kemp. New York, Grove Press, 1959. 123 p. $1.25

This is a very good English translation of the contemporary Mexican classic. It should be required reading for those who study Mexico.

1082

Sábato, Ernesto. *El túnel.* Edited by Louis C. Pérez. New York, Macmillan, 1965. 124 p. (Macmillan modern Spanish-American literature series) $2.50

First published in 1948, this is the story of a man who announces that he committed a crime. He becomes progressively more insane as he tells the story, and his madness is metaphysical: he is like a man lost in a tunnel. This is a textbook edition of an influential contemporary novel, with notes and vocabulary.

1083

Sable, Martin Howard. *Communism in Latin America; an international bibliography: 1900-1945, 1960-1967,* by Martin H. Sable, with the assistance of M. Wayne Dennis. Los Angeles, Latin American Center, University of California, 1968. 220 p. (University of California. Latin American Center Reference series, no. 1-A) $2

Supplements Ludwig Lauerhass' *Communism in Latin America: a bibliography (1945-1960).* Sable's work includes over 2,000 items in 22 languages, most of which are available in major libraries. The entries have been arranged chronologically and by area.

1084

Sable, Martin Howard. *A guide to Latin American studies.* Los Angeles, Latin American Center, University of California, 1967. 2 v. (lxxv, 783 p.) (California. University at Los Angeles. Latin American Center. Reference series, no. 4) $25

This oversize reference work is an annotated bibliography which covers the humanities, as well as the social, natural, and applied sciences. It contains 51,024 entries of English, Spanish, and Portuguese sources. The introduction is in English and Spanish. Includes bibliographies. [Charles Fleener]

1085

Safford, Frank. *Latin America: a culture area in perspective,* Leften S. Stavrianos, general editor. Boston, Allyn and Bacon, 1970. 94 p. illus. (part col.), maps, ports. $1.40

Reviews Latin America's cultural background and is intended for the general reader. Includes a brief bibliography.

1086

Salinas, Raul, and Lillian Faderman, comps. *From the barrio; a Chicano anthology.* New York, Canfield Press; distributed by Harper & Row, 1973. 298 p. $3.95

This compilation of writings by and about Chicanos is intended as a textbook for the study of the Mexican Americans in the U.S. Includes a select bibliography.

1087

Salkey, Andrew, comp. *Island voices; stories from the West Indies.* New York, Liveright, 1970. 256 p. $2.45

This collection of contemporary short stories from the West Indies includes such authors as V. S. Naipaul, Samuel Selvon, and John Hearns.

1088

Samora, Julian, ed. *La raza: forgotten Americans; papers in memory of Charles de Young Elkus.* Notre Dame, Ind., University of Notre Dame Press, 1969. xvii, 218 p. $2.50

In the U.S. Southwest there are more than four million Spanish-speaking citizens. The seven authors of the essays in this volume deal with religion, political activity, civil rights, and the emerging middle class. The editor summarizes the current status of the Chicanos and suggests paths for future development. Includes bibliographies.

1089

Sánchez, Florencio. *Representative plays.* Translated from the Spanish by Willis Knapp Jones. Rev. by Glenn Barr. Washington, Pan American Union, 1961. 362 p. (UNESCO collection of representative works: Latin American series) $2.50

Considered one of Spanish America's greatest playwrights, Sánchez produced the 11 plays included here between 1903 and 1909. Included are the classics *My son the lawyer (M'hijo el dotor), The immigrant girl (La gringa), Down the gully (Barranca abajo),* and *Our children (Nuestros hijos).*

1090

Sánchez, George Isadore. *Mexico,* by George I. Sánchez. Consulting editor: Lindley J. Stiles. Boston, Ginn, 1970. 112 p. illus., maps. (Today's world in focus) $1.60

A general and concise text about Mexico intended for young readers or for survey courses. Contains a brief bibliography.

1091

Sánchez, José. *Academias y sociedades literarias de Mexico.* Chapel Hill, University of North Carolina Press, 1951. 277 p. (North Carolina. University. Studies in the Romance languages and literatures, no. 18) $6.50

Contains a historical listing of Mexican literary societies. Of great interest for the specialist. Bibliographical references included.

1092

Sánchez, Ricardo. *Canto y grito mi liberación (y lloro mis desmadrazgos...); pensamientos, gritos, orgullos, penumbras poéticas, ensayos, historietas, hechizos almales del son de mi existencia...* Illus. by Manuel G. Acosta. Garden City, N.Y., Anchor Press, 1973. 159 p. illus. $2.95

Contains poems, short stories, and essays by a Chicano author who attempts to describe his newly found identity.

1093

Sánchez-Reulet, Aníbal, ed. *Homenaje a Rubén Darío. Memoria del XIII Congreso Internacional de Literatura Iberoamericana (Primera Reunión)...* Los Angeles, University of California Press, 1973. 356 p. illus. $3.50

Contains papers presented at a conference held in January of 1967 to honor the Nicaraguan poet Rubén Darío. The contributors are important literary figures and specialists in Spanish American poetry. Contains bibliographical references.

1094

Sanders, Thomas G. *Mexico 1974; demographic patterns and popualtion policy.* New York, American Universities Field Staff, 1974. 28 p. (North America series, II, 1; Mexico) $2

Surveys recent demographic patterns and government policy in Mexico.

1095

Sanders, William T., and Barbara J. Price. *Mesoamerica: the evolution of civilization.* New York, Random House, 1969. xix, 265 p. illus., maps. (Studies in anthropology) $4.50

The authors analyze factors and processes of growth that shaped the cultural history of Mexico and Guatemala in pre-Columbian times. This is a valuable book for the theory of civilization, pointing out that nowhere is the societal structure of several layers of ancient culture as well documented as in Mesoamerica and Peru. Includes a bibliography.

1096

Sanderson, Ivan Terence. *Caribbean treasure,* by Ivan T. Sanderson, with thirty-two illustrations by the author. New York, Pyramid Publications, 1963. 292 p. illus. $.75

Describes the fascinating world of the Caribbean jungle animals. It was first published in 1939.

1097

Sarfatti, Magali. *Spanish bureaucratic-partrimonialism in America.* Berkeley, University of California, Institute of International Studies, 1966. 129 p. tables. $2

Describes the main characteristics of the Spanish bureaucratic patrimonial systems during the colonial period. Using a generalized Weberian model of patrimonial authority, the author has examined the interrelationships between normative and structural, theoretical and empirical aspects of the Spanish traditional system.

1098

Sarmiento, Domingo Faustino. *Life in the Argentine Republic in the days of the tyrants; or civilization and barbarism.* Translated by Mrs. Horace Mann. New York, Hafner, 1960. xxxvi, 400 p. front. $3.95

Mrs. Mann's English translation of *Civilización i barbarie: vida de Juan Facundo Quiroga* (1845) was first published in 1868. Sarmiento's book provides an interesting insight into the first decades of Argentina as an independent nation. It also occupies an important place in Spanish-American literature.

1099

Sarmiento, Domingo Faustino. *Life in the Argentine Republic in the days of the tyrants; or civilization and barbarism.* With a biographical sketch of the author by Mrs. Horace Mann. New York, Macmillan, 1961. 288 p. $1.50

See above.

1100

Sarmiento, Domingo Faustino. *Travels; a selection.* Translated from the Spanish by Inés Muñoz. Washington, Pan American Union, 1963. 297 p. (UNESCO collection of representative works: Latin American series) $1.50

Contains a selection of travel accounts by Sarmiento. He undertook the trips from 1845 to 1848 as a representative of the Chilean government. The selection is taken from the three-volume work dealing with the U.S., which he regarded as a model for Argentina.

1101

Sasser, Elizabeth Skidmore. *Architecture of ancient Peru.* Illus. by Nolan E. Barrick. Cover design by Elizabeth Sasser. Lubbock, International Center for Arid and Semi-Arid Land Studies, Texas Technological College, 1969. 79 p. illus., map. $2.95

The scope of this survey extends from the Chavín Cult around 900 B.C. to the Imperialist Period of the Inca until the arrival of the Spaniards in the 16th century. An important and useful contribution. Includes a bibliography.

1101A

Sauer, Carl Ortwin. *The early Spanish Main.* Berkeley, University of California Press, 1973. xii, 306 p. illus., maps. $2.45

An important contribution by one of the outstanding students of Latin American geography. Reviews the basic literature on Spanish colonization for the 1492-1518 period, including the discovery, later Columbian voyages, settlement of the islands, and expansion to the mainland. Exceptionally rich in geographical and ethnohistorical insight. [HLAS 28:448a]

1102

Sauer, Carl Ortwin. *Land and life; a selection from the writings of Carl Ortwin Sauer,* edited by John Leighly. Berkeley, University of California Press, 1973. 435 p. maps (1 fold.) $3.95

Provides an excellent and representative selection of the writings by an outstanding Latin Americanist who devoted his research chiefly to the discovery and conquest period. Includes bibliographical references.

1103

Sauer, Carl Ortwin. *Northern mists.* Berkeley, University of California Press, 1972. 204 p. illus., map. $2.95

Includes a very good description and analysis of the discovery of the Pacific Northwest and northern Mexico. Contains bibliographical footnotes.

1104

Sauer, Jonathan D. *Geographic reconnaissance of seashore vegetation along the Mexican gulf coast.* Baton Rouge, Louisiana State University Press, 1967. x, 59 p. illus. (Louisiana State University Studies. Coastal studies series, no. 21) $2.50

Studies vegetation along the Mexican gulf coast, focusing on the fringe kept open by waves, salt, and wind-driven sand. Includes photographs, appendixes, and a bibliography.

1105

Sawyer, Alan Reed. *Ancient Peruvian ceramics: the Nathan Cummings Collection.* With drawings by Milton F. Sonday, Jr., and photos by William F. Pons and William E. Lyall. New York Metropolitan Museum of Art; distributed by New York Graphic Arts Society, Greenwich, Conn., 1966. 144 p. illus. (part mounted col.), maps. $3.95

A valuable documentation of the various ceramic styles in Peru, complete with annotated illustrations and well-written text. Each design motif is drawn in its complete form beside a photograph of the original piece of pottery, making this an unusual and scholarly volume.

1106

Sawyer, Alan Reed. *Tiahuanaco textile design,* by Alan R. Sawyer. New York, Museum of Primitive Art, 1970. Distributed by the New York Graphic Arts Society. 195 p. illus. (The Museum of Primitive Art Studies, no. 3) $1.50

The text explains the many attractive textile designs from Tihuanaco which are reproduced here.

1107

Schaedel, Richard, and Vera Rubin, comps. *Research and resources in Haiti.* New York, Teachers College Press, 1973. 312 p. $3.50

The papers included in this work were originally presented at a conference sponsored by the Institute of Latin American Studies at the University of Texas and the Research Institute for the Study of Man. The topics covered range from demography to Afro-Latin music and linguistics. Includes bibliographical references.

1108

Schell, Rolfe F. *De Soto didn't land at Tampa.* Maps and cover design by the author. Rev. ed. Fort Myers Beach, Fla., Island Press, 1966. 96 p. maps. $1

This is a description of De Soto's arrival in Florida, intended for the lay reader.

1109

Schmidt, James Norman, and Margaret Fox Schmidt. *A shopper's guide to Mexico: where, what, and how to buy.* Newly rev. and updated. Garden City, N.Y., Dolphin Books, 1973. 272 p. (A Dolphin handbook, C-466) $1.95

First published in 1959 under the title *In Mexico: where to look, how to buy Mexican popular arts and crafts,* this new edition expands on the topic on how to buy wisely and well in Mexico.

1110

Schmitt, Karl Michael, and David D. Burks. *Evolution or chaos; dynamics of Latin American government and politics.* With an introd. by Ronald M. Schneider. New York, Praeger, 1963. xii, 320 p. $2.95

Presents a useful overview of Latin American politics up to the end of 1962, with good analysis of political parties and pressure groups. Includes a bibliography.

1111

Schneider, Ronald M. *An atlas of Latin American affairs.* Text by Ronald M. Schneider; maps by Robert C. Kingsbury. New York, Praeger, 1965. 136 p. maps. (Praeger paperbacks, P-124) $1.95

A collection of 60 maps by Kingsbury and text by Schneider presenting Latin America's current political, economic, social and cultural panorama. [AUFS 1967:8156]

1112

Schneider, Ronald M. *The political system of Brazil; emergence of a "modernizing" authoritarian regime, 1964-1970.* New York, Columbia University Press, 1971. xviii, 431 p. $3.95

A thorough investigation of the political forces that shaped Brazilian politics during the six-year period that saw the João Goulart, Castelo Branco, and Costa a Silva regimes. A well-researched and necessary study on this period in Brazilian history.

1113

Scholes, Walter Vinton. *Mexican politics during the Juárez regime; 1855-1872.* Columbia, University of Missouri Press, 1969. 190 p. (University of Missouri. Studies, v. 30) $2.50

Presents a scholarly interpretation of the Mexican political scene during the second half of the 19th centruy, as it was influenced by the Reform Program.

Concludes that the political power of the Church was circumscribed in such situations as attaining freedom of speech and of the press. [Charles Fleener]

1114
Schulz, Herbert Clarence, Norma B. Cuthbert, and Haydée Noya. *Ten centuries of manuscripts in the Huntington Library.* San Marino, Calif., Huntington Library, 1962. 87 p. illus., facsims., maps. (*Its* Huntington Library Publications) $1.50

Describes this valuable archive of materials relating to Europe and the Americas. Especially noteworthy are the items relating to Spanish rule in America.

1115
Schurz, William Lytle. *The civilization of Latin America.* New York, Dutton, 1964. 429 p. maps. $1.95

Presents a popularized general study of Latin America, its history and culture. It was first published in 1954, and it should be acquired by most public and college libraries.

1116
Schurz, William Lytle. *Latin America; a descriptive survey.* Completely rev. and brought up-to-date. New York, Dutton, 1964. 373 p. illus., maps. $1.95

This is a revised edition of a 1941 work. This readable introductory text contains good personal insights into the history, land, and society of Latin America. Includes a bibliography.

1117
Schurz, William Lytle. *The Manila galleon.* New ed. New York, Dutton, 1959. 453 p. illus., maps. $2.45

First published in 1939, this is an account of the Acapulco-Manila galleon trade from 1565 to 1815. Contains interesting descriptions of the navigation of the Pacific and the Spanish empire in the Orient. Includes a bibliography.

1118
Scobie, James R. *Argentina: a city and a nation.* 2d ed. New York, Oxford University Press, 1971. 323 p. illus., maps. (Latin American histories) $2.50

An excellent general survey of Argentine history which emphasizes the economic, cultural, and social factors involved in the rivalry between Buenos Aires and the provinces. The author interprets Argentina's long struggle for unity. Includes a very good, 26-page select bibliography.

1119
Scott, Robert Edwin. *Mexican government in transition.* Rev. ed. Urbana, University of Illinois Press, 1964. 345 p. (Illini books, IB-20) $2.25

Contains a good analysis of the changing pattern of government in Mexico over the past half century. This could be a useful text for courses in Mexican politics. Includes a bibliography.

1120
Scott, Stuart D. *Dendrochronology in Mexico.* Tucson, University of Arizona Press, 1966. 80 p., illus., maps. (Papers of the Laboratory of Tree Ring Research, no. 2) $4.50

The recent excavations at Casas Grandes in Chihuahua, Mexico, stimulated tree-ring studies in Mexico. The study initiated at this site was expanded to include the entire body of archeological wood in the Mexican collections of the Tree-Ring Research Laboratory at the University of Arizona. Includes a bibliography.

1121

Segal, Aaron, and Kent C. Earnhardt. *Politics and population in the Caribbean.* New York, International Publications Service, 1973. 341 p. illus. $7.50

This work studies the political problems and the society of the Caribbean islands. Contains a bibliography.

1122

Semmel, Bernard. *Democracy versus Empire: the Jamaica riots of 1865, and the Governor Eyre Controversy.* New York, Doubleday, 1969. 200 p. $1.45

A thorough study of the 1865 Jamaica riots and their political implications. This is an important contribution to Caribbean studies. Contains a bibliography.

1123

Senior, Clarence Ollson. *The Puerto Ricans; strangers, then neighbors.* Foreword by Hubert H. Humphrey. Chicago, Quadrangle Books, 1965. 128 p. illus., maps. $1.95

Analyzes the problems of education, job discrimination, and social acceptance which confront the Puerto Ricans in the U.S. mainland. It also points out what progress has been made by the mid-1960's. Includes an insightful foreword and an endorsement by the B'nai B'rith. Includes a bibliography.

1124

Senior, Clarence Ollson. *Santiago Iglesias: labor crusader. A historical and interpretive biography.* With a foreword by Herman Badillo. Hato Rey, P.R., Inter-American University, 1973. $2.95

Depicts the life, work, and achievements of this remarkable Puerto Rican labor leader of the first half of the 20th century. Available in separate English and Spanish versions.

1125

Senior, Clarence Ollson. *Santiago Iglesias; apóstol de los trabajadores.* Illustrated by Myrna Rodriguez. Hato Rey, P.R., Inter-American University Press, 1973. $2.95

This is the Spanish-language version of the above. The translation by Jesús Benítez is very good.

1126

Servin, Manuel P., comp. *The Mexican-Americans; an awakening minority.* Beverly Hills, Calif., Glencoe Press, 1970. 245 p. (The insight series) $2.85

Includes six new historical studies in addition to various previously published selections, with a bibliography and references. Of great interest to libraries specializing in Chicano studies.

1127

Sexton, James D. *Education and innovation in a Guatemalan community: San Juan la Laguna.* Los Angeles, Latin American Center, University of California, 1972. 72 p. (Latin American studies, v. 19) $2.50

Studies the education patterns in San Juan la Laguna, one of Guatemala's Indian communities. The various attitudes toward education and acculturation are examined and the results of the study are neatly summarized. This is an important study of social anthropology. Contains a bibliography.

1128

Sexton, Patricia Cayo. *Spanish Harlem; anatomy of poverty.* New York, Harper & Row, 1966. xiii, 208 p. map. $1.60

The author probes into the many problems of the Puerto Rican slum dwellers in New York City. Contrasts cultural and socioeconomic facets of Puerto Ricans living in a big industrial city. Includes bibliographical references.

1129

Shafer, Robert Jones. *Mexico; mutual adjustment planning.* Pref. by Bertram M. Gross. Syracuse, N.Y., Syracuse University Press, 1966. xxiv, 214 p. (National planning series, 4) $4.25

This is a probing and comprehensive view of the evolution of economic planning in Mexico. Includes a description of the structure of various levels of planning and relates his study to key planning and general development issues.

1130

Shapiro, Norman R., and E. S. Simha, comps. *Negritude; black poetry from Africa and the Caribbean.* Edited and translated from the French by Norman R. Shapiro, with an introd. by William Cartey. Bilingual ed. New York, October House, 1970. 240 p. $2.95

Includes a representative selection of black poets from both sides of the Atlantic, who write in French. Contains a bibliography.

1131

Shapiro, Samuel, ed. *Cultural factors in inter-American relations.* Notre Dame, Ind., University of Notre Dame Press, 1968. 368 p. $3.45

These papers, delivered at the 5th annual meeting of the Catholic Inter-American Cooperation Program in St. Louis (1968) addressed themselves to the problems facing Latin America and to the general question of inter-American cultural relations. Lyle McAlister, John Plank, and Eugene McCarthy were among the contributors.

1132

Shapiro, Samuel, ed. *Integration of man and society in Latin America.* Notre Dame, Ind., University of Notre Dame Press, 1968. xiii, 356 p. $3.25

Includes papers presented at the 4th annual meeting of the Catholic Inter-American Cooperation Program. The authors are J. Mayone Stycos (on population problems), Arturo Bonilla (on trade unions), Henry Landsberger (labor), and others. Contains bibliographical references.

1133

Sherlock, Philip Manderson. *Belize; a junior history.* London, Collins, 1969. 112 p. illus., maps. $2.95

This history of Belize from pre-Columbian times to the present is intended for junior high and high school use throughout the English-speaking portions of the hemisphere.

1134

Sherlock, Philip Manderson. *West Indies,* by Philip Sherlock. New York, Walker, 1966. 215 p. maps, plates. (New nations and peoples) $3.50

This interpretive history and analysis hails from Trinidad. The author studies the 10 islands' achievements as a whole in light of the special economic and political difficulties which face these societies. [Charles Fleener]

1135

Sherwood, Frank P. *Institutionalizing the grass roots in Brazil; a study in comparative local government.* San Francisco, Chandler Pub. Co., 1967. xii, 173 p. (Chandler publications in political science) $3.75

Discusses both general and specific problems. The approach is methodical. The U.S. experience is the usual base of comparison, but other national cases are also used. [HLAS 31:7334]

1136

Sierra, Justo. *Political evolution of the Mexican people;* with notes and a new introd. by Edmundo O'Gorman. Prologue by Alfonso Reyes. Translated by Charles Ramsdell. Austin, University of Texas Press, 1970. xx, 406 p. (The Texas Pan-American series) $2.95

This classic synthesis written on the eve of the Mexican Revolution greatly influenced the revolutionary leaders. Sierra was the first historian to write about the rights of the people. Translation of *La evolución política del pueblo mexicano.*

1137

Sigmund, Paul E., ed. *The ideologies of the developing nations.* 2d rev. ed. New York, Praeger, 1972. 483 p. $3.95

One-fourth of this work is devoted to Latin America. It is valuable because it makes available English translations of writings and speeches by leading figures of the region such as Haya de la Torre, Betancourt, Frei, Latendorf, Kubitschek, and Castro, expressing their political theories. Includes a bibliography.

1138

Sigmund, Paul E., ed. *Models of political change in Latin America.* New York, Praeger, 1970. xiv, 338 p. $3.95

Mexico, Bolivia, and Cuba were chosen by the author as models of regimes that derived their political character from revolution. Argentina, Brazil, and Peru are examples of military regimes, and Colombia, Venezuela, and Chile are presented as the leading constitutional democracies. It should be kept in mind that Mexico is now a democracy and that Bolivia is currently under military rule.

1139

Silen, Juan Angel. *We, the Puerto Ricans; a story of oppression and resistance.* Translated by Cedric Belfrage. New York, Monthly Review Press, 1971. 134 p. illus. $1.75

Essays arguing for the complete independence of Puerto Rico.

1140

Silverberg, Robert. *Lost cities and vanished civilizations.* New York, Bantam Books, 1964. 177 p. illus. $.60

This work was first published in 1962 in hard cover. Chichén Itzá is one of the lost cities studied.

1141

Silverman, Bertram, comp. *Man and socialism in Cuba; the great debate.* Edited and with an introd. by Bertram Silverman. New York, Atheneum, 1973. xiv, 382 p. $3.95

Presents 17 essays on the transition to communism, economic organization, the function of finance under socialism, and socialist theory and practice. Fidel Castro, Che Guevara, Luis Alvarez Rom, and Joaquín Infante are some of the authors of the essays. Includes bibliographical references.

1142

Silvert, Kalman H. *The conflict society: reaction and revolution in Latin America.* Rev. ed. New York, American Universities Field Staff, 1966. xiv, 289 p. $2.25

First published in 1961, this revised edition contains several new essays entitled "National political change in Latin America," "The costs of antinationalism," "Argentina," "The university students," and "Peace, freedom, and stability in the Western Hemisphere." A valuable source of information on contemporary Latin America. Contains bibliographical footnotes.

1143

Simmen, Edward, comp. *The Chicano; from caricature to self-portrait.* New York, New American Library, 1971. xiv, 318 p. (A Mentor book, MY-1069) $1.25

Contains sketches and studies on Mexican Americans and various issues concerning this ethnic group. Contains a good bibliography for further reading.

1144

Simmen, Edward, comp. *Pain and promise; the Chicano today,* edited and with an introd. by Edward Simmen. New York, New American Library, 1972. 348 p. (A Mentor book, MY1139) $1.25

Contains essays on the problems faced by Chicanos, written by prominent spokesmen and others specializing in ethnic minorities. Robert R. Haro contributed a valuable article entitled "A bibliographic essay."

1145

Simon, Kate. *Mexico; places and pleasures.* New York, World Pub. Co., 1971. xiv, 386 p. illus., maps (on lining papers) $5.95

This is a sophisticated and well-written guidebook to Mexico, emphasizing important places to visit and giving sufficient cultural background for the traveler to sustain his interest.

1146

Simon and Schuster. Editorial Staff. *Portugal.* New York, 1971. 245 p. illus., maps. $3.50

Covers all there is to see in Portugal. The various points of interest are rated with one, two, or three stars. Includes a very good set of maps and illustrations.

1147

Simplified Travel, Inc. *The real Mexico and South America.* New York, Bantam Books, 1973. 205 p. illus., maps. $1.95

This is a travel guide which contains many suggestions for hotels, excursions, and other information for tourists.

1148

Simpson, George Eaton. *Religious cults of the Caribbean: Trinidad, Jamaica and Haiti.* Rev. and enl. Rio Piedras, Institute of Caribbean Studies, University of Puerto Rico, 1970. 308 p. illus. (Caribbean monograph series, no. 7) $9

Presents the author's more important articles on West Indian religious cults. Four selections deal with Trinidad, four with Jamaica, including two papers on the Rastafari movement, and five on Haiti, all of which concentrate on Vodun. [HLAS 33:1472]

1149

Simpson, Lesley Bird. *Many Mexicos.* 4th ed. rev. Berkeley, University of California Press, 1959. xiii, 389 p. illus., map. $1.95

Professor Simpson, long a student of Mexico and a thorough scholar and observer of Mexican life, has turned out one of the truly good books about Mexico and its history. It was first published in 1952. Includes a bibliography.

1150

Sinclair, Andrew. *Che Guevara.* Edited by Frank Kermods. New York, Viking Press, 1970. 128 p. (Modern Masters) $1.95

The author has prepared a study of Guevara's ideas and influence on Latin American politics. Includes a bibliography.

LATIN AMERICA

1151

Singletary, Otis A. *The Mexican War.* Chicago, University of Chicago Press, 1960. 181 p. (The Chicago history of American civilization) $1.95

This is a brief, readable account of the Mexican War. No new ground is broken, and the author plunges directly into the events of 1845 with only a scant six pages devoted to the historical background. [HLAS 25:3324]

1152

Skidmore, Thomas E. *Politics in Brazil, 1930-1964; an experiment in democracy.* New York, Oxford University Press, 1968. xviii, 446 p. maps. $2.50

A thorough review of Brazilian politics and government during a crucial period of Brazilian history. Based on extensive scholarly research, it is a major contribution to the field of Brazilian studies. Includes bibliographical references.

1153

Slater, Jerome. *A reevaluation of collective security: the OAS in action.* Columbus, Ohio State University Press, 1965. 56 p. (The Social Science Program of the Mershon Center for Education in National Security, the Ohio State University. Pamphlet series no. 1) $1.50

Contends that collective security is workable under certain circumstances and that some appropriate revisions of the theory of collective security will be necessary. Contains bibliographical footnotes.

1154

Smiley, Terah L., Stanley A. Stubbs, and Bryant Bannister. *Foundation for the dating of some late archaeological sites in the Rio Grande area; New Mexico, based on studies in tree-ring methods and pottery analyses.* Tucson, University of Arizona Press, 1953. 66 p. illus., maps. (Arizona. University. Bulletin, v. 24, no. 3. Laboratory of Tree-Ring Research. Bulletin, no. 6) $1

Studies archeological dating in the Rio Grande region of New Mexico. A very important monograph.

1155

Smith, Buckingham. *Narratives of the career of Hernando de Soto,* by a Gentleman of Elvas. Introd. by A. Lythe. Gainesville, Fla., Kallman Pub. Co., 1965. 243 p. illus. $2.25

Examines the career of Hernando de Soto, one of the early explorers of Florida.

1156

Smith, Donald Eugene, ed. *Religion, politics, and social change in the Third World; a sourcebook.* Edited with introductory notes by Donald Eugene Smith. New York, Free Press, 1974. xv, 286 p. $3.95

About one-third of these essays and documents deal with the dynamic relationships that link religion, politics, and social change in Latin America. Includes introductory notes and a bibliography.

1157

Smith, Robert Freeman, ed. *Background to revolution: the development of modern Cuba.* New York, Knopf, 1966. xi, 224 p. (Borzoi books on Latin America) $2.50

A selection of essays concerning Cuban history of the past three centuries showing that from the beginning of European contact the island has captured the interest of foreign powers that believed Cuba was vital to their interest. It provides historical perspective to counteract simplistic views of Cuba's political history. Includes suggestions for further reading.

1158

Smith, Robert Freeman, ed. *United States and Cuba: business and diplomac* *1917-1961.* New Haven, Conn., College and University Press, 1962. 256 p. $2.25

Published in 1961, this is a review of U.S.-Cuban relations since 1898. Speci attention is given to the important problems raised by the interplay of privat business and governmental agencies in the formulation of foreign policy. Th author has made extensive use of official documents and archival sources. [HLA 24:3551]

1159

Smith, Thomas Lynn, ed. *Agrarian reform in Latin America.* Edited with a introductory essay by T. Lynn Smith. New York, Knopf, 1965. ix, 218 p. tables (Borzoi books on Latin America) $2.50

The editor's introduction and 19 essays survey the development of concern abou agrarian reform and current programs being undertaken in Latin America. Brazi and Colombia receive special emphasis. Includes a good bibliography.

1160

Smith, Thomas Lynn. *Latin American population studies.* Gainesville, University o Florida Press, 1961. 83 p. maps, tables. (University of Florida monographs. Socia sciences, no. 8) $2

The author presents a thorough compilation and analysis of demographic data fo Latin America as a whole, amply supported by graphs and tables. The principal topics treated are the number and distribution of inhabitants, age and sex composition, rate of reproduction, rural-urban migration, and population growth. Bibliographical footnotes included.

1161

Smith, Thomas Lynn. *The process of rural development in Latin America,* by T. Lynn Smith. Gainesville, University of Florida Press, 1969. 87 p. illus., map. (University of Florida monographs. Social sciences, no. 33) $2

An important study about recent rural developments in Latin America which will be of great interest to area specialists. Includes bibliographical references.

1162

Smith, Thomas Lynn. *Studies of Latin American societies,* by T. Lynn Smith. Garden City, N.Y., Anchor Books, 1970. xvii, 412 p. $1.95

The emphasis is on societal structures and the rapid changes that are taking place in Latin America. Includes a bibliography.

1163

Snow, Peter G. *Argentine radicalism; the history and doctrine of the Radical Civic Union.* Iowa City, University of Iowa Press, 1965. 137 p. (University of Iowa. Monograph) $2.75

Traces the history of the Unión Cívica Radical, one the most important political parties of 20th-century Argentina. It closely studies factionalism within the party and the evolution of divergent doctrines of radicalism. This is a scholarly contribution, with a good bibliography.

1164

Snow, Peter G. *Political forces in Argentina.* Boston, Allyn and Bacon, 1971. 157 p. (The Allyn and Bacon series in Latin American politics) $3.50

This succinct text explains and describes political currents in Argentina during the last century. It is a thoughtful and scholarly work, with a bibliography.

1165

Solnick, Bruce B. *West Indies and Central America to 1898.* Philadelphia, Philadelphia Book Co., 1973. 311 p. maps. $3.95

This is a textbook describing the history and society of the West Indies and Central America from the colonial period to the end of the 19th century. Contains a bibliography.

1166

Sousa Sánchez, Mario. *Las colecciones botánicas de C. A. Purpus en México; período 1898-1925.* Berkeley, University of California Press, 1969. 36 p. (University of California publications in botany, v. 51) $1.50

Describes the botanical collection of an important Mexican specialist. Contains illustrations and a thorough bibliography.

1167

Soustelle, Jaques. *The daily life of the Aztecs on the eve of the Spanish conquest.* Translated from the French by Patrick O'Brien. Stanford, Calif., Stanford University Press, 1970. xxiv, 321 p. maps. $2.95

English translation of *La vie côtidienne des Azteques á la veille de la conquète espagnole* (1955), which is an ethnology of Aztecs at the time of first European contact, largely as described in native codices and early histories. Contains a good bibliography.

1168

South America travel digest. 9th ed. Hollywood, Calif., Paul, Richmond, 1973. 159 p. illus. $4.95

This is an annual publication of the South American Travel Organization. It contains basic information on travel through South America.

1169

Spasek, Edward. *It's fun to fly in Mexico!* San Francisco, Avion Aids Co; sales agent Aviation Book Co., Glendale, Calif., 1967. xii, 163 p. illus., maps. $1.95

For the private pilot, this book will suggest interesting places to visit in Mexico. It provides much useful information on flying in the country, such as conversion tables for gas, radio data, and useful words for pilots. Includes a glossary and a select bibliography.

1170

Spell, Lota May Harrigan. *Pioneer printer; Samuel Bangs in Mexico and Texas.* Austin, University of Texas Press, 1973. xii, 230 p. facsims, maps. $2.25

This is a detailed study of the life and career of the man who printed or helped to print the first document known to have been published in Texas. It traces the progress of the press in early Texas and in three other Mexican states. Contains an appendix of documents and a thorough bibliography.

1171

Spicer, Edward Holland. *Cycles of conquest; the impact of Spain, Mexico and the United States on Indians of the Southwest, 1533-1960.* Drawings by Hazel Fontana. Tucson, University of Arizona Press, 1962. xii, 609 p. illus., maps. $5.95

This is a handsome volume on how the Indian tribes of the Southwest fared under the various groups of conquerors who came to their lands. Contains bibliographic notes.

1172

Spiess, Lincoln Bunce, and Thomas Stanford. *An introduction to certain Mexican musical archives.* Detroit, Information Coordinators, 1969. 85, 99 p. facsims. (Detroit studies in music bibliography, 15) $3.50

> This is an invaluable description of important musical archives in Mexico. Contains a thorough bibliography.

1173

Spratling, William Philip. *A small Mexican world,* by William Spratling. With ports. and decorations by the author. Foreword by Diego Rivera. Introd. by Lesley Byrd Simpson. Boston, Little, Brown, 1964. 198 p. illus. $1.95

> Originally published in 1932 under the title *Little Mexico,* this is the account of a trip through rural Mexico in 1931 by a m n who was a longtime resident of that country. It is an interesting narrative pι nctuated by sharp insights. Includes charcoal drawings by the author.

1174

Stastny, Francisco. *Breve historia del arte en el Perú.* New York, Wittenborn, 1967. 57 p. illus., port. $2

> This is a succinct Spanish-language survey of Peruvian art with attractive illustrations. Includes a bibliography.

1175

Stavenhagen, Rodolfo, ed. *Agrarian problems and peasant movements in Latin America.* Garden City, N.Y., Doubleday, 1970. xi, 583 p. map. $2.45

> Includes papers by anthropologists, economists, political scientists, and sociologists, from a wide range of nationalities. The essays provide the reader with aspects of the agrarian problems and the situation in which more than 100,000,000 peasants find themselves in Latin America. Includes bibliographical references.

1176

Stein, Stanley J., and Barbara H. Stein. *The colonial heritage of Latin America: essays on economic dependence in perspective,* by Stanley J. and Barbara H. Stein. New York, Oxford University Press, 1970. 222 p. $1.50

> The authors present a series of essays with a social and economic approach, trying to pinpoint the coordinates of sustained backwardness in a dependent colonial area. They have selected broad chronological periods to achieve their aim. Includes a bibliography.

1177

Stein, Stanley J. *Vassouras, a Brazilian coffee county, 1850-1900.* New York, Atheneum, 1971. 289 p. tables. $3.25

> This is a scholarly economic history of a principal coffee producing region in Brazil. It contains a thorough bibliography. This work should be noted by all libraries that wish to acquire a basic Latin American collection, as well as by economic historians.

1178

Steinbeck, John. *The log from the Sea of Cortez; the narrative portion of the book, Sea of Cortez,* by John Steinbeck and E. F. Ricketts, 1941, here reissued with a profile "About Ed Ricketts." New York, Bantam Books, 1973. ixvii, 282 p. map. $1.25

> Describes the Nobel Prize-winning U.S. author's expedition through many little harbors and barren coasts of the Gulf of California to collect and preserve the marine invertebrates of the littoral.

1179

Steiner, Stanley. *La raza: the Mexican-Americans,* by Stan Steiner. New York, Harper & Row, 1970. xii, 432 p. plates, ports. $1.95

The author has drawn skillful portraits of many of the more influential Mexican-American leaders, such as César Chavez, Rodolfo "Corky" Gonzales, Reies López Tijerina, and others. He describes in a journalistic style the cultural, social, and economic environment of the Chicanos in the Southwest. Includes a bibliography.

1180

Stephen, John Lloyd. *Incidents of travel in Central America, Chiapas, and Yucatán.* Illus. by Frederick Catherwood. New York, Dover Publications, 1969. 2 v. illus., maps, plans, ports. $3 each

This is another complete edition of the famous travelog by a prominent American traveler and amateur archeologist. The original edition appeared in 1841. Catherwood's beautiful illustrations have been reproduced in the present edition.

1181

Stephens, John Lloyd. *Incidents of travel in Yucatán.* New York, Dover Publications, 1963. 2 v. illus. (part fold.), maps, plans. $2.50 each

Originally published in 1841 as *Incidents of travel in Central America, Chiapas, and Yucatán,* this is an abridged edition which deals with the portions devoted to Yucatán. It is a classic travelog by a well-known American traveler and amateur archeologist of the 19th century and is a major contribution to modern Maya research.

1182

Sterling, Phillip, and Maria Brau. *Quiet rebels: four Puerto Rican leaders: José Celso Barbosa, Luis Muñoz Rivera, José de Diego, Luis Muñoz Marín.* Illustrated by Tracy Sugerman. New York, Doubleday, 1968. 118 p. col. illus., map. (Zenith books) $2.95

Biographical sketches of four prominent Puerto Rican leaders.

1183

Sterling Pub. Co., editors. *Caribbean English-speaking islands in pictures.* New York, Sterling Pub. Co., 1974. 64 p. illus., map. (Visual geography series) $1.50

This descriptive booklet will be useful for the classroom and for the traveler. It does not include the Spanish, French, Dutch, or U.S. islands of the Antillean area.

1184

Sterling Pub. Co., editors. *Ecuador in pictures.* New York, Sterling Pub. Co., 1974. 64 p. illus., map. (Visual geography series) $1.50

Provides factual information and illustrative material on this Andean country.

1185

Sterling Pub. Co., editors. *Honduras in pictures.* Rev. ed. New York, Sterling Pub. Co., 1972. 64 p. illus. map. (Visual geography series) $1.50

Provides a succinct pictorial and textual description of this Central American country.

1186

Sterling Pub. Co., editors. *Jamaica in pictures.* New York, Sterling Pub. Co., 1974. 64 p. illus. (Visual geography series) $1.50

Provides a succinct, profusely illustrated description of Jamaica, its history, government, and culture. Intended for classroom use, as well as for the traveler.

1187
Sterling Pub. Co., editors. *Puerto Rico in pictures.* New York, Sterling Pub. Co., 1973. 64 p. illus., map. (Visual geography series) $1.50

Puerto Rico is described here with attractive illustrations and informative textual material on the history, demography, and economy of the island.

1188
Stevens, Hugh, and Jim Hefley. *Miracles in Mexico.* Chicago, Moody Press, 1971. 214 p. illus. $1.95

Describes religious conversions and other similar events among new Christians in Mexico.

1189
Stevenson, Robert Murrell. *Music in Mexico; a historical survey.* New York, Apollo Editors, 1973. 300 p. illus. $2.75

Traces the development of music in Mexico. This is a very important contribution, based on thorough research by a specialist. Includes bibliographical references.

1190
Stimson, Frederick Sparks. *Cuba's romantic poet: the story of Plácido.* Chapel Hill, University of North Carolina Press, 1964. 150 p. (University of North Carolina Studies in Romance languages and literatures, no. 47) $5

This is a scholarly biography of one of the most popular Cuban poets, Gabriel de la Concepción Valdés, better known by his pseudonym "Plácido." Professor Stimson describes Plácido's Cuba, the main events of the poet's life (1809-1844), and his work.

1191
Stimson, Frederick Sparks, and Ricardo Navas-Ruiz, comps. *Literatura de la América hispánica; antología e historia.* New York, Dodd, Mead, 1971. 2 v. $5.95

The first volume covers the colonial period and independence, and the second the contemporary period. Each selection is preceded by biographical and critical information on the author. Intended for intermediate and advanced students of Spanish, with notes and vocabulary.

1192
Stoetzer, O. Carlos. *The Organization of American States: an introduction.* New York, Praeger, 1965. 213 p. illus., tables. (Praeger university series, U-582) $1.95

This is a historical overview of the OAS. Over half of the book consists of the texts of pertinent documents through which the OAS operates. The work was originally published for German university students under the title *Panamerika. Idee und Wirklichkeit; die Organisation der Amerikanischen Staaten* (1964).

1193
Strand, Mark, comp. *New Poetry of Mexico, 1915-1966.* New York, Dutton, 1974. 278 p. $4.95

This is a representative selection of modern Mexican poetry. Each poem appears in the original Spanish with English translations on facing pages. Includes biographical and bibliographical references.

1194

Strout, Richard Robert. *The recruitment of candidates in Mendoza Province, Argentina.* Chapel Hill, University of North Carolina Press, 1968. 159 p. (The James Sprunt studies in political science, v. 50) $4.50

Investigates how different parties in Mendoza, Argentina, recruited their legislative-gubernatorial candidates from 1962 to 1965. The aim is to test certain assertions about the social backgrounds of the candidates, the role of the oligarchy, and emerging changes in the political process. [Charles Fleener]

1195

Stycos, J. Mayone. *Children of the Barriada; a photographic essay on the Latin American population problem.* New York, Grossman Publishers, 1970. 196 p. illus. $3.95

The author illustrates, through interviews and photographs, the conditions in a Latin American slum, making a strong case for serious efforts at improved birth control.

1196

Stycos, J. Mayone, and Jorge Arias, eds. *Population dilemma in America.* New York, Columbia Books, 1966. xiii, 249 p. illus., maps. $2.45

Contains 11 papers on population problems in Latin America presented as background reading at the 1965 Pan American Assembly on Population in Cali, Colombia, sponsored by the Pan American Assembly of Columbia University, New York.

1197

Suárez, Andrés. *Cuba: Castroism and communism, 1959-1966.* With a foreword by Ernst Halperin. Translated by Joel Carmichael and Ernst Halperin. Cambridge, Massachusetts Institute of Technology Press, 1969. xviii, 266 p. (Massachusetts Institute of Technology Center for International Studies. Studies in International Communism, 12) $2.45

This highly praised work surveys the course of political events in Cuba from early revolutionary days to the mid-1960's. It is a comprehensive, objective, and scholarly book on Fidel Castro's Cuba. Contains bibliographical footnotes.

1198

Suassuna, Ariano. *The rogues' trial; the crimes of John Cricket and other rogues; their trial and the intercession of Mary, Our Lady of Mercy. A satire on human frailties in the form of a miracle play based on ballads and folktales of northeastern Brazil.* Translated by Dillwyn F. Ratcliff. Berkeley, University of California Press, 1963. $1.50

English translation of the prize-winning play *Auto da Compa decida* (1957) in which the playwright combines the technique of a puppet show, the miracle play, and the commedia dell'arte with Brazilian folklore. Although based on the 15th-century *auto* of Gil Vicente, this social satire is thoroughly Brazilian in feeling.

1199

Sumner, William Graham. *The conquest of the United States by Spain, and other essays.* Chicago, H. Regnery, 1965. 250 p. $1.45

One of the essays in this work describes Spain's colonization of North America.

1200

Sumwalt, Martha Murray. *Colombia in pictures.* New York, Sterling Pub. Co., 1970. 64 p. illus., maps, ports. (Visual geography series) $1.25

This is an attractively illustrated description of the Andean country, with information on the people, their history and government.

1201

Sundel, Alfred. *Christopher Columbus; a concise biography.* New York, American R.D.M. Corp., 1968. 67 p. illus., maps. $1

This is a popularized account of the efforts by Columbus to gain support in his enterprise and of his four voyages to the New World.

1202

Sundel, Alfred. *History of the Aztecs and the Mayas and their conquest.* New York, American R.D.M. Corp., 1967. illus., maps. $1

Describes the two great nations of Middle America and their conquest. Intended for the generalist.

1203

Sunset. *Mexico,* by the editors of Sunset books and Sunset magazine. 5th rev. ed. Menlo Park, Calif., Lane Books, 1974. 160 p. illus. (A Sunset travel book) $2.95

An attractively illustrated guide to Mexico, with much helpful information for the motorist as well as other travelers.

1204

Sunset. *Sunset Mexican cookbook,* by the editors of Sunset books and Sunset magazine. Menlo Park, Calif., Lane Books, 1974. 149 p. illus. (Sunset books) $1.95

Contains interesting, illustrated, and easy-to-follow recipes of Mexican cookery adapted for the North American kitchen.

1205

Swan, Bradford Fuller. *Early printing in the Caribbean.* Edited by C. Clair. New York, A. Schram, 1971. 420 p. illus. $8.25

Surveys early printing in the Caribbean area.

1206

Szulc, Tad. *Latin America.* New York, Atheneum, 1966. 185 p. map. (A New York Times byline book) $1.65

A *New York Times* correspondent introduces the reader to the changing Latin American scene. It is a popularized essay divided into background, the present and the future, and Latin America and the world.

1207

Szulc, Tad, ed. *The United States and the Caribbean.* Edited by Tad Szulc. Englewood Cliffs, N.J., Prentice-Hall, 1971. 212 p. (A Spectrum book) $2.45

This timely collection of essays covers such topics as the politics and social customs of the Caribbean, the Hispanic Caribbean, and the Caribbean and North America. The contributing editors include Caribbean, U.S., and English scholars and journalists. The essays attempt to study the new Caribbean reality.

1208

Syvrud, Donald E. *Foundations of Brazilian economic growth.* Stanford, Calif., Hoover Institution Press, 1974. 141 p. $4.95

Describes and studies the causes of Brazilian economic growth since 1964. An understanding of Brazil's economic policies may offer some lessons for other developing countries. Contains bibliographical notes.

1209

Tambs, Lewis A., and others, eds. *Latin American government leaders.* Tempe, Center for Latin American Studies of Arizona State University, 1970. 60 p. $2

> The editors have assembled 350 biographies of political and governmental leaders in 12 Latin American countries. A much needed and useful reference work.

1210

Tannenbaum, Frank. *Peace by revolution; Mexico after 1910.* Drawings by Miguel Covarrubias. New York, Columbia University Press, 1966. 316 p. illus., maps. (A Columbia paperback, 68) $2.95

> Tannenbaum's excellent appraisal of the Mexican Revolution was first published in 1933. He emphasizes the two decades following 1910.

1211

Tannenbaum, Frank. *Slave and citizen; the Negro in the Americas.* New York, Random House, 1963. xi, 128 p. $1.65

> First published in 1946, it rests on the thesis that when the moral equality of the Negro was accepted by the governing society, slavery was peacefully abolished, but when that egalitarianism was lacking, social change and abolition were produced by force, war, or revolution.

1212

Tannenbaum, Frank. *Ten keys to Latin America.* New York, Random House, 1966. 237 p. $1.95

> The key subjects in this collection of essays are race and religion. Emphasis is placed on current problems and their historical roots by a sympathetic critic who has spent a lifetime studying such matters.

1213

Tarn, Nathaniel, ed. *Con Cuba: an anthology of Cuban poetry.* New York, Grossman, 1969. 144 p. $2.95

> Cuba, according to the editor, is a land "where poets are as abundant as trees and books as leaves." This collection presents 30 Cuban poets, more than half of them born after 1935. They range from Felix Pita (b. 1909) to Lina de Feria and Eduardo Lolo (b. 1945). The poems appear in the original Spanish with English translations.

1214

Tardy, William T. *Tres novelas latinoamericanas.* Skokie, Ill., National Textbook Corp., 1972. 211 p. $1.25, five or more $1 each

> A textbook edition of three Latin American novels aimed at the intermediate level. Contains notes and vocabulary.

1215

Tarkesian, Sarkis A. *A comparative study of the Mexican-American graduate and dropout.* San Francisco, R. & E. Associates, 1971. 131 p. $7

> Originally presented as the author's thesis at the University of Southern California in 1967, this monograph surveys the academic accomplishments or failure of a group of Mexican Americans. This is an important contribution, with a bibliography.

1216

Tate, Bill. *Guadalupe Hidalgo 1848.* Truchas, N.M., Tate Gallery Publications, 1973. 89 p. illus. $2.50

Discusses the historical setting at the time of the Guadalupe Hidalgo Treaty when New Mexico became part of the U.S.

1217
Tate, Bill. *Mountain chants: the secret of the Penitentes.* Truchas, N.M., Tate Gallery Publications, 1970. 59 p. illus. $3

In this brief study the author describes several rites of the Penitentes, a sacred Spanish-American brotherhood.

1218
Tate, Bill. *The Penitentes of the Sangre de Cristos: an American tragedy.* 2d ed. Truchas N.M., Tate Gallery Publications, 1968. 56 p. illus., facsims., maps. $3

The Penitentes are members of a secret and ancient Spanish-American brotherhood who live in the mountains of northern New Mexico and southern Colorado. The author, who lives among the Penitentes in the village of Truchas attempts to portray the Penitentes' way of life.

1219
Tate, Bill. *Truchas: village with a view; life in a Spanish village.* Truchas, N.M., Tate Gallery Publications, 1969. 49 p. illus., map. $3

The author, who is an artist, moved to Truchas in 1963. This personal essay about his experiences contains prose, poetry, recipes, and drawings.

1220
Taylor, Alice, ed. *Focus on South America.* New York, Praeger, 1973. 274 p. illus (Focus series) $3.95

This economic geography of South America also contains sections on political geography, rural development, demography, urbanization, the Andean Common Market, and other contemporary topics. The chapters by Kempton Webb on Brazil and by James J. Parsons on Colombia are especially good. Includes bibliographies.

1221
Taylor, Barbara Howland. *Mexico: her daily and festive breads.* Illus. arranged by the author and photographed by Merle G. Wachter. Edited by Ruth S. Lamb. Claremont California, Creative Press, 1969. 98 p. illus. $6.95

In words and pictures, the author describes the varieties of breads of Mexico and interprets what they tell about the country and the people. Many attractive illustrations enhance the text. Contains a bibliography.

1222
Taylor, Martin C. *Gabriela Mistral's religious sensibility.* Berkeley, University o California Press, 1968. 191 p. port. (University of California publications in modern philology, v. 87) $7

Studies the Hebraic, Christian, and mythological themes in Gabriela Mistral's four books of poetry: *Desolación, Ternura, Tala,* and *Lagar.* An appendix offers a numerical concordance of different themes and the poems in which they appear This is an important contribution, with a bibliography.

1223
Taylor, Philip Bates. *The Venezuelan golpe de estado of 1958: the fall of Marcos Pérez Jiménez.* Washington, Institute for the Comparative Study of Political Systems, 1968 98 p. tables. (Political studies series, no. 4) $2

Analyzes the barracks revolt which brought down the dictatorship of Pérez Jiménez. Venezuelan society and politics, as well as the nature of the dictatorship are studied. Professor Taylor concludes that "Venezuela has burst from its shell of past authoritarianism with enormous energy."

1224

Tebbel, John William, and Ramón Eduardo Ruiz. *South by Southwest; the Mexican-American and his heritage,* by John Tebbel and Ramón Eduardo Ruíz. Illustrated by Earl Thollander. New York, Doubleday, 1969. 122 p. illus., maps, port. (Zenith books) $1.45

A thoughtful study of Mexican Americans and their cultural heritage.

1225

Terry, Robert H., comp. *Comparative readings on Latin America.* Berkeley, Calif., McCutchan Pub. Co., 1969. 188 p. 2 maps. $3.95

Contains essays by Frank Tannenbaum, Hubert Herring, Victor L. Urquidi, and others. The readings deal with social, economic, and diplomatic topics. Includes bibliographic references.

1226

Texas. University. Institute of Latin American Studies. *Latin American research and publications at the University of Texas at Austin, 1893-1969.* Foreword by Stanley Ross. Austin, 1972. 79 p. $3.75

Lists current publications and research sponsored by the University of Texas at Austin. Of great interest to libraries and graduate students.

1227

Thomas, Aaron Joshua. *The Dominican Republic crisis, 1965; background paper and proceedings.* A. J. Thomas, Jr., and Ann Van Wynen Thomas, authors of the working paper. John Carey, editor. Dobbs Ferry, N.Y. Published for the Association of the Bar of the City of New York by Oceana Publications, 1967. x, 164 p. $2.45

Analyzes the Dominican crisis of 1965 and the intervention of the Inter-American Peace Force. Includes a bibliography.

1228

Tomasek, Robert Dennis, ed. *Latin American politics; studies of the contemporary scene.* 2d ed. rev. and updated. Garden City, N.Y., Doubleday, 1970. xiv, 584 p. $2.45

First published in 1966, this is a new edition of a selection of essays which present a many-sided view of the power groups, the political process, and the violent nature of Latin American politics. Chosen from the writings of well-known authorities, they provide a good background for the understanding of Latin American politics. Includes bibliographical references.

1229

Thompson, Edward Herbert, and J.R. Murie. *High Priest's grave: Chichén Itzá, Yucatán, Mexico.* New York, Kraus Reprints, 1970. 320 p. illus. $5

An archeological study of the Maya grave, with attractive illustrations.

1230

Thompson, Edward Herbert. *People of the serpent; life and adventure among the Mayas.* New York, Putnam, 1965. xv, 301 p. (Capricorn 123) $1.65

This is a book of personal memoirs, essentially a volume on archeology, written by one of the most famous explorers of Yucatán, the archeologist who established the ritual significance of the Sacred Cenote of Chichén Itzá.

1231

Thompson, John Eric Sidney. *Maya hieroglyphic writing; an introduction.* 3d ed
Norman, Oklahoma University Press, 1971. xxii, 347 p. illus. (Civilization of the
American Indian series, no. 56) $9.95

An admirable new edition of Thompson's massive studies on the history of
decipherment, sources, and subject matter, composition and nature of th
hieroglyphs, origins, as well as stylistic changes and the implications of unity and
regionalism. Excellent illustrations enhance the text. Includes bibliographies
[HLAS 35: 942]

1232

Thiesenhusen, William C. *Chile's experiments in agrarian reform.* Madison, University of
Wisconsin Press, 1966. xi, 304 p. maps, tables. (University of Wisconsin Land Tenur
Center. A Research paper, no. 10) $3

Analyzes several land reform experiments in Chile where the traditiona
latifundia-minifundia agrarian structure still predominates. It is predicated on th
idea that when a more inclusive agricultural restructuralization comes, technician
will benefit from having studied how reform works on a small scale.

1233

Tinkle, Lon. *The Alamo: thirteen days to glory.* New York, New American Library
1958. 176 p. illus. $.75

This is a factual yet considerably dramatized day-by-day account of the 183
battle for the Alamo.

1234

Tolstoy, Paul. *Surface survey of the northern valley of Mexico; the classic and
post-classic periods.* Philadelphia, American Philosophical Society, 1958. 101 p. illus.
map. (Transactions of the American Philosophical Society, new ser., v. 48, pt. 5) $2

A thorough study of classic and postclassic periods of art in northern Mexico
Contains a bibliography.

1235

Topling, Robert Brent. *The abolition of slavery in Brazil.* New York, Atheneum, 1975
378 p. illus. $3.95

Surveys the abolition of slavery in Brazil in a scholarly and careful study
Contains bibliographical references.

1236

Tornöe, Johannes Kristoffer. *Columbus in the Arctic, and the Vineland literature.* New
York, Humanities Press, 1965. 92 p. maps (1 fold.) $4.50

The author assumes that the sagas of the Norse discovery can be interpreted a
factual reports of historical events. He further states that first-hand knowledge o
North America persisted in Europe for many centuries. Thus he theorizes tha
Columbus actually knew about North America before "accidentally" discovering
the Western Hemisphere. Contains a bibliography. [Charles Fleener]

1237

Torres Restrepo, Camilo. *Revolutionary priest; the complete writings and messages o
Camilo Torres.* Edited and with an introd. by John Gerassi. Translators: June de
Cipriano Alcántara and others. New York, Random House, 1971. xi, 460 p. $2.45

Presents the writings by a Colombian priest, who moved gradually to the left unti
he died in 1966 with a guerrilla band in north central Colombia. Torres wa
deeply committed to social and economic reforms. Includes a brief bibliography

174

1238

Torres Ríoseco, Arturo, ed. *Antología de la literatura hispanoamericana;* Selección, comentarios, notas y glosario de Arturo Torres-Ríoseco. 2d ed. New York, Appleton-Century-Crofts, 1961. xv, 311 p. $3.25

A very useful and representative anthology of Spanish-American literature. It includes samples from novels, short stories, essays, and poetry by great literary figures.

1239

Torres Rioseco, Arturo. *The epic of Latin American literature.* Berkeley, University of California Press, 1959. 277 p. $2.25

Originally published in 1942, this is an excellent survey of the history of Latin American literature from the colonial period to the mid-20th century. It includes a chapter on Brazilian literature.

1240

Trend, John Brande. *Bolivar and the independence of Spanish America.* New York, Harper and Row, 1970. xii, 287 p. port., maps. $1.45

A fresh view of Simón Bolívar and the independence of South America is presented here. It will be very useful for studying the independence period.

1241

Tulchin, Joseph S. *Problems in Latin American history; the modern period.* New York, Harper & Row, 1973. 529 p. $5.95

An interdisciplinary survey of Latin America based on both primary and secondary sources. The topics deal with developmental economics, militarism, U.S.-Latin American relations, ideologies of left and right, dictatorship, and others. Includes bibliographies.

1242

Turner, Frederick C. *The dynamic of Mexican nationalism.* Chapel Hill, University of North Carolina Press, 1968. xii, 350 p. $2.95

An important study of the nature and some of the functions of nationalism in Mexican society by a political scientist. He analyzes the extent to which nationalism has been relevant in Mexican national life, particularly since the Revolution of 1910. Includes bibliographical references.

1243

Turner, Mary C. *La empresa del libro en America Latina.* New York, Bowker, 1970. 451 p. $15.95

Surveys Latin American publishing. This will be a useful work for persons engaged in acquisitions.

1244

Tyson, George F., ed. *Toussaint L'Ouverture.* Englewood Cliffs, N.J., Prentice-Hall, 1973. 185 p. (Great lives observed) $2.45

The editor has assembled many almost unavailable sources, some of the Haitian independence leader's own writings, as well as diverse evaluations by Toussaint's contemporaries and by later historians. A clear and informed introduction puts the period in perspective. Includes a bibliography.

1245

Ugalde, Antonio, and others. *The urbanization process of a poor Mexican neighborhood,* by Antonio Ugalde with Leslie Olson, David Schers and Miguel Von Hoegen. Austin,

Institute of Latin American Studies, University of Texas, 1974. 68 p. (A special publication of the Institute of Latin American Studies, University of Texas) $2

> Studies a migrant barrio, San Felipe del Real Adicional, in Ciudad Juárez. The study finds that the traditional family is a vehicle of modernization. Contains a bibliography.

1246

Ulibarri, Richard O. *American interest in the Spanish Southwest, 1803-1848.* San Francisco, R. and E. Research Associates, 1974. 127 p. $12

> A detailed account, with good references, of U.S. interest in the northern outpost of the waning Spanish colonial empire. Includes a bibliography.

1247

Ulibarri, Sabine R. *Tierra amarilla; cuentos de Nuevo México. Stories of New Mexico.* Translated from the Spanish by Thelma Campbell Nason. Illus. by Kercheville. Albuquerque, University of New Mexico Press, 1971. x, 167 p. $3.45

> This bilingual edition contains the following short stories: "My wonderful horse," "The stuffing of the Lord," "The Frater family," "Get that straight," "Forge without fire," and "Man without name."

1248

Ulloa, Antonio de, and Jorge Juan y Santacilia. *A voyage to South America.* The John Adams translation abridged. Introd. by Irving A. Leonard. New York, Knopf, 1964. 245 p. (Borzoi books on Latin America) $2.95

> A translation of a controversial 18th-century report emphasizing defects in the Spanish empire in its waning days. Two young Spanish officers describe their visits to the important Spanish cities and settlements of South America. Does not include the scientific reports of the expedition. Contains a bibliography.

1249

United Nations. Economic Commission for Latin America. *Economic bulletin for Latin America.* Washington, 1964- $2.50

> This is a biennial publication, containing a wealth of information and statistical data.

1250

U.S. Agency for International Development. Office of Technical Cooperation and Research. *A study of present and needed book activities in national development: Chile.* Pittsburgh, University of Pittsburgh, School of Education, 1967. 141 p. $1

> This report is the result of a survey in which a team of four researchers investigated the needs for and potentials of textbooks in the Chilean educational system.

1251

U.S. Agency for International Development. Office of Technical Cooperation and Research. *A study of present and needed book activities in national development: Peru.* Pittsburgh, University of Pittsburgh, School of Education, 1967. 141 p. $1

> Surveys who is publishing, distributing, and utilizing books in the various educational and developmental programs in Peru. Recommendations are also made for future projects to encourage Peruvian publishing.

1251A

U.S. Congress. House. Committee on Foreign Affairs. Subcommittee on Inter-American Affairs. *Inter-American relations; a collection of documents, legislation, descriptions of inter-American organizations, and other material pertaining to inter-American affairs.* Washington, U.S. Govt. Print. Off., 1973. 780 p. $4.80

Designed to provide Members of Congress with a single source of important reference material relating to inter-American affairs. The material was compiled and selected by Barry Sklar and Virginia Hagen of the Congressional Research Service, Library of Congress, with the assistance of the Permanent Mission of the U.S. to the Organization of American States.

1252

Urquidi, Víctor. *Free trade and economic integration in Latin America; the evolution of a common market policy.* Translated from the Spanish by Marjory M. Urquidi. Berkeley, University of California Press, 1962. 190 p. $3.75

A Mexican economist traces the steps leading to the Central American integration treaties and the organization of LAFTA. This is an English translation of *Trayectoria del mercado común latinoamericano* (1960), with a bibliography, chronology, and the text of the Treaty of Montevideo.

1253

Usigli, Rodolfo. *Corona de luz; pieza antihistórica en tres actos.* Edited by Rex Edward Ballinger. New York, Appleton-Century-Crofts, 1967. 217 p. illus. $3.10

This is a very good play centering around a historical theme, first published in 1965. The present edition contains glossary, notes, and vocabulary for intermediate and advanced students of Spanish, as well as for drama classes.

1254

Usigli, Rodolfo. *Corona de sombra; pieza antihistórica en tres actos.* Edited by Rex Edward Ballinger. New York, Appleton-Century-Crofts, 1961. 206 p. illus. $2.80

Usigli is probably the most professional Mexican playwright. He called *Corona de sombra* (1943) an anti-historical work with a historical theme: the tragic fate of Maximilian and Carlota. This is a textbook edition of the play, with notes and vocabulary.

1255

Usigli, Rodolfo. *El gesticulador; pieza para demagogos en tres actos.* Edited by Rex Edward Ballinger. New York, Appleton-Century-Crofts, 1963. 178 p. illus. $2.80

According to the preface "this textbook edition of *El Gesticulador* (1937) is designed for English-speaking students of Hispanic-American literature with an interesting play by the most distinguished playwright of Mexico." Contains notes and vocabulary.

1256

Uslar Pietri, Arturo. *Catorce cuentos venezolanos.* Philadelphia, Center for Curriculum Development, 1969. 320 p. $2.75

Presents narratives from the early and later years of Uslar Pietri. The prose is rich in lyric metaphors, symbols, and sensuality. Contains notes and vocabulary.

1257

Uslar Pietri, Arturo. *Las lanzas coloradas;* with introd., notes, exercises, and vocabulary by Donald Devenish Walsh. New York, Norton, 1964. 219 p. $3.95

This historical novel by the Venezuelan writer was first published in 1931. It describes in rich prose and in a fictionalized form the wars of independence with the figure of Bolívar vaguely outlined. Contains excellent psychological portraits of the different characters. Includes notes, exercises, and a vocabulary.

1258

Vaillant, George Clapp. *Aztecs of Mexico; origin, rise, and fall of the Aztec nation.* Rev. by Suzannah B. Vaillant. Baltimore, Penguin Books, 1964. xxii, 312 p. illus., maps, tables. $2.95

This is a revised edition of a book published in 1941. This work comes closest to becoming the standard account of Central Mexican archeology and the culture of the native people of the area at the time of European contact. The archeological portion has been considerably revised to reflect a new research. Includes a bibliography.

1259

Valdés, Nelson, and Edwin Lieuwen, comps. *The Cuban revoltuion; a research-study guide, 1959-1969.* Albuquerque, University of New Mexico Press, 1971. 230 p. $3.95

Contains 3,839 items essential for scholars working in the humanities and social sciences. Includes official documents, books, periodicals, newspapers, eyewitness reports, and dissertations. This is the first systematic and comprehensive guide which includes most of the relevant sources. Recommended for most Latin American collections.

1260

Valdez, Luis, and Stan Steiner, comps. *Aztlán; an anthology of Mexican-American literature.* New York, Vintage Books, 1973. xxxii, 410 p. (A Marc Corporation book) $2.45

The introductory essay describes cultural trends as well as recent developments in Mexican-American literature. The anthology presents a good selection of relevant Mexican and Chicano literature in various forms.

1261

Valero, Helena, *Yanoama; the narrative of a white girl kidnapped by Amazonian Indians,* as told to Ettore Biocca. Photographs by the missionary Luigi Cicci and by Ettore Biocca. Translated from the Italian by Dennis Rhodes. New York, Dutton, 1970. 382 p. illus, map. $3.45

This fascinating first-hand account of life among the Amazonian Indians contains dramatic photographs depicting the customs and rituals of the tribe. Helena Valero lived for many years with the Yanoáma in the unexplored forest between Brazil and Venezuela.

1262

Vallejo, César Abraham. *César Vallejo; an anthology of his poetry,* with an introd. and notes by James Higgins. Oxford, New York, Pergamon Press, 1970. 183 p. (The Commonwealth and international library. Latin American division) $4

In addition to a thorough introduction, it includes selections from *Los heraldos negros* (1919), *Trilce* (1922), *Poemas humanos* (1939), and *España, aparta de mí este cáliz* (1939). Includes a bibliography of works by and about Vallejo.

1263

Vallejo, César Abraham. *Poemas humanos.* Translated by Clayton Eshleman. New York, Grove Press, 1969. xxv, 326 p. port. $2.95

Poemas humanos was first published posthumously in Paris in 1939. The poems were inspired by the Spanish civil war. The poet expressed through his verses the great pity he felt for the oppressed and turned his hopes toward redemption through Marxism. This is a bilingual edition.

1264

Vallejo, César Abraham. *Spain, let this cup pass from me.* Translated by Alvaro Cardona-Hine. Fairfax, Calif., Red Hill Press, 1974. 51 p. $2.50

English translation of *España, aparta de mí este cáliz*, in which Vallejo expounds on his own rebellion and that of insurgent Spain.

1265

Vallejo, César Abraham. *Trilce*. Translated from the Spanish by David Smith, introd. by Fernando Alegría. New York, Grossman, 1974. 121 p. $5.95

Published in 1922, *Trilce* is in the words of the critic Enrique Anderson-Imbert "pure poetic rebellion." Written in free verse and devoid of syntax, it is considered Vallejo's most important book.

1266

Vallier, Ivan. *Catholicism, social control, and modernization in Latin America*. Englewood Cliffs, N.J., Prentice-Hall, 1970. x, 171 p. tables. (Modernization of traditional societies series) $3.15

Analyzes how Catholicism is affecting the process of change in Latin America. A number of individuals such as Dom Helder Cámara, Camilo Torres, Ivan Illich, and others have become symbols for the "new church." Includes a bibliography.

1267

Van Deusen, Glyndon G. *The life of Henry Clay*. Boston, Little, Brown, 1967. 448 p. facsims., plates, ports. $2.95

Latin America remains on the periphery of this classic biography of one of the earliest advocates for Latin independence in the U.S. Some interesting background information on U.S. attitudes towards Latin America is given for the 1800-50 period. It was first published in 1937. [Charles Fleener]

1268

van Loon, Hendrick Willem. *Fighter for freedom: Jefferson and Bolívar*, written and illustrated by Hendrick Willem van Loon. New York, Dodd, Mead, 1962. 243 p. illus. $2.25

Originally published in 1943 as two works under the titles *Thomas Jefferson* and *The life and times of Simón Bolívar*, respectively, this edition combines the two towering figures. It is a popular treatment for the general public.

1269

Vargas Llosa, Mario. *The green house*. Translated from the Spanish by Gregory Rabassa. New York, Avon, 1973. 405 p. $1.95

Translation of *La casa verde* (1965) which first appeared in English in 1968. This novel won the 1966 International Rómulo Gallegos Award. It is a highly complex and structured novel, in which the author explores the Piura region and the Amazon jungle while depicting the entwined lives of the different characters. He is adept at presenting crisp dialog and has a sharp eye for detail. The translation is excellent.

1270

Vazquez, Richard. *Chicano*. New York, Avon Books, 1973. 117 p. $1.25

Readings on the situation of the Chicanos in the U.S. which describe problems and progress to date.

1271

Vela, Irma. *Bailes a colores*. Austin, Tex., American Universal Artforms Corp., 1974. 211 p. illus. $10

Describes Latin American modern and folk dances. Contains attractive illustrations.

1272

Velázquez, León de. *Mexican cookbook for American homes.* New York, Corner Book Shop, 1974. 213 p. $5

This is an attractive cookbook of Mexican dishes and pastry with clear instructions, adapted for the American kitchen.

1273

Véliz, Claudio, ed. *Obstacles to change in Latin America.* New York, Oxford University Press, 1969. 263 p. $1.95

Contains papers presented at the Conference on Obstacles to Change in Latin America, London, 1965. The contributors include Torcuato Di Tella, Celso Furtado, Orlando Fals Borda, Víctor Urquidi, and Felipe Herrera. The papers are provocative and interesting.

1274

Véliz, Claudio, ed. *The politics of conformity in Latin America.* London, New York, issued under the auspices of the Royal Institute of International Affairs [by] Oxford University Press, 1970. x, 291 p. $2.25

The eight essays and excellent introduction in this volume examine the principal political problems of development in Latin America. The topics include social change, peasants, the military, university students, and others. Includes bibliographical references.

1275

Veríssimo, Erico. *Gato preto em campo de neve.* Edited by L. Kasten and Claude E. Leroy. New York, Harcourt, Brace and World, 1969. 296 p. (Galaxy book, GB-328) $2.95

A Brazilian author describes U.S. social life and customs, as well as landscapes, in a fascinating narrative.

1276

Violette, Paul E. *Shelling in the sea of Cortez.* Tucson, Ariz., Dale Stuart King, 1964. 95 p. illus. $1.95

This is a handsomely illustrated guide to mollusks and shellfish in the Gulf of California.

1277

Violich, Francis, and Juan B. Astica. *Desarrollo de la comunidad y el progreso de planificación urbana en la América Latina.* Translated from the Spanish by Sergio Seelenberger and Winston C. Estremadoiro. Los Angeles, Latin American Center, University of California, 1971. xiii, 167 p. (Latin American studies series, v. 17) $3.50

This perceptive work on the cities of Latin America and housing was first published in English as *Community development and the urban planning process in Latin America* (1967).

1278

Vivian, R. Gordon, and others. *Kin Kletso, a Pueblo Three community in Chaco Canyon, New Mexico, and tree-ring dating of the archaeological sites in the Chaco Canyon region.* Albuquerque, University of New Mexico Press, 1974. 2 v. illus. maps. $5

Contains a thorough archeological description of this New Mexico site, together with a detailed account of tree-ring dating. Includes bibliographical notes.

1279

Vivian, R. Gordon. *Three-C site; an early Pueblo II ruin in Chaco Canyon, New Mexico,* by Gordon Vivian. Albuquerque, University of New Mexico Press, 1965. 48 p. illus., map. (University of New Mexico publications in anthropology, no. 13) $2

This is an archeological study of an important Pueblo site in New Mexico, with scholarly notes and illustrations.

1280

Vogt, Evon Zartman. *The Zinacantecos of Mexico; a modern Maya way of life.* New York, Holt, Rinehart and Winston, 1970. xii, 113 p. illus., maps. (Case studies in cultural anthropology) $2.75

Zinacantan is one of 21 Tzotzil-speaking towns in Chiapas in the highlands near the Guatemalan border. The Zinacantecos have been converted to Catholicism. Their life is highly ceremonialized; the Catholic observances and rites have smoothly synthesized with Mayan usages. The result is an elaborate and unique, highly integrated cultural system. This is an important contribution to cultural anthropology.

1281

Von Hagen, Victor W. *The Aztec; man and tribe.* Illustrated by Alberto Beltrán. New York, New American Library, 1958. 222 p. illus. (Mentor: Ancient civilizations, MD-236) $1.25

This is a popularized account of late pre-Hispanic central Mexican native culture, with a brief archeological background. It is an error-studded and superficial work. It contains fine-line drawings which capture the spirit of the Aztec pictorial style. [HLAS 22:612]

1282

Von Hagen, Victor W. *Desert kingdoms of Peru.* New York, New American Library, 1969. 190 p. illus., maps. $1.50

Describes the kingdoms of ancient Peru in a popularized style.

1283

Von Hagen, Victor W. *Realm of the Incas.* Illustrated by Alberto Beltrán. New York, New American Library, 1961. 223 p. illus. (Mentor books: Ancient civilizations, MP-355) $1.25

Deals with the ancient cultures of Peru culminating with the Incas. A brief discussion of the geographical and historical background of pre-Incan cultures is followed by discussion of the Incas and their achievements. Unfortunately, it often overstretches the data and contains some inaccuracies. [HLAS 21:340]

1284

Von Hagen, Victor W. *The world of the Maya.* Illustrated by Alberto Beltrán. New York, New American Library, 1960. 224 p. illus. (Mentor: Ancient civilizations, MD-300) $1.25

Popular account of pre-Hispanic Maya civilization, based in part on documentary sources. Contains some errors of fact and interpretations. [HLAS 24:1161]

1285

Von Lazar, Arpad. *Latin American politics; a primer.* With a foreword by Federico Gil. Boston, Allyn and Bacon, 1971. xviii, 157 p. (The Allyn and Bacon series in Latin American politics) $2.95

This is an introductory volume in a series on Latin American political systems. It is a concise study of complex political, economic, and social problems. Prof. Gil's introduction outlines essential trends in contemporary Latin America.

1286
Wagenheim, Kal. *Puerto Rico: a profile.* Foreword by Piri Thomas. New York, Praeger, 1970. xv, 286 p. illus., maps, ports. (Praeger country profile series) $2.95

Describes the history of Puerto Rico with emphasis on the cultural and sociological aspects of the islands. Contains attractive illustrations and a bibliography. Intended for survey courses and public library collections.

1287
Wagley, Charles. *Amazon town; a study of man in the tropics.* With a new epilogue by the author. Illus. by João José Rescála. New York, Knopf, 1964. xi, 325 p. illus. (Borzoi books on Latin America) $2.95

First published in 1953, this work describes a small community on the lower Amazon river system. It is of great value in understanding the relationship of humans and their institutions to the tropical habitat. A new epilog brings the work up to date. Contains a bibliography.

1288
Wagley, Charles. *An introduction to Brazil.* New York, Columbia University Press, 1965. xi, 322 p. illus., maps. $2.95

A well-known anthropologist provides here a basic book on Brazil. Includes a good bibliography.

1289
Wagley, Charles. *The Latin American tradition; essays on the unity and the diversity of Latin American culture.* New York, Columbia University Press, 1968. 242 p. $3.95

Contains papers and essays written between 1951 and 1964. All of them have been previously published, but most are not easily available. It provides a good retrospective view of interpretive anthropological thinking on Latin America by an important specialist. Contains a bibliography. [HLAS 30:163]

1290
Wagley, Charles, and Marvin Harris. *Minorities in the New World; six case studies.* New York, Columbia University Press, 1964. xvi, 320 p. $2.45

This is an incisive work on Indians, Negroes, Jews, and other minority groups in the Americas. Because the book was first published in 1958, the chapter on blacks in the U.S. is outdated. Includes a bibliography.

1291
Wagner, C. Peter. *Latin American theology; radical or evangelical? The struggle for the faith in a young church.* Grand Rapids, Mich., Eerdmans, 1970. 118 p. $2.45

The associate director of the Andes Evangelical Mission describes the current crisis in theological circles in the Latin American Protestant churches. The author analyzes the radical left and concludes that the theology of its exponents has become secularized. Contains a bibliography. [Charles Fleener]

1292
Wagner, C. Peter. *The Protestant movement in Bolivia.* South Pasadena, Calif., William Carey Library, 1970. xxii, 240 p. illus., maps, ports. $3.95

Analyzes the Protestant churches' history and perspectives in Bolivia. Includes a bibliography.

1293
Wakefield, Dan. *Island in the city; Puerto Ricans in New York.* New York, Corinth Books, 1960. 149 p. $1.95

Presents a disturbing journalistic account of Spanish Harlem and other Puerto Rican ghettos. It was first published in 1959.

1294

Waldo, Myra. *Travel guide to South America*. Rev. ed. New York, Macmillan, 1972. 456 p. maps. $3.95

This is a useful guidebook for those who wish to travel through South America. It points out places of interest and contains helpful information on the various countries.

1295

Walker, Nell. *The life and work of Manuel Gutiérrez Nájera*. Columbia, University of Missouri Press, 1971. 83 p. port. (The University of Missouri studies; a quarterly of research, vol. II, no. 2) $1.25

Presents a thorough analysis of a Mexican poet and short story writer, pioneer of the modernista movement in the second half of the 19th century. Contains a bibliography.

1296

Wallace, Alfred Russell. *A narrative of the travels on the Amazon and Rio Negro*. 2d ed. With a new introd. by H. Lewis McKinney. New York, Dover, 1972. xxvi, 363 p. illus. $3.50

This is a reprint of the 1889 edition of this classic account of exploring two great rivers of the Southern Hemisphere. Includes bibliographical references.

1297

Wallace, George, and Inger Wallace. *Mexican cookbook*. Concord, Calif., Nitty Gritty Productions, 1971. 173 p. illus. $3.95

Contains almost all the favorite and some less well-known Mexican dishes and desserts. Handsome illustrations enhance the text.

1298

Wallach, Kate, comp. *Union list of basic Latin American legal materials*. South Hackensack, N.J., Published for the American Association of Law Libraries, by F. B. Rothman, 1971. 64 p. (AALL publications series, no. 10) $6.75

This is an important and welcome bibliography of essential Latin American legal materials and their locations. Of great interest to law libraries.

1299

Walsh, Donald Devenish, and Lawrence B. Kiddle, comps. *Cuentos americanos con algunos poemas;* illus. by Howard Willar. 3d ed. New York, Norton, 1970. 210 p. illus., map. $3.25

This anthology was first published in 1948 under the title *Cuentos y versos americanos*. Contains excerpts from the writings of Gregorio López y Fuentes, Alberto Guillén, Alfonsina Storni, Horacio Quiroga, Arturo Uslar Pietri, and others. Contains notes and vocabulary. Intended for the early intermediate reader of Spanish.

1300

Walters, Elsa Hopkins, and E. B. Castle. *Principles of education with special reference to teaching in the Caribbean*. New York, Humanities Press, 1967. 211 p. $3

Intended for students in teachers' colleges of the English-speaking West Indies. Examples and illustrations have been taken from Dr. Walter's decade of first-hand experience in Caribbean schools.

1301

Waltrip, Rufus, and Lela Waltrip. *The Mexican-American story*. Introd. by Joseph Montoya. Boulder, Colo., Shields Pub. Co., 1974. 311 p. illus. $4.95

> Discusses the cultural, economic, and social adjustment of Mexican Americans in the contemporary U.S. Contains bibliographical notes.

1302

Wauchope, Robert, ed. *The Indian background of Latin American history; the Maya, Aztec, Inca and their predecessors*. New York, Knopf, 1970. 211 p. (Borzoi books on Latin America) $3.15

> This excellent selection of readings treats a wide range of ancient cultures. The editor has concentrated on the native civilizations that most concern Latin Americanists. The introduction summarizes the earlier cultures that preceded those described in the readings. Includes a bibliography.

1303

Wauchope, Robert. *Lost tribes and sunken continents*. Chicago, University of Chicago Press, 1962. 155 p. illus. $2.95

> Discusses the origins of the Indians in the Americas, their probable arrival, and acculturation throughout the varied geographical and climactic regions. Includes a bibliography.

1304

Wauchope, Robert. *They found the buried cities; exploration and excavation in the American tropics*. Chicago, University of Chicago Press, 1965. 382 p. illus., ports. $4.50

> Relates the early excavations of the Maya ruins in Mexico and Central America, with information on the explorers. This is a very readable and scholarly account, with bibliographies.

1305

Weaver, Charles Edwin. *Paleontology of the Jurassic and Cretaceus of west central Argentina*. Seattle, University of Washington Press, 1970. xv, 594 p. 62 plates (incl. maps) (Memoirs of the University of Washington, vol. I) $15

> Originally published in 1931, this is a scholarly monograph on certain aspects of paleontology in west central Argentina. Contains a bibliography.

1306

Weaver, Jerry L., comp. *Latin American development; a selected bibliography, 1950-1967*. Santa Barbara, Calif., American Bibliographical Center, Clio Press, 1969. 87 p. (Bibliography and reference series, no. 9) $7.25

> Lists articles and books dealing with the political, economic, and social development of Latin America. It contains 1,853 entries classified by region and arranged alphabetically by author. [Charles Fleener]

1307

Weaver, Jerry L., comp. *The political dimensions of rural development in Latin America; a selected bibliography, 1950-1967*. Long Beach, California State College, 1968. x, 92 p. $5

> Contains 1,506 entries dealing with various facets of rural development in Latin America. This is a welcome research tool for the study of rural conditions. [Charles Fleener]

1308

Weaver, Muriel Porter. *Tlapacoya pottery in the Museum collection*. New York, Museum of the American Indian, Heye Foundation, 1967. xi, 48 p. illus., maps, 41 plates. (Indian notes and monographs; a series of publications related to the American aborigines, no. 56) $3.50

An attractively illustrated volume featuring the Tlapacoya, Mexico, collection at the Museum of the American Indian. Includes references.

1309

Webb, Kempton Evans. *Brazil,* by Kempton E. Webb. Boston, Ginn, 1970. 122 p. illus. (part col.), maps, ports. $1.95

Provides a general treatment of Brazil's history, geography, economy, and culture. It is a useful introduction to the country for survey courses. Contains a bibliography.

1310

Webb, Kempton Evans. *Geography of Latin America; a regional analysis,* by Kempton E. Webb. Englewood Cliffs, N.J., Prentice-Hall, 1972. xiv, 126 p. illus. (Foundations of world regional geography series) $2.95

This is a brief geographic description of Latin America, intended for survey courses. Includes a bibliography.

1311

Weber, David J., comp. *Foreigners in their native land; historical roots of the Mexican Americans.* Foreword by Ramon Eduardo Ruiz. Albuquerque, University of New Mexico Press, 1973. xi, 288 p. illus. $4.95

Includes essays and documents on the history and cultural background of Mexican Americans in the U.S. The introduction presents a concise view of the Spanish culture in an Anglo-Saxon setting. Includes a bibliography.

1312

Weinberg, Albert Katz. *Manifest destiny; a study of nationalist expansionism in American history.* Chicago, Quadrangle Books, 1963. xiii, 559 p. $2.95

Based on public records, newspaper accounts, and diplomatic correspondence. It contains data on U.S.-Mexican relations, the Spanish American War, the Panama Canal, and "dollar diplomacy." Includes bibliographical notes.

1313

Werstein, Irving. *1898: the Spanish-American War and the Philippine insurrection told with pictures.* New York, Cooper Square Publishers, 1966. 191 p. illus., maps. $2.50

This is an illustrated popularized account of the Spanish-American War and the insurrection in the Philippine Islands.

1314

West, Robert Cooper. *The Tabasco lowlands of southeastern Mexico,* by Robert C. West, N. P. Psuty and B. G. Thom. Baton Rouge, Louisiana State University Press, 1969. xv, 193 p. illus., maps. (Louisiana State University Studies. Coastal studies series, no. 27) $4

An important study of the Tabasco region of Mexico, based on extensive field research. It contains a thorough bibliography.

1315

Whitaker, Arthur Preston. *Argentina.* Englewood Cliffs, N.J., Prentice-Hall, 1964. 184 p. (The Modern nations in historical perspective [Latin American subseries]) $1.95

Two chapters on the 19th century serve as an introduction to this political survey of Argentina from 1880 to 1960. Contains a good bibliography.

185

1316

Whitaker, Arthur Preston, ed. *Latin America and the enlightenment; essays,* by Arthur P. Whitaker and others. Introd. by Federico de Onís. 2d ed. Ithaca, N.Y., Cornell University Press, 1965. 156 p. $1.75

> Originally published in 1942, this standard volume contains a collection of essays by such prominent Latin Americanists as John Tate Lanning, Harry Bernstein, Roland D. Hussey, etc. A new essay by Charles Griffin and an updated bibliography have been added to the present edition.

1317

Whitaker, Arthur Preston. *The Spanish-American frontier, 1783-1795; the westward movement and the Spanish retreat in the Mississippi Valley.* With an introd. by Samuel Eliot Morison. Lincoln, University of Nebraska Press, 1969. 255 p. maps. $1.95

> First published in 1927, this is a thorough analysis of Spanish rule in the Southwest during the end of the 18th century and the gradual displacement of Spanish power by the westward movement. Contains a bibliography.

1318

Whitaker, Arthur Preston. *The U.S. and the independence of Latin America, 1800-1830.* New York, Norton, 1964. 632 p. $3.25

> Based on official records, documentary evidence, and contemporary sources, this work focuses on the diplomatic role of the U.S. in encouraging independence movements in Latin America. It was first published in 1941. Contains bibliographies.

1319

Whitaker, Arthur Preston. *The Western Hemisphere idea; its rise and decline.* Ithaca, N.Y., Cornell University Press, 1965. 194 p. $1.95

> Contains eight essays which provide stimulating and important discussions of the validity of ideas underlying past and present inter-American relations and relations of these concepts to those of global or other regional groupings. Includes a bibliography.

1320

Whitted, Gerald. *Pan Am's new guide to the Caribbean, Central America, South America, U.S.A., and Canada.* New York, Pan American Publications, 1973. 278 p. illus. $1.50

> Introduces the air traveler to the Americas.

1321

Whitten, Norman E., and John F. Szwed, comps. *Afro-American anthropology; contemporary perspectives.* Foreword by Sidney Mintz. New York, Free Press, 1970. x, 468 p. illus. $5.95

> Contains articles by prominent anthropologists dealing with Afro-Latins. The topics covered include ethnohistory and self-image, cultural and linguistic ambiguities, patterns of performance, and others. These articles were originally presented at a 1967 symposium at the American Anthropology Association meeting of that year. Includes bibliographies.

1322

Whitten, Norman E. *Black frontiersman; a South American case.* Cambridge, Mass., Schenkman Pub. Co., 1974. 211 p. $4.95

> Discusses the sociocultural changes of blacks in northwestern Ecuador. Includes a bibliography.

1323

Whitten, Norman E. *Class, kinship, and power in an Ecuadorean town; the Negroes of San Lorenzo.* Stanford, Calif., Stanford University Press, 1965. 238 p. $4

This is an excellent sociocultural analysis of change in a city of largely black population and tradition, which is being brought into the national social system. The black traditional system, although changing, is still intact, viable, and flexible. The analysis is made from a national rather than a subcultural point of view. Includes a bibliography. [HLAS 29:1715]

1324

Wiarda, Howard J. *Dictatorship and development; the methods of control in Trujillo's Dominican Republic.* Gainesville, University of Florida Press, 1968. 224 p. map. (Latin American monographs, 2d series, no. 5) $3.75

Focuses on the methods and nature of Rafael Trujillo's dictatorial control of the Dominican Republic from 1930 to 1961. The author offers some conclusions concerning the legacy bequeathed to the island republic by Trujillo's rule. Contains a good bibliography.

1325

Wilbur, W. Allan. *The Monroe doctrine.* Boston, Heath, 1965. 180 p. (New dimensions in American history) $2.08

Presents selections from documents and from secondary sources tracing the history of the Monroe doctrine. Includes a chronology of the evolution of this doctrine. A teacher's edition is also available from the publisher. Includes bibliographies.

1326

Wilcock, John, and Jim Tuck. *Mexico on 5 or 10 dollars a day.* New ed. New York, A. Frommer, 1974. 211 p. illus. $2.95

A guidebook to travel in Mexico, which contains much helpful information concerning lodging, shopping, travel in Mexico.

1327

Wilder, Thornton Niven. *The bridge of San Luis Rey.* New York, Washington Square Press, 1960. 117 p. illus. $.75

First published in 1927, this novel was inspired by a short play by Prosper Merimée, *Le carrosse du Saint Sacrament.* The novel is set in colonial Lima of the 18th century. It centers around a group of people precipitated into a gulf when a bridge breaks.

1328

Wilgus, Alva Curtis, and Raul d'Eça. *Latin American history; a survey of political, economic, social, and cultural events from 1492 to the present.* 5th ed. New York, Barnes & Noble, 1963. 466 p. illus. (College outline series) $2.75

This is a completely revised edition of an outline history which first appeared in 1939. The previous editions were entitled *An outline history of Latin America.* Includes bibliographies.

1329

Wilkerson, Loree A. R. *Fidel Castro's political programs from reformism to Marxism-Leninism.* Gainesville, University of Florida Press, 1965. 100 p. (Latin American monographs 2d series, no. 1) $2

This is a scholarly monograph on the evolution of Castro's programs from the tenets of orthodoxy to communism. Includes a good bibliography.

1330
Wilkie, James Wallace. *Elitelore*. Los Angeles, Latin American Center, University of California, 1973. 87 p. (Latin American studies, v. 22) $3.25

Surveys the upper classes or elite groups in Latin America. This insightful study contains a good bibliography.

1331
Wilkie, James Wallace. *The Mexican Revolution: Federal expenditure and social change since 1910;* with a foreword by Howard F. Cline. 2d ed. rev. Berkeley, University of California Press, 1970. xxx, 337 p. illus. $3.65

Studies the degree of social change and the persistence of poverty in Mexico during four periods: political revolution (1910-30), social revolution (1930-40), economic revolution (1940-60), and balanced revolution since 1960. Examines closely the contrast between projected and actual budgetary expenditures. The author concludes that social change for the masses really began after 1940. An excellent foreword and an important bibliography enhance this valuable contribution. The first edition appeared in 1967. [HLAS 30:1466]

1332
Wilkie, James Wallace. *New hypotheses for statistical research in recent Mexican history.* Los Angeles, Latin American Center, University of California, 1974. 112 p. $.75

This is an important contribution to historiography, describing statistical tools for historical research. Contains a helpful bibliography.

1333
Wilkie, James Wallace, and Albert L. Michaels, comps. *Revolution in Mexico; years of upheaval, 1910-1940.* New York, Knopf, 1969. xiii, 300 p. illus., map. (Borzoi books on Latin America) $3

These carefully selected excerpts from North American and Mexican scholars, journalists, and political figures ably characterize three periods of the Revolution: armed struggle, the rule of the Northern dynasty, and the Cárdenas era. Includes a bibliography. [HLAS 32:1735]

1334
Wilkie, James Wallace. *Statistics and state policy.* Los Angeles, Latin American Center, University of California, 1974. 112 p. $4.50

Discusses various statistical policies within the political context of Latin America. Contains many bibliographical notes.

1335
Williams, Edward J. *The political themes of inter-American relations.* Belmont, Calif., Duxbury Press, 1971. 178 p. $2.50

Describes major trends in inter-American relations during the last 150 years. The topics examined are imperialism, U.S.-Russian rivalry in the hemisphere, distribution of U.S. aid, and the economic disparity between the U.S. and the countries of Latin America. Contains a bibliography.

1336
Williams, Howell, and others. *Geologic reconnaissance of southeastern Guatemala.* Berkeley, University of California Press, 1964. 62 p. illus., maps (part fold.) (University of California publications in geologic sciences, v. 50) $2.50

This is a thorough geologic description of the southeastern portion of Guatemala, with maps, illustrations, and a bibliography.

1337

Williams, Howell, and A. R. McBirney. *Volcanic history of Honduras*. Berkeley, University of California Press, 1971. 71 p. illus., maps. $2.50

Studies the history of volcanic activity in the mountains of Honduras. Contains a bibliography.

1338

Williams, Miller, comp. *Chile: an anthology of new writings*. Kent, Ohio, Kent State University Press, 1968. 1 v. (unpaged) $1.95

This anthology of poetry, one play, and two short stories gives an insight into contemporary Chilean literature. The following writers have been included, among others: Miguel Arteche, Efraín Barquero, Enrique Linn, Pablo Neruda, and Nicanor Parra. The translations are very good. Facsimiles of the authors' signatures have been added.

1339

Williams, Simon, and James A. Miller. *Credit systems for small-scale farmers; case histories from Mexico*. New ed. Austin, Bureau of Business, University of Texas, 1973. xxi, 260 p. (Studies in Latin American business, no. 14) $3

This is a useful addition to a very good series on Latin American business. It presents case studies of agricultural credit to small-scale Mexican farmers. Includes bibliographical references.

1340

Wilson, Carter. *Crazy February; death and life in the Mayan highlands of Mexico*. Berkeley, University of California Press, 1974. 253 p. $2.45

First published in 1965, this novel conveys ethnographic information through a story involving the reader in the dynamics of life of the Maya people of Chamula in the mountains of southeastern Mexico. The book's title comes from the fact that February is the month of the carnival.

1341

Winnie, William W. *Latin American development; theoretical, sectoral, and operational approaches*. Los Angeles, Latin American Center, University of California, 1967. xv, 255 p. (Latin American studies, v. 8) $5

This is the result of a project sponsored by the OAS and the Peace Corps through the Chancellor's Committee on International and Comparative Studies of the University of California at Los Angeles. Includes a thorough bibliography.

1342

Winsberg, Morton D. *Colonia Baron Hirsch, a Jewish agricultural colony in Argentina*. Gainesville, University of Florida Press, [1964] 71 p. illus., maps. (University of Florida monographs. Social Sciences, no. 19) $2

A thorough study of a colony of northern European Jews in Argentina from 1905 to 1962. The emphasis is on the sociological aspects of the community. Includes bibliographical footnotes.

1343

Winsberg, Morton D. *Modern cattle breeds in Argentina; origins, diffusion, and change*. Lawrence, Center of Latin American Studies, University of Kansas, 1968. 59 p. illus., maps. (University of Kansas. Center of Latin American Studies. Occasional publications, no. 13) $2

Explains the diffusion of modern breeds of cattle throughout Argentina, the high concentration of distinct breeds within physical regions, and the reasons for the popularity of various breeds and their fluctuation. Includes a bibliography.

1344

Wise, Sidney Thomas. *Invest and retire in Mexico*. Garden City, N.Y., Dolphin Books, 1973. xi, 200 p. illus. $3.95

> Presents good suggestions on investments in Mexico, and describes the country for the tourist or the person who might wish to live there.

1345

Wolf, Eric Robert, and Edward C. Hansen. *The human condition in Latin America*. New York, Oxford University Press, 1972. x, 369 p. illus. $3.95

> Presents an interesting analysis of social and economic conditions in Latin America, with extensive documentation and a good bibliography.

1346

Wolf, Eric Robert. *Peasant wars of the twentieth century*. New York, Harper & Row, 1969. xv, 328 p. maps. $3.45

> Compares peasant rebellions in Latin America and elsewhere. Suggests that one can rely most on "middle" peasants and "free" lower class peasants (territorially remote from urban centers) for revolutionary movements but only when certain motivating events have occurred. Includes a bibliography.

1347

Wolf, Eric Robert. *Peasants*. Englewood Cliffs, N.J., Prentice-Hall, 1966. xii, 116 p. illus. (Foundations of modern anthropology series) $2.40

> Discusses the changing patterns of farmers and the inhabitants of rural areas when they are faced with increasing industrialization and urbanization of their societies. Includes bibliographical references.

1348

Wolf, Eric Robert. *Sons of the shaking earth*. Chicago, University of Chicago Press, 1959. 302 p. illus. $1.95

> An exciting and authoritative account of the peoples and cultures of Middle America from the earliest times to the present. The presentation of the archeological evidence, particularly in the valley of Mexico, is first-rate. The author's ideas on the importance of irrigation in Mexican prehistory are significant. Includes a bibliography. [HLAS 23:159]

1349

Wolfe, Bertram David. *The fabulous life of Diego Rivera*. New York, Stein and Day, 1969. 457 p. illus. $3.95

> Diego Rivera (1886-1957) is generally considered one of Mexico's most important contemporary artists. The present work deals with the artistic and personal life of this figure. It has 164 black-and-white illustrations of persons and paintings. Includes a bibliography.

1350

Wolff, Egon. *Paper flowers; a play in six scenes*. Translated by Margaret Sayers Peden. Columbia, University of Missouri Press, 1971. 78 p. (A breakthrough book) $3

> This is an English translation of *Flores de papel* which won the Casa de las Américas prize in 1970. Wolff is a well-known Chilean playwright. This play centers around man's need for love. It also reflects Wolff's sensitivity to social reality. Contains vocabulary.

1351

Womack, John. *Zapata and the Mexican Revolution*. New York, Random House, 1970. 480 p. illus. (Vintage books) $2.95

This highly readable, scholarly book won the 1970 Bolton Prize of the Conference on Latin American History. It presents the revolution in Morelos as an exciting story of simple people caught up in a great moment of history. Zapata emerges as the cunning campesino and charismatic leader who guides his people through a successful revolution. Includes a bibliography.

1352

Wood, Bryce. *The making of the Good Neighbor policy.* New York, Norton, 1967. x, 438 p. $3.75

First published in 1961, this work traces the origins of the Good Neighbor policy to the U.S. intervention in Nicaragua in 1926-27, based on documentation and previously unpublished material from the archives of the State Department and the F. D. Roosevelt Library at Hyde Park, N.Y. It will probably remain as the standard reference work on the period. Includes bibliographical references.

1353

Wood, Robert, Brother. *Missionary crisis and challenge in Latin America.* New York, Herder and Herder, 1964. 92 p. $1.25

This is a thoughtful study about the shortage of priests in Latin America and an analysis of the many challenges which the contemporary church faces. Includes bibliographical references. [Charles Fleener]

1354

Wood, Eugene. *How to retire in Mexico.* San Diego, Calif., R. R. Knapp, 1967. 126 p. illus., maps (part fold.) $1.95

Outlines the economic and other advantages of retiring in Mexico. It contains useful information on food, lodging, places to see, real estate, and customs of the country.

1355

Woodward, Ralph Lee. *Class privilege and economic development. The Consulado de Comercio of Guatemala, 1793-1871.* Chapel Hill, University of North Carolina Press, 1966. xviii, 155 p. (The James Sprunt studies in history and political sciences, v. 48) $2.50

This carefully researched monograph describes the functions and operations of the Consulado of Guatemala and analyzes the extent and significance of its role in the economic and political history of Central America. Contains a bibliography.

1356

Woodward, Ralph Lee, comp. *Positivism in Latin America, 1850-1960: are order and progress reconcilable?* Lexington, Mass., Heath [1971] xviii, 130 p. (Problems in Latin American civilization) $2.50

A good introduction precedes selections from Arciniégas, Ardao, Alberdi, Zea, Costa, Rosa, and Romero. Includes a bibliography. [HLAS 34:1474]

1357

Woodyard, George W., ed. *Modern stage in Latin America.* New York, Dutton, 1974. 312 p. $3.45

Contains six modern Latin American plays, with brief essays about the plays and the playwrights.

1358

Worcester, Donald Emmet. *Brazil: from colony to world power.* New York, Charles Scribner's Sons, 1973. 277 p. illus. $3.95

Offers a chronological study of the political history of Brazil, with emphasis on the Empire period. Intended for undergraduate courses. Contains a bibliography.

1359

Worcester, Donald Emmet, and Wendell G. Schaeffer. *The growth and culture of Latin America.* 2d ed. New York, Oxford University Press, 1970-71. 2 v. maps. $4.50

The first edition of 1956 has been updated in the present one. This textbook synthesizes a great body of recent monographic material and reflects modern trends of historiography. It is especially useful for coverage of 17th-century developments. Includes bibliographies.

1360

Worcester, Donald Emmet. *Sea power and Chilean independence.* Gainesville, University of Florida Press, 1962. 87 p. (University of Florida monographs. Social science series, no. 15) $2

Based on published sources, this is a balanced treatment of a topic whose significance extends beyond the independence of Chile. Includes a bibliography.

1361

Wyckoff, Lydia L. *Nicaragua pottery sequence in the Museum collection.* New York, Museum of the American Indian, 1973. 98 p. illus. $2.50

Attractive illustrations enhance the descriptions of pre-Columbian pottery found in the Museum of the American Indian. Contains bibliographical notes.

1362

Yañez, Agustín. *Al filo del agua.* Austin, University of Texas Press, 1970. 209 p. illus. $2.75

First published in 1947, this is Yañez' best known book. It depicts the atmosphere in a small Mexican village on the eve of the Mexican Revolution. In masterful strokes the author has etched the deep religiosity and the collective lethargy of the people.

1363

Yañez, Agustín. *The edge of the storm.* Translated by Ethel Brinton. Illustrated by Julio Prieto. Austin, University of Texas Press, 1971. x, 332 p. (The Texas Pan-American series) $2.95

Al filo del agua (1947) was translated into English in 1963. It brings back to life the theme of the Mexican Revolution years after it has ceased to be useful for novelistic purposes. The translation is very good.

1364

Yates, Donald A., and John B. Dalbor, eds. *Imaginación y fantasía; cuentos de las Américas.* Rev. ed. New York, Harcourt, Brace, and World, 1970. 378 p. $3.25

Includes a selection of Spanish-American short stories, aimed at the beginning and intermediate levels of instruction.

1365

Yates, Donald A., Joseph Sommers, and Julian Palley, comps. *Tres cuentistas hispanoamericanos: Horacio Quiroga, Francisco Rojas González, Manuel Rojas.* New York, Macmillan, 1969. x, 211 p. $3.25

Includes several short stories by a Uruguayan, a Mexican, and a Chilean, providing a good cross-section of idioms and social customs. Each of these authors treats the countryside and the psychology of the people with insight. Includes biobibliographical sketches of the authors.

1366

Ynigo, Alexander. *Mexican-American children in an integrated elementary school.* San Francisco, R. & E. Research Associates, 1974. 105 p. $7

Originally prepared as a thesis in 1957, this study surveys the social adjustment and academic factors affecting Mexican-American children in an Anglo-American environment. Includes a bibliography.

1367

Yoder, Howard W. *This is Latin America.* New York, Friendship Press, 1961. 34 p. illus. $.85

Introduces the reader to Protestant work in Latin America. Intended to give a basis for understanding this area.

1368

Young, Jordan M., ed. *Brazil 1954-64: end of a civilian cycle.* New York, Facts on File, 1972. 197 p. (Interim history) $4.45

Presents a factual analysis of Brazil's political, economic, and social history from the downfall of Getulio Vargas to the assumption of power by Alencar Castelo Branco.

1369

Zárate, Agustín de. *Discovery and conquest of Peru; translation of Books I to IV of Augustín de Zárate's History...* compiled and translated with and introd. by J. M. Cohen. Harmondsworth, England, Penguin, 1968. 282 p. maps. (The Penguin classics) $1.95

In addition to Zárate's remarkable first-hand chronicle, the translator has interpolated material by six other persons who took part in the conquest, as well as material by Cieza de León and Garcilaso de la Vega. Translation of *Historia del descubrimiento y conquista del Perú* (1955).

1369A

Zeh, Erwin. *Brazil.* Tokyo, Palo Alto, Calif., Kodansha International; distributed by Harper & Row, New York, 1974. 138 p. illus. (This beautiful world) $2.75

An attractively illustrated travel book on South America's largest country.

1370

Zeitlin, Maurice, and Robert Scheer. *Cuba: tragedy in our hemisphere.* New York, Grove Press, 1963. 316 p. $1.95

Describes the Cuban Revolution. The authors have traveled to Cuba since Castro came to power. The book is based on documents and news sources. Contains bibliographical references.

1371

Zeitlin, Maurice. *Revolutionary politics and the Cuban working class.* New York, Harper & Row, 1970. 306 p. $1.95

First published in 1967, this book is based on data drawn from interviews with industrial workers in revolutionary Cuba during the 1962-66 period.

1372

Zelayeta, Elena Emilia. *Elena's fiesta recipes.* Rev. ed. Foreword by Helen E. Brown. Los Angeles, W. Ritchie Press, 1968. 126 p. illus. $1.95

Assembles a wonderful variety of recipes for Mexican dishes and some Central American favorites.

1373

Zelayeta, Elena Emilia. *Elena's secrets of Mexican cooking.* New York, Doubleday, 1970. 204 p. illus. $1.95

Includes a good assortment of recipes and hints on how to master Mexican cooking.

1374

Zorrilla de San Martín, Juan. *Tabaré; an Indian legend of Uruguay.* Translated by Walter Woen. Washington, Pan American Union, 1956. 366 p. $2.75

An English translation of *Tabaré* by the Uruguayan poet and essayist Juan Zorrilla de San Martín (1885-1931). The protagonist is a mestizo born of a Charrúa chief and a captive Spanish woman. It is an epic poem about the Spanish spiritual conquest of the Indians.

spain and portugal

1375
Abbruzzese, Marghierita. *Goya.* New York, Grosset and Dunlap, 1970. 100 p. $1.50

Contains an overview of the Spanish painter's work and an introduction to his life and times.

1376
Abreu-Gómez, Ermilo, and Joseph S. Flores. *Historias de Don Quijote.* New York, Van Nostrand, 1970. 261 p. $2.75

This is a textbook edition of stories from *Don Quijote* to be used in Spanish-language courses.

1377
Aceves, Joseph B. *Social change in a Spanish village.* Cambridge, Mass., Schenkman Pub. Co., 1973. xii, 145 p. illus. (The Schenkman series on socio-economic change) $2.95

Introduces the reader to the problems of rural Spain and presents a detailed ethnographic study of the Castillian village of El Pinar, near Valladolid. The author outlines the resistance to change in the village, coupled with an eager acceptance of the same.

1378
Adams, Nicholson Barney, and John E. Keller. *History of Spanish literature; a brief survey.* Paterson, N.J., Littlefield, Adams, 1962. 206 p. map. (The New Littlefield college outline series, no. 38) $1.95

Presents a succinct overview of Spanish literature from the early Middle Ages to the 20th century. A well-written and successful work.

1379
Agoncillo, Teodoro A. *A short history of the Philippines.* New York, New American Library, 1969. 319 p. (A Mentor book, MW-963) $1.50

This short history of the Philippines includes detailed information about the period from the time of contact to 1899, during which the Philippines were part of the Spanish colonial empire.

1380
Agostini de del Rio, Amelia A., ed. *Flores del romancero.* Englewood Cliffs, N.J., Prentice-Hall, 1970. 276 p. $4.25

"Romances" are brief epic-lyric poems recited or sung with the accompaniment of musical instruments. This book provides an excellent sampling of Spanish popular ballads and poems from the earliest medieval romances through those of the 17th century. Includes a bibliography and a glossary of terms.

1381
Ainaud de Lasarte, Juan. *Romanesque Catalan art.* Panel painting. New York, Tudor Pub. Co., 1965. 95 p. illus. $2.25

A brief introduction prefaces the 15 small but excellent reproductions of superb examples of romanesque panel paintings that still survive in Catalonia.

1382
Alarcón, Pedro Antonio de. *El sombrero de tres picos.* Edited by Edmund V. de Chasca. 2d ed. Columbus, Ohio, Xerox College, 1969. 322 p. illus. $3.95

Alarcón's most successful novel was based on a popular ballad, *El molinero de Arcos.* It deals with a tale of a corregidor's love for a miller's wife, set in the early 19th century. The descriptions of a small town and its people are humorous.

1383
Alarcón, Pedro Antonio de. *El sombrero de tres picos. Adapted from the story by Pedro Antonio de Alarcón,* and edited with notes, direct-method exercises and vocabulary by James P. Wickersham Crawford. New York, Macmillan, 1969. 200 p. $1.95

A good textbook edition of *The three cornered hat.*

1384
Alarcón, Pedro Antonio de. *The three cornered hat. A modern translation,* with notes, edited by Glenn Wilbern. New York, American RDM, 1966. 250 p. $1.25

This is an English-language textbook edition of the Alarcón classic work.

1385
Alarcón, Pedro Antonio de. *The three cornered hat.* Translated by Harriet de Onís. Woodbury, N.Y., Barron's, 1964. 198 p. $1.25

Mrs. de Onís has given us an excellent translation of this witty, charming Spanish classic. It is intended for classroom use.

1386
Alas, Leopoldo. *La Regenta,* by Clarín [pseud.] Philadelphia, Center for Curriculum Development, 1969. 240 p. $2.40

A textbook edition of one of the most important novels written in Spain in the 19th century. First published in 1885, it depicts life in Oviedo (Vetusta in the book) and revolves around a love story in which La Regenta, a married woman, is the coveted prize. The novel is reminiscent of Flaubert and Zola.

1387
Alas, Leopoldo. *Su único hijo,* by Clarín [pseud.] Philadelphia, Center for Curriculum Development, 1970. 131 p. $1.20

Clarín's second full-length novel, first published in 1890, is presented here in abridged form. In this novel one can find naturalistic influences as well as the idealistic tendency which began to affirm itself in the author's work toward the end of the century.

1388
Alberti, Rafael. *Selected poems.* Edited and translated by Ben Belitt. Introd. by Luis Monguió. Berkeley, University of California Press, 1966. x, 219 p. illus. $1.75

Contains a bilingual edition of some 50 poems by Alberti which originally appeared between 1929 and 1954. The poet's own drawings serve as illustrations. Monguió's introduction captures the poet's life and work.

1389
Aldecoa, Ignacio. *Santa Olaja de Acero y otras historias.* Philadelphia, Center for Curriculum Development, 1968. 167 p. $1.20

Aldecoa is one of the most influential novelists of present-day Spain. He returns to a traditional posture in this novel.

1390
Alexius, Saint. *Legend; see* Allen, Joseph H. D., 1392

1391
Allen, John Jay. *Don Quixote, hero or fool; a study in narrative technique.* Gainesville, University of Florida Press, 1969. 90 p. (University of Florida monographs. Humanities, no. 29) $2

The author analyzes widely divergent critical opinions toward Don Quixote throughout the history of literature. Includes bibliographical footnotes.

1392
Allen, Joseph H. D., ed. *Old Portuguese versions of the Life of Saint Alexis; Codices Alcobacenses 36 and 266.* Urbana, University of Illinois Press, 1970. 67 p. illus. $3

This is a very thorough linguistic, semantic, and textual study of the Codices Alcobacenses. Both codices are presented at the end of the analysis, and 21 black-and-white plates of the texts themselves enhance the work.

1393
Alpern, Hymen, ed. *Three classic Spanish plays: Sheep well, by Lope de Vega; Life is a dream, by Calderón de la Barca; None beneath the king, by Rojas Zorrilla.* New York, Washington Square Press, 1963. x, 229 p. (The ANTA series of distinguished plays, W660) $.60

Includes English translations of three well-known and important plays of the Spanish Golden Age: *Fuente ovejuna,* by Lope de Vega; *La vida es sueño,* by Calderón de la Barca; and *Del rey abajo ninguno,* by Rojas Zorrilla.

1394
Alpert, Michael, ed. *Two Spanish picaresque novels.* Edited and translated by Michael Alpert. Baltimore, Penguin Books, 1969. 214 p. (Penguin classics L211) $1.45

Presents new translations of *El Lazarillo de Tormes* (1554) and Francisco Quevedo's *Vida del Buscón* (1626). Both classics depict social conditions in 16th- and 17th-century Spain, and each has rascal heroes living by their wits.

1395
Alvarez Harvey, Maria Luisa. *Cielo y tierra en la poesía lírica de Manuel Altolaguirre.* Hattiesburg, University and College Press of Mississippi, 1972. 143 p. $2.95

This in-depth literary analysis approaches Altolaguirre's work from a philosophical as well as a poetic point of view. A bibliography and list of poems studied complete this work.

1396
Anderson-Imbert, Enrique, and Lawrence B. Kiddle, eds. *Veinte cuentos españoles del siglo XX.* Edited, with introd., notes, and vocabulary by Enrique Anderson-Imbert and Lawrence B. Kiddle. New York, Appleton-Century-Crofts, 1970. 303 p. $3.75

Presents a selection of Spanish short stories of the 20th century, with notes and vocabularies.

1397
Appolonio, Umbro. *Picasso.* Translated from the Italian by Cesare Foligno. New York, Crown Publishers, 1965. 26 p. illus. (10 mounted color plates) $1.45

This handsomely illustrated book reproduces representative works by the great Spanish master.

1398

Armistead, Samuel G., and Joseph H. Silverman, eds. *Judeo-Spanish ballads from Bosnia;* with the collaboration of Biljana Sljvić-Simsić. Philadelphia, University of Pennsylvania Press, 1971. x, 129 p. (University of Pennsylvania publications in folklore and folklife, no. 4) $6.50

> Exiled from the mainstream of Hispanic culture at the end of the Middle Ages, Judeo-Spanish language and folk literature became a living, contemporary document of late 15th-century linguistic forms. This documentary publication does not analyze individual ballads.

1399

Arnett, Willard Eugene. *George Santayana.* New York, Washington Square Press, 1968. 184 p. (The Great American thinkers series) $.75

> This is a lucid and succinct study of the life and works of the Spanish-born philosopher who spent most of his life in the U.S.

1400

Arnheim, Rudolf. *Picasso's Guernica; the genesis of a painting.* Berkeley, University of California Press, 1962. 139 p. illus. $5.95

> Describes and analyzes the sketches and stages that came to form Picasso's famous painting, "Guernica." It is a fascinating and insightful work on the creative process. Very good illustrations enhance the text.

1401

Arrabal, *Fernando. The architect and The emperor of Assyria.* Translated from the French by Everart d'Haroncourt and Adele Shank. New York, Grove Press, 1970. 93 p. (Evergreen original E486) $2.40

> Includes English translations of two plays by the most controversial and avant-garde Spanish playwright.

1402

Arrabal, Fernando. *Guernica and other plays.* Translated from the French by Barbara Wright. New York, Grove Press, 1969. 126 p. (Evergreen original E521) $1.95

> Includes English translations of *Labyrinth, Picnic on the battlefield,* and *Tricycle,* in addition to *Guernica,* by the internationally acclaimed Spanish playwright.

1403

Atkinson, William C. *History of Spain and Portugal.* Baltimore, Penguin Books, 1969. 382 p. illus. (The Pelican history of the world) $1.45

> Presents a useful survey of the history of the Iberian peninsula from the earliest period until 1956.

1404

Ayala, Francisco. *La cabeza del cordero.* Edited by Keith Ellis. Englewood Cliffs, N.J., Prentice-Hall, 1968. 196 p. $4.25

> A textbook edition of four short stories by one of the outstanding Spanish writers of fiction. The Spanish civil war is at the center of these stories. Ayala examines the tragic effects of civil conflicts on society and the resulting deterioration of human relationships. Includes an extensive vocabulary.

1405

Ayala, Francisco. *Muertes de perro.* Philadelphia, Center for Curriculum Development, 1969. 150 p. $1.20

> A textbook edition of Ayala's novel about an invalid intellectual and his tortuous inner life. Includes vocabularies and a glossary of terms.

1406

Ayala, Francisco. *El rapto.* Edited by Phyllis Zatlin Boring. New York, Harcourt Brace Jovanovich, 1971. xii, 132 p. $2.50

Intended as a reader for intermediate Spanish courses, it also serves as a good introduction to the Spanish contemporary novel. Ayala is one of the major figures of 20th-century Spanish literature. Includes a bibliography and vocabularies.

1407

Baker, J. F., and I. Almeida Ariza, eds. *España a la vista.* New York, Pergamon Press, 1970. 200 p. illus. $2.50

Provides travel information and a cursory glance at Spanish culture and civilization.

1408

Barnes, Richard G., ed. *Three Spanish sacramental plays.* Translated and with an introd. by R. G. Barnes. San Francisco, Chandler Pub. Co., 1969. x, 103 p. (Chandler editions in drama) $2.25

Includes *For our sake*, by Lope de Vega; *King Belshazzar's feast*, by Calderón de la Barca; and *The bandit queen*, by Maestro Josef de Valdivielso. Barnes' introduction describes the "auto sacramental" and synthesizes the careers of the three playwrights.

1409

Baroja y Nessi, Pío. *El árbol de la ciencia.* Edited by Gerard C. Flynn. New York, Appleton-Century-Crofts, 1970. xxii, 314 p. $2.75

Pío Baroja is considered, after Benito Pérez Galdós, the leading novelist of modern Spanish literature. First published in 1911, this novel deals with the incongruities of the modern world and its growing technology. Includes vocabularies.

1410

Baroja y Nessi, Pío. *El árbol de la ciencia.* Philadelphia, Center for Curriculum Development, 1969. 200 p. $1.20

Textbook edition of above.

1411

Baroja y Nessi, Pío. *Las ciudades; César o nada; El mundo es ansí; La sensualidad pervertida.* Philadelphia, Center for Curriculum Development, 1972. 463 p. $2.40

These short stories by Baroja reflect his theories about the intellect and nature and are quite his pessimism about the possibility of improving people and society. Includes notes and vocabulary.

1412

Baroja y Nessi, Pío. *Cuentos.* Philadelphia, Center for Curriculum Development, 1972. 215 p. $1.20

Includes several short stories by this leading Spanish novelist well known for his dynamic style and practical approach to life.

1413

Baroja y Nessi, Pío. *The restlessness of Shanti Andía, and selected stories.* Translated by Anthony and Elaine Kerrigan. New York, New American Library, 1962. 330 p. (Signet, CT149) $.75

An English translation of a fast-moving novel about the wonderings of a Basque sailor. Also included are six short stories and an extensive introduction to the world of Pío Baroja by Anthony Kerrigan.

1414

Barrett, Linton Lomas, ed. *Five centuries of Spanish literature; from the Cid through the Golden Age.* New York, Dodd, Mead, 1968. 352 p. $6.25

Includes representative selections of Spanish prose and poetry from the Middle Ages through the 17th century. This is a helpful anthology.

1415

Barrios, Miguel de. *La poesía religiosa.* Columbus, Ohio State University Press, 1962. 357 p. $5

Miguel de Barrios was the pseudonym of Daniel Levi de Barrios (1635-1701), born in Montilla, Spain. He lived in Amsterdam during most of his life. In his writings, this convert to Catholicism from Judaism returns to a primitive mysticism. Kenneth R. Scholberg edited these religious poems. Includes bibliographies.

1416

Barrow, Leo L., and Charles F. Olmstad. *Aspectos de la literatura española.* Columbus, Ohio, Xerox College, 1972. xiv, 186 p. $4.25

Examines 10 main aspects of the Spanish novel, as well as the 10 most important elements in Spanish poetry in an effort to study Spanish literature in depth. Examples are given. Includes bibliographies, glossaries, and a vocabulary.

1417

Basdekis, Demetrios. *Miguel de Unamuno.* New York, Columbia University Press, 1970. 48 p. (Columbia essays on modern writers, 44) $1

This essay provides a succinct analysis of the writings of the great Spanish philosopher and novelist. Includes a bibliography.

1418

Beene, Gerrie, and Lourdes Miranda King. *Dining in Spain.* Rutland, Vt., C.E. Tuttle, 1969. 197 p. $2.50

The recipes in this book are authentic and more than half of them are the specialities served in Madrid's most distinctive restaurants. It includes a guide to and a description of the wines of Spain.

1419

Bell, Aubrey Fitz Gerald. *Baltasar Gracián.* New York, Hispanic Society of America, 1968. 100 p. $2

This is a study of Baltasar Gracián y Morales, Spanish moral philosopher and naturalist of the 17th century, and his concern for ethical principles and rules of conduct for leaders.

1420

Bell, Aubrey Fitz Gerald. *Benito Arias Montano.* New York, Hispanic Society of America, 1969. 120 p. $2

Presents Arias Montano, theologian, writer, philosopher, and naturalist of 16th-century Spain. He knew several oriental languages and was one of the most erudite men of his times. He was professor of oriental languages at the Escorial Monastery and the author of many learned treatises. Includes a bibliography.

1421

Bell, Aubrey Fitz Gerald. *Cervantes.* New York, Macmillan, 1961. 247 p. $.95

The author bases his biography largely on the works of Cervantes, searching his words for a revelation of the poet and the philosopher.

1422

Bell, Aubrey Fitz Gerald. *Diogo do Couto*. New York, Hispanic Society of America, 1972. 82 p. (Hispanic notes and monographs. Portuguese series, vi) $2

Couto was a historian of the Portuguese conquests in India, a prose writer, and poet. He continued the *Decadas* begun by João de Barros. This is a valuable biography of the life and times of Couto. Includes bibliographical notes.

1423

Bell, Aubrey Fitz Gerald. *Fernán López*. New York, Hispanic Society of America, 1969. 90 p. $2

Biography of a Portuguese chronicler of the 15th century, whose works about the reigns of Pedro I, Fernando I, and Juan I are outstanding.

1424

Bell, Aubrey Fitz Gerald. *Francisco Sánchez, el Brocense*. New York, Hispanic Society of America, 1972. xii, 166 p. $2

This is a good biography of a man whom Menéndez y Pelayo called "the father of general grammar and of the philosophy of language." He was one of the great scholars of 16th-century Spain, who was famous as a humanist in the later Renaissance. Includes bibliographic notes.

1425

Bell, Aubrey Fitz Gerald. *Gaspar Corrêa*. New York, Hispanic Society of America, 1972. 93 p. $2

Corrêa was one of the great historians of India in 16th-century Portugal. His *Lendas da India* was not published until 1858. None of the historians of India have given us slices of life as has Corrêa. This is a very good biography of the historian.

1426

Bell, Aubrey Fitz Gerald. *Gil Vicente*. New York, Hispanic Society of America, 1967. 140 p. $2

Gil Vicente (1470?-1536?) was a Renaissance dramatist and lyric poet, born in Portugal, who wrote most of his works in Spain. He wrote over 40 plays of which only seven were in Portuguese. This is a good biography and analysis of Vicente and his works.

1427

Bell, Aubrey Fitz Gerald. *Juan Ginés de Sepúlveda*. New York, Hispanic Society of America, 1969. 106 p. $2

Biography of a philosopher and outstanding classicist of the 16th century. Erasmus considered him the most erudite man of the century. His works on philosophy and theology were controversial and created heated polemics. Includes a bibliography.

1428

Bell, Aubrey Fitz Gerald. *Luis de Camões*. New York, Hispanic Society of America, 1969. 152 p. illus. $2

Camões (1524-1580) is considered Portugal's greatest poet. Some critics consider that Camões reached his height as a lyric poet. Undoubtedly, his best known work remains *Os Lusíadas*, an epic poem of the Portuguese empire. This is a handsome, brief study on Camões.

1429

Benavente y Martínez, Jacinto. *Bonds of interest. Los intereses creados*. Translated by J.

G. Underhill. Edited, rev., and with an introd. by Hymen Alpern. Bilingual ed. New York, Ungar, 1967. 160 p. $1.75

This play was first published in 1907 by the Spanish Nobel Prize-winning playwright Benavente (1886-1954). This is a charming allegorical morality play, generally considered Benavente's masterpiece. Includes vocabularies.

1430
Benavente y Martínez, Jacinto. *Los malhechores del bien.* Edited by Irving A. Leonard and Robert K. Splauding. New York, Macmillan, 1963. xxvii, 126 p. (The Macmillan Hispanic series) $1.95

This is a textbook edition, with notes and vocabulary, of a play written in 1905 in which Benavente shows great depth and intensity.

1431
Benavente y Martínez, Jacinto. *La malquerida.* Edited, with introd., notes, and vocabulary by Paul T. Manchester. New York, Appleton-Century-Crofts, 1959. xxxii, 143 p. $2.65

This is a rustic tragedy, simple and masterful in its dramatic structure. It was first published in 1913.

1432
Benedikt, Michael, and George S. Wellworth, eds. *Modern Spanish theater; an anthology of plays.* New York, Dutton, 1969. xx, 416 p. $2.95

Includes eight 20th-century Spanish plays which combine the theater of anguish with the theater of magic. Valle-Inclán, García Lorca, Casona, and Arrabal are represented among these dramas which span the 1913-63 period. Includes music of songs in some of the plays.

1433
Benson, Frederick R. *Writers in arms; the literary impact of the Spanish Civil War.* Foreword by Salvador de Madariaga. New York, New York University Press, 1971. xxx, 345 p. map. (New York University studies in comparative literature, 1) $2.95

Examines the major influence of the Spanish civil war on European and American literature. It considers those writers who were active participants in the conflict and whose writings illuminate the various perspectives of this cataclysm. Includes bibliographies.

1434
Bentley, E., ed. *Six Spanish plays: The Celestina, by Fernando de Rojas; The siege of Numantia, by Miguel de Cervantes; Fuenteovejuna, by Félix Lope de Vega; The trickster of Seville, by Tirso de Molina; Love after death; [and] Life is a dream, by Calderón de la Barca.* New York, Doubleday, 1969. 380 p. $2.50

Contains the six most important plays of the Golden Age of Spanish literature. This attractive edition includes bibliographies.

1435
Berger, John. *The success and failure of Picasso.* Baltimore, Penguin Books, 1965. 210 p. illus. (incl. ports.) $2.25

Picasso's life and work from his "Blue Period" through Cubism, and up to the present, are depicted in this ambitious study of the man and the artist. The 120 illustrations add depth to both the biographical and critical aspects of the work.

1436
Bertrand, Louis, and Charles Petrie. *History of Spain.* Translated by Warre B. Wells. 2d

ed., rev. and continued to the year 1945. New York, Macmillan, 1972. xv, 431 p. illus., maps. $2.95

First published in 1937, this standard Spanish history consists of four main sections: Moslem Spain; discovery and conquest of the New World; absolute monarchy and Reformation; and Spain since the reign of Philip II. Includes a bibliography.

1437

Birmingham, David. *The Portuguese conquest of Angola.* New York, Oxford University Press, 1965. 51 p. maps. $1

A brief survey of the establishment of Portuguese hegemony in Angola from 1483 to the late 18th century. Includes a bibliography.

1438

Blanco Aguinaga, Carlos, ed. *Lista de los papeles de Emilio Prados en la Biblioteca del Congreso de los Estados Unidos de América.* Con pref. de Howard F. Cline. Baltimore, Johns Hopkins Press, 1967. xiv, 47 p. port. $3.50

After the death of the Spanish poet Emilio Prados in 1962, his papers were deposited in the Library of Congress, where they were cataloged and microfilmed. Professor Blanco arranged the papers and prepared the present listing. The papers include drafts of poems and autobiographical material from 1925 to 1962. Includes an appendix listing Prados' works.

1439

Blasco Ibañez, Vicente. *Blood and sand.* Translated by Frances Partridge. Introd. by Isaac Goldberg. New York, Ungar, 1964. 240 p. $1.45

English translation of *Sangre y arena* which was first published in 1908 and immediately went on to become a bestseller. It is a romantic and picturesque novel with a bullfighter as the protagonist.

1440

Blasco Ibañez, Vicente. *Reeds and mud.* Translated by Lester Beberfall. Boston, Branden Press, 1972. 194 p. $1.95

English translation of *Cañas y barro* (1902), one of the author's regional Valencian novels, which depicts local types and customs with naturalistic detail.

1441

Blaud, Henry C. *The Basques.* San Francisco, R. and E. Research Associates, 1974. 116 p. $8

One of the few historical and sociological studies on this ethnic group, originally presented as a thesis in 1957. Contains a bibliography.

1442

Booton, Harold W. *Architecture of Spain.* Chester Springs, Pa., Dufour, 1970. 130 p. illus. $1.95

This is an attractive book, with handsome illustrations, about Spanish architecture.

1443

Bosquet, Alain. *Conversations with Dali.* Translated from the French by Joachim Neugroschel. New York, Dutton, 1969. 123 p. $1.45

English translation of *Entretiens avec Salvador Dali.* Typically mercurial and quotable Daliisms abound here, as well as shrewd and knowing observations on the history and craft of painting. Also includes Dali's essay "The Conquest of the irrational'' in which he comments on the place of surrealism in 20th-century culture.

1444

Boxer, Charles R. *Four centuries of Portuguese expansion, 1415-1825; a succinct survey.* Berkeley, University of California Press, 1961. 102 p. illus., map. $1.65

The text of four lectures given by the author in South Africa in 1960. Some documentation has been added to the present edition. Includes bibliographies.

1445

Brademas, Stephen John. *Anarcosindicalismo y revolución en España; 1930-1937.* Traducción castellana de Joaquín Romero Maura. Barcelona, Editorial Ariel, 1974. 295 p. $3

Based on the author's dissertation at Oxford, this is a scholarly study of the different labor factions during the republican and early civil war periods of Spain. Contains a massive bibliography. The translation into Spanish is excellent. An English version is scheduled to appear in 1976.

1446

Bradford, Saxtone E. *Spain in the world.* Princeton, N.J., Van Nostrand, 1962. 121 p. maps. (Van Nostrand searchlight book, no. 3) $1.95

A somewhat outdated analysis of Spain as a cultural and political entity in the modern world.

1447

Braider, Donald. *Private life of El Greco.* New York, Dell, 1969. 461 p. illus. $1.25

Studies the tormented life of a great artist whose life seemed cursed with misfortune. He witnessed the depletion of his family fortunes, the mental collapse of María, his young bride, and the public condemnation of the woman he loved. Although born in Greece, he has become identified with Spain. His paintings put on canvas the counter-Reformation period of Spain.

1448

Brandi, Karl. *The Emperor Charles V; the growth and destiny of a man and a world-empire.* Translated from the German by C.V. Wedgewood. New York, Humanities Press, 1968. 655 p. $4

First published in 1939, this excellent biography of Charles V stresses his role as emperor rather than king of Spain. Unfortunately the annotations and bibliography of the original German edition are not included here.

1449

Brault, Gerard J., ed. *Celestine: a critical ed. of the first French translation (1527) of the Spanish classic La Celestina,* with an introd. and notes by Gerard J. Brault. Detroit, Wayne State University Press, 1963. 264 p. (Wayne State University studies no. 12. Humanities) $8

The full title of the Spanish classic is *La tragicomedia de Calisto y Melibea,* published in Burgos in 1499. This is a valuable scholarly contribution to medieval literature.

1450

Braymer, Nan, and Lillian Lowenfels, eds. and trs. *Modern poetry from Spain and Latin America.* New York, Corinth Books, 1964. 63 p. $1.45

Contains translations of representative selections by modern Spanish and Spanish American poets.

1451

Brenan, Gerald. *The literature of the Spanish people; from Roman times to the present day.* New York, World Pub. Co., 1957. 494 p. $4.05

This is a succinct history of Spanish literature from its origins to the present.

1452

Brenan, Gerald. *The Spanish labyrinth, an account of the social and political background of the Civil War.* 2d ed. Cambridge, England, University Press, 1960. xx, 384 p. maps. $2.45

First published in 1943, this history of Spain covers the 1874-1936 period. It focuses on the four decades preceding the Spanish Civil War. Includes a bibliography.

1453

Brent, Albert. *Leopoldo Alas and La Regenta; a study in nineteenth century Spanish prose fiction.* Columbia, University of Missouri Press, 1971. 135 p. $2.50

First published in 1951, this is a thorough stylistic and subject study of *La Regenta* (1884-85) which depicts every stratum of the cathedral city of Oviedo. The author analyzes Clarín's accurate psychological analysis. Contains a bibliography.

1454

Brokenau, Franz. *Spanish cockpit: an eye-witness account of the political and social conflict of the Spanish civil war.* Ann Arbor, University of Michigan, 1963. 303 p. $2.95

Originally published in 1937, this book was written by a political analyst. It describes the specific characteristics of the Spanish conflict and paints a gripping picture of those critical years.

1455

Buchanan, Milton A., ed. *Spanish poetry of the Golden Age.* Edited, with an introd. and notes by Milton A. Buchanan. 2d ed. rev. Toronto, University of Toronto Press, 1966. 149 p. $4

Includes 113 poems by writers ranging from the Marqués de Santillana (1398-1458) to Sor Juana Inés de la Cruz (1651-1695). The poems appear in Spanish but are exhaustively annotated in English footnotes.

1456

Buero Vallejo, Antonio. *En la ardiente oscuridad, drama en tres actos.* Edited by Samuel A. Wofsy. With an introd. by Juan R. Castellano. New York, Scribner, 1964. 196 p. illus. $2.95

This play can easily be adapted to performances by Spanish classes. The setting of the play is an institution for the blind, with most inmates being blind from birth. An atmosphere of carefree optimism prevails, and a love affair blooms. Contains notes and vocabulary.

1457

Buero Vallejo, Antonio. *Las cartas boca abajo.* Edited by Félix G. Ilárraz. Englewood Cliffs, N.J., Prentice-Hall, 1971. 302 p. $3.50

One of the author's most acclaimed tragedies, it deals with some of the negative aspects of contemporary Spanish society. It won the Premio Nacional de Teatro of Spain in 1958. The play centers around the failure of a mediocre professor. Contains notes, vocabulary, and an introduction.

1458

Buero Vallejo, Antonio. *El concierto de San Ovidio*. Edited with notes and vocabulary by Pedro N. Trakas. Introd. by Juan R. Castellano. New York, Scribner, 1965. 215 p. (The Scribner Spanish series) $2.95

This is an annotated textbook edition of this contemporary Spanish play set in a home for the blind in Paris in 1771. The blind are asked by the director of the home to give a concert. It is a moving psychological drama with excellent dialog. First produced in 1962.

1459

Buero Vallejo, Antonio. *Dos dramas de Buero Vallejo: Aventura en lo gris; dos actos y un sueño. Las palabras en la arena; tragedia en un acto*. Edited with an introd., notes, and exercises by Isabel Magaña Schewill. New York, Appleton-Century-Crofts, 1967. xi, 259 p. illus., port. $3.65

The first play included in this work was written in 1949 and produced in 1963. The second drama was also written in 1949, and it deals with an adultery based on a biblical episode. This is an annotated textbook edition with a vocabulary.

1460

Buero Vallejo, Antonio. *Historia de una escalera; drama en tres actos*. Edited by J. Sánchez. New York, Scribner, 1955. 179 p. illus. (The Scribner Spanish series for colleges) $2.95

This is a play depicting the life and customs of people in the vicinity of Madrid. The characters belong to the Spanish lower middle class and the play represents the dilemma between hope and despair of those struggling with poverty. Contains notes and vocabulary.

1461

Buero Vallejo, Antonio. *Madrugada; episodio dramático en dos actos*. Edited by Donald Bleznick and Martha T. Halsey. Waltham, Mass., Blaisdell Pub. Co., 1969. xxviii, 111 p. port. (A Blaisdell book in the modern languages) $2.75

Contains an annotated textbook edition of Buero Vallejo's play, dealing with the lives of lower middle class people in Madrid. The central theme is the inheritance of the main female character. The play was written and produced in 1953.

1462

Buero Vallejo, Antonio. *Las Meninas; fantasía velazqueña en dos partes*. Edited with introd. and notes by J. Rodríguez-Castellano, vocabulary by Helen K. Castellano. New York, Scribner, 1963. 237 p. $2.95

Buero Vallejo's historical play presents an episode in the life of the Spanish court painter Diego Velázquez. The central theme is a trial by the Inquisition. The characterizations in this important play are excellent. Includes notes and vocabulary.

1463

Buero Vallejo, Antonio. *Un soñador para un pueblo; versión libre de un episodio histórico en dos partes*. Editado con introducción, notas y vocabulario, por M. Manzanares de Cirre. New York, Norton, 1966. 131 p. illus. $1.85

First presented on the stage in 1958, this play deals with the struggle of the individual against society. The setting is Spain during the reign of Charles III.

1464

Buñel, Luis. *Buñel: three screenplays*. New York, Grossman, 1970. $3.50

Includes the screenplays of *Viridiana, The exterminating angel,* and *Simon of the desert.*

1465

Burnshaw, Stanley, ed. *The poem itself; 45 modern poets in a new presentation, the French, German, Spanish, Portuguese, Italian poems, each rendered literally in an interpretive discussion.* Associate editors: Dudley Fitts, Henri Peyre, John Frederick Nims. New York, Schocken Books, 1967. 337 p. $2.95

First published in 1960, this work includes 10 important poets from Spain and Portugal: Rosalía Castro, Miguel de Unamuno, Antonio Machado, Juan Ramón Jiménez, León Felipe, Fernando Pessoa, Pedro Salinas, Jorge Guillén, Federico García Lorca, and Rafael Alberti. Highly recommended for serious students of modern comparative literature. The selection of poets from the Iberian peninsula is representative; the editors include a major poetic figure of the 19th century in Rosalía Castro, who is not widely known outside her homeland because she wrote mostly in Gallegan (the dialect of her native Galicia) rather than in Castilian Spanish.

1466

Busoni, Rafaello. *The man who was Don Quixote; the story of Miguel de Cervantes.* Written and illustrated by Rafaello Busoni, editorially assisted by Johanna Johnston. New York, Avon Books, 1973. 209 p. illus. $.60

This charming children's book tells the story of Miguel de Cervantes through the elaborate adventures of Don Quixote. Each event in his life is beautifully illustrated by Rafaello Busoni. Highly recommended for children with an interest in history and literature.

1467

Butler, Richard. *The life and world of George Santayana.* Chicago, H. Regnery, 1960. 205 p. $1.45

Studies the life and work of George Santayana, the Spanish philosopher who spent most of his life in the United States.

1468

Byne, Arthur, and M. Stapley. *Decorated wooden ceilings in Spain.* New York, Hispanic Society of America, 1960. 90 p. illus. $2

An attractive description of decorated wooden ceilings in Spain.

1469

Byne, Arthur, and M. Stapley. *Spanish interiors and furniture.* With a brief text by Mildred Stapely. New York, Dover Publications, 1969. xxii p. 300 photographs and drawings. $6

Spanish interior decorative schemes and furniture are presented here with taste and an excellent sense of history.

1470

Caballero, Fernán [pseud.] *La gaviota.* Edited by G. W. Umprey and F. Sánchez y Escribano. Boston, Heath, 1970. 321 p. $3.50

Fernán Caballero (1796-1877) was Cecilia Bohl de Faber, born in Switzerland, the daughter of a Spanish mother and German father. She had lived in Andalusia from the age of 17. She wrote her first novel, *La gaviota*, in 1849 in French and translated it into Spanish.

1471

Caballero, Fernán [pseud.] *La gaviota. The sea gull.* Translated by J. MacLean. Woodbury, N.Y., Barron Educational Series, 1966. 246 p. $1.75

This is a textbook edition of *La gaviota* (1849), a romantic story of a peasant girl who marries a German surgeon, becomes an opera singer, falls in love with a bullfighter, and after the deaths of both husband and lover, marries a village barber.

1472

Cabat, Louis, and Robert Cabat. *The Hispanic world; a survey of the civilizations of Spain and Latin America.* New York, Oxford Book Co., 1969. 179 p. illus. $2

Presents the Hispanic cultural background to prepare those who wish to study the Spanish language. Suitable for high school or college freshmen. Also available in a Spanish edition entitled *Mundo hispánico* ($2).

1473

Calderón de la Barca, Pedro. *El alcalde de Zalamea.* Edited with introd., and notes by Peter N. Dunn. Oxford, New York, Pergamon Press, 1969. 380 p. (The Commonwealth and International library) $2.95

This is a textbook edition of Calderón's most famous tragedy dealing with honor. Contains notes and vocabulary.

1474

Calderón de la Barca, Pedro. *Four plays: Secret vengeance for secret insult; The phantom lady; The mayor of Zalamea; The devotion to the cross.* Translated by Edwin Honig. New York, Hill and Wang, 1969. 302 p. $1.95

Professor Honig has prepared excellent English translations of these plays. *A secreto agravio secreta venganza* (1635) is a tragedy dealing with the defense of honor; *La dama duende* (1629) is an amusing comedy revolving around love, intrigue, and honor; *El alcalde de Zalamea* (1642) is also a tragedy about defending honor; and *La devoción a la cruz* (1633) is a theological play.

1475

Calderón de la Barca, Pedro. *Life is a dream.* Translated by William E. Colford. Woodbury, N.Y., Barron's Educational Series, 1960. 101 p. $1.25

This is a textbook edition of Calderón's beautiful allegorical drama, whose central character is Segismundo. Through him the playwright explores the mysteries of human destiny, the illusory nature of everyday existence, and the conflict between predestination and free will.

1476

Calderón de la Barca, Pedro. *The mayor of Zalamea (El alcalde de Zalamea).* Translated and introd., by William E. Colford. Woodbury, N.Y., Barron's Educational Series, 1961. 131 p. (Barron's Educational Series) $1.25

A useful textbook edition with notes, glossary, and vocabulary.

1477

Calderón de la Barca, Pedro. *Tragedias one: La vida es sueño; La hija del aire; El mayor monstruo del mundo.* Philadelphia, Chilton, 1969. $1.80

A textbook edition of the well-known masterpiece *La vida es sueño*, as well as the historical comedy about Semiramis, Queen of Ninive entitled *La hija del aire* (1653), and the religious play *El mayor monstruo del mundo* (1637).

1478

Calderón de la Barca, Pedro. *Tragedias 3: Los cabellos de Absalón; Devoción de la cruz; El mágico prodigioso; Las cismas de Inglaterra.* Introd. by Francisco Ruiz Ramón. Philadelphia, Center for Curriculum Development, 1970. 539 p. $2.40

Presents four religious tragedies of the Spanish Golden Age.

1479

Calderón de la Barca, Pedro. *La vida es sueño; and El alcalde de Zalamea.* Introd. and notes by Sturgis E. Leavitt. New York, Dell Pub. Co., 1962. 239 p. $.50

This is a textbook edition, with notes and vocabulary, of Calderon's two masterpieces.

1480

Calvo Sotelo, Joaquín. *La muralla, comedia dramática en dos partes, dividida cada uno en dos cuadros.* Editores Robina E. Henry and Enrique Ruiz-Fornells. New York, Appleton-Century-Crofts, 1962. 112 p. $1.95

A textbook edition of this contemporary Spanish play.

1481

Camões, Luís Vaz de. *The Lusiads;* translated by William C. Atkinson. Harmondsworth, England, Penguin, 1952. 248 p. (The Penguin classics L26) $1.95

A very good English translation of the famous Portuguese epic, which celebrates Portugal's global empire and the exploits of the navigators. Contains bibliographical references.

1482

Cannon, W. C., ed. *Modern Spanish poems.* New York, Macmillan, 1969. 289 p. $2.25

An anthology of modern Spanish poems which includes the most outstanding modern poets, starting with the late 19th century.

1483

Cano, José Luis, ed. *Tema de España en la poesía española contemporánea.* Philadelphia, Center for Curriculum Development, 1964. 300 p. $3.95

The editor has prepared a representative anthology of contemporary Spanish poetry.

1484

Carbonell, Reyes. *El hombre sobre el armario y otros cuentos.* Prólogo de Juan Antonio de Zunzunegui. Edited by Leonard C. de Morelos and Adela Lafora. New York, Harper & Row, 1967. xv, 230 p. $3.25

Contains the title story, as well as *El reloj, Ay! literatura,* and *El loro,* by a Valencian short story writer.

1485

Carreira, Antonio. *Social and economic organization of the people of Portuguese Guinea.* Riverside, N. J., C.C.M. Information Corp., 1974. 264 p. $11

Analyzes and describes social stratification and economic structure in Portuguese Guinea. Contains bibliographical references.

1485A

Carter, Henry Hare; *see Liuro de Josep Abaramatia. The Portuguese book of Joseph of Arimathea,* 1698

1486

Casona, Alejandro. *Los árboles mueren de pie.* Edited by J. Castellano. New York, Holt, Rinehart & Winston, 1973. 220 p. $4.40

This is a Spanish-language edition of Casona's popular comedy revolving around a Spanish family. Includes notes and vocabulary.

1487

Casona, Alejandro. *El caballero de las espuelas de oro.* Edited by José A. Balseiro and Eliana Suárez-Rivero. New York, Oxford University Press, 1968. xxxiv, 130 p. $1.95

The most famous era of Spanish culture, the Golden Age, comes to life in this play by Casona based on the life of Francisco Quevedo. The editors' preface and introduction provide a rich background for students of Spanish literature.

1488

Casona, Alejandro. *Corona de amor y muerte.* Edited by José A. Balseiro and J. Riis Owre. New York, Oxford University Press, 1969. 269 p. $2.75

The play centers around several romantic entanglements and is suited for staging as a classroom play by intermediate and advanced Spanish classes.

1489

Casona, Alejandro. *Nuestra Natacha.* Edited by William H. Shoemaker. New York, Appleton-Century-Crofts, 1968. 200 p. $1.95

This is a textbook edition of a cheerful contemporary Spanish play.

1490

Castañeda, James A. *A critical edition of Lope de Vega's Las paces de los reyes y judía de Toledo.* Chapel Hill, University of North Carolina Press, 1962. 265 p. facsims. (North Carolina. Studies in the Romance languages and literatures, no. 40) $5

The general theme is the hypothetical love affair of Alfonso VIII of Castile and the Jewess of Toledo. The author examines the historical background and the literary treatments of the legend. Includes a bibliography.

1491

Cela, Camilio José. *La colmena.* The complete novel edited with notes and vocabulary by José Ortega. New York, Las Americas Pub. Co., 1966. 311 p. $4

A textbook edition of Cela's most ambitious novel. The editor has added a vocabulary in the form of footnotes and an appendix of all the madrileñismos and other idiomatic expressions. Recommended for advanced Spanish courses.

1492

Cela, Camilo José. *La familia de Pascual Duarte.* Edited by Harold L. Bodreau and John W. Kronik. New York, Appleton-Century-Crofts, 1967. 175 p. illus. $2.45

This is a Spanish edition of Cela's masterful book which had a powerful impact on the Spanish novel of the post-civil war period. Includes a vocabulary and is eminently suited for classroom use.

1493

Cela, Camilo José. *The family of Pascual Duarte.* Translated and with an introd. by Anthony Kerrigan. 13th ed., rev. New York, Avon Books, 1964. 144 p. $1.45

English translation of *La familia de Pascual Duarte* (1942), a probing account of the harsh life of a poor Spanish family. There is a great deal of existential despair in Pascual who killed the things he loved the most. Pascual is an anti-hero trying to escape his spiritual crisis. This novel introduced a literary movement known as tremendismo reflecting the anguish of everyday life. It also marked the revival of the picaresque novel, breaking with the innocuous forms of the decade preceding the mid-1940's.

1494

Cela, Camilo José. *The hive.* Translated by J. M. Cohen, in consultation with Arturo Barrea. With an introd. by Arturo Barrea. New York, Noonday Press, 1965, 247 p. (Noonday, 276) $1.95

English translation of *La colmena* (1951) which critics consider Cela's best book. He presents Madrid in the 1940's in the wake of the civil war where hunger is a stark reality. The characters' tormented existence reflects a penetrating examination of Hispanic values.

1495

Cela, Camilo José. *Mrs. Caldwell speaks to her son. Mrs. Caldwell habla con su hijo,* in the authorized English version by J. S. Bernstein. Ithaca, N. Y., Cornell University Press, 1968. xxvi, 206 p. $2.45

Cela wrote this work in 1953. He used the technique of letters written by Mrs. Caldwell to her dead son. The brief chapters on an incestuous mother-son relationship are subtle and poetic.

1496

Cervantes Saavedra, Miguel de. *Deceitful marriage and other exemplary novels.* A new translation with a foreword by Walter Starkie. New York, New American Library, 1970. 320 p. (A Signet classic, CT-157) $.75

This is a new translation of *El casamiento engañoso* with a foreword by Walter Starkie. Spain's greatest novelist wrote this work in a realistic style.

1497

Cervantes Saavedra, Miguel de. *Don Quijote de la Mancha.* New York, Macmillan, 1960. 410 p. $2.50

Cervantes' masterpiece was published in 1605 under the title *El ingenioso hidalgo don Quijote de la Mancha,* the story of a naive country gentleman who decides to become a knight errant. The book is a satire of the romances of chivalry.

1498

Cervantes Saavedra, Miguel de. *Don Quijote de la Mancha.* Edited by W. Tardy. Skokie, Ill., National Textbook Corp., 1969. 301 p. $1.25; 5 or more copies $1 each

This is a textbook edition of *Don Quijote.* . . .

1499

Cervantes Saavedra, Miguel de. *Don Quixote de la Mancha.* Translated by Charles Jarvis. Abridged and edited with an introd. by Lester G. Crocker. New York, Washington Square Press, 1957. 446 p. $.95

A handsome abridged edition of Cervantes' classic in English translation.

1500

Cervantes Saavedra, Miguel de. *Don Quixote de la Mancha.* Translated by John M. Cohen. Baltimore, Penguin Books, 1961. 390 p. $1.95

This is an English translation of the Spanish masterpiece.

1501

Cervantes Saavedra, Miguel de. *Don Quixote de la Mancha.* Translated by Pierre A. Motteux. Introd. by Henry Grattan Doyle. New York, Modern Library, 1959. 836 p. $1.45

The perceptive introduction and concise biographical notes on Cervantes are very helpful in reading this excellent edition. Includes a bibliography of select titles.

1502

Cervantes Saavedra, Miguel de. *Don Quixote.* Translated by Peter Motteux. New York, Airmont, 1968. 799 p. $1.75

Raymond R. Canon provides a brief biographical sketch of the author. The publisher elliptically reveals that this version is "Ozell's revision of the translation of Peter Motteux." [Charles Fleener]

1503

Cervantes Saavedra, Miguel de. *Don Quixote de la Mancha.* Translated and edited by

Walter Starkie. New York, New American Library, 1968. 501 p. (Signet, CV-622) $1.95

This is an unabridged edition with a perceptive and useful introduction by the translator.

1504

Cervantes Saavedra, Miguel de. *Don Quixote of la Mancha*. Translated and edited by Walter Starkie. New York, New American Library, 1968. 324 p. (Mentor books, MY-1163) $1.25

This is an abridged edition in which the translator provides an excellent introduction to the life and times of Cervantes.

1505

Cervantes Saavedra, Miguel de. *Exemplary novels of Cervantes*. Cranbury, N.J., Barnes, 1960. 143 p. illus. $1.25

First published in 1952, this selection includes *The generous lover, The little gypsy,* and *The jealous Estremaduran,* from Cervantes' immortal *Novelas ejemplares* (1613), a collection of 12 short stories in the style of the Italian novella but with an ethical purpose.

1506

Cervantes Saavedra, Miguel de. *Interludes*. New translation, with foreword by Edwin Honig. New York, New American Library, 1969. 220 p. $.75

This is an outstanding translation of *Entremeses* (1615), with an insightful foreword on the work of Cervantes.

1507

Cervantes Saavedra, Miguel de. *The portable Cervantes*. Translated and edited by Samuel Putnam. New York, Viking Press, 1968. 420 p. $3.50

First issued in 1949, this well-known translation includes both parts of *Don Quijote,* complete, with all omitted passages covered by editorial summaries. Also included are two exemplary novels and *Foot in the stirrup,* as well as an excellent introduction by Putnam.

1508

Cervantes Saavedra, Miguel de. *Rinconete and Cortadillo*. Boston, Branden Press, 1972. 97 p. $.85

This is a textbook edition of one of Cervantes' exemplary novels.

1509

Cervantes Saavedra, Miguel de. *Selections from Don Quixote*. Translated and edited by Florence Fishman. Woodbury, N. Y., Barron's Educational Series, 1970. 390 p. $1.95

A useful textbook edition of selections from *Don Quijote,* with notes, glossary, and vocabularies.

1510

Cervantes Saavedra, Miguel de. *Six exemplary novels*. Translated and edited by Harriet de Onís. Woodbury, N. Y., Barron's Educational Series, 1967. 297 p. illus $2.50

Includes *Dialogue of the dogs (Coloquio de los perros), Master glass (Licenciado Vidriera), Gypsy maid (La gitanilla), Rinconete y Cortadillo, Jealous hidalgo (El celoso extremeño),* and *The illustrious kitchen maid (La ilustre fegona),* which are six of the 12 short stories which Cervantes published under the title *Novelas ejemplares* in 1613.

1511

Cervantes Saavedra, Miguel de. *Tales from Don Quixote.* New York, Pyramid Books, 1970. 280 p. $.35

> Contains selected stories from *Don Quixote* in English translation, with bibliographical references.

1512

Chapman, Charles Edward. *A history of Spain; founded on the Historia de España y de la civilización española of Rafael Altamira.* New York, Free Press, 1965. xv, 559 p. (Free Press paperbacks) $2.95

> An excellent history emphasizing Spain in America from 1492 to 1808. It is a good cultural and political history of great interest for students of Spain.

1513

Chase, Gilbert. *The music of Spain.* 2d ed. New York, Dover, 1959. 383 p. illus. $2.50

> This is a historical study of Spanish music from the Middle Ages to the present.

1514

Chilcote, Ronald H., ed. *Emerging nationalism in Portuguese Africa; a bibliography of documentary ephemera through 1965.* Stanford, Calif., Hoover Institution on War, Revolution and Peace, 1969. 114 p. (Hoover Institution Bibliographical series, 39) $4

> A useful bibliography on nationalism in the Portuguese territories of Africa.

1515

Chilcote, Ronald H. *Portuguese Africa.* Englewood Cliffs, N. J., Prentice-Hall, 1968. x, 149 p. (A Spectrum book: The modern nations in historical perspective) $1.95

> Analyzes Portuguese policy in its various stages of conquest, pacification, and colonization in the African territories of Angola, Moçambique, Portuguese Guiné, and the islands of Cape Verde, Santo Tomé, and Principe over the last 500 years. Attempts to give both the African and Portuguese perspectives. Includes a bibliography.

1516

Church, Margaret. *Don Quixote: the knight of La Mancha.* New York, New York University Press, 1971. xxxvi, 179 p. $2.95

> Intended for the general reader of *Don Quixote,* this book gives a chapter by chapter analysis of structural, thematic, and stylistic nuances of this famous Spanish classic.

1517

El Cid Campeador. *The epic of the Cid.* Translated by Gerald Markley. Indianapolis, Bobbs-Merrill, 1961. 132 p. $1.45

> The translator provides a concise introduction to the classic epic of Spain's national hero of the Middle Ages, Rodrigo Díaz de Vivar (1040?-1099). The name "El Cid" is derived from the Arabic title "Sidi" meaning my lord. The epic appeared in 1140.

1518

El Cid Campeador. *Poem of the Cid.* Translated by William S. Merwin. New York, New American Library, 1962. 301 p. (Mentor books, MQ-995) $.95

> This bilingual edition contains an English verse translation of the epic with the Spanish text edited by Ramón Menéndez Pidal.

1519

El Cid Campeador. *Poem of the Cid.* Translated by Lesley Byrd Simpson. Berkeley, University of California Press, 1965. 304 p. $1.95

This textbook edition is a good translation of the epic, depicting the legendary exploits of the solider-hero Rodrigo Díaz de Vivar.

1520

El Cid Campeador. *Poem of the Cid; a modern translation with notes,* edited by G. Willbern; translated by Paul Blackburn. New York, R.D.M. Corp., 1966. 155 p. (Study master. Publication T-44) $1.95

An abbreviated textbook edition of the Spanish epic.

1521

El Cid Campeador. *Poems of the Cid selections.* Translated by Leonard E. Amaud. Great Neck, N.Y., Barron's Educational Series, 1972. 135 p. $.95

Provides selections from *El Cid.*

1521A

Clarín [pseud.] ; *see* Alas, Leopoldo

1522

Clark, Fred M. *Objective methods for testing authenticity and the study of ten doubtful comedias attributed to Lope de Vega.* Chapel Hill, University of North Carolina Press, 1971. 185 p. (University of North Carolina studies in the Romance languages and literatures, no. 106) $5

Examines the orthoepy and rhyme patterns of 10 plays attributed to Lope de Vega. The author has accumulated all the possible non-Lopean elements to find out whether they provide sufficient evidence to consider them as written by other authors.

1523

Clarke, Dorothy Clotilde. *Allegory, decalogue, and deadly sins in La Celestina.* Berkeley, University of California Press, 1969. 310 p. $4.50

The author analyzes and presents the allegories in this remarkable Spanish medieval drama.

1524

Cohen, John Michael, ed. *The Penguin book of Spanish verse.* Rev. ed. Baltimore, Penguin Books, 1960. 472 p. $1.75

Ranging from *El Cid* to Claudio Rodríguez (b. 1934), more than 100 poets are represented in this anthology in prose translation. Many Latin American poems are also included. This is a bilingual edition.

1525

Coleman, John A. *Other voices; a study of the late poetry of Luis Cernuda.* Chapel Hill, University of North Carolina Press, 1969. 185 p. (Studies in the romance languages and literatures, no. 81) $3.50

Studies the post-1936 poetry of Luis Cernuda. The poet's approach is the "the suppression of the subjective in poetry, and the concomitant elaboration of objective, dramatic voices which define the trajectory between the first and third persons, the lyric and the dramatic." Includes a bibliography.

1526

Colford, William E., ed. *Classic tales from modern Spain.* Woodbury, N. Y., Barron's Educational Series, 1964. 201 p. $1.50

Contains short stories by 19th- and 20th-century authors ranging from Gustavo Adolfo Bécquer to Vicente Blasco Ibañez.

1527

Connell, Geoffrey, ed. *Spanish poetry of the grupo poético de 1927.* Elmsford, N. Y., Pergamon Press, 1974. 326 p. $3.95

Includes poetry by Rafael Alberti and other Spanish poets who were known as the "Group of '27."

1528

Contreras, Alonso de. *Vida, nacimiento, padres y crianza del Capitán Alonso de Contreras.* Philadelphia, Chilton Book Co., 1969. 199 p. $.90

A textbook edition of the autobiography of the famous Spanish adventurer and soldier of fortune of the 17th century. Includes vocabulary and notes.

1529

Corredor, José María. *Conversations with Casals,* translated from the French by André Mangeot. With an introd. by Pablo Casals and an appreciation by Thomas Mann. New York, Dutton, 1957. 240 p. illus., ports. $1.55

The great Spanish musician gives his opinions on music, politics, and a variety of other subjects. He emerges as a warm, intelligent, and direct human being. The French original *Conversations avec Pablo Casals* appeared in 1954.

1530

Corrigan, Robert Willoughby, ed. and tr. *Masterpieces of the modern Spanish theater.* New York, Macmillan, 1967. 384 p. $1.50

J. Benavente's *Witches' Sabbath,* G. Martínez Sierra's *Cradle song,* F. García Lorca's *Love of Don Perlimplín,* and A. Buero Vallejo's *Death thrust* are the plays included in this anthology.

1531

Cox, Ralph Merritt. *The Rev. John Bowle; the genesis of Cervantean criticism.* Chapel Hill, University of North Carolina Press, 1971. 123 p. (University of North Carolina studies in the Romance languages and literatures, no. 99) $5

The author's primary concern is to bring out of obscurity the Rev. John Bowle who brought forth the first truly learned edition of *Don Quixote* 170 years after its publication in Spain. A must for Cervantes scholars.

1532

Crabb, Daniel M. *Critical study guide to Cervantes' Don Quixote.* Totowa, N. J., Littlefield, Adams, 1966. 122 p. map. $1

An introduction and chapter-by-chapter summary of the most important Spanish classic, which will be of help to students of Spanish literature.

1533

Daix, Pierre. *Picasso.* New York, Praeger, 1965. 271 p. illus. (Praeger world of art profiles) $3.95

This is an illustrated edition which includes a good selection of Picasso's works as well as an introduction to the artist's life and work.

1534

Damase, Jacques. *Pablo Picasso.* Translated by Hayden Barnes. New York, Barnes and Noble, 1965. 90 p. (Art series illustrated) $.95

Includes 72 illustrations, 24 of which are color reproductions. The introduction gives a concise survey of the life and work of the artist.

1535
Davidson, Basil. *In the eye of the storm; Angola's people.* Garden City, N. Y., Anchor Press, 1973. xiv, 386 p. maps. $2.95

Discusses the history of Angola and the role of Portugal, as well as the emergent nationalism and guerrilla activities. Includes a bibliography.

1536
Davies, Reginald Trevor. *The golden century of Spain, 1501-1621.* New York, Harper and Row, 1967. xi, 325 p. illus., maps. $2.75

This is an excellent study of 16th century Spain by a noted English historian, especially valuable for its emphasis on economic and social aspects. Maps, illustrations, and a thorough bibliography enhance the text.

1537
Delano, Lucille K. *Oh lovely Spain!* Rock Hills, S. C., Lucille K. Delano, 1973. 350 p. illus. $10

The author visited Spain both before and after the civil war. Her most recent trip took place in 1970. She displays a fine sense of Spanish history and culture and adds much local color to her descriptions of the most interesting and enjoyable places for tourist to see. Includes a bibliography.

1538
Delibes, Miguel. *El camino.* Edited by José Amor y Vásquez, and Ruth H. Kosoff. New York, Harcourt, Brace and World, 1960. 244 p. illus. $3.60

A textbook edition of Delibes' novel which appeared in 1950 and is considered among the best Spanish novels of the last two decades.

1539
Delibes, Miguel. *La partida.* Philadelphia, Center for Curriculum Development, 1954. 162 p. $1.50

First published in 1954, this is a widely read Spanish novel. The characters are firmly delineated and represent specific psychological types. This is an annotated textbook edition, with notes and vocabulary.

1540
Delibes, Miguel. *Viejas historias de Castilla la Vieja.* Philadelphia, Center for Curriculum Development, 1964. 85 p. illus. $1.20

Describes the Spanish province of Castilla la Vieja. Attractive photographs enhance the text.

1541
De Onís, Harriet, ed. *Cuentos y narraciones en lengua española.* New York, Washington Square Press, 1961. 304 p. $.60

Contains substantially the same collection of stories as appeared in the English translation in the editor's *Spanish short stories and tales,* first published in 1954. See next entry.

1542
De Onís, Harriet, ed. *Spanish short stories and tales.* New York, Washington Square Press, 1964. 288 p. $.60

These short stories have been selected for their literary value and their intrinsic interest.

1543

Deyermond, A. D. *A literary history of Spain.* New York, Barnes & Noble, 1973. 3 v. $4 each

Presents a succinct literary history of Spain aimed at the undergraduate level. Contains a bibliography.

1544

Diaz, Janet Winecoff. *The major themes of existentialism in the works of Ortega y Gasset.* Chapel Hill, University of North Carolina Press, 1970. 233 p. (University of North Carolina. Studies in the Romance languages and literatures, no. 94) $6.50

The author approaches the Spanish philosopher's major works "from the perspective of a positive hypothesis of existentialist concepts, with an attempt made to relate his principal publications to an overall philosophy of life." An important scholarly work with a thorough bibliography.

1545

Diffie, Bailey W. *Prelude to empire: Portugal overseas before Henry the Navigator.* Lincoln, University of Nebraska Press, 1960. xxii, 321 p. illus. (A Bison book original, BB108) $2.25

Demonstrates the importance of the Portuguese overseas experience before 1415 to the subsequent period of the great discoveries. This is a scholarly and interesting work with extensive annotations, an index, and a brief bibliography.

1546

Dixon, R.A.N. *Spain.* drawings by Barbara Crocker. Chicago, Rand McNally, 1967. 96 p. illus. (some col.), col. maps. $1

Describes Spain, chiefly from the geographical point of view. Contains attractive illustrations.

1547

Duffy, James. *Portugal in Africa.* Harmondsworth, England, Baltimore, Penguin Books, 1962. 239 p. illus., maps. (Penguin African Library, AP3) $.95

The author surveys Portuguese Africa from the explorations of the 15th century to the growing colonial problems of the Salazar regime. Includes bibliography.

1548

Durán, Manuel, and Federico Alvarez, eds. *Voces españolas de hoy.* Under the general editorship of Robert G. Mead, Jr. New York, Harcourt, Brace & World, 1965. 216 p. $4.50

Planned for the intermediate Spanish student, this work contains poems, stories, essays, and a long play. The authors range from León Felipe and Blas de Otero, to Vicente Aleixandre and Alfonso Sastre. Includes biographical sketches of the authors, notes, and vocabulary.

1549

Durgnat, Raymond. *Luis Buñuel.* Berkeley, University of California Press, 1969. 144 p. front. (port.), illus. $2.45

This is a study of the acclaimed contemporary film director's work.

1550

Ebersole, Alva Vernon, comp. *Cinco cuentistas contemporáneos.* Edited by A. V. Ebersole in collaboration with Jorge Campos. Englewood Cliffs, N. J., Prentice-Hall, 1969. 213 p. ports. $3.50

Includes contemporary Spanish short stories by J. Campos, D. Sueiro, C. Ianzo, M. Fraile, and F. García.

1551

Elliott, John H. *The old world and the new, 1492-1650.* (The Wiles lectures, 1969). New York, Cambridge University Press, 1970. 180 p. $1.95

Discusses the intellectual, economic, and social consequences of the discovery and settlement of America for early modern Europe. Analyzes the way in which contact with new lands and peoples challenged a number of traditional assumptions about astronomy, geography, history, and the nature of man.

1552

Elliott, John H. *Imperial Spain, 1469-1716.* New York, New American Library, 1966. 406 p. illus. $.95

This book by a prominent English Hispanist is of great interest to students of history. It presents a synthetic account of the most important years of the Spanish empire without detailed narrative. Includes a bibliography.

1553

Enggass, Robert, and Jonathan Brown, eds. *Italy and Spain, 1600-1750; sources and documents.* Englewood Cliffs, N. J., Prentice-Hall, 1970. xi, 239 p. illus. (Sources and documents in the history of art series) $4.50

This college text consists of translations with introductions of important source materials relevant to the art of Spain. Includes bibliographical footnotes.

1554

Eoff, Sherman Hinkle. *The modern Spanish novel; comparative essays examining the philosophical impact of science on fiction.* New York, New York University Press, 1961. 280 p. $1.95

A probing study of the influence of science on late 19th-century and modern European literature. The authors thoroughly studied in these essays include José María Pereda, Leopoldo Alas, Emilia Pardo Bazán, Vicente Blasco Ibañez, Benito Pérez Galdós, Pío Baroja, Miguel de Unamuno, and Ramón Sender.

1555

Espronceda y Delgado, José de. *El diablo mundo; El estudiante de Salamanca; Poesías.* Philadelphia, Center for Curriculum Development, 1970. 247 p. $1.20

Contains textbook editions of *El diablo mundo,* an unfinished poem; *El estudiante de Salamanca,* a verse legend; and a sampling of poems by Spain's great romantic poet of the 19th century noted for his lyricism and emotional power. Includes vocabularies.

1556

Estep, Gerald A. *Social placement of the Portuguese in Hawaii as indicated by factors in assimilation.* San Francisco, R. and E. Research Associates, 1974. 135 p. $8

A sociological study of the social mobility of the Portuguese ethnic group in Hawaii. Includes a bibliography.

1557

Fabian, Donald L. *Tres ficciones breves.* Boston, Houghton Mifflin, 1968. 162 p. $3.50

Includes three short stories: "El tesoro del holandés" by Pío Baroja, "Nada menos que todo un hombre" by Miguel de Unamuno, and "La cruz del diablo" by Gustavo Adolfo Bécquer. The book is intended for intermediate Spanish courses and includes notes and vocabularies.

1558

Feis, Herbert. *The Spanish story; Franco and the nations at war*. New York, Norton, 1966. xii, 282 p. (The Norton library, N-339) $1.85

First published in 1948, this is a history of Spain's diplomatic and trade relations with the allied and axis powers during World War II, written by a Pulitzer Prize-winning historian.

1559

Ferrater Mora, José. *La filosofía actual*. Philadelphia, Chilton Education Series, 1969. 188 p. $1.20

The author outlines his thoughts and comments on modern philosophy.

1560

Ferrater Mora, José. *Unamuno, a philosophy of tragedy*. Translated by Philip Silver. Berkeley, University of California Press, 1962. 135 p. $1.50

Presents and examines Unamuno's philosophy. This is an English translation of *Unamuno: bosquejo de una filosofía* published in 1957. Includes a good bibliography.

1561

Ferreira, Eusébio da Silva. *My name is Eusébio*, by Eusébio da Silva, assisted by Fernando F. Garcia. Translated by Derrik Low. New Rochelle, N. Y., Soccer Associates, 1968. 166 p. illus. $2.50

Entertainingly and accurately written story of the great soccer player from Moçambique. Well-chosen illustrations, including the World Cup, enhance the text. English translation of *Meu nome é Eusébio*.

1562

Fitzmaurice-Kelly, Julia. *Antonio Perez*. New York, Hispanic Society of America, 1970. 170 p. $2

First published in 1922, this is a biography of Antonio Pérez (1534-1611), a Spanish writer and politician who had been secretary to Philip II. After a court scandal he fled to Aragón and died in exile in France. He corresponded with major European political figures of his era.

1563

Fitzmaurice-Kelly, Julia. *Cervantes in England*. New York, Haskell House, 1970. 180 p. $1.95

Studies the impact of Cervantes' works on the intellectual and literary life of England.

1564

Flores, Ángel, ed. *Great Spanish short stories*. Selected and introduced by Angel Flores. New York, Dell, 1962. 304 p. $.60

The editor has included 17 short stories by Spanish and Latin American writers, including pieces by Azorín, Valle-Inclán, López y Fuentes, Borges, and Rulfo. Contains an excellent introduction.

1565

Flores, Ángel, comp. *Selecciones españolas; a basic Spanish reader*. New York, Bantam Books, 1967. 231 p. (A Bantam monolingual edition) $1.25

Included are selections from the works of Spanish and Spanish American writers such as Benito Lynch, Azorín, Borges, Ricardo Palma, Luis Taboada, José María Bárcenas, and others. Includes notes.

1566

Flores, Angel, ed. *Spanish stories; cuentos españoles; stories in the original Spanish,* with English translations. New York, Bantam Books, 1960. 339 p. (A Bantam dual lingual book) $.95

>This is a bilingual edition of stories by 13 masters of the Spanish language from Spain and Latin America. It includes Cervantes, Alarcón, Clarín, Borges, Cela, and Goytisolo, as well as an excellent introduction by the editor.

1567

Floyd, Troy S., ed. *The Bourbon reformers and Spanish civilization: builders or destroyers?* Edited and translated with an introd. by Troy S. Floyd. Boston, Heath, 1966. xx, 87 p. (Problems in Latin American civilization) $2.50

>The essays presented here attempt to analyze the complex and enduring historical debate over the Bourbon rulers of Spain (1700-1808). The readings were drawn from the writings of Spanish and Latin American political figures and scholars of the 18th and 19th centuries. Includes bibliographical footnotes.

1568

Fraker, Charles F. *Studies on the Cancionero de Baena.* Chapel Hill, University of North Carolina Press, 1970. 460 p. (University of North Carolina. Studies in the Romance languages and literatures, no. 61) $5

>A thorough, scholarly work on the *Cancionero de Baena* which appeared in 1445. It is one of the earliest Castilian anthologies of songs and lyric poetry. Includes bibliographies.

1569

Franco, Jean, ed. *Short stories in Spanish; cuentos hispánicos.* Baltimore, Penguin Books, 1966. 204 p. (Penguin parallel texts) $.95

>This is a bilingual edition of eight short stories by Camilo José Cela and other contemporary Spanish writers. Includes a bibliography.

1570

Frank, Bruno A. *A man called Cervantes.* New York, Popular Library, 1970. 301 p. $.60

>A popular and well-written introduction to Cervantes and his times.

1571

Froissart, Jean. *The chronicles of England, France, Spain, etc.* Introd. by Charles W. Dunn. New York, Dutton, 1961. 616 p. illus. (A Dutton everyman paperback, D75) $2.75

>Contains a condensed version of Froissart's chronicles, which have been ranged with historical romances like Ivanhoe. Froissart was born in 1337 at Valenciennes. The chronicles deal with the history, culture, and politics of the 14th century.

1572

Frothingham, Alice Wilson. *Barcelona glass in Venetian style.* New York, Hispanic Society of America, 1972. 49 p. illus. (Hispanic notes & monographs, essays, studies, and brief biographies) $2

>Barcelona glassmakers, like others in Europe, imitated the art perfected by the Venetians. This work traces the development of glassmaking in Barcelona. The work is enhanced by excellent illustrations.

1573

Frothingham, Alice Wilson. *Hispanic glass, with examples in the collection of the Hispanic Society of America...* with 125 illustrations. New York, Hispanic Society of America, 1961. xviii, 204 p. illus., plates. (Hispanic notes and monographs; essays, studies, and brief biographies. Catalogue series) $1.50

In 1248 King Alfonso the Wise began to disseminate among his subjects the craft of glassmaking. This book traces the history of Spanish glass and presents superb examples from different eras and from several parts of the country. Contains a bibliography.

1574

Gagliardo, John G. *Enlightened despotism.* New York, Crowell, 1967. 118 p. (Europe since 1500: a paperback series) $2.25

Surveys recent historical research concerning the era of enlightened despotism in Western European history (1760-90). Charles III of Spain and the Marquis de Pombal of Portugal are closely examined. Includes a good select bibliography.

1575

Ganivet, Ángel. *Los trabajos del infatigable creador Pío Cid.* Philadelphia, Center for Curriculum Development, 1965. 389 p. $2.35

This novel is a spiritual autobiography of Ganivet, first published in 1898. It analyzes the intrinsic qualities of the Spanish character.

1576

Gaquere, François. *Children of Fatima.* Boston, Daughters of St. Paul, 1970. 79 p. illus. $.35

Describes briefly the Fatima shrine's history as a devotional center in Portugal and in Europe.

1577

García, Salvador. *Las ideas literarias en España entre 1840 y 1850.* Berkeley, University of California Press, 1971. xiii, 206 p. (University of California publications in modern philology, v. 98) $4.50

Analyzes the 1840-50 decade in Spanish literature which saw the decline of romanticism. The author examines numerous literary journals, theater production, the novel, and *costumbrismo.* A very important contribution, with a critical chapter, annexes, and bibliography.

1578

García Lorca, Federico. *Five plays; comedies and tragicomedies.* Translated by James Graham-Lujan and Richard L. O'Connell. New York, New Directions, 1968. 246 p. $1.75

Includes *The shoemaker's prodigious wife, The love of Don Perimplín and Belisa in the garden, Doña Rosita, the spinster, Billy club puppets,* and *The butterfly's evil spell.* The last is an incomplete play which was Lorca's first, and serves as an appendix demonstrating the author's development. Prof. Francisco García Lorca provides a good introduction to his brother's work. Includes melodies used in the plays.

1579

García Lorca, Federico. *Gypsy ballads of García Lorca.* Translated by Rolfe Humphries with three historical ballads. Bloomington, Indiana University Press, 1968. 64 p. (Indiana University poetry series) $1.45

Romancero gitano (1928) made García Lorca an immediate success. Many of his ballads were soon recited everywhere, were sung by common people, and enriched the treasure of traditional poetry. The poet took his subjects from the people and incorporated them into his stream of living art.

1580

García Lorca, Federico. *Obras escogidas.* Introd. and noted by Eugenio Florit. New York, Dell, 1967. 208 p. (The Laurel language library. Spanish series) $.95

Includes a selection of poems by Spain's most intense and original poet of this century.

1581

García Lorca, Federico. *Poet in New York.* Complete Spanish text, with a new translation by Ben Bellitt. Introd. by Ángel del Río. New York, Grove Press, 1961. 192 p. port. $1.95

García Lorca's trip to the United States (1929-30) is reflected in his *Poeta en Nueva York* (1940?). It describes the impression the modern city made upon the poet. It shows the influence on him of many contemporary trends, especially surrealism. The work exudes rich imagery, a sense of reality, and the dramatic pace that is the hallmark of the poet's work.

1582

García Lorca, Federico. *Selected poems.* Edited by Francisco García Lorca and Donald M. Allen. Norfolk, Conn., New Directions, 1970. 180 p. (The new classics series) $1.50

This bilingual edition contains selections from *Libro de poemas* (1921), *Poema del cante jondo* (1921), *Primeras canciones* (1921-24), *Romancero gitano* (1924-27), *Poeta en Nueva York* (1929-30), *Llanto por Ignacio Sánchez Mejía* (1935), *Seis poemas gallegos* (1935), and *Diván del Tamarit* (1936). The translations of these representative selections are very good.

1583

García Lorca, Federico. *Three tragedies.* Translated by James Graham-Lujan and Richard L. O'Connell. New York, New Directions, 1961. 212 p. $1.75

Contains *Blood wedding, Yerma,* and *The house of Bernardo Alba.* An introduction by the poet's brother, Francisco García Lorca, provides an interesting personal glimpse of Federico as a dramatist.

1584

García Lorca, Federico. *Tree of song.* Translated from the Spanish by Allan Brilliant. Santa Barbara, Unicorn Press, 1971. 31 p. illus. (Unicorn keepsake series) $2

This bilingual edition contains a brief selection of poems by García Lorca.

1585

García Lorca, Federico. *La zapatera prodigiosa. Farsa violenta en dos actos.* Edited with introd., excercises, notes, and vocabulary by Edith F. Helman. New York, Norton, 1968. 192 p. illus. $2.35

This play represents one of the highest attainments of contemporary poetic theater in the tradition of Spanish classic and romantic tragicomedy.

1586

García-Mazas, José. *El poeta y la escultora; la España que Huntington conoció.* 2d ed. New York, Hispanic Society of America, 1962. x, 525 p. illus., ports. (Hispanic Society of America publications) $2.50

An attractive volume about the careers of Archer Huntington and his wife, founders of the magnificent library and museum, the Hispanic Society of America. The work concentrates on the Huntingtons' sojourn in Spain.

1587

García Montoro, Adrian, and Sergio A. Rigol. *En torno al poema; de Bécquer a Miguel*

Hernández. New York, Harcourt, Brace, Jovanovich, 1974. 259 p. $4.75

Surveys Spanish poetry from Gustavo Adolfo Bécquer of the second half of the 19th century to Miguel Hernández (1910-1942). Includes bibliographies.

1588

García Pavón, Francisco. *Antología de cuentistas españoles contemporáneos (1939-1966).* Madrid, Editorial Gredos, 1966. 454 p. $5.75

Includes selected short stories by 29 prominent Spanish writers, among these, Camilo José Cela, Ana María Matute, Carmen Laforet, Ignacio Aldecoa, Miguel Buñuel, Ricardo Domenech, and others.

1589

Gasser, Manuel. *Joan Miró.* Translated by Haydn Barnes. New York, Barnes & Noble, 1965. 90 p. illus. (part col.) (Barnes & Noble art series) $.95

The Catalonian painter is represented by 24 excellent color reproductions and a large number of black-and-white illustrations of his work. The brief text relates his life's work through the 1960's. [Charles Fleener]

1590

Gaudin, Lois Frances. *Bibliography of Franco-Spanish literary relations (until the XIXth century).* New York, Burt Franklin, 1973. 71 p. (Burt Franklin bibliography and reference series, 470. Selected essays and texts in literature and criticism, 187) $12.50

This is a reprint of the 1930 edition of a most useful compilation of books and articles written on the period of the Middle Ages to the 1800's.

1591

Gilot, Françoise, and Carlton Lake. *Life with Picasso.* New York, New American Library, 1965. 350 p. illus. $.95

One of Picasso's great loves describes, with rare wit and insight, her life with the artist.

1592

Giner de los Ríos, Francisco. *Ensayos;* selección, edición y prólogo de Juan López-Morillas. Philadelphia, Center for Curriculum Development, 1974. 230 p. $1.20

Juan López-Morillas' insightful introduction makes this collection of Giner's essays worthwhile. Giner expounds on traditional humanist topics in the true manner of the essayist, and the chronological table of Giner's life is very useful. Includes bibliographic footnotes.

1593

Gironella, José María. *Los cipreses creen en Dios.* New York, Harcourt, Brace, and World, 1969. 353 p. $3.75

In this novel about the Spanish civil war, the author captures the enormous toll in human suffering and tragedy paid by the Spanish people during this crucial period of their history.

1594

Gladfelter, Bruce G. *Meseta and campiña landforms in central Spain; a geomorphology of the Alto Henares Basin.* Chicago, University of Chicago Press, 1971. xii, 204 p. illus., maps. (University of Chicago. Dept. of Geography. Research paper no. 130) $4.50

This is scholarly piece of research on the geologic formations of the Alto Henares

Basin. Includes excellent maps, illustrations, and a bibliography. Of great interest to the specialist.

1595

Goldstein, David, comp. *The Jewish poets of Spain, 900-1250,* translated with an introduction and notes by David Goldstein Rev. and expanded ed. Harmondsworth, England, Penguin, 1971. 218 p. index. (The Penguin classics) $1.95

This is a very interesting anthology of Spanish Jewish poetry translated into English. The introduction is written from the historical and literary perspectives, and the short but complete synopses of the poets' lives make the collection worthwhile.

1595A

Goldston, Robert. *The civil war in Spain.* Greenwich, Conn., Fawcett Publications, 1969. 221 p. $.75

The author presents a clear, brief introduction to the Spanish civil war. Starting with "How war came" through 11 chapters to "The fall of the republic," he analyzes the war and those who fought it.

1596

Gómez-Moreno, Carmen. *Medieval art from private collections;* a special exhibition at the Cloisters, October 30, 1968, through January 5, 1969. Introd. and catalogue by Carmen Gómez-Moreno. New York, Metropolitan Museum of Art, 1969. 1 v. (chiefly illus.) $8.75

This is a handsomely illustrated book about medieval art in which the Luso-Hispanic world is well represented. The captions and explanatory text are very good.

1597

Góngora y Argotes, Luis. *Poems;* selected, introduced and annotated by R.O. Jones. New York, Cambridge University Press, 1966. 162 p. $2.25

Góngora (1561-1627) was the most complex poet of the Golden Age. His collected poems were first published in 1627. From 1580 to 1612 his poetry was chiefly lyrical. After 1612 his work shows signs of increasing complexity which culminates in his later unique baroque style. The introduction is a scholarly essay on the author and his work. Includes a select bibliography.

1598

Goya y Lucientes, Francisco. *Los caprichos;* with a new introd. by Philip Hofer. New York, Dover Publications, 1969. 87 p. illus. (incl. port.), plates. $2.75

Contains good reproductions of Goya's *Los caprichos* with English and Spanish captions.

1599

Goya y Lucientes, Francisco. *The disasters of war;* with a new introd. by Philip Hofer. New York, Dover Publications, 1967. 12 p. illus., 83 plates. $1.95

Reproduces 83 plates by Goya that depict the Spanish nationalist uprising against the French puppet king Joseph Bonaparte (1808-14). Goya denounces war through his art. Hofer's bilingual introduction examines the artist's work. Translation of *Los desastres de la guerra* (1863).

1600

Goya y Lucientes, Francisco. *The disparates, or proverbios.* Introd. by Philip Hofer. New York, Dover Publications, 1969. 64 p. illus. $2.75

In this oversized volume the last of Goya's four main series are reproduced. The

18 etchings, variously known as *Los proverbios* or *Los disparates* [follies] were probably executed in 1819. Includes three proofs and a preliminary drawing for a *Disparates* subject. First published in 1864.

1601

Goya y Lucientes, Francisco. *Drawings of Goya in the Prado Museum,* by Xavier de Salas. Translated and edited by Stephen Longstreet. Alhambra, Calif., Borden Pub. Co., 1969. 1 v. (unpaged) illus. (Master draughtsman series) $1.75

Includes representative drawings by the Spanish master. The reproductions are very good.

1602

Goya y Lucientes, Francisco. *Goya;* edited by E. L. Ferrari. New York, New American Library, 1970. 120 p. illus. $.95, durabind edition $2.25

Illustrates the most salient works of Goya with explanatory text and an introduction which analyzes the artist's work. Contains bibliographical references.

1603

Goya y Lucientes, Francisco. *Goya.* Edited by F.S. Wight. New York, H.F. Abrams, 1970. 110 p. illus. (An Abrams art book) $.95

Includes reproductions of representative selections by the Spanish master.

1604

Goya y Lucientes, Francisco. *La tauromaquia and The bulls of Bordeaux.* Introd. by Philip Hofer. New York, Dover Publications, 1969. 120 p. illus. $3

Forty plates of *La tauromaquia* and four lithographs of *The bulls of Bordeaux* are included in this splendid volume. This work is an important addition to any collection of books on Spanish art.

1605

Goytisolo, Juan. *Fiestas.* Introd. and notes by Kessel Schwartz. New York, Dell Pub. Co., 1964. 255 p. (The Laurel language library. Spanish series) $.95

Ramón Sender, a major Spanish novelist, said of *Fiestas* that it was "a model of harmony, sharpness, love of things and beings, originality of vision. . ." providing a "contrast between Spanish official and real life." A glossary of unusual terms and phrases is appended.

1606

Goytortúa Santos, Jesús. *Lluvia roja;* edited with introd., notes, exercises, and vocabulary by Donald D. Walsh. New York, Appleton-Century-Crofts, 1961. xii, 195 p. $2.45

A textbook edition of this incisive contemporary Spanish novel.

1607

Goytortúa Santos, Jesús. *Pensativa;* edited, with introd., notes, cuestionario and vocabulary by Donald D. Walsh. New York, Appleton-Century-Crofts, 1962. xiv, 202 p. $2.45

This is a textbook edition, with notes and vocabulary, of a fast-moving contemporary Spanish novel. Of interest to students of Spanish literature.

1608

Gracián y Morales, Baltasar. *Art of wordly wisdom.* Translated from the Spanish by Joseph Jacobs. New York, F. Ungar, 1960. 197 p. $1.25

Arte de ingenio (1642) by the great Spanish prose stylist, explains the literary theory of "conceptismo."

1609
Gracián y Morales, Baltasar. *The best of Gracián.* A new translation by Thomas G. Corvan. New York, Philosophical Library, 1964. 84 p. $.95

Contains selections from the essays and allegorical works of the influential Spanish moralist and stylist of the 17th century.

1610
Greco, El. *El Greco.* Edited by John F. Matthews. New York, Harry N. Abrams, 1969. 90 p. illus. $.95

An attractive, illustrated work which succinctly covers the life and work of El Greco.

1611
Green, Otis Howard. *Spain and the Western tradition; the Castilian mind in literature from El Cid to Calderón.* Madison, University of Wisconsin, 1963-66. 4 v. $2.95 each

This extensive work surveys Spanish literature within the Western world from the Middle Ages to the Golden Age. It is a very important contribution to the field. Includes bibliographies.

1612
Gris, Juan. *Juan Gris: dessins and guaches.* Edited by Leiris Gallery. New York, Wittenborn, 1965. 70 p. illus. (part col.) $3.50

Contains handsome reproductions of representative works by the contemporary Catalan painter.

1613
Guillén, Claudio, ed. *Lazarillo de Tormes. El Abencerraje.* Introd. and notes by Claudio Guillén. New York, Dell, 1966. 187 p. $.75

La vida de Lazarillo de Tormes y sus fortunas (1554) gained instant success and ushered in the picaresque novel. The book exudes humor and iconoclastic satire. *El Abencerraje,* a contemporary of the former, is a poetic novel about the exploits of the chivalrous Moor. The editor presents the 1554 Antwerp edition of *Lazarillo* and the 1565 *Abencerraje* of Antonio Villegas. The spelling has been modernized.

1614
Guillén, Jorge. *Affirmation: a bilingual anthology 1919-1966.* Translated with notes by Julian Palley. Introd. by Jorge Guillén. Norman, University of Oklahoma Press, 1968. xvi, 208 p. $2.95

The selections in this bilingual anthology are well chosen and translated faithfully from the original Spanish. The introduction is a translation of Guillén's own essay on writing, and a select bibliography is included at the end of the volume.

1615
Guillén, Jorge. *Cántico: a selection.* Edited by Norman Thomas de Giovanni. Boston, Little, Brown, 1965. 291 p. illus. $2.95

The poet himself, who devoted 31 years to writing *Cántico,* chose the 50 poems for this edition. They appear in the original Spanish, with English translations on the facing pages. Guillén said *"Cántico* is an act of attentiveness. Despite many obstacles it tends toward serenity, toward joy, with wonder and with gratitude. Experience of being, affirmation of life, of this life on earth which has a value in itself."

1616
Guillén, Jorge. *Guirnalda civil.* Cambridge, Mass., Halty Ferguson, 1970. 33 p. $3

This collection of poems is dedicated to Leopoldo Alas, who was assassinated in 1937. They deal in great part with Spanish civil strife and its effect on the Spanish psyche.

1617

Gulf Coast History and Humanities Conference, 2d, University of West Florida, 1970. *Spain and her rivals on the Gulf Coast: proceedings.* Edited by Earle W. Newton and Ernest F. Dibble. Pensacola, Fla., Historic Pensacola Preservation Board, 1971. 143 p. illus. $3

Contains the papers presented at a conference sponsored by the University of West Florida dealing with Spain's role in the northern Caribbean from the 16th through the 19th centuries. Includes bibliographical references.

1618

Guttman, Allen. ed. *American neutrality and the Spanish Civil War.* Boston, Heath, 1970. 243 p. (Problems in American civilization, readings selected by the Dept. of American Studies, Amherst College) $2.25

Examines U.S. diplomacy during the 1936-40 period. Contains a select bibliography.

1619

Haggart, Stanley Mills, and Darwin Porter. *Dollar-wise guide to Portugal.* New York, A. Frommer, 1971. 225 p. illus. $2.50

Emphasizes accommodations and entertainment for the economy-minded tourist.

1620

Haggart, Stanley Mills, and Darwin Porter. *Spain on five and ten dollars a day.* 1971 rev. ed. New York, A. Frommer, 1972. 288 p. illus. $2.95

Although some of the prices may have changed during the recent inflation, this is a very useful guide pointing out reasonably priced accommodations. It also contains good travel tips.

1621

Hale, John Rigley. *Renaissance exploration.* New York, Norton, 1972. 110 p. illus. (some col.), maps. $5.95

Deals chiefly with 15th- and 16th-century exploration, devoting generous space to Columbus' and Vasco da Gama's exploits. It extends through the 18th century. Provides an excellent profile of European society during the age of exploration and contains a very good bibliography.

1622

Halperin, Don A. *The ancient synagogues of the Iberian peninsula.* Gainesville, University of Florida Press, 1969. 86 p. illus., plans. (University of Florida monographs. Social sciences, no. 38) $2

Studies in detail ancient synagogues of Spain and Portugal. This scholarly monograph contains a good bibliography.

1623

Hart, Thomas, and Carlos Rojas, eds. *La España moderna; vista y sentida por los españoles.* Englewood Cliffs, N.J., Prentice-Hall, 1969. xiii, 341 p. illus. $8

Provides reading material for a semester's work in intermediate college Spanish. Selections from a wide range of writers have been included, such as Unamuno, Antonio Machado, Juan Ramón Jiménez, Américo Castro, Ramón Menéndez Pidal, and many others. Includes exercises and an extensive vocabulary.

1624
Hartzfeld, Helmut Anthony. *Critical bibliography of the new stylistics applied to the Romance literatures, 1900-1966.* Berkeley, University of California Press, 1968. 2 v. $7

> Volume 1 covers the 1900-52 period, and volume 2 deals with 1953-66. This is an important and invaluable contribution, of great interest to the specialist.

1625
Hatheway, Maruja. *Authentic Spanish cooking.* New York, Paperback Library, 1973. 183 p. illus. $.75

> Contains many good recipes from Spain with clear directions for preparation.

1626
Hauben, Paul J., ed. *The Spanish Inquisition.* New York, Wiley, 1969. xiii, 140 p. (Major issues in history) $2.95

> The editor's extensive introduction is followed by eight readings which are historiographical and descriptive in scope. The second set of selections includes sources and trial records of the Inquisition. This volume serves as an introduction to the nature and history of the Holy Office. [Charles Fleener]

1627
Hawkes, John Ryder, and Moira Hawkes. *Spain.* New Rochelle, N.Y., Soccer Associates, 1965. 100 p. illus., maps. (Holiday factbook) $1

> Introduces Spain to the traveler and the casual visitor.

1628
Hemingway, Ernest. *Death in the afternoon.* New York, Scribner, 1960. 487 p. illus. $2.95

> This is a paperback edition of Hemingway's splendid study on the Spanish bullfight. It explains the spectacle both emotionally and esthetically. First published in 1922.

1629
Hemingway, Ernest. *Fifth column and four unpublished stories of the Spanish civil war.* New York, Scribner, 1969. 151 p. $2.45

> Ernest Hemingway's interesting account of his personal experiences during the Spanish civil war in form of fiction is presented here with hitherto unpublished short stories.

1630
Hemingway, Ernest. *Fifth column and four stories of the Spanish civil war.* New York, Bantam Books, 1973. 162 p. $1.25

> See above.

1631
Hemingway, Ernest. *For whom the bell tolls.* New York, Scribner, 1962. 352 p. $1.95

> Hemingway's classic novel about the Spanish civil war will interest all those who study that period. The Nobel Prize-winning novelist captured the essence of Spain during its bitter and agonizing struggle.

1632
Hemingway, Ernest. *The sun also rises.* New York, Scribner, 1970. 284 p. $1.65

> This is one of Hemingway's earliest novels, set in northern Spain and in Paris.

There are descriptions of landscapes in Spain, which surfaced with greater force in his subsequent novels.

1633

Herr, Richard. *Eighteenth-century revolution in Spain.* Princeton, N.J., Princeton University Press, 1969. 484 p. illus., maps. $3.45

Scholarly and valuable guide to Spanish history in the late 18th and early 19th centuries. Professor Herr presents a view of the Spain of Charles III and Charles IV, which includes political, religious, and economic aspects, as well as the social and cultural life. Includes bibliographies.

1634

Herr, Richard. *Modern Spain.* Berkeley, University of California Press, 1974. 306 p. $3.65

A very good, scholarly political history of modern Spain, this book traces the country's rapid transformation from an agrarian society to a fast-growing industrial one. Includes a bibliography.

1635

Hesse, Everett Wesley, and Harry F. William, eds. *Vida de Lazarillo de Tormes y de sus fortunas y adversidades.* Introd. by Américo Castro. Rev. ed. Madison, University of Wisconsin Press, 1960. 84 p. $1.50

See *Lazarillo de Tormes.*

1636

Highfield, John Roger Loxdale, comp. *Spain in the fifteenth century, 1369-1516; essays and abstracts by historians of Spain.* Translated from the Spanish by Frances M. López-Morillas. New York, Harper & Row, 1972. 488 p. $4.95

Includes 14 representative essays by Jaime Vicens Vives, José María Font y Rius, Ramón Menéndez Pidal, Marcel Bataillon, and several other prominent historians. This excellent compilation includes several bibliographies.

1637

Hispanic Society of America, New York. *Studies in memory of Ramón Menéndez Pidal,* by the Hispanic Society of America in cooperation with the editors of the Hispanic Review. New York, 1971. 100 p. illus., plates. $4

Contains articles on various aspects of the works of the great Spanish scholar by Homero Serís, Ciriaco Morón Arroyo, Theodore Beardsley, Samuel G. Armistead, and others.

1638

Hoenerbach, Wilhelm, ed. and tr. *Spanische-Islamische Urkunden, aus der Zeit der Nasriden und Moriscos.* Berkeley, University of California Press, 1965. xxxxiv, 397 p. 103 facsims. (University of California publications. Near Eastern studies, v. 3) $12

Presents important notarial documents from Moslem Spain in German translation, with numerous scholarly annotations and references. Includes a thorough introduction and a bibliography. An important contribution.

1639

Holiday editors. *Travel guide to Spain.* Rev. ed. New York, Random House, 1971. 278 p. illus., col. maps (part fold.) (A Holiday Magazine travel guide, v. 7) $1.95

An attractive guide for visitors and tourists, containing useful information.

1640

Holt, Marion, ed. *Modern Spanish stage; four plays.* New York, Hill and Wang, 1970. xxvi, 278 p. (A Mermaid drama book) $2.45

> This anthology includes Antonio Buero Vallejo's *The concert at St. Ovide* (1958), Alfonso Sastre's *Condemned squad* (1953), José López Rubio's *The blindfold* (1954), and Alejandro Casona's *The boat without a fisherman* (1945). The translations are excellent. Includes vocabularies.

1641

Honig, Edwin. *García Lorca.* Rev. ed. New York, New Directions, 1963. 239 p. (A New Directions paperbook, 102) $1.80

> Professor Honig surveys Federico García Lorca's life and work, including both poetry and drama. The introduction is excellent and sheds new light on this important Spanish literary figure.

1642

Houghton, Norris, ed. *The Golden Age.* New York, Dell Pub. Co., 1963. 349 p. (Laurel masterpieces of continental drama, v. 1) $.95

> Includes Lope de Vega's *Sheep well*, Calderón de la Barca's *Life is a dream*, and *The Cid* by Corneille. These plays are representative of Spanish Golden Age theater at its finest.

1643

Huntington, Archer M. *Turning pages.* New York, Hispanic Society of America, 1950. 74 p. $1

> Includes poetry and essays by the prominent North American philanthropist and Hispanophile.

1644

Huntington, Archer M. *Versos.* New York, Hispanic Society of America, 1952. 98 p. illus. $5

> Selected poems by Archer Huntington who spent his life disseminating the Spanish culture in the U.S.

1645

Ilie, Paul, comp. *Documents of the Spanish vanguard.* Chapel Hill, University of North Carolina Press, 1969. 451 p. (University of North Carolina. Studies in the Romance languages and literatures, no. 78) $11.50

> The editor has chosen the most relevant essays, addresses, and lectures on the history and criticism of the literary vanguard in contemporary Spain. Contains bibliographical notes.

1646

Ilie, Paul. *The surrealist mode in Spanish literature; an interpretation of basic trends from post-romanticism to the Spanish vanguard.* Ann Arbor, University of Michigan Press, 1968. 242 p. $5

> An important literary history of Spanish literature during the late 19th and first half of the 20th century. Contains a thorough bibliography.

1647

Irving, Washington. *Tales of the Alhambra.* Adapted for young readers by Robert C. Goldston. Illustrated by Stephane. New York, Avon Books, 1972. 153 p. $.60

> This is an abridged edition of the charming 19th-century classic adapted for young people.

1648

Isidorius, Saint, Bishop of Seville. *Isidore of Seville; the medical writings;* an English translation with an introd. and commentary by William D. Sharpe. Philadelphia, American Philosophical Society, 1964. 75 p. (Transactions of the American Philosophical Society, new series, v. 54, pt. 2) $2

A scholarly, annotated edition of writings by Isidore of Seville in the field of medicine. Isidore was a noted scientist in 7th-century Spain. Contains a thorough bibliography.

1649

Isidorius, Saint, Bishop of Seville. *Isidore of Seville's history of the kings of the Goths, Vandals and Suevi.* Translated by Guido Donini and Gordon B. Ford, Jr. New York, Humanities Press, 1967. 45 p. $4

This is the first translation into English of Isidore of Seville's chronicle of the history of the West Goths from A.D. 256 to 624, entitled *Historia de regibus Gothorum, Vandalorum et Suevorum* (A.D. 624). The translation is excellent, and there are notes clarifying the text.

1650

Jackson, Gabriel. *The making of medieval Spain.* New York, Harcourt, Brace, Jovanovich, 1972. 216 p. (History of European civilization library) $3.95

Presents a succinct analysis of the cultural, political, economic, and social forces that shaped Spain during the Middle Ages. This is an important contribution and includes a good bibliography.

1651

Jackson, Gabriel, comp. *The Spanish civil war; domestic and international conspiracy.* Edited, with an introd. by Gabriel Jackson. Boston, Heath, 1967. 112 p. (Problems in European civilization) $2.25

Contains a representative selection of articles and news reports from the *New York Times* covering the Spanish civil war.

1652

Jackson, Gabriel, comp. *The Spanish civil war; domestic and international conspiracy.* Edited, with an introd. by Gabriel Jackson. New York, Franklin Watts, 1972. 113 p. $2.45

Another edition of the above entry.

1653

Jackson, Gabriel. *The Spanish republic and the civil war, 1931-1939.* Princeton, N.J., Princeton University Press, 1967. xiii, 578 p. illus., maps. $3.45

Traces the history of Spain during the second republic and through the onset of the civil war. The author analyzes modern Spain to discover the roots of the disaster that overwhelmed the republic. He also studies the structure of Spanish society. Includes a bibliography. [Charles Fleener]

1654

Jardiel Poncela, Enrique. *Una noche de primavera sin sueño; comedia humorística en tres actos.* Edited by Francisco C. Lacosta. New York, Appleton-Century-Crofts, 1967. 108 p. $2.20

This edition of a humorous contemporary Spanish play is intended for classroom use. It contains numerous notes and vocabularies.

1655

Jiménez, Juan Ramón. *Forty poems of Juan Ramón Jiménez.* Translated by Robert Bly. Madison, Minn., Sixties Press, 1969. 286 p. illus. $2

Includes excellent translations of representative poems by the Nobel Prize-winning contemporary Spanish poet.

1656
Jiménez, Juan Ramón. *Platero and I.* New translation by William H. and Mary Roberts, with an introd. by William H. Roberts. New York, New American Library, 1960. 231 p. $.75

Jiménez was awarded the Nobel Prize in literature in 1956. He is considered, together with Antonio Machado, the foremost lyric poet of contemporary Spain. *Platero* is a prose poem of rare beauty and sensitivity, first published in 1917.

1657
Jiménez, Juan Ramón. *El Platero y yo.* Illustrated by Rafael A. Ortega. Introd. by Arturo del Hoyo. Philadelphia, Center for Curriculum Development, 1972. 349 p. $5.60

This is an annotated textbook edition of the Spanish classic.

1658
Jiménez, Juan Ramón. *Platero y yo; trescientos poemas.* Austin, University of Texas Press, 1964. 310 p. $1.75

In addition to the outstanding prose poem *El Platero y yo,* this attractive volume contains many other important poems by Jiménez. Includes a select bibliography.

1659
Joannes XXI, Pope. *Tractatus syncategorematum and selected anonymous treatises,* by Peter of Spain. Translated by Joseph P. Mullally, with an introd. by Joseph P. Mullally and Roland Houde. Milwaukee, Wis., Marquette University Press, 1964. 156 p. (Mediaeval philosophical texts in translation, no. 13) $3.50

Peter of Spain was born in Lisbon in the early 13th century; he became a leading philosopher of his age and was elected pope in 1276. The present work makes it possible for scholars to appreciate the continuity of formal logic and the progress of medieval over classical logic in the tracts of Peter of Spain. Contains bibliographical footnotes.

1660
Johnson, Harold Benjamin, comp. *From reconquest to empire; the Iberian background to Latin American history.* Edited with an introd. by H.B. Johnson, Jr. New York, Knopf, 1970. 230 p. (Borzoi books on Latin America) $2.95

The selection includes essays ranging from medieval to modern colonization, the elements of conquest and settlement, to the ethos of medieval Iberia. It provides a thorough background to the economic and social history of Spain. Includes bibliographies.

1661
Jones, Joseph Ramón. *Una década de Césares.* Chapel Hill, University of North Carolina Press, 1966. 527 p. $12

Antonio de Guevara (1480?-1545) of Spain was a courtier, writer, and priest. His works were very popular in Spain and throughout Europe and England. This is an exhaustive study of Guevara's work. Includes a bibliography.

1662
Jones, Royston O. *The Golden Age: prose and poetry; the sixteenth and seventeenth centuries.* New York, Barnes & Noble, 1971. xvii, 233 p. (A literary history of Spain, v. 2) $4

Presents a concise and readable literary history of the most important literary figures of the 16th and 17th centuries. Intended as a review text in courses of Spanish literature. Includes bibliographies.

1663

Jones, Willis Knapp, comp. *Spanish one act plays in English: a comprehensive anthology of Spanish drama from the 12th century to the present,* translated by Willis Knapp Jones . . . with an introd. by Hayward Keniston. New York, Barron's Educational Series, 1969. 296 p. $1.95

This compact anthology of Spanish drama in English translation is of great interest to public and college libraries, as well as specialized reference collections.

1664

Jovellanos, Gaspar Melchor de. *Diarios.* Philadelphia, Center for Curriculum Development, 1971. 310 p. $1.50

Excerpts from Jovellanos' diary covering the years 1790-1801 give the reader an intimate picture of the Spanish statesman and reformer's inner life and of the society of his time. This textbook edition contains notes, vocabulary, and a brief bibliography.

1665

Juan de la Cruz, Saint. *Ascent of Mount Carmel.* Translated and edited with a general introd. by E. Allison Peers. 3d rev. ed. Garden City, N.Y., Doubleday, 1958. 386 p. $1.45

Translation of *La subida del Monte Carmelo* (1578-83), which is a remarkable work of St. John of the Cross, the purest lyric poet and the most metaphysical among the European mystics. *Ascent* consists of eight canciones, each followed by prose commentary in which the poet explains his verse.

1666

Juan de la Cruz, Saint. *Dark night of the soul.* Translated and edited, with an introd. by E. Allison Peers from the critical edition by P. Silverio de Santa Teresa. 3d rev. ed. Garden City, N.Y., Doubleday, 1959. 193 p. $1.25

Translation of *Noche oscura del alma* (1579), in which St. John expressed the pinnacle of mystical experience. His poetry radiates light, beauty, love, and it transcends the bounds of reality. Professor Peers' introduction enhances this important edition.

1667

Juan de la Cruz, Saint. *Living flame of love.* Translated, edited and with an introd. by E. Allison Peers from the critical ed. by P. Silverio de Santa Teresa. Garden City, N.Y., Doubleday, 1962. 272 p. $1.95

Translation of *O llama de amor viva* (1594). It is an allegorical song, a categorical affirmation of absolute love. St. John's lyricism and methaphysical labyrinths have been compared to such great poets as Sappho, Cafavy, and Emily Dickinson. The introduction provides a scholarly capsule of St. John.

1668

Juan de la Cruz, Saint. *Poems of St. John of the Cross.* Translated by Roy Campbell. New York, Grosset and Dunlap, 1968. 109 p. $1.95

Includes all the known poems of St. John. The original texts are followed by excellent translations.

1669

Juan de la Cruz, Saint. *The poems of St. John of the Cross.* Original Spanish texts and

English version newly revised and rewritten by John Frederick Nims, with an essay by Robert Graves. Rev. ed. New York, Grove Press, 1959. 147 p. $1.95

> Robert Graves asserts that St. John had "duende," or divine presence, to an unprecedented degree in his poetry. He states with García Lorca that "no poem, whether written for love of God, or love of woman, is worth much if it lacks duende." The translations are excellent.

1670
Juan de la Cruz, Saint. *The poems of St. John of the Cross. Masterpieces of Christian mystic poetry.* New York, New Directions, 1974. 151 p. $2.45

> Assembles very good translations of the complete poems by the Spanish mystic.

1671
Juan de la Cruz, Saint. *Spiritual canticle.* 3d rev. ed. Translated, edited, and with an introd. by E. Allison Peers, from the critical edition of P. Silverio de Santa Teresa. Garden City, N.Y., Image Books, 1961. 520 p. (A Doubleday Image book, D-110) $1.45

> *El cántico espiritual* (1578) was inspired by Solomon's *Song of Songs* as translated from the Hebrew by another great Spanish mystic, Fray Luis de León. St. John wrote part of *Cántico* while imprisoned in a Toledo dungeon. This work constitutes St. John's most ambitious poem. The poem itself is one of the most successful long lyrics in world literature. The sources include not only Hebrew folk culture, but also Spanish, Portuguese, and Moorish popular ballads.

1672
Kamen, Henry Arthur Francis. *Spanish Inquisition.* New York, New American Library, 1966. x, 339 p. illus., map. $3.95

> Interprets the role and impact of the activities of the Holy Office in Spain. Bibliographical references included in a section entitled "Notes."

1673
Kanki, Keizo. *Goya.* Palo Alto, Calif., Kodansha International, 1969. 154 p. illus. (part col.) (This beautiful world, v. 10) $2.75

> Analyzes the style, techniques, and aims of Goya. The illustrations, some in color, are excellent.

1674
Keller, John Esten, ed. *The book of the wiles of women.* Translated by John Esten Keller. Chapel Hill, University of North Carolina Press, 1956. 60 p. (North Carolina. University. Studies in the Romance languages and literatures, no. 27) $3.50

> An English version of an anonymous collection of oriental tales about the "deceits and wiles of women," translated from the Arabic into Spanish in 1253 by order of the Infante Fadrique, younger brother of Alfonso X, king of Spain. This work had a decisive influence on early Spanish medieval literature. Includes an important bibliography.

1675
Keller, John Esten, ed. *Libro de los engannos et los assyamientos de las mugeres.* Chapel Hill, University of North Carolina Press, 1953. xiii, 56 p. (North Carolina. University. Studies in the Romance languages and literatures, no. 20) $3.50

> These 24 oriental tales became a part of Spanish literature. The plots revolve around a charge of attempted seduction brought by a vindictive queen against her stepson, who had spurned her advances. At his trial seven wise men speak in his defense, relating stories about the perfidy of women. These tales have strongly influenced the Arcipreste de Talavera's writings. Includes a thorough bibliography.

1676

Keller, John Esten. *Motif-index of medieval Spanish exempla.* Knoxville, University of Tennessee Press, 1949. xvii, 67 p. $2

Exemplum (in Spanish ejemplo or fábula) is a medieval didactic or moral tale of the 13th through the 15th centuries. They are usually grouped into a series of stories within a story known as the "frame." The origins of most of these tales can be traced to Sanskrit, Persian, Arabic, Greek, and Latin sources. Includes a select bibliography.

1677

Kirkpatrick, Frederick Alexander. *The Spanish conquistadores.* Cleveland, World Book Pub. Co., 1968. xiii, 366 p. maps. (The pioneer histories) $2.95

Originally published in 1934, this work was the first single volume to contain a succinct survey of the explorations and expeditions of the Spaniards in the New World. It covers the period from Columbus' first voyage to Juan de Garay's founding of Buenos Aires.

1678

Kirsner, Robert. *The novels and travels of Camilo José Cela.* Chapel Hill, University of North Carolina Press, 1963. 187 p. (University of North Carolina. Studies in Romance languages and literatures, no. 43) $5

A major study of Cela's six novels: *La familia de Pascual Duarte, Pabellón de reposo, Nuevas andanzas y desventuras de Lazarillo de Tormes, La colmena, Mrs. Caldwell habla con su hijo,* and *La Cátira,* as well as his books of travels. Cela describes his travels in Spain using a quasi-novelistic form with rare artistic insight and objectivity. Contains a good bibliography.

1679

Klingender, F.D. *Goya in the democratic tradition.* New York, Schocken Books, 1968. xvi, 235 p. illus., tables. $2.95

First published in 1948, this work studies Goya's works in search of a key to the interpretation of Spanish history during the reigns of Charles III, Charles IV, and Ferdinand VII. The author uses 122 figures to illustrate this work. [Charles Fleener]

1680

Kyd, Thomas. *The Spanish tragedy.* Edited by Thomas W. Ross. Berkeley, University of California Press, 1968. 128 p. (The Fountainwell drama texts, 6) $1.65

This was one of the most famous plays in Elizabethan England, which exerted its influence on other plays of its era, especially *Hamlet.* The play is sheer fantasy although loosely based on the rivalry between Spain and Portugal.

1681

Lacy, Allen. *Miguel de Unamuno: the rhetoric of existence.* New York, Humanities Press, 1970. 382 p. $10.50

This remarkable study analyzes the Spanish philosopher's work and art.

1682

Lado, María Dolores. *Las guerras carlistas y el reinado isabelino en la obra de Ramón del Valle-Inclán.* Gainesville, University of Florida Press, 1966. 73 p. (University of Florida monographs, no. 18) $2

Valle Inclán did not attempt to make his novels a vehicle for political ideology; he simply accurately reflected certain periods of Spanish history in his writings, especially the Carlist wars. This important contribution contains a select bibliography.

1683

Laín Entralgo, Pedro. *Entre nosotros, comedia dramática*. Philadelphia, Center for Curriculum Development, 1973. 167 p. $1.20

Of particular interest in this edition of Laín Entralgo's three-act comedy is his "confidencia previa" or introductory remarks which tell how he began writing plays. A must for those who know Laín Entralgo only through his serious work.

1684

Laforet, Carmen. *Nada*. Edited by Edward R. Mulvihill and Roberto G. Sánchez. New York, Oxford University Press, 1958. 269 p. $2.95

First published in 1944 by a then unknown Spanish writer, this work won the first Eugenio Nadal Prize. It is an autobiographical novel narrated by Andrea, who tells what happens to her among her uncles and aunts in a society disintegrating after the Spanish civil war.

1685

Laforet, Carmen. *Un noviazgo*. Edited by Carolyn L Galerstein. Indianapolis, Odyssey Press, 1973. xiii, 90 p. $1.95

First published in 1953, this long short story depicts masterfully the psychological complexities of a 50-year-old Spanish spinster. The author is one of Spain's most remarkable contemporary novelists. This edition is intended for intermediate and advanced Spanish classes, with notes and vocabularies.

1686

La Souchère, Elena de. *Picasso; Antibes*. New York, Tudor, 1962. 102 p. illus. (Little art library) $.95

A personal reminiscence of the author is included in the brief introduction to these 15 color reproductions from the Picasso Museum in Antibes.

1687

Lazarillo de Tormes. *The life of Lazarillo de Tormes, his fortunes and adversities*. A modern translation with notes by James Parson. Introd. by Glen Wilbern. New York, American R.D.M. Corp., 1966. 96 p. (A Study master publication T-47) $1.25

English translation of the 1554 Spanish picaresque novel in which the roguish protagonist criticizes his times with mock seriousness. The entire tale is told by Lazarillo in a double perspective of self-concealment and self-revelation. Includes a good bibliography.

1688

Lazarillo de Tormes. *The life of Lazarillo de Tormes, his fortunes and adversities*. Translated from the Spanish, with notes and an introd. by Harriet de Onís. Great Neck, N.Y., Barron's Educational Series, 1959. xviii, 74 p. $1.25

Translation of *La vida de Lazarillo de Tormes y de sus fortunas y adversidades* (1554). Its authorship has been attributed to Hurtado de Mendoza, but modern scholarship has conclusively rejected this theory. This edition contains good notes, and the translation is excellent.

1689

Lazarillo de Tormes. *The life of Lazarillo de Tomes, his fortunes and adversities*. Translated by J. Gerald Markley. Introd. by Alan G. Holaday. Indianapolis, Bobbs-Merrill, 1960. 68 p. $.95

An abridged English version of the classic Spanish picaresque novel which ranks with the *Celestina* and *Don Quijote* as a realistic masterpiece.

1690

Lazarillo de Tormes. *The life of Lazarillo de Tormes; his fortunes and misfortunes as told by himself.* Translated and with an introd., by Robert S. Rudder. With a sequel by Juan de Luna. Translated by Robert S. Rudder with Carmen Criado de Rodríguez Puértolas. New York, Ungar, 1974. xxi, 245 p. illus. $2.95

> This new translation of *Lazarillo* is accompanied by Juan de Luna's witty sequel with its trenchant critique of Spanish society. Includes notes.

1691

Lazarillo de Tormes. *La segunda parte de la vida de Lazarillo de Tormes; sacada de las corónicas antiguas de Toledo,* por H. de Luna. Edited by Elmer R. Sims. Austin, University of Texas Press, 1958. 138 p. $1.95

> This is a Spanish-language edition, based on the first edition with notes and bibliography.

1692

Lazarillo de Tormes. *La vida de Lazarillo de Tormes y de sus fortunas y adversidades.* Edited by Everett W. Hesse and Harry F. Williams. Introd. by Américo Castro. Rev. ed. Madison, University of Wisconsin Press, 1969. 84 p. $1.50

> The notes and introduction in this Spanish version of *Lazarillo* are scholarly and illuminate for the reader the background of 16th-century Spain, as well as facets in the character of Lazarillo and his various masters. Includes a bibliography.

1693

Lea, Tom. *Brave bulls.* Boston, Little, Brown, 1969. 224 p. illus. $1.95

> Describes the art and techniques of bullfights.

1694

Leigh, Mitch. *Man from La Mancha; a musical play,* written by Dale Wasserman. Lyrics by Joe Darion. Music by Mitch Leigh. With an introd. by John Bettenbender. New York, Dell, 1969. 126 p. illus. $.60

> This musical play is based on Don Quixote, the classical Cervantes hero. It became one of the most highly regarded musical revues of the 1960's, both in the U.S. and abroad.

1695

Lera, Angel María de. *Los clarines del miedo.* Abridged, edited by Robert W. Hatton. Columbus, Ohio, Xerox College, 1971. xxiv, 216 p. $4.50

> A contemporary story about Spanish bullfighting set in a lively and colorful ambiance. This edition includes a preface and biographical material on the author in English as well as exercises in Spanish or English.

1696

Lich, Fred, ed. *Goya in perspective.* Englewood Cliffs, N.J., Prentice-Hall, 1973. 180 p. illus. (Spectrum) $2.45

> Nine essays and excerpts from other books which form a good overview of the artist and his work. Designed for undergraduates as well as for college and specialized libraries.

1697

Lima, Robert. *An annotated bibliography of Ramón del Valle-Inclán.* University Park, Pennsylvania State University Libraries, 1973. 401 p. illus. (Bibliographical series, no. 4) $5

This is the first complete bibliography of the Spanish writer since Rubia Barcia's *A bio-bibliography and inconography of Valle Inclán, 1866-1936* appeared in 1960. It includes works by and about Valle Inclán. This listing is clear and well organized. Highly recommended for college and public libraries.

1698
Liuro de Josep Abaramatia. The Portuguese book of Joseph of Arimathea; paleographical ed., with introd., linguistic study, notes, plates, and glossary by Henry Hare Carter. Chapel Hill, University of North Carolina Press, 1967. 464 p. facsims. (North Carolina. University. Studies in the Romance languages and literatures, no. 71) $11.50

This work is based on Codex 643 of the Portuguese National Archives of the Torre do Tombo, which deals with the first part of the quest for the Holy Grail. Contains a bibliography.

1699
Livermore, Harold V. *A history of Spain.* 2d ed. New York, Funk and Wagnalls, 1967. 484 p. maps. $2.95

A thorough and valuable history of Spain intended for use in college courses. Includes a good bibliography.

1700
Livermore, Harold V. *A new history of Portugal.* New York, Cambridge University Press, 1967. xi, 365 p. front., 13 plates, maps, table. $2.95

Traces the political history of Portugal, from pre-Roman Lusitania to the republic's loss of Goa in 1962. It is a well-balanced, dispassionate, and comprehensive survey. This is the best history of Portugal available in English.

1701
Longland, Jean R. *Selections from contemporary Portuguese poetry: a bilingual selection.* Illustrated by Anne Marie Jauss. Foreword by Ernesto Guerra Da Cal. New York, Harvey House, 1966. 96 p. illus. $2.95

Through excellent English translations from as many as 28 modern and nearly modern poets, along with the original versions, a little bibliographical detail, and some delightful illustrations, Miss Longland provides a thorough introduction to contemporary Portuguese poetry.

1702
López Estrada, Francisco, and John Esten Keller. *Antonio Villegas' El abencerraje.* A collaboration of Francisco López Estrada and John Esten Keller, translator. Chapel Hill, University of North Carolina Press, 1964. 86 p. (University of North Carolina. Studies in comparative literature, no. 33) $3.50

A study of this early 16th-century narrative based on a theme from Moorish romances, which was erroneously attributed to Antonio de Villegas or to Jorge de Montemayor. Includes a bibliography.

1703
López Rubio, José. *La otra orilla; comedia en tres actos.* Edited by Anthony M. Pasquariello and John V. Falconieri. New York, Appleton-Century-Crofts, 1958. 137 p. $2.60

López Rubio is a poetic humorist and writes what Spanish critics have defined as "teatro de evasión." This play takes place within the space of three hours. It is an amusing and swiftly paced play. Contains notes, vocabulary, and questionnaires for classroom use.

1704

López Rubio, José. *Un trono para Cristy; comedia en tres actos,* original de José López Rubio. Edited by Gerald E. Wade. New York, Dodd, Mead, 1960. 146 p. $2.60

One of the most successful comedies by a prominent Spanish playwright. It was first staged in Madrid in 1956. The present edition of this humorous play has been adapted for use in intermediate Spanish classes. Contains notes, questionnaires, and vocabulary.

1705

López Rubio, José. *Una madeja de lana azul celeste.* Edited by Virgil Alexander Warren and Nelson Augusto Cavazos. Englewood Cliffs, N.J., Prentice-Hall, 1969. 192 p. $3.75

First staged in Madrid in 1951, this play has been praised by Spanish critics as the perfect light comedy. The seven characters engage in sparkling dialogs. This edition is intended for intermediate students of Spanish. Contains notes and vocabulary.

1706

López Rubio, José. *La venda en los ojos; comedia en tres actos.* Edited by Marion P. Holt. New York, Appleton-Century-Crofts, 1966. 131 p. $2.60

This play is a serious comedy which deals with the failure of a marriage. The female protagonist chooses to fail in life and pretend madness to escape from her predicament. Contains notes and a vocabulary.

1707

Lott, Robert E. *The structure and style of Azorín's El caballero inactual.* Athens, University of Georgia Press, 1963. 108 p. (University of Georgia monographs, 10) $2.75

An attempt to provide a thorough interpretation of one of the most complex novels of Azorín. The author also analyzes the work's significance and esthetic structure. [Charles Fleener]

1708

Loyola, Ignatius de, Saint. *Spiritual exercises of Saint Ignatius.* Translated by A. Mottola. Introd. by R.W. Gleason. New York, Doubleday, 1969. 251 p. $.95

English translation of St. Ignatius' *Ejercicios espirituales,* an influential book written during the period of Reformation by the founder of the Jesuits.

1709

Luis de Granada. *Wisdom's workshop.* St. Louis, Mo., Herder, 1970. 267 p. $1

Luis de Granada (1504-1588) was a Spanish mystic, writer, and translator who wrote in Latin, Portuguese, and Spanish. This work includes fragments from his *Suma de la vida cristiana.*

1710

Lyon, Richard Colton, ed. *Santayana on America: essays, notes, and letters of American life, literature and philosophy.* New York, Harcourt, Brace and World, 1968. xxxvii, 307 p. (An Original harbinger book) $3.75

These essays, notes, and letters were written over a 60-year period, 1890-1951. The editor has divided them according to subject, thus the reader is allowed to observe George Santayana discourse on "The American intellect," "The American will," and "The American imagination."

1711

McCrary, William Carlton. *The goldfinch and the hawk: a study of Lope de Vega's El*

Caballero de Olmedo, by William C. McCrary. Chapel Hill, University of North Carolina Press, 1970. 362 p. $5

This is a thorough critical edition of *El caballero de Olmedo* a historical play. Contains a good bibliography.

1712
McCullough, Flavia M. *The Basques in the Northwest.* San Francisco, R. and E. Research Associates, 1974. 146 p. $8

Studies a small but unusual group of settlers hailing from Spain, who have made their home in the Rocky Mountain states. Includes a bibliography.

1713
MacCurdy, Raymond R. *Francisco de Rojas Zorrilla and the tragedy.* Albuquerque, University of New Mexico Press, 1958. xiii, 161 p. (University of New Mexico publications in language and literature, no. 13) $2.50

Some 40 or 50 authentic plays of Rojas' survive, 16 of which may be considered tragedies. The author states that "to a large degree Rojas' tragic art represents a return to Spanish tragedy as it was cultivated . . . before Lope de Vega forged the new, all purposeful *comedia.*" Includes bibliographical notes.

1714
Machado y Ruiz, Antonio. *Juan de Mairena: epigrams, maxims, memoranda, and memoirs of an apocryphal professor, with an appendix of poems from the Apocryphal songbooks.* Edited and translated by Ben Belitt. Berkeley, University of California Press, 1963. xxxi, 135 p. $1.50

A very good English translation of *Juan de Mairena; sentencias, donaires, apuntes y recuerdos de un profesor apócrifo* (1936), which consists of philosophic aphorisms and prose fragments by the great Spanish lyric poet.

1715
McVan, Alice Jane. *Antonio Machado with translations and selected poems.* New York, Printed by order of the Trustees of the Hispanic Society of America, 1959. 249 p. ports. (Hispanic notes & monographs; essays, studies, and brief biographies) $1.50

Contains selected poems of the great Spanish poet Antonio Machado in the original Spanish with English translations, as well as a biographic and critical sketch on the author. Includes a bibliography.

1716
Madariaga, Salvador de. *Don Quixote: an introductory essay in psychology.* Ref. ed. New York, Oxford University Press, 1968. 185 p. (Oxford paperbacks, no. 23) $1.50

Madariaga wrote *Guía del lector del Quijote* in 1926 and published his own English translation in 1934 in London. He is the product of three cultures and writes in Spanish, English, and French; all translations of his books are his own. He is the most cosmopolitan of Spain's 20th-century intellectuals.

1717
Madariaga, Salvador de. *The fall of the Spanish Empire.* New rev. ed. New York, Collier Books, 1963. 414 p. $1.50

First published in 1947, this is the continuation of *The rise of the Spanish-American empire.* Madariaga maintains that strife between brothers caused the end of the Spanish empire, especially when the Creole brothers, restless under a tyrannical Spanish father, turned to foreign but equally tyrannical inspiration for revolt. Includes a good bibliography.

1718

Madariaga, Salvador de. *The rise of the Spanish-American empire.* New York, Free Press, 1965. xix, 408 p. illus. port., map (on lining papers) $2.95

> Not too critical of sources, weak in many aspects of institutional life, and somewhat apologetic about Spain, this book is written from a first-hand examination of contemporary accounts by one of Spain's most interesting historians. Madariaga makes many stimulating interpretations and presents Spain to the outside world during the formation of its vast overseas empire.

1719

Madariaga, Salvador de. *Selecciones de Madariaga.* Edited by Frank Sedwick and Elizabeth Van Orman. Englewood Cliffs, N.J., Prentice-Hall, 1969. 208 p. port. $4.25

> Contains selections from the author's *Ingleses, franceses, españoles* (1929); *Bosquejo de Europa* (1951); and *El enemigo de Dios* (1929). All of these works represent Madariaga's most penetrating analysis of national and psychological traits. This textbook edition is intended for second- and third-year students of Spanish. Contains a vocabulary.

1720

Marías, Julián. *History of philosophy.* Translated from the Spanish by Stanley Applebaum and Clarence C. Strowbridge. New York, Dover, 1967. xviii, 505 p. $3

> A translation of the bestselling Spanish survey of western philosophy *Historia de la filosofía* (1966). The main topics treated are Greek, Christian, medieval, and modern philosophy. Marías was a disciple of Ortega y Gasset. A special preface to the English edition and a bibliography are included.

1721

Marías, Julián. *Meditaciones sobre la sociedad española.* Philadelphia, Center for Curriculum Development, 1971. 149 p. $1.20

> Textbook edition of a noted philosopher's description of Spanish society.

1722

Marías, Julián. *Modos de vivir; un observador español en los Estados Unidos; selections from the writings of Julián Marías.* Edited by Edward R. Mulvihill and Roberto G. Sánchez. New York, Oxford University Press, 1964. xiii, 182 p. $2.50

> Spain's most influential philosopher of the second half of the 20th century surveys the U.S. in a manner reminiscent of De Tocqueville's famed account.

1723

Marín, Diego. *Vida española.* 3d ed. New York, Appleton-Century-Crofts, 1970. 238 p. illus. $4.15

> Contains short chapter on Spanish life and culture for the intermediate student of Spanish. Includes notes and vocabulary.

1724

Martinez Sierra, Gregorio. *Mamá; comedia en tres actos.* Edited with introduction, notes and vocabulary by Donald Devenish. New York, Norton, 1952. 189 p. $2.95

> A noted play by Spain's well-known playwright and poet, *Mamá* became a considerable popular success when it was first produced in 1912. Martinez Sierra shows sharp psychological insight in delineating his characters.

1725

Mattingly, Garrett. *The armada.* Boston, Houghton Mifflin, 1962. 443 p. illus. $2.65

This is an account of the 1588 Spanish attempt to conquer England, first published in 1959. It provides a good background to 16th-century Latin America.

1726
Mattingly, Garrett. *Catherine of Aragon*. New York, Random House, 1960. 415 p. $2.40

An excellent and well-researched biography of the Spanish princess who became Henry VIII's first wife. First published in 1942.

1727
Mattingly, Garrett. *The Invincible Armada and Elizabethan England*. Charlottesville, University Press of Virginia. $1.50

The author discusses the interpretations, which have been substantially revised during the last half century, of the defeat of the Spanish Armada.

1728
Matute, Ana María. *Doce historias de la Artámila*. Edited by Manuel Durán and Gloria Durán, under the general editorship of Robert G. Mead, Jr. New York, Harcourt, Brace, and World, 1965. xi, 172 p. illus. $3.75

Ana María Matute is Spain's most gifted contemporary short story writer. She depicts places, people, and events with humor and warmth.

1729
Matute, Ana María. *Fiesta al noroeste*. Edited by Luis Alpera. Englewood Cliffs, N.J., Prentice-Hall, 1971. 100 p. $2.95

Describes a dramatic episode in the Artámila region, masterfully depicting rural personages and their lives. This novel was first published in 1952 and was awarded the Café Girón literary prize of that year. This edition contains notes and vocabulary.

1730
Mezerik, Avrahm G. *Goa: Portuguese colonial policy, Indian campaign, U.N. record, chronology*. New York, International Review Service, 1962. 55 p. maps. (International review service, v. 8, no. 70) $5

Reviews Portuguese colonial policy towards Goa. Includes a good bibliography.

1731
Michel, Joseph, ed. *Valle-Inclán; páginas selectas*. Edited by Joseph Michel. Englewood Cliffs, N.J., Prentice-Hall, 1969. x, 198 p. $3.50

This text is intended as an introduction to the life and work of Valle-Inclán. The preface avoids being labored and yet presents the major events of Valle-Inclán's life as well as the distinguishing features of his literary style. The footnotes, usually on vocabulary and idiomatic expressions, are in English or in Spanish, whichever the author considers most appropriate. Includes a bibliography.

1732
Micheletti, Emma. *Velázquez*. New York, Grosset & Dunlap, 1969. 120 p. illus. $1.50

A handsome edition about the work of the famous Spanish painter, illustrated with 80 full-color drawings.

1733
Micheli, Mario de. *Picasso*; translated from the Italian by Pearl Sanders. New York, Grosset and Dunlap, 1967. 80 p. illus. (part col.) (The New Grosset art library, 4) $1.50

Describes succinctly the life and work of Pablo Picasso with representative illustrations of his work covering many stages of his evolution as an artist. Contains a bibliography.

1734

Michener, James Albert. *Iberia; Spanish travels and reflections,* by James A. Michener. Photos by Robert Vavra. Greenwich, Conn., Fawcett Publications, 1968. 960 p. illus., geneal. tables, maps (part col.), ports. $1.95

A well-known American author gives his interpretation of that complex and magnificent country which is Spain. He brings fresh insights to many of the hidden places which tourists never seem to find. Photographs by Robert Vavra enhance the text.

1735

Mihura, Miguel. *Carlota.* Edited by Edith B. Sublette. New York, Odyssey Press, 1963. xii, 146 p. $1.65

A contemporary play set in today's Spain by a young Spanish dramatist. Includes a bibliography.

1736

Mihura, Miguel. *Mi adorado Juan, comedia en dos actos.* Edited by John V. Falconieri and Anthony M. Pasquariello. Boston, Ginn-Blaisdell, 1964. xvii, 110 p. illus. $3.50

Textbook edition of a contemporary Spanish play. Contains a good bibliography.

1737

Miles, George Carpenter. *Coinage of the Umayyads of Spain.* Published in cooperation with the Hispanic Society of America. New York, American Numismatic Society, 1971. 2 v. plates. (Hispanic numismatic series, monograph, no. 1) $10

This is an important monographic study of certain Moslem coins used in Spain under the Umayyad Caliphate. Contains representative illustrations, as well as a good bibliography.

1738

Miles, George Carpenter. *Coinage of the Visigoths of Spain; Leovigild to Achila.* Published in cooperation with the Hispanic Society of America. New York, American Numismatic Society, 1962. xv, 519 p. illus., fold. maps. (Hispanic numismatic series, monograph, no. 2) $10

This scholarly study records and studies 3,461 Gothic Iberian coins in the collection of the Hispanic Society of America and other depositories. Contains illustrations of forgeries, and a thorough bibliography.

1739

Miles, George Carpenter. *Coins of the Spanish-Muluk al-Tawa'if.* Published in cooperation with the Hispanic Society of America. New York, American Numismatic Society, 1971. xi, 168 p. 15 plates. (Hispanic numismatic series, monograph, no. 3) $4.50

An important numismatic expert presents here a study of Spanish Moslem coins, with illustrations and a bibliography.

1740

Miller, Samuel Jefferson Taylor, and John P. Spielman. *Cristóbal Rojas y Spínola, Cameralist and Irenicist, 1626-1695.* Philadelphia, American Philosophical Society, 1962. 108 p. (Transactions of the American Philosophical Society, new series, 52) $2.50

Rojas y Spínola was the bishop of Tina for the second half of the 17th century and strove for the reunification of Catholics and Protestants. This is a good biography with a thorough bibliography.

1741
Minter, William. *Portuguese Africa and the West.* New York, Monthly Review Press, 1974. 200 p. illus., maps. $2.95

The author states in the preface that he wants to "spell out American complicity in Portugal's colonial wars." He asserts that Portugal has the tacit backing of NATO and the West in its colonial policies. Includes a bibliography.

1742
Miró, Joan. *Miró.* Introd. by Jacques Dupin. Translated from the French by Edward Marsh. New York, Tudor, 1967. 24 [5] p. illus. (part col.), plates. $1.25, durabind $2.25

Contains representative illustrations of the work by the great Catalan painter, with excellent introductory material about this contemporary artist.

1743
Miró Joan. *Nineteen forty to nineteen fifty-five.* Edited by Guy Weelen. New York, Tudor Pub. Co., 1969. 24 p. illus. $.49

The editor has selected works for the 1940-55 period and illustrated and commented on this phase of Miró's production.

1744
Miró, Joan. *Miró: Nineteen twenty-four to nineteen forty.* Edited by Guy Weelen. New York, Tudor Pub. Co., 1969. 1 v. illus. $.49

Concentrates on the period mentioned in the title as the most productive in the career of the artist. Contains interesting illustrations of lithographs, paintings, and other works.

1745
Moffitt, John F. *Spanish painting.* New York, Dutton, 1973. 159 p. illus. (Studio/Vista pictureback) $2.75

Explores the character of Spanish painting within the familiar historical periods from prehistoric times to the present. Attractive illustrations enhance this highly recommended book.

1746
Moon, Harold K. *Alejandro Casona; playwright.* Provo, Utah, Brigham Young University Press, 1970. 80 p. (Charles E. Merrill monograph series on the humanities and social sciences, v. 2, no. 1) $1.50

Reviews the work of Casona, who achieved in his lifetime perhaps greater international renown than any other Spanish playwright, with the possible exception of García Lorca. The author uses specific works to illustrate certain general characteristics. Includes bibliographical references.

1747
Munch, Peter A. *The song tradition of Tristan da Cunha.* Bloomington, Indiana University, Research Center, 1971. 149 p. $8

An interesting analysis of musical tradition in the island of Tristan da Cunha settled by Portuguese mariners, New England whalers, and several other groups. The contemporary genetic and anthropological composition of the population is rather unique and worthy of study.

1748

Nach, James. *Portugal in pictures.* New York, Sterling Pub. Co., 1970. 64 p. illus., maps, ports. (Visual geography series) $1.50

An illustrated booklet on the land, geography, history, people, and culture of Portugal. Intended for school use and for travelers who wish to acquaint themselves with the country.

1749

Namikawa, Banri. *Spain.* Tokyo, Palo Alto, Calif., Kodansha International, 1971. 138 p. col. illus., map. (This beautiful world, v. 19) $2.75

This superbly illustrated tour book gives a view of Spain seldom seen in such works. The author is sensitive to the charm and beauty of the land and people and approaches his study from the regional as well as local perspective. Highly recommended.

1750

Nelson, Lowry, comp. *Cervantes; a collection of critical essays.* Englewood Cliffs, N.J., Prentice-Hall, 1969. 176 p. (Twentieth century views; A Spectrum book) $1.95

A number of noted contemporary critics, such as Thomas Mann, Leon Spitzer, W. H. Auden, and the editor present their views on the great Spanish writer, analyzing *Don Quixote,* as well as Cervantes' lesser known works. Includes a bibliography.

1750A

Newberry Library, Chicago; *see* Welsh, Doris Varner, ed., 1932

1751

Newmark, Maxim. *Dictionary of Spanish literature.* Paterson, N.J., Littlefield, Adams, 1963. 352 p. (Midcentury reference library) $2.25

This convenient reference work includes basic data on authors, their works, and short critical evaluations of each, as well as succinct coverage of literary schools and currents. This is an important work for libraries and for those specializing in Spanish literature.

1752

Norman, Barbara. *The Spanish cookbook.* New York, Bantam Books, 1967. 197 p. $.95

The author has selected representative recipes of Spanish food and adapted them for the U.S. kitchen.

1753

Norris, Frank Pelletier. *La coronica troyana; a medieval Spanish translation of Guido de Colonna's Historia destructionis Troiae.* Edition, studies, notes and glossary by Frank Pelletier Norris, II. Chapel Hill, University of North Carolina Press, 1970. 176 p. facsims. (Studies in the Romance languages and literatures, no. 90) $6.50

Based on the original medieval Spanish manuscript at El Escorial, MS L.III.16, this is a scholarly, annotated edition of *Historia de la destrucción de Troya.*

1754

Nowell, Charles E. *The great discoveries and the first colonial empires.* Ithaca, N.Y., Cornell University Press, 1954. 150 p. illus., maps. (The Development of Western Civilization: narrative essays in the history of our tradition from its origins in ancient Israel and Greece to the present) $1.95

Describes the historical and cultural background of the first colonial empires. This is a good summary of the age of discovery. Includes a good bibliography.

1755

Nowell, Charles E. *Portugal*. Englewood Cliffs, N.J., Prentice-Hall, 1973. xii, 178 p. maps. (The modern nations in historical perspective; A Spectrum book) $2.45

A concise history of Portugal which attempts to interpret the historical, cultural, social, and economic experience of the country. Contains a bibliography.

1756

O'Hara, Frank. *New Spanish paintings and sculpture: Rafael Canogan and others.* Exhibition. Garden City, N.Y., Doubleday, 1960. 59 p. illus. $1.95

Presents the catalog of an exhibition of the works of 16 contemporary Spanish artists. The director of the exhibit provides the text which is accompanied by 44 pages of black-and-white illustrations. Includes a bibliography.

1757

Ornstein, Jacob, ed. *Luis de Lucena; repetición de amores.* Chapel Hill, University of North Carolina Press, 1954. 130 p. (North Carolina University. Studies in the Romance languages and literatures, no 23) $5

A scholarly, well-researched, annotated edition of Luis de Lucena's work. Includes a bibliography.

1758

Ortega y Gasset, José. *Concord and liberty.* Translated from the Spanish by Helene Weyl. New York, Norton, 1966. 182 p. $1.95

This English translation was first published in 1946. The book contains essays by Spain's influential philosopher who embodied more than any other writer the spirit of the first three decades of the 20th century. He has made extensive comments on every important subject of our time.

1759

Ortega y Gasset, José. *Dehumanization of art and other essays on art, culture, and literature.* Princeton, N.J., Princeton University Press, 1968. 204 p. (Princeton paperbacks, 128) $2.45

Five essays in which Ortega expresses his incisive views on the arts and literature in the 20th century. "Dehumanization of art" and "Notes on the novel" appeared in 1925, "On point of view in the arts" and "In search of Goethe from within" were first published in 1949, and "The self and the other" in 1952. Contains bibliographical footnotes.

1760

Ortega y Gasset, José. *History as a system, and other essays toward a philosophy of history.* With an afterword by John William Miller. New York, Norton, 1961. 269 p. $1.85

Translation of *La historia como sistema* which was first published in English in 1941 under the title *Toward a philosophy of history.* Ortega expresses in these essays his views on history.

1761

Ortega y Gasset, José. *Man and crisis.* Translated from the Spanish by Mildred Adams. New York, Norton, 1958. 217 p. $1.95

An English translation of *En torno a Galileo* in which he writes on the impact of science on human thought.

1762

Ortega y Gasset, José. *Man and people.* Translated from the Spanish by Willard Trask. New York, Norton, 1957. 272 p. $1.95

These essays deal with the place of the individual within a mass society. Ortega feels that the individual, rather than follow circumstances blindly, modifies them in a continuous interplay.

1763

Ortega y Gasset, José. *Meditations on Quixote.* With an introd. and notes by Julián Marías. Translated from the Spanish by Evelyn Rugg and Diego Marín. 1st American ed. New York, Norton, 1961. 192 p. $1.95

Ortega's first book, *Meditaciones del Quixote* (1914), outlines his philosophy. He conceives the ego as the first reality surrounded by circumstances, and he defines circumstances as silent things which are in one's immediate surroundings. Includes bibliographical references.

1764

Ortega y Gasset, José. *Mission of the university.* New York, Norton, 1967. 194 p. $1.25

An essay on the aims and purposes of the university is presented in a systematic form. Includes bibliographical references.

1765

Ortega y Gasset, José. *The modern theme.* Introd. by José Ferrater Mora. New York, Harper & Row, 1961. 152 p. $1.75

Translation of *El tema de nuestro tiempo* (1923) in which Ortega systematized his purely philosophical thought based on life itself. To the pure reason of idealism he opposed a "vital reason," constantly affected by the circumstances of life.

1766

Ortega y Gasset, José. *On love; aspects of single theme.* Translated by Toby Talbot. New York, World Pub. Co., 1969. 241 p. $2.95

An essay on love by the Spanish philosopher who was very influential during the first half of the 20th century. He embodied, perhaps more than any other writer of our time, the contemporary spirit. The original Spanish is entitled *Estudios sobre el amor* (1939).

1767

Ortega y Gasset, José. *The origin of philosophy.* Authorized translation from the Spanish by Toby Talbot. New York, Norton, 1967. 125 p. $1.25

Essays on the origins of philosophy which had great impact on Latin American thought of this century. Includes bibliographical footnotes.

1768

Ortega y Gasset, José. *La redención de las provincias.* Philadelphia, Chilton Educational Series, 1967. 171 p. $.90

A series of essays, articles, and speeches published in 1931, in which Ortega expounded his ideas on current political events in Spain of that period. Contains notes.

1769

Ortega y Gasset, José. *The revolt of the masses.* Authorized translation from the Spanish by Toby Talbot. New York, Norton, 1957. 190 p. $1.50

First published in 1932 under the title *La revolución de las masas,* this remains Ortega's most widely read book. In it he explains modern society as an inversion of values due to a crisis in European culture and the preponderance of mass culture. Contains bibliographical footnotes.

1770
Ortega y Gasset, José. *Some lessons in metaphysics.* Translated by Mildred Adams. New York, Norton, 1970. 158 p. $1.95

> English translation of *Unas lecciones de metafísica,* in which Ortega explains his ideas on metaphysics and the basis of his philosophical thought.

1771
Ortega y Gasset, José. *Sus mejores páginas.* Edited by Manuel Durán. Englewood Cliffs, N.J., Prentice-Hall, 1966. 250 p. $3.95

> Professor Durán has selected a representative series of essays by the influential Spanish philosopher and essayist. Contains important bibliographical notes.

1772
Ortega y Gasset, José. *What is philosophy?* Translated from the Spanish by Mildred Adams. New York, Norton, 1961. 252 p. $1.85

> Contains a series of lectures given by Ortega in Madrid and Buenos Aires, containing most of his themes and thoughts on society, culture, and philosophy.

1773
Orwell, George. *Homage to Catalonia.* New York, Harcourt, Brace and World, 1952. 232 p. (Harvest book, 162) $1.95

> A memoir of the British novelist's experiences as a journalist and soldier in the Spanish civil war. It is also a record of the author's disillusionment with totalitarian communism. Lionel Trilling, in his introduction to this edition, calls this work "one of the most important documents of our time." [Charles Fleener]

1774
Palacio Valdés, Armando. *José.* Translated by Harriet De Onís. Great Neck, N.Y., Barron's Educational Series, 1961. 189 p. $1.50

> Palacio Valdés (1853-1938) was a Spanish short story writer, novelist, and essayist. He achieved fame in 1885 with *José,* a novel of fishermen and the sea.

1775
Pardo Bazán, Emilia. *Los pazos de Ulloa.* Philadelphia, Center for Curriculum Development, 1962, 102 p. $1.20

> One of Pardo Bazán's best novels, it first appeared in 1886. It is a Zolaesque study of social decay in a rural Galician setting.

1776
Parker, Jack Horace, and Arthur M. Fox, eds. *Lope de Vega studies, 1937-63; a critical survey and annotated bibliography.* Toronto, University of Toronto Press, 1970. 366 p. $6

> This is a thoroughly annotated bibliography of works about the great Spanish Golden Age dramatist written between 1937 and 1962.

1777
Parry, John Horace. *The age of reconnaissance.* New York, New American Library, 1964. 383 p. illus. $1.25

> Excellent study of European expansion from 1450 to 1650 by an expert in maritime history. Includes a good bibliography.

1778
Parry, John Horace. *The establishment of European hegemony 1415-1715; trade and*

exploration in the age of the Renaissance. New York, Harper and Row, 1961. 202 p. $1.45

A succinct history of European expansion, emphasizing economic motivations. Includes a good bibliography.

1779

Parry, John Horace, ed. *European reconnaissance.* New York, Harper and Row, 1970. 219 p. maps. $1.65

A history of European maritime expansion. Hispanists should note the exploits of the Spanish and Portuguese mariners and explorers. Includes a bibliography.

1780

Paso, Alfonso. *La corbata.* Ed. by E.B. Sublette. New York, Odyssey Press, 1967. 146 p. $1.65

Alfonso Paso is a contemporary Spanish playwright. This is an annotated edition of one of his most popular dramas.

1781

Pattison, Walter Thomas, and Donald W. Bleznick, comps. *Representative Spanish authors.* 3d ed. New York, Oxford University Press, 1971. 2 v. illus. $7.50

The first edition appeared in 1942. Volume 1 extends from the Middle Ages to the 18th century, and volume 2 brings Spanish literature to the present. The generous selections give the student an ample view of the literature of Spain. Includes vocabularies.

1782

Payne, Robert, ed. *The civil war in Spain, 1936-1939.* New York, Fawcett World Library, 1968. 336 p. maps, tables. $.95

The editor has selected eyewitness accounts by participants including George Orwell, John Dos Passos, and Arthur Koestler.

1783

Payne, Stanley G. *Falange: a history of Spanish fascism.* Stanford, Calif., Stanford University Press, 1966. 316 p. $2.95

Presents an excellent history of Spanish fascism from 1931 to 1959 with special emphasis on the 1936-45 period. Includes bibliographies.

1784

Payne, Stanley G. *Franco's Spain.* New York, Crowell, 1967. 142 p. tables. $1.95

An analysis of Spain's evolution under Franco's regime, presenting the country within the broader European context. The author includes a brief biography of Franco and also surveys to some extent the Spanish civil war which is used as the historical background for the development of the regime. Includes bibliographies.

1785

Payne, Stanley G. *The Spanish Revolution.* New York, Norton, 1970. 398 p. maps. $3.25

A thorough and important book on the Spanish Revolution. It traces the forces that brought about the Revolution, such as the socialists, the military, and other segments of society. It also analyzes the legacy of the 19th century within the broad political spectrum of Spain between World Wars I and II. Includes bibliographies.

1786

Penrose, Roland. *Picasso: his life and work.* 2d ed. New York, Schocken Books, 1962. 410 p. illus. (Schocken paperbacks, SB 31) $4.95

Explores the work and life of Pablo Picasso. The illustrations are representative of many periods of the artist's work.

1787
Pérez Galdós. Benito. *El amigo manso.* Edited by Denah Lida. New York, Oxford University Press, 1963. 330 p. $3.50

This is a realistic novel, written in a naturalistic style, which centers around a Quixotesque personage.

1788
Pérez Galdós, Benito. *Compassion.* Translated from the Spanish *Misericordia* by Toby Talbot. New York, Ungar, 1962. 282 p. $1.75

Deals with the decline of an aristocratic family in Madrid in the late 19th century and the rise of the new middle class.

1789
Pérez Galdós, Benito. *Compassion,* by Galdós. A modern translation with notes by Joan MacLean. Introd. by Glen Willbern. New York, American R.D.M. Corp., 1966. 159 p. (A Study master publication T-42) $1.95

See above.

1790
Pérez Galdós, Benito. *Las de bringas.* Edited by Ricardo Gullón. Englewood Cliffs, N.J., Prentice-Hall, 1971. 321 p. $3.95

This is the complete text of Galdós' realistic novel, with notes and vocabulary. It will be very useful in intermediate to advanced Spanish courses.

1791
Pérez Galdós, Benito. *La desheredada.* Philadelphia, Chilton Books, 1964. 246 p. $1.80

Perhaps Pérez Galdós' greatest novel, this work deals with the heroine's delusions that she is of noble birth which eventually lead to her ruin. It was first published in 1881.

1792
Pérez Galdós, Benito. *Doña Perfecta.* Translated and introd. by Harriet de Onís. Great Neck, N.Y., Barron's Educational Series, 1960. 235 p. $1.25

Pérez Galdós decried bigotry and radicalism in this novel published in 1876.

1793
Pérez Galdós, Benito. *Doña Perfecta,* por Benito Pérez Galdós. Introd. and notes by Rodolfo Cardona. New York, Dell, 1965. 281 p. (The Laurel language library) $.50

See above.

1794
Pérez Galdós, Benito. *Marianela;* edited by Nicholson B. Adams. Boston, Ginn-Blaisdell, 1951. 197 p. illus. $3

An abridged version of Pérez Galdós' widely read classic novel. It revolves around a romantic love story. This is a textbook edition, with notes and vocabulary.

1795
Pérez Galdós, Benito. *Marianela: a story of Spanish love.* Translated from the Spanish of B. Pérez Galdós by Helen W. Lester. New York, Barnes and Noble, 1961. 295 p. $1.50

An English translation of Pérez Galdós' well-known novel.

1796

Pérez Galdós, Benito. *Miau.* Translated by John Michael Cohen. Baltimore, Penguin Books, 1966. 282 p. $1.75

The great Spanish novelist displays his concern for the individual in relation to society. The protagonist is a civil servant in Madrid who has lost his post and is gradually driven to distraction and suicide. It was first published in 1888.

1797

Pérez Galdós, Benito. *La sombra de Galdós; libro de lectura, repaso y conversación.* Edited by Rodolfo Cardona. New York, Norton, 1964. xxxiv, 245 p. $2.95

Includes selections from Pérez Galdós' works.

1798

Pérez Galdós, Benito. *Tormento.* Philadelphia, Chilton Books, 1967. 175 p. $.90

This novel was first published in 1886; it is written in the style of literary realism for which Pérez Galdós became well known.

1799

Pérez Galdós, Benito. *Torquemada en la hoguera. Torquemada en la cruz. Torquemada en el Purgatorio. Torquemada y San Pedro.* Philadelphia, Chilton Books, 1969. 392 p. $1.80

An annotated textbook edition of the Torquemada series published between 1889 and 1895. These works deal with the ethical decay resulting from avarice.

1800

Pérez Galdós, Benito. *Tristana.* Translated from the Spanish by R. Selden Rose. Peterborough, N.H., R.R. Smith, 1961. 143 p. $1.95

This short novel is a masterful study of possessiveness carried to the point of vice. It presents a microcosmic view of Spanish culture and values.

1800A

Pérez Galdós, Benito; *see also* Weber, Robert J., 1931

1801

Picasso, Pablo. *Drawings of Picasso.* Edited by Arthur Miller. Alhambra, Calif., A. Borden, 1961. 48 p. (chiefly illus.) (Master draughtsman series) $1.75

Excellent reproductions of Picasso's most representative works at a reasonable price.

1802

Picasso, Pablo. *Pablo Picasso; blue and rose periods.* Text by William S. Lieberman. New York, H.N. Abrams, 1971. 40 p. illus., col. plates. (Great art of the ages) $1.95

The paintings reproduced here begin with his second trip to Paris, 1899-1902, during which the color blue dominated his palette, and go on to his rose period. These early works are classics. The reproductions are excellent.

1803

Picasso, Pablo. *Picasso; Barcelona to the pink period.* New York, Tudor, 1971. 1 v. (chiefly illus.) $.49

Traces the early work of Picasso through the first decade of this century.

1804

Picasso, Pablo. *Picasso; dessins 1959-1960. Galerie Louise Leiris, 30 novembre-31 décembre. Paris 1960.* New York, Wittenborn, 1960. 1 v. (chiefly illus., part col.) $4

Contains drawings and gouaches in the series entitled *Romancero deu picador*, with handsome reproductions.

1805

Picasso, Pablo. *Picasso: dessins 1966-1967, Galerie Louise Leiris.* New York, Wittenborn, 1968. 74 p. (chiefly illus., part col.) (Galerie Louise Leiris. Catalogue no. 21, série A) $4.50

Contains reproductions of 82 drawings by Picasso which were exhibited by the Louise Leiris Gallery. The reproductions are excellent.

1806

Picasso, Pablo. *Picasso: Les Ménines 1957. Galerie Louise Leiris, 22 mai-27 juin. Paris 1959.* New York, Wittenborn, 1959. 1 v. (chiefly illus., part col.) (Galerie Louise Leiris. Catalogue no. 10, série A) $4

Presents Picasso's paintings inspired by *Las meninas* of Velásquez, as well as nine paintings entitled *Les pigeons* and several luminous Mediterranean landscapes.

1807

Picasso, Pablo. *Picasso; peintures 1955-1956. Galerie Louise Leiris, mars-avril 1957. Paris 1957.* New York, Wittenborn, 1957. 1 v. (chiefly illus., part col.) (Galerie Louise Leiris. Catalogue no. 1, série A) $4.50

Presents reproductions of 50 paintings by the great Spanish master, among these the *Femme dans l'atelier* series, and the famous *Femme assise près de la fenêtre*. The paintings were exhibited in 1957.

1808

Picasso, Pablo. *Picasso; 45 gravures sur linoleum, 1958-1960. Galerie Louise Leiris, 15 juin-13 juillet, 1960. Catalogue de l'exposition Picasso.* New York, Wittenborn, 1961. 45 plates (part col.) $4.50

Presents 45 linoleum cuts by the great master, some in color.

1809

Picasso, Pablo. *The sculptor's studio: etchings.* With an introd. by William S. Lieverman. New York, Museum of Modern Art; distributed by the New York Graphic Arts Society, 1952. 23 p. illus. $2.50

Contains etchings by Picasso.

1810

Pitt-Rivers, Julian Alfred. *The people of the Sierra.* 2d ed. Chicago, University of Chicago Press, 1971. xxviii, 274 p. $1.95

Originally presented as the author's thesis at Oxford in 1954, this excellent monograph studies the people of Alcalá de la Sierra in Andalusia. It analyzes patterns of daily life and thus provides insight into the social structure of southern Spain. Includes bibliographical references.

1811

Plaidy, J. *The Spanish Inquisition: its rise, growth, and end.* New York, Citadel Press, 1970. 392 p. illus. $3.95

A loosely organized, superficial study of the Spanish Inquisition, with bibliographical references.

1812

Polt, John Herman Richard, ed. *Juan Pablo Forner y Segarra: Los gramáticos, historia chinesca.* Ed. crítica por John H.R. Polt. Berkeley, University of California Press, 1970. 256 p. (University of California publications in modern philology, v. 95) $3

This is a new edition of the work of an 18th-century Spanish polemicist who studied the Chinese grammarians, in part to refute Juan de Iriarte, another figure of the Spanish enlightenment. Contains a good prolog, notes, and a bibliography. This is an important contribution.

1813

Prestage, Edgar D. *Francisco Manuel de Mello.* New York, Hispanic Society of America, 1969. 110 p. illus. $2

Studies the life and works of Francisco Mello [i.e. Melo], a Portuguese literary figure of the 17th century who spent a considerable part of his life in Spain. He became famous for his voluminous historical and literary writings.

1814

Proske, Beatrice Gilman. *Pompeo Leoni; work in marble and alabaster in relation to Spanish sculpture.* New York, Hispanic Society of America, 1956. 49 p. illus. (Hispanic notes and monographs; essays, studies, and brief biographies) $2

Pompeo Leoni, son of Leone Leoni, sculptor to Emperor Charles V, came to Spain in 1556 with the royal party. He settled permanently in Spain and became the most influential sculptor in Spain of the 16th century. This handsomely illustrated work is a succinct analysis of the artist's work.

1815

Puhl, Louis James. *The spiritual exercises of St. Ignatius: based on studies in the language of the autograph.* Chicago, Loyola University Press, 1968. 216 p. $2

A clear, idiomatic translation of the *Spiritual exercises* of the Spanish saint and founder of the Jesuit order. This edition was first published in 1955.

1816

Puzzo, Dante Anthony. *The Spanish civil war.* Edited by L.L. Snyder. New York, Van Nostrand, 1969. 191 p. (An Anvil original, 102) $1.95

A brief historical study of the Spanish civil war, intended for classroom use. It relies on some documents as well as on newspaper reports. Contains a useful bibliography.

1817

Randolph, Donald Allen. *Don Manuel Cañete, cronista literario del romanticismo y del posromanticismo en España.* Chapel Hill, University of North Carolina Press, 1972. 268 p. (University of North Carolina. Studies in the Romance languages and literatures, no. 115) $6.50

A scholarly critical study of the work of the most influential literary critic of 19th-century Spain who was a poet, newspaperman, critic, and essayist. It also provides, for the first time, ample biographical information.

1818

Rennert, Hugo Albert. *The Spanish stage in the time of Lope de Vega.* New York, Dover Publications, 1963. xv, 403 p. $3.50

First published by the Hispanic Society of America in 1909, this is a scholarly study of the various aspects of Spanish drama, including staging, costumes, and actors during the 16th and 17th centuries.

1819
Rey, Agapito, and Antonio García Solalinde. *Ensayo de una bibliografía de las leyendas troyanas en la literatura española.* Bloomington, Indiana University Press, 1969. 103 p. (Indiana University publications. Humanities series, no 6) $1

First published in 1942 by the prominent Spanish medievalist who has been residing in the U.S. for the past 30 years, this is an annotated bibliography of Trojan legends in Spanish literature. Contains a general bibliography as well.

1820
Rey, Agapito. *El libro de los cien capitulos.* Edición de Agapito Rey. Bloomington, Indiana University Press, 1960. xxii, 92 p. (Indiana University Humanities series, no. 44) $4

A new edition of the medieval work *Libro de los cient capitulos.*

1821
Reuter, Wolfgang. *The Lipizzaners and the Spanish Riding School.* Translated by J.M. Abbot. North Hollywood, Calif., Wilshire Book Co., 1973. 78 p. illus. $2

A profusely illustrated book about Vienna's famed Spanish Riding School founded in 1580 by the Archduke Charles, who dispatched officials to Spain to buy breeding stock for new studs. In those days the Spanish horse played a similar role to that played by the English thoroughbred in this century. A very attractive and informative book.

1822
Rexroth, Kenneth, ed. *Thirty Spanish poems of love and exile.* San Francisco, City Lights Pocket Bookshop, 1968. 31 p. (The Pocket poets series, no. 2) $1

Included are Rafael Alberti, Jorge Guillén, Pablo Neruda, Federico García Lorca, and Antonio Machado. The editor says that "only some of these poets were born in Spain. None of them lives there today." [Charles Fleener]

1823
Ricart, Domingo. *Juan de Valdés y el pensamiento religioso europeo en los siglos 16 y 17.* Lawrence, University of Kansas Press, 1971. 223 p. $2.50

Juan de Valdés was a philosopher, religious writer, and literary critic in 16th-century Spain. His writings were controversial and, fearing the Inquisition, he went to Rome in 1531. This work studies Valdés' influence on European philosophy.

1824
Richards, Vernon. *Lessons of the Spanish Revolution, 1936-1939.* Enlarged ed. New York, Chip's Bookshop, 1973. 240 p. $3.75

This is an enlarged edition of the work with the same title published in 1953. The author is more interested in seeking the reasons for the defeat of the Revolution than for Franco's military victory. The study relies on official documents. Includes a bibliography and a lengthy bibliographical postscript.

1825
Rikhoff, Jean, ed. *The Quixote anthology;* edited by Jean Rikhoff in collaboration with Kam and Richard Tiernan. New York, Grosset and Dunlap, 1961. 372 p. (The Universal library. UL 120) $2.45

A carefully edited anthology of the famous Spanish epic.

1826
Rincon, E. *Coplas satíricas y dramáticas en la edad media.* Philadelphia, Center for Curriculum Development, 1967. 187 p. $1.20

Contains a very good selection of Spanish medieval satiric and dramatic ballads.

1827
Río, Amelia Agostini de del, ed. *Flores del romancero.* Englewood Cliffs, N.J., Prentice-Hall, 1970. 288 p. $3.95

The editor has assembled outstanding ballads from their origins to the present to illustrate the development in theme, technique, style, and length. The text also indicates the influence of ballads on other literary genres.

1828
Rivers, Elías L., ed. and tr. *Renaissance and Baroque poetry of Spain with English prose translations.* New York, Dell Pub. Co., 1966. 351 p. (The Laurel language library. Spanish series) $3.95

This is a bilingual edition of Spanish poetry of the 15th and 16th centuries with a good introduction by the editor.

1829
Rivers, Elías L., ed. *36 Spanish poems.* Boston, Houghton Mifflin, 1957. 72 p. $1.90

A choice and interesting selection of Spanish poetry.

1830
Rodriguez, Alfred, and William Rosenthal, eds. *The modern Spanish essay.* Waltham, Mass., Blaisdell Pub. Co., 1969. xvi, 129 p. (A Blaisdell books in modern languages) $3.25

Includes essays by Unamuno, Ortega y Gasset, Madariaga, Azorín, Eugenio d'Ors, Marañón, Francisco Ayala, Laín Entralgo, and Julián Marías. Each selection is preceded by a brief sketch of the author and his work. Also contains notes and vocabularies.

1831
Rodriguez-Moñino, Antonio R., and María Brey Mariño, eds. *Catálogo de los manuscritos poéticos castellanos existentes en la Biblioteca de The Hispanic Society of America (siglos XV, XVI, y XVII).* New York, Hispanic Society of America, 1965-66. 3 v. facsims., ports. $12

The first two volumes contain an annotated catalog and content notes of 248 manuscripts of Spanish poetry, with 128 facsimile reproductions and portraits. The third volume provides a thorough bibliographic history of this magnificent collection.

1832
Rojas, Fernando de. *La Celestina; a novel in dialogue.* Translated from the Spanish by Lesley Bird Simpson. Berkeley, University of California Press, 1962. x, 162 p. illus., facsim. $1.95

This is a very good modern translation of the classic Spanish drama that expresses the ribald elements with the sentimentality that is its very essence.

1833
Rojas, Fernando de. *Celestina; a play in twenty-one acts attributed to Fernando de Rojas.* Translated from the Spanish by Mack Hendricks Singleton. Madison, University of Wisconsin Press, 1962. 316 p. $2.95

A scholarly version of the Spanish drama that includes all the original editorial sources, such as letters, prologs, a modern preface, and a critical bibliography. Survey of Celestina studies in the 20th century and the selected bibliography prepared by Cándido Ayllón are included.

SPAIN AND PORTUGAL

1834
Rojas, Fernando de. *La Celestina; tragicomedia de Calisto y Melibea.* Prologue by Stephen Gilman. Edited by Dorothy Severun. Philadelphia, Center for Curriculum Development, 1970. 274 p. $1.20

An analytical presentation of the classic Spanish 15th-century masterpiece which many critics consider second only to *Don Quijote*. It was first published in 1499. Celestina is the central character who with her devious ways persuades Melibea to respond to Calisto, her suitor. Includes bibliographical references.

1835
Rojas, Fernando de. *Celestine: a critical ed. of the first French translation (1527) of the Spanish classic La Celestina,* with an introd. and notes by Gerard J. Brault. Detroit, Wayne State University Press, 264 p. facsims. (Wayne State University studies, no. 12. Humanities) $8

A thoroughly analyzed and annotated edition of the first French translation of the *Tragicomedia de Calisto y Melibea*, which will be of great interest to students of medieval Spanish literature.

1836
Rojas, Fernando de. *The Spanish bawd: La Celestina; being the tragicomedy of Calisto and Melibea.* Translated and edited by John Michael Cohen. Baltimore, Penguin Books, 1964. 247 p. (Penguin classics, L142) $1.25

A very good English translation of this great work of Spanish literature.

1837
Rojas Vila, Carlos, ed. *De Cela a Castillo-Navarro; veinte años de prosa española contemporánea.* Edited, with introd., notes and vocabulary by Carlos Rojas. Englewood Cliffs, N.J., Prentice-Hall, 1965. 213 p. $4.95

Presents a remarkable selection of Spanish prose by Cela, Laforet, Gironella, Delibes, Matute, Salvador, Romero, Cunqueiro, Juan Goytisola and Castillo-Navarro. Their themes reflect major trends in modern fiction—the plight of human existence and the collapse of normative values.

1838
Rojas Zorrilla, Francisco de. *Del rey abajo ninguno.* Edited by Raymond R. MacCurdy. Englewood Cliffs, N.J., Prentice-Hall, 1970. 128 p. $2.95

Rojas Zorrilla (1607-1648) was one of the outstanding dramatists of the Spanish Golden Age. This play, first published in 1650, deals with the conflict between two national ideals, loyalty to the king and personal honor. The introduction explains the Spanish code of honor.

1839
Romera-Navarro, Miguel. *Autógrafos cervantinos; estudio.* Austin, University of Texas Press, 1954, 76 p. facsims. (The University of Texas Hispanic studies, v. 6) $2.50

Analyzes 10 genuine autographs by Miguel de Cervantes which date from the 1589-94 period.

1840
Romera-Navarro, Miguel. *Estudios sobre Gracián.* Austin, University of Texas Press, 1950. 146 p. (The University of Texas Hispanic studies, v. 2) $3.50

A noted Hispanist presents a thorough analysis of Gracián's style. Contains bibliographical footnotes.

256

1841
Roth, Cecil. *The Spanish Inquisition.* New York, Norton, 1964. 316 p. illus. $1.95

First published in 1937, this book attempts to trace the history of the Spanish Inquisition. Appendixes provide transcripts of a trial for heresy.

1842
Roy, Gregor. *Cervantes' Don Quixote.* New York, Monarch Press, 1965. 106 p. $1

A guide for the college student. The plot is discussed, characters are analyzed, and possible examination questions are suggested and answered. [Charles Fleener]

1843
Ruiz, Juan, Arcipreste de Hita. *Libro de buen amor.* Edited, with an introd. and English paraphrase, by Raymond S. Willis. Princeton, N.J., Princeton University Press, 1972. xcvi, 479 p. front. $9.50

The Arcipreste was the greatest poet of the medieval "mester de clerecía" school. This work is essentially a collection of 12 narrative poems each recounting a love affair. His aim is to educate the reader in spiritual as well as carnal love. He also presents humorous satire of medieval life. Contains a bibliography.

1844
Ruiz Iriarte, Víctor. *El carrusell; comedia en dos actos y siete cuadros.* Edited by Marion P. Holt. New York, Appleton-Century-Crofts, 1970. xx, 121 p. music, port. $2.45

This comedy was first represented in Madrid in 1964 to considerable critical acclaim. It reflects contemporary Madrid society and the generation gap between young people and the adult world. This edition is designed for language instruction at the intermediate college level and is suited for class discussion. Contains a bibliography.

1845
Ruiz Iriarte, Víctor. *Esta noche es la víspera.* Edited by Judith S. Merrill. New York, Odyssey Press, 1972. 115 p. $1.65

A popular play by Spain's acclaimed playwright. It is a humorous play, presented here with notes and vocabulary.

1846
Ruiz Iriarte, Víctor. *Juego de niños, comedia en tres actos.* Edited with introd., notes, pattern drills, exercises, and vocabulary by Isabel Magaña Schevill. Englewood Cliffs, N.J., Prentice-Hall, 1965. xxviii, 168 p. port. $4.25

This play received the Premio Nacional de Teatro in 1952. It is an amusing and sensitive comedy by a contemporary Spanish playwright. This edition is intended as an intensive language text for intermediate college Spanish, providing opportunities for class drills.

1847
Ruiz Iriarte, Víctor. *Tres telecomedias de España.* Edited by Marion P. Holt and George Woodyard. Lexington, Mass., Heath, 1971. xi, 129 p. $2.95

Includes three plays written for television: *Amador, el optimista, El presidente y la felicidad,* and *Sala de espera.* The three are light comedies, presented here with notes and vocabulary for intermediate courses.

1848
Saavedra, Ángel de. *Don Álvaro, o La fuerza del sino.* New York, Harcourt, Brace & World, 1972. xv, 245 p. $3.95

Better known as "El Duque de Rivas," this romantic author wrote the famous play *Don Álvaro, o La fuerza del sino* (1831, 1835), depicting a hero harassed by fate. It later inspired Verdi's opera *La forza del destino* (1862). This edition contains notes and vocabulary.

1849
Salinas, Pedro. *El defensor.* Philadelphia, Chilton Educational Division, 1969. 195 p. $.90

Salinas (1892-1951) was one of the most outstanding Spanish lyric poets of the 20th century. In 1936 he established residence in the U.S. and taught at Johns Hopkins University, the University of Puerto Rico, and Wellesley College. He wrote an intellectual type of poetry in which outward simplicity was arrived at through complex mental processes.

1850
Salinas, Pedro. *Reality and the poet in Spanish poetry.* Introd. by Jorge Guillén. Baltimore, Johns Hopkins Press, 1940. 165 p. $1.95

A lucid critical work in which Salinas states that "the poet places himself before reality . . . in order to create something else." Included are critical essays on *El Cid,* Calderón de la Barca, Garcilaso, Góngora, and San Juan de la Cruz. Jorge Guillén's 30-page introduction on his good friend and fellow poet is excellent. The English text of these lectures is by Edith Fishtine Helman.

1851
Sallese, Nicholas Francis, and José A. Pérez. *España: vida y literatura* por Nicholas F. Sallese y José A. Pérez. New York, Van Nostrand Reinhold, 1969. xii, 271 p. $4.95

Written primarily for the intermediate, college-level student of Spanish, this composite history of Spanish literature gives detailed and specific information on the evolution of the Spanish literary style through the ages. Important authors are given special attention, and modern writers each receive biographical paragraphs. Includes a selective glossary. This can also be used as a reference work.

1852
Salter, Cedric. *Introducing Spain.* Rev. ed. New York, Transatlantic Arts, 1971. 210 p. illus., maps. $2.45

Describes Spain in general terms.

1853
Sánchez, José, ed. *Nineteenth-century Spanish verse.* New York, Appleton-Century-Crofts, 1972. xxvi, 374 p. $3.25

The editor has collected representative poems with explanatory material for the study of Spanish verse of this period, beginning with costumbrismo, covering the great era of romanticism, and ending with modernismo and ultramodernismo. The Duque de Rivas, José de Espronceda, José Zorrilla, Gertrudis Gómez de Avellaneda, Juan Ramón Jiménez, Rubén Darío, Gustavo Adolfo Bécquer, Federico García Lorca, and several others. The work includes a note on Spanish versification and a selected bibliography on the poetry of the 19th century.

1854
Sánchez Silva, J.M. *Marcelino pan y vino.* Edited by E.R. Mulvihill and R.G. Sánchez. New York, Oxford University Press, 1967. 121 p. $1.95

A book based on the Spanish folk tale which became an internationally acclaimed, award-winning motion picture of Spain.

1855
Santayana, George. *Character and opinion in the United States,* New York, Norton, 1967. x, 233 p. $1.65

Santayana (1863-1952) was born in Spain but lived most of his life in Boston. In this work he deals with conflict of materialism and idealism in American life. Late 19th-century New England is his point of departure for a penetrating analysis of American civilization.

1856

Santayana, George. *The last Puritan: a memoir in the form of a novel.* New York, Scribner's, 1964. 602 p. $2.45

This fictionalized autobiography, first published in 1936, is the only novel written by Santayana. In it he analyzes the New England character and comments on the moral and material idols of the 20th century. [Charles Fleener]

1857

Santayan, George. *Persons and places: the background of my life.* New York, Scribner's, 1963. 262 p. $1.45

The great Spanish-born philosopher writes of his early years in Spain, his arrival in the U.S., and ends with his graduation from Harvard. The book contains many interesting comments on late 19th-century Spain. [Charles Fleener]

1858

Santayana, George. *The sense of beauty: being the outline of aesthetic theory.* New York, Dover, 1955. xii, 268 p. illus. $1

First published in 1896, the author discusses here "why, when, and how beauty appears, what conditions an object must fulfill to be beautiful, what elements of our nature make us sensitive to beauty." The book is written in an elegant literary style. [Charles Fleener]

1859

Santayana, George. *Soliloquies in England and later soliloquies.* New introd. by Ralph Ross. Ann Arbor, University of Michigan Press, 1967. 264 p. (Ann Arbor paperbacks AA 123) $2.25

Contains 55 essays written from 1914 to 1921 when Santayana was at Oxford. The essays show the thoughts of a detached philosopher and a superb stylist. [Charles Fleener]

1860

Sastre, Alfonso. *Escuadra hacia la muerte; drama en dos partes.* Edited by Anthony M. Pacquariello. New York, Appleton-Century-Crofts, 1967. 115 p. port. $2.45

This play was first performed in Madrid in 1953 to great acclaim. It deals with the fate of six soldiers awaiting an offensive in an isolated forester's cabin during an imaginary third world war. It is an important drama centering around the dilemma of living and dying. Includes a bibliography, notes, vocabulary, and an introduction by the playwright.

1861

Sastre, Alfonso. *Guillermo Tell tiene los ojos tristes. Muerte en el barrio. Asalto nocturno.* Philadelphia, Center for Curriculum Development, 1972. 237 p. port. $1.40

A textbook edition of three plays by a contemporary Spanish playwright. It is intended for use in literature and advanced Spanish classes. Contains notes and vocabularies. The plays were first published in 1967.

1862

Schapiro, Jacob Salwyn. *Anticlericalism; conflict between church and state in France, Italy, and Spain.* Princeton, N.J., Van Nostrand, 1967. 207 p. (An Anvil original, 91) $1.75

The author outlines the history of Roman Catholic anticlericalism through the modern periods of Spain, France, and Italy. Included also are 44 readings, six of which deal exclusively with Spain. Includes bibliographies. [Charles Fleener]

1863

Schaub-Koch, Émile. *Obra animalista y monumental de Anna Hyatt Huntington.* Translated by Antonio Gomes da Rocha Madahil. New York, Hispanic Society of America, 1971. 109 p. illus. $1.50

Analyzes the work of sculptress Anna Hyatt Huntington, wife of Archer M. Huntington, the great Hispanophile philanthropist. Contains excellent illustrations and a select bibliography.

1864

Schierbeek, Bert. *Spain.* Chicago, Follett Pub. Co., 1967. 128 p. illus. (part col.) (The World in color) $1.65

A general description of Spain.

1865

Schiller, Johann Christoph Friedrich von. *Don Carlos, Infante of Spain; a drama in five acts.* Translated by Charles E. Passage. New York, F. Ungar Pub. Co., 1969. xxvii, 216 p. $2.25

An English translation of the historical drama on the Prince of Asturias by the great German poet of the 18th century. Contains bibliographies.

1866

Scholberg, Kenneth R. *Pierre Bayle and Spain.* Chapel Hill, University of North Carolina Press, 1958. 40 p. (University of North Carolina. Studies in the Romance languages and literatures, no. 33) $3.50

Pierre Bayle (1647-1706) was an erudite and controversial French philosopher and theologian and one of the most interesting men of his time. This book explores Bayle's impact on Spanish thought of the period. Includes a bibliography.

1867

Scholberg, Kenneth R., ed. and trans. *Spanish life in the late Middle Ages,* selected and translated by Kenneth R. Scholberg. Chapel Hill, University of North Carolina Press, 1965. 180 p. (University of North Carolina. Studies in the Romance languages and literatures, no. 57) $4

This collection of prose writings from 15th-century Castile focuses on the court of Juan II. The pieces describe the land and the people, political and intellectual life, warfare, knighthood, and daily life.

1868

Schonberg, Jean Louis. *A la recherche de Lorca.* Port Washington, N.Y., Paris Publications, 1971. 381 p. $8.50

An important study about the life and the work of the great Spanish poet.

1869

Sender, Ramón José. *Crónica del alba.* Edited by Florence H. Sender. New York, Appleton-Century-Crofts, 1970. 212 p. $2.65

Textbook edition of the contemporary Spanish novelist's work which was published in 1942. The novel goes back to Sender's childhood days in Aragón, portraying with humor and tenderness the unfolding of a boy's character.

1870
Sender, Ramón José. *Jubileo en el zócalo: retablo conmemorativo,* by Ramón J. Sender. Edited by Florence Hall. New York, Appleton-Century-Crofts, 1964. 215 p. map (on lining papers) $2.65

Sender's vigorous novelistic style is well represented in this novel.

1871
Sender, Ramón José. *Seven red Sundays.* New York, Collier-Macmillan, 1967. 192 p. $.95

This is an English translation of *Siete domingos rojos* (1932), which deals with an abortive worker's revolution in Madrid.

1872
Sender, Ramón José. *Tres ejemplos de amor y una teoría.* Philadelphia, Center for Curriculum Development, 1969. 181 p. $2

An annotated, textbook edition of one of Sender's novels.

1873
Seneca, Lucius Annaeus. *Thyestes.* Translated by Moses Hadas. Indianapolis, Bobbs-Merrill, 1957. 32 p. (Library of liberal arts series, no. 76) $.50

The Hispanic-born philosopher and spokesman for Roman stoicism is here represented by one of his finest tragedies. The late Moses Hadas' translation is excellent. [Charles Fleener]

1874
Serís, Homero. *Guía de nuevos temas de literatura española; transcrita, editada y cotejada por D.W. McPheeters.* New York, Hispanic Society of America, 1973. 324 p. $4

Contains scholarly essays on suggested topics and areas for further investigation into Spanish literature from the 7th to the early 20th century. This careful work by a major figure in Spanish bibliography is of interest to those directing dissertations of graduate students. Includes bibliographical notes.

1875
Serís, Homero. *Manual de bibliografía de la literatura española.* New York, Hispanic Society of America, 1962. 2 v. $3.50

Originally published in 1954, this is an extensive bibliography of Spanish literature, organized by subject. Excellent reference tool.

1876
Simon and Schuster, editors. *Simon and Schuster travel guide to Spain and Portugal.* New York, Cornerstone Press; distributed by Simon and Schuster, 1974. 192 p. illus. $2.95

An attractive travel guide to the Iberian Peninsula, with illustrations.

1877
Smith, Christopher Colin, ed. *Spanish ballads.* Oxford, New York, Pergamon Press, 1964. 220 p. (The Commonwealth and international library) $2.95

The introductory essay explains that Spanish ballads have an absolute uniformity of form, are extremely well preserved, and have, from the 15th century, enjoyed the interest of scholars and poets. The essay also analyzes the structure, style, and history of ballads. This edition contains a selection of 70 ballads, mostly from *Primavera y flor de romances,* first published in 1856 and revised in 1899 by the great Spanish scholar Marcelino Menéndez y Pelayo. Contains bibliographical notes and a glossary.

1878

Spaulding, Robert Kilburn. *How Spanish grew.* Berkeley, University of California Press, 1962. xii, 259 p. $1.50

First published in 1943, this is an interesting history of the evolution and structure of the Spanish language within its cultural context. Includes bibliographies.

1879

Squire, Christy. *Spain in pictures.* New York, Sterling Pub. Co., 1970. 64 p. illus., maps, ports. (Visual geography series) $1.25

A visual description of Spain and its people and culture, with attractive and contemporary illustrations.

1880

Stansky, Peter, and William Abraham. *Journey to the frontier: the roads to the Spanish Civil War.* New York, Norton, 1970. xviii, 430 p. illus. $2.45

Julian Bell and John Cornford, the subjects of this dual biography, were among the thousands of Europeans and Americans who made their way to Spain in the 1930's to fight for the Republic. It is a striking account of life and death in the Spanish Civil War.

1881

Stipp, John, C. Warren Hollister, and Allen W. Dirrim. *The rise and development of Western civilization.* New York, Wiley, 1971. 3 v. illus., maps. $7.95 each

The first volume covers Western civilization's rise from its Mediterranean beginnings to 1500. Volume 2 deals with the 1300 through 1850 period. The third volume ranges from 1815, the aftermath of the Congress of Vienna, to the present. Includes bibliographical references.

1882

Strongin, Theodore, comp. *Casals.* Illustrated by Vytas Valaitis. New York, Grossman, 1966. 112 p. illus. $3.50

Vytas Valaitis photographed Pablo Casals, the great Spanish cellist, at work and at play. Theodore Strongin provided the introduction and a biography of Casals.

1883

Sturman, Marianne. *Don Quixote notes.* Lincoln, Nebr., Cliff's Notes, 1964. 89 p. $1

This essay presents a dicussion of the action and thought of *Don Quixote* and a concise interpretation of its artistic merits and significance. Chapter summaries and selected questions are included.

1884

Suárez, Francisco. *Disputation six on formal and universal unity.* Translated by J.F. Ross. Milwaukee, Wisc., Marquette University Press, 1964. 123 p. $3.50

Francisco Suárez (1548-1617), the Spanish theologian and philosopher, was the most important figure of the second flowering of scholasticism. His principal work, *Disputationes metaphysicae* (of which the present work is a portion) was used for over a century as the textbook in philosophy in most European universities, Protestant and Catholic alike.

1885

Suárez, Francisco. *On the various kinds of distinctions.* Translated by Cyril Vollert.

Milwaukee, Wisc., Marquette University Press, 1947. 67 p. (Medieval philosophical texts in translation, no. 4) $1.50

This is a work dealing with philosophy by the influential Spanish thinker of the late 16th century. Includes bibliographies.

1886
Sutton, Denys. *Diego Velásquez.* New York, Barnes and Noble, 1967. 89 p. 54 illus. (part col.) (Barnes and Noble art series, no. 627) $.95

Contains over 50 illustrations, almost half in color. The accompanying text is concise, and it describes the life and work of this great Spanish painter of the 17th century.

1887
Tardy, William Thomas, ed. *Dos novelas picarescas.* Skokie, Ill., National Textbook Corp., 1968. 129 p. $1; five or more $.85 each

Includes textbook editions of two Spanish picaresque novels, with notes, questionnaires, and vocabulary. Includes a brief bibliography.

1888
Téllez, Gabriel de. *El burlador de Sevilla y convidado de piedra,* and *La prudencia en la mujer,* por Tirso de Molina [pseud.] Introd. and notes by Raymond MacCurdy. New York, Dell, 1965. 288 p. (Laurel language library Spanish series) $.95

Tirso de Molina (1584-1648) was a famous Spanish dramatist of the Lope de Vega school. *El burlador de Sevilla* . . . (1630), his most acclaimed play, was the first Don Juan drama in world literature. *La prudencia en la mujer* (1633) is a historical play. Contains bibliographical references.

1889
Terry, Arthur. *An anthology of Spanish poetry, 1500-1700,* with notes and introd. Oxford, New York, Pergamon Press, 1965-68. 2 v. (Commonwealth and international library) v. 1: $2.95; v. 2: $3.50

The first part covers the peak of the Golden Age, 1500-80, dominated by Garcilaso de la Vega, Luis de León, Herrera, Aldana, and San Juan de la Cruz. The second volume presents the Renaissance and Baroque phase in Spanish literature (1580-1700). This is an important anthology in which only complete poems have been included.

1890
Terry, Arthur. *Catalan literature.* New York, Barnes & Noble, 1972. xix, 136 p. (A literary history of Spain) $4

The authors presents a detailed history and literary criticism of Catalan literature from the medieval period to the present. This useful work is enhanced by a bibliography. It will be a welcome addition to library collections with an interest in Iberian literature.

1891
Thomas, Hugh. *The Spanish civil war.* New York, Harper & Row, 1963. 720 p. illus., maps, tables. $3.45

A comprehensive account, with a good summary of the historical antecedents of the war. It is amply illustrated with maps and photographs. Includes a bibliography. [Charles Fleener]

1892
Thompson, Corrie, ed. *Cinco comedias.* Skokie, Ill., National Textbook Corp., 1969. 162 p. $1; 5 or more $.85 each

Includes annotated, abridged editions of five Spanish plays.

1893
Tilles, Solomon, ed. *Puntos de vista: voces de España e Hispanoamerica.* New York
Harper & Row, 1971. xvii, 213 p. $4.50

The essays included are by José Ortega y Gasset, José Antonio Primo de Rivera
José Manuel Rodríguez Delgado, Julián Marías, Daniel Cossío Villegas, Lui
Quintanilla, Gonzalo Baéz-Camargo, Fidel Castro, José Comblín, Alfonso Caso
and Domingo Faustino Sarmiento. The texts have been abridged, but they have
not been rewritten or changed in any other way. Contains a vocabulary.

1894
Tirso de Molina; *see,* Téllez, Gabriel de, 1888

1895
Traverso, Edmundo. *The Spanish-American War: a study in policy change.* Boston
Heath, 1968. 140 p. (New Dimensions in American history) $2.80

Reexamines the Spanish-American War and U.S. policy. Contains a bibliography

1896
Trend, John Brande. *The civilization of Spain.* 2d ed. ¡London, New York, etc., Oxford
University Press, 1967. 138 p. 4 maps. (Oxford paperbacks university series, opus 19
$1.75

In six essays Professor Trend outlines the history of Spain and her cultura
achievements. This is a scholarly and lucid survey ranging from the Phoenicians to
the *Falange.* The text stops at the civil war, but a revised bibliography by Henry
Kamen lists the principal secondary sources for the study of Hispanic history and
culure into the 1960's. [Charles Fleener]

1897
Trend, John Brande. *Luis Milán and the vihuelistas.* New York, Hispanic Society of
America, 1969. 128 p. illus. $2

The vihuela is an ancient Spanish musical instrument used by troubadours
somewhat similar to the Spanish guitar. It was especially popular in 16th-century
Spain. Luis Milán wrote a definitive work on vihuela history and music, entitled
Libro de música de vihuela de mano. . . (1536).

1898
Turnbull, Eleanor Laurelle. *Ten centuries of Spanish poetry; an anthology in English
verse with original texts from the 11th century to the Generation of 1898.* With
introductions by Pedro Salinas. Baltimore, Johns Hopkins University Press, 1969. xv
452 p. (Johns Hopkins paperback JH-54) $3.95

An anthology in English translation tracing the original Spanish texts of the vast
panorama of Spanish poetry from its origins in the Mazarabic ballads of the 11th
century to the leading figures of the Generation of 1898. A very important and
useful work.

1899
Turner, Raymond. *Gonzalo Fernández de Oviedo y Valdés; an annotated bibliography.*
Chapel Hill, University of North Carolina Press, 1967. xvii, 61 p. (University of
North Carolina studies in the Romance languages and literatures, no. 66) $3.50

Contains a thorough annotated bibliography of the life and writings of an early
chronicler of Spanish explorations and conquests in the New World.

1900

Unamuno y Jugo, Miguel de. *Abel Sánchez and other stories.* Translated with an introd. by Anthony Kerrigan. Chicago, H. Regnery, 1956. 216 p. (A Gateway edition, 6034) $1.95

Includes three stories in English translation by the great Basque philosopher, essayist, poet, and novelist—*Abel Sánchez* (1917), *The madness of Doctor Montarco* (1921), and *Saint Emmanuel the Good, martyr* (1933). Contains notes and a glossary.

1901

Unamuno y Jugo, Miguel de. *The agony of Christianity.* Translated with an introd. by Kurt F. Reinhardt. New York, Ungar, 1960. 155 p. (Selected books on religion and philosophy) $1.95

La agonía del cristianismo was first published in 1930. It is an important and influential work on ethics and values in the modern world.

1902

Unamuno y Jugo, Miguel de. *Dos novelas cortas: San Manuel Bueno, mártir [and] Nada menos que todo un hombre.* Edited by James Russell Stamm and Herbert Eugene Isar. Boston, Ginn, 1961. 127 p. illus. $4.25

Two vigorous and trenchant novels are presented here in a textbook edition, with notes and vocabulary. The author's ideas on idealism versus materialism run through all his works of fiction.

1903

Unamuno y Jugo, Miguel de. *Relatos de Unamuno.* Edited by Eleanor Krane Paucher. New York, Appleton-Century-Crofts, 1969. xii, 199 p. illus., port. $3.40

An annotated, textbook edition of essays and short stories by one of Spain's most important contemporary literary figures.

1904

Unamuno y Jugo, Miguel de. *San Manuel Bueno, mártir, y Como se hace una novela.* Philadelphia, Center for Curriculum Development, 1973. 211 p. $1.20

A useful annotated textbook edition of a novel and an essay by Unamuno. Contains vocabularies and exercises, intended for intermediate to advanced students of Spanish.

1905

Unamuno y Jugo, Miguel de. *Three exemplary novels.* Edited by Angel del Rio. Translated by Angel Flores. New York, Grove Press, 1956. 227 p. (An Evergreen book, E-30) $2.95

Includes the English translations of three outstanding short novels by Unamuno: *The marquis of Lumbría, Two mothers,* and *Nothing less than a man.* This trilogy was first published in 1920. Unamuno examines here the Spanish psyche and characterizes many intrinsic Spanish values.

1906

Unamuno y Jugo, Miguel de. *La tía Tula.* Edited by Elaine D'Entremont. Englewood Cliffs, N.J., Prentice-Hall, 1975. 198 p. $2.95

The introduction states that "the protagonist of *La tía Tula* (1921) is the best example of the emergence of the woman character and the tensions that underlie her struggles." This is an edition with notes and vocabulary intended for beginning and intermediate courses. Includes a bibliography.

1907
Unamuno y Jugo, Miguel de. *La tía Tula.* Edited by Elaine Graybill. New York Appleton-Century-Crofts, 1974. 184 p. $2.95

> Centers around an old maid and her relationship to her family, masterfully depicting inner conflicts. Contains notes and a vocabulary.

1908
Unamuno y Jugo, Miguel de. *Tragic sense of life.* With an introductory essay by Salvador de Madariaga. Translated by J. Crawford Flitch. New York, Dover, 1967. xxxv, 332 p. $2.50

> This is Unamuno's most highly regarded essay, in which he states "my work . . . is to combat all those who live resigned, be it to Catholicism, to rationalism, or to agnosticism; it is to make everyone live fearfully and hungrily." The original title is *Del sentimiento trágico de la vida* (1913).

1909
Unamuno y Jugo, Miguel de. *Tres novelas de Unamuno.* Edited by Demetrios Basdekis. Englewood Cliffs, N.J., Prentice-Hall, 1971. 118 p. port. $2.95

> Includes *Nada menos que todo un hombre, El marqués de Lumbría,* and *La novela de don Sandalio, jugador de ajedrez.* The editor has added a concise introduction, as well as notes and vocabulary.

1910
Unamuno y Jugo, Miguel de. *Unamuno: sus mejores páginas.* With introductions, notes, and bibliography. Edited by Philip Metzidakis. Englewood Cliffs, N.J., Prentice-Hall, 1970. x, 395 p. (Modern Spanish and Latin American authors series) $4.25

> This edition includes selections from several of Unamuno's incomparable essays, short stories, and poetry.

1911
Valdés, Mario J. *Death in the literature of Unamuno.* Urbana, University of Illinois Press, 1964. 173 p. (Illinois studies language and literature, 54) $1.25

> An important and thorough monographic study on the theme of death throughout Unamuno's works. Contains bibliographical footnotes.

1912
Valera y Alcalá Galiano, Juan. *Pepita Jiménez.* Edited by Alberto Romo. New York, Regents Pub. Co., 1970. 210 p. $1.25

> An abridged, textbook edition in Spanish of a novel originally published in 1874. Contains notes and vocabularies.

1913
Valera y Alcalá Galiano, Juan. *Pepita Jiménez.* Introd. and translation by Harriet de Onís. Great Neck, N.Y., Barron's Educational Series, 1964. 181 p. $1.25

> Juan Valera (1824-1905) was one of Spain's most important 19th-century regional novelists. *Pepita Jiménez* was his first and most famous novel. It is a psychological study of the victory of passionate love over divine aspirations. The translation is excellent and the introduction places the novel in a historical and cultural context.

1914
Valle Inclán, Ramón del. *Luces de bohemia; Divinas palabras.* New York, Dell, 1969. 244 p. $1

> Valle Inclán (1866-1936) was a Galician novelist, poet, and playwright of the Generation of 1898. *Luces de bohemia* (1921) deals with the literary and

bohemian world that the author loved. *Divinas palabras* is a novel, first published in 1919.

1915

Vega Carpio, Lope Félix de. *La batalla del honor.* Edited with notes and an introd. by Henryk Ziomek. Athens, University of Georgia Press, 1972. 169 p. $4.50

This edition is based on the 1608 manuscript now at the Biblioteca Nacional in Madrid. It is a melodrama of love and jealousy in a French court setting, with the theme of honor recurring throughout. Lope de Vega used history with great dexterity. The introduction contains much useful information on the playwright, his style, and his times. Includes a bibliography.

1916

Vega Carpio, Lope Félix de. *Castigo sin venganza.* Edited by C. A. Jones. New York, Pergamon Press, 1966. 136 p. (The Commonwealth and international library) $2.95

An annotated Spanish-language edition of a popular romantic comedy by Lope de Vega.

1917

Vega Carpio, Lope Félix de. *A critical and annotated edition of Lope de Vega's Las almenas de Toro,* by Thomas E. Case. Chapel Hill, University of North Carolina Press, 1971. 217 p. facsims. (North Carolina. University. Studies in the Romance languages and literatures, no. 104) $9

The basic text for this comedy is a manuscript found in the Biblioteca Nacional, Madrid, listed as 107. The central personages are Doña Elvira, Infanta of Castile, and El Cid. The editor's scholarly introduction and notes are of great interest.

1918

Vega Carpio, Lope Félix de. *El duque de Viseo.* Philadelphia, Center for Curriculum Development, 1969. 121 p. $1.20

An annotated textbook edition of a play by Spain's most acclaimed dramatist of the Golden Age and its most important literary figure after Cervantes. Lope de Vega was born in 1562 and died in 1635.

1919

Vega Carpio, Lope Félix de. *Five plays: Peribañez; Fuente ovejuna; The dog in the manger; The knight from Olmedo; Justice without vengeance.* Edited by R. D. Pring-Mill. Translated by Jill Booty. New York, Hill and Wang, 1967. 345 p. $2.45

Contains English translations of five major plays by Lope de Vega, with notes and vocabulary.

1920

Vega Carpio, Lope Félix de. *Fuente ovejuna.* Translated by William E. Colford. Woodbury, N.Y., Barron's Educational Series, 1968. 201 p. $2.25

A bilingual edition of this historical drama which deals with the epic revenge of an entire village of hardworking peasants against their feudal lord. Contains notes and vocabulary.

1921

Vega Carpio, Lope Félix de. *Fuenteovejuna;* simplified and adapted by Alberto Romo, with exercises for study and vocabulary drill. The vocabulary range of the book is 875 words. New York, Regents Pub. Co., 1971. 124 p. illus., port. $1.25

A textbook edition of the classic Spanish play, ideally suited for classroom use on the intermediate Spanish level.

1922

Vega Carpio, Lope Félix de. *Lope de Vega's Lo que pasa en una tarde; a critical, annotated edition of the autography manuscript,* by Richard Angelo Picerno. Chapel Hill, University of North Carolina Press, 1971. 190 p. (University of North Carolina Studies in the Romance languages and literatures, no. 105) $5

> The object of Lope's lively comedy of manners and intrigue is to get Doña Blanca married to Don Juan in the face of many obstacles. This scholarly edition is based on the manuscript located in the Biblioteca Nacional of Madrid. It is also studied in comparison with four other annotated editions. Contains a thorough bibliography.

1923

Vega Carpio, Lope Félix de. *El peregrino en su patria.* Edited by Myron A. Peyton. Chapel Hill, University of North Carolina Press, 1971. 610 p. facsims. (North Carolina. University. Studies in the Romances languages and literatures, no. 97) $14

> The editor based this annotated, critical edition on the autograph manuscript in the Biblioteca Nacional in Madrid.

1924

Vega Carpio, Lope Félix de. *La prueba de los amigos.* Edited with notes and an introd. by Henryk Ziomek. Athens, University of Georgia Press, 1973. vii, 173 p. $4.50

> Based on the autograph manuscript of 1604, now at the Biblioteca Nacional in Madrid, this edition analyzes all critical assumptions relevant to the play. Friendship is the main theme in this play, while disguises, recognitions and surprises contribute elements of intrigue. Includes a bibliography.

1925

Vicens Vives, Jaime. *Approaches to the history of Spain.* Edited and translated by Joan Connelly Ullman. 2d ed. corr. and rev. Berkeley, University of California Press, 1970. xxviii, 189 p. geneal. tables, maps. (Campus, 22) $2.45

> This is a very good English translation of *Aproximación a la historia de España* which appeared in 1952. Vicens Vives writes about the history of Spain from the social and economic viewpoints. This title will be of great interest to all who study Spain. Includes bibliographical notes.

1926

Vilar, Pierre. *Spain; a brief history.* Translated by Brian Tate. Oxford, New York, Pergamon Press, 1967. 140 p. (Pergamon Oxford Spanish series) $3

> Translation of *Histoire de l'Espagne* which is a succinct analysis of the history of this Iberian country. Contains a bibliography.

1927

Waldo, Myra. *Flavor of Spain; a basic cookbook.* New York, Macmillan, 1965. 188 p. illus. $1.50

> Includes many well-known and some unusual items of Spanish cuisine, with directions for their preparation.

1928

Wasserman, Marvin, and Carol Wasserman, comps. *Prosa de la España moderna.* New York, AMSCO School Publications, 1974. 214 p. $3

> Includes prose selections from the writings of contemporary Spanish authors. Contains notes and references.

1929

Watson, Foster. *Luis Vives, el gran valenciano.* New York, Hispanic Society of America,

1969. 126 p. illus. (Hispanic notes and monographs, essays, studies and brief biographies issued by the Hispanic Society of America, IV) $2

Luis Vives (1492-1540) was a Spanish philosopher and humanist from Valencia. His works on education made him famous during his century. Mr. Watson presents here an outline of Vives' life and writings.

1930

Weber, Frances Wyers. *Literary perspectivism of Ramón Pérez de Ayala.* Chapel Hill, University of North Carolina Press, 1966. 108 p. (North Carolina. University. Studies in the Romance languages and literatures, no. 60) $5

Analyzes the abstract symbolism and other facets of Ramón Pérez de Ayala's writings. Contains bibliographical footnotes.

1931

Weber, Robert J. *The Miau manuscript of Benito Pérez Galdós; a critical study.* Berkeley, University of California Press, 1964. 155 p. (University of California publications in modern philology, v. 72) $3.50

This exhaustive critical study is based on two manuscript versions of *Miau* dated 1887 and 1888, respectively. Contains a thorough bibliography.

1932

Welsh, Doris Varner, ed. *Catalog of the William B. Greenlee collection of Portuguese history and literature and the Portuguese materials in the Newberry Library.* Chicago, Newberry Library, 1959. 342 p. $3

A useful catalog of an exceptional collection of Portuguese literature and history, most of them rare materials, at the Newberry Library in Chicago.

1933

Whelen, Guy. *Miró, 1940-1955.* New York, Tudor Pub. Co., 1960. 87 p. illus. $.95

Contains a few drawings and 14 color prints of the Barcelona-born surrealist painter. The author provides a background sketch of Joan Miró's life and work.

1934

Whelpton, Peter. *Portugal.* Chicago, Rand McNally, 1967. 96 p. illus. (part col.), maps. (A Rand McNally pocket guide) $1

An illustrated travel guide which describes the most important points of interest and gives advice on travel, shopping, and other helpful hints.

1935

Wentinck, Charles. *El Greco.* Translation: Albert J. Fransella. New York, Barnes & Noble, 1964. 89 p. illus. (part col.) (Barnes & Noble art series) $2.95

The author has selected 54 very good color reproductions of the Spanish master's paintings. A brief text explains El Greco's difficult life and the artistic influences on his style.

1936

Young, Howard Thomas. *Juan Ramón Jiménez.* New York, Columbia University Press, 1967. 48 p. $1.50

Analyzes the life and work of Spain's Nobel Prize-winning poet who became famous as a leading modernist and great lyricist. Includes bibliographical references.

1937

Young, Howard Thomas. *The victorious expression; a study of four contemporary*

Spanish poets: Miguel de Unamuno, Antonio Machado, Juan Ramón Jiménez, Federico García Lorca. Madison, University of Wisconsin Press, 1964. xxiii, 223 p. $2.95

Studies the four most important contemporary Spanish poets. The author reaches beyond the poetry to analyze the poets themselves. Includes bibliographical references.

1938
Zobel de Ayala, Fernando. *Casas Colgadas, Cuenca Museum; Spanish abstract art.* New York, Wittenborn, 1967. 151 p. illus. $4.50

A brief bilingual introduction describes this collection of abstract art housed in the Hanging Houses of Cuenca, Spain. Sculptures and paintings comprise the greater part of this work. The more than 80 illustrations are in black and white. [Charles Fleener]

1939
Zobel, Fernando. *Museo de arte abstracto español, Cuenca.* New York, Wittenborn, 1972. 125 p. illus. $6

Profusely illustrated guide to a museum of modern Spanish art in Cuenca, Spain.

1940
Zorrilla y Moral, José. *Don Juan Tenorio.* Edited by N. B. Adams. New York, Appleton-Century-Crofts, 1970. 221 p. $2.75

Zorrilla (1817-1893) was a Spanish romantic dramatist and lyric poet who wrote *Don Juan Tenorio* in 1844. This play became his greatest stage success. Zorrilla made his Don Juan into a warm and sympathetic character. This edition contains notes and vocabulary.

1941
Zunzunegui, Juan Antonio de. *Cuentos y patrañas,* edited by Rex Edward Ballinger. New York, Appleton-Century-Crofts, 1966. xiii, 203 p. $2.80

First published in 1942, Zunzunegui calls some of these farcical short narratives "patrañas" or tall tales. They are filled with lively humor. The setting is the Bilbao region in the author's native Basque country. This textbook edition includes vocabulary and exercises.

1942
Zunzunegui, Juan Antonio de. *Esta oscura desbandada.* Philadelphia, Center for Curriculum Development, 1972. 333 p. $1.95

The author achieved a solid literary reputation in Spain and Latin America shortly after the Spanish civil war. The present work, published in 1952, won the coveted Premio del Círculo de Bellas Artes of Madrid that same year. This novel centers around a Spanish family and displays the author's great creative talent. This edition contains notes and a vocabulary.

Dictionaries, grammars, readers, and textbooks

1943
Abreu, Maria Isabel, and Cléa Rameh. *Português contemporâneo.* Edited by Richard J. O'Brien. Rev. ed. Washington, Georgetown University Press, 1972. 2 v. illus. v. 1, $4.50; v. 2, $5.50

> The authors have prepared a linguistically based grammar of Brazilian Portuguese emphasizing everyday speech patterns. This is a very useful learning aid, containing colorful and practical dialogs.

1944
Adler, Kurt. *Phonetics and diction in singing: Italian, French, Spanish, German.* Minneapolis, University of Minnesota Press, 1973. 161 p. illus., music. (Minnesota paperbacks, 6) $4

> Contains much helpful information on phonetics and diction applied to singing.

1945
Aid, Frances M. *Semantic structures in Spanish; a proposal for instructional materials.* Washington, Georgetown University Press, 1973. $2.95

> A pioneer effort in gathering in one work instructional materials relating to semantic structures in Spanish. A welcome tool for teachers as well as researchers.

1946
Aliandro, Hyginio, ed. *The English-Portuguese pocket dictionary: over 26,000 vocabulary entries and expressions.* New York, Pocket Books, 1961. 381 p. (A Cardinal giant CG-750) $.95

> This item and the following are companion volumes. They are compact and useful reference tools.

1947
Aliandro, Hyginio, ed. *The Portuguese-English pocket dictionary; over 30,000 vocabulary entries and expressions.* New York, Pocket Books, 1960. xxviii, 311 p. (Cardinal giant, CG-754, reference, 4) $.95

> See above.

1948
Altabe, David F. *Temas y diálogos.* New York, Holt, Rinehart and Winston, 1970. 171, xxii p. illus. $4.50

> Contains readings and dialogs designed for intermediate Spanish courses. Contains notes and vocabularies.

1949
Anderson, Arthur J. *Rules of the Mexican language; classical Náhuatl grammar.* Logan, Utah State University Press, 1974. 215 p. $8

A clear, scholarly, and most valuable Náhuatl grammar which will be a welcome tool for scholars and researchers.

1950
Anderson, Gerald F., ed. *Lecturas intermedias; prosas y poesía,* edited by Gerald F. Anderson, Ned J. Davison, and Robert L. Smith. New York, Harper & Row, 1965. 333 p. $5.50

Provides the student of intermediate Spanish with a good selection of writings by outstanding Spanish and Spanish-American writers. Each page contains a vocabulary along the right-hand margin.

1951
Anderson, James, and Jo Ann Creore, eds. *Readings in Romance linguistics.* New York, Humanities Press, 1973. 472 p. $15

Covers the past 20 years, offering a good selection of influential essays. The editors present selections from the new trends in research, such as functional structuralism, glossematics, and generative transformation grammar. Includes bibliographies.

1952
Andrews, James Richard, and Charles M. Vance. *Patterns for reading Spanish.* New York, Appleton-Century-Crofts, 1964. xii, 378 p. $4.95

This book is intended for graduate students and others who wish to learn to read Spanish without learning to write or speak it. It points out the importance of recognizing patterns as the key to translation.

1953
Andrian, Gustave W., ed. *Modern Spanish prose; an introductory reader with a selection of poetry.* 2d ed. New York, Macmillan, 1969. xi, 233 p. $3.95

First published in 1964 under the title *Modern Spanish prose and poetry,* this work includes a representative sampling of contemporary Spanish poetry and prose.

1954
Andújar, Julio I. *Mastering Spanish verbs.* New York, Regents Pub. Co., 1968. 229 p. tables. $1.50

This thorough text describes Spanish verb forms and contains drills and exercises.

1955
Andújar, Julio I, and Robert James Dixson. *Sound teaching; a laboratory manual of everyday Spanish.* New York, Regents Pub. Co., 1969. 306 p. tables. $1.75

This laboratory manual accompanies the authors' *Workbook in everyday Spanish.* Contains exercises and spelling as well as pronouncing aids.

1956
Andújar, Julio I., and Robert James Dixson. *Workbook in everyday Spanish.* New York, Regents Pub. Co., 1968. 2 v. $1.25 each

A useful book of exercises for Spanish students.

1957
Angel, Juvenal Lodoño, and Robert James Dixson. *Método directo de conversación en español.* New York, Regents Pub. Co., 1966. 2 v. $1.50 each

The authors have prepared a thorough guide to Spanish conversation. This will be a useful tool for beginning and intermediate Spanish students.

1958

Angel, Juvenal Lodoño. *Tests and drills in Spanish grammar.* New York, Regents Pub. Co., 1966. 280 p. $1.50

This is a bilingual review of Spanish grammar.

1959

Arjona, Doris King, and Edith F. Helman, eds. *Cuentos contemporáneos.* New York, Norton, 1972. xxiii, 182 p. (Norton Spanish series, vol. 5) $2.30

The editors have assembled Spanish short stories of the 19th and 20th centuries for students of intermediate Spanish. The authors include Armando Palacio Valdés, Ramón del Valle Inclán, Azorín, Emilia Pardo Bazán, Ramón Gómez de la Serna, Ramón Perez de Ayala, and others.

1960

Auerbach, Erich. *Introduction to the Romance languages and literatures: Latin, French, Spanish, Provençal, Italian.* Translated by Guy Daniels. New York, Capricorn Books, 1961. 291 p. (A Capricorn original CAP44) $1.65

An English translation of *Introduction aux études de philologie romance* (1959). It outlines the history and philology of the Romance languages and also sketches briefly each language's literature.

1961

Babcock, Sandra S. *The syntax of Spanish reflexive verbs; the parameters of the middle voice.* The Hague, Mouton, 1970. 96 p. (Janua linguarum, Series practica, 105) $6.50

In the generative grammar approach, this work studies voice relations in natural languages. An important monograph. Includes a bibliography.

1962

Barrett, Linton Lomas. *Barron's simplified approach to Cervantes' Don Quixote.* Woodbury, N.Y., Barron's Educational Series, 1971. 150 p. (Barron's book notes) $.95

An annotated and greatly simplified edition intended to aid those studying the great Spanish classic.

1963

Batchelor, Courtnay Malcolm, ed. *Cuentos de acá y allá.* 2d ed. Boston, Houghton Mifflin, 1968. 395 p. $2.95

Contains short stories by Juan Bosch, Vicente Blasco Ibañez, Manuel Rojas, Rufino Blanco-Fombona, Juan Natalicio González, Gregorio López y Fuentes, Azorín, and others. This is a useful book for advanced college-level Spanish courses.

1964

Bills, Garland D., Bernardo Vallejo, and Rudolph C. Troike. *An introduction to spoken Bolivian Quechua.* Austin, Published for the Institute of Latin American Studies by the University of Texas Press, 1971. xxii, 449 p. illus., map. (Special publication of the Institute of Latin American Studies, University of Texas) $7.50

Most of the Quechua in use today is derived directly from classical Quechua. Bolivian Quechua is one of the most closely related dialects to the language of classical Cuzco. This is a thorough introduction to Bolivian Quechua; a companion set of tape recordings is also available. Thus for the first time we have a coordinated set of audio-lingual materials for an intensive college-level course in Bolivian Quechua.

1965

Boggs, Ralph Stelle. *Basic Spanish pronunciation.* New York, Regents Pub. Co., 1967. 195 p. $1.25

A useful guide to Spanish-language study.

1966

Bolinger, Dwight L., and others. *Writing modern Spanish: a student manual for modern Spanish.* 2d ed. New York, Harcourt, Brace and World, 1969. $3.95

Teacher's manual is sent free on request. Contains rules for writing Spanish.

1967

Bourne, Marjorie A., James B. Silman, and Josephine Sobrino. *Español: la teoría y la práctica.* New York, Holt, Rinehart, and Winston, 1971. xii, 288 p. illus. $4.25

This textbook is intended for students with one year of Spanish or more. The emphasis is placed on the structure of the language as well as the uses of verbs. The text is complete with reading passages, questions, drills and exercises. Charming drawings illustrate the text.

1968

Bowen, J. D., and R. P. Stockwell. *Patterns of Spanish pronunciation.* Chicago, University of Chicago Press, 1969. 279 p. $2.75

Contains a guide to the most frequent patterns in Spanish pronunciation. Dialogs, exercises, and notes have been added.

1969

Brenes, Edin, and D. H. Patterson. *¡Conversemos! A first book for Spanish conversation.* New York, Appleton-Century-Crofts, 1952. 146 p. plates. $2.50

Intended for review of Spanish conversation.

1970

Brown, Charles Bennett, and Milton L. Shane, comps. *Brazilian-Portuguese idiom list, selected on the basis of range and frequency of occurrence,* compiled and edited by Charles B. Brown and Milton L. Shane. Nashville, Tenn., Vanderbilt University Press, 1961. xii, 118 p. $2

A useful list of the most frequently used Portuguese idioms in Brazil.

1971

Brown, R. F. *Putnam's contemporary Spanish-English, English-Spanish dictionary.* New York, Putnam, 1973. 465 p. $2.95

Concise bilingual dictionary containing approximately 40,000 entries.

1972

Bruton, J. G. *Ejercicios de español.* Oxford, New York, Pergamon Books, 1968. 119 p. (Pergamon Oxford Spanish series) $2.50

A compilation of drills and exercises intended for intermediate Spanish classes.

1973

Buffum, Mary E. *Construction of object pronouns in the work of modern Spanish writers.* Columbia, University of Missouri Press, 1930. 46 p. $1.25

This is a detailed study of the object pronoun in the works of some of Spain's leading writers. Most useful for students of linguistics. Includes a bibliography.

1974
Burnett, Jane. *Crucigramas para estudiantes.* Skokie, Ill., National Textbook Corp., 1969. 92 p. $1.25

> Contains crossword puzzles which help the student to learn Spanish and acquire a wider vocabulary.

1975
Cabat, Luis, and Robert Cabat. *Unified Spanish: a review text for grammar and civilization.* Enl. ed. New York, Oxford Books, 1963. 331 p. $1.60

> In addition to the text of the authors' *The Hispanic world* (1961), this volume contains a Spanish grammar.

1976
Cabrillo, Angel, George E. Starnes, and Alden R. Hefler. *Spanish, a first course.* New York, Odyssey Press, 1960. 336 p. illus. $.95

> Presents the essentials of Spanish grammar in lessons short enough to be prepared by the student in two hours or less.

1977
Calvo, Juan A., and Carlos Gómez del Prado. *Veta hispana; panorama de la civilización española.* New York, Appleton-Century-Crofts, 1972. xii, 345 p. illus. $3.50

> Contains readings intended to acquaint the student of Spanish with the history and culture of Spain. Includes notes, glossary, and vocabularies.

1978
Casa, Frank Paul. *En busca de España.* Under the general editorship of Robert G. Mead, Jr. New York, Harcourt, Brace & World, 1968. 237 p. illus. $3.95

> Presents selections from the writings of Spanish novelists and essayists. Includes notes and vocabulary.

1979
Cassell's compact Spanish-English, English-Spanish dictionary. Compiled by Brian Dutton, L.P. Harvey, and Roger M. Walks. New York, Dell, 1972. xv, 444 p. $.95

> A handy Spanish-English dictionary for the student, the translator, or the traveler.

1980
Castillo, Carlos, and Otto F. Bond, eds. *University of Chicago Spanish dictionary: English-Spanish, Spanish-English.* Chicago, University of Chicago Press, 1968. xxxvi, 226 p. $1.85

> A succinct and useful bilingual dictionary, intended for the student.

1981
Castillo, Carlos, and Otto F. Bond, eds. *University of Chicago Spanish-English, English-Spanish Dictionary.* New York, Washington Square Press, 1968. 220 p. $.75

> A compact and useful reference for the student of Spanish or the traveler.

1982
Caycedo de Naber, Cecilia. *Pasatiempos para ampliar el vocabulario.* Skokie, Ill., National Textbook Co., 1968. 4 v. illus. $4 each.

> *Pasatiempos* comprises four puzzle booklets designed to offer progressively more difficult exercises to Spanish students. These puzzles are intended primarily for students in first- to fourth- year Spanish courses.

1983
Cohen, Leon J., and A.C. Rogers. *Say it in English for Spanish-speaking people.* New York, Dover, 1957. 134 p. $.75

A helpful aid to learn English speech patterns, intended for those whose native language is Spanish. Includes notes and exercises.

1984
Cohen, Leon J., and A.C. Rogers. *Say it in Spanish.* New York, Dover, 1954. 128 p. illus. (Dover say it series) $.75

An exercise book with vocabulary to learn Spanish.

1985
Corona Bustamante, Francisco. *Spanish/English-English/Spanish dictionary.* New York, Doubleday, 1973. 1072 p. $5.95

This is a useful and thorough bilingual dictionary for classroom use and research.

1986
Cortina Academy of Languages. *Brazilian-Portuguese conversation course.* Rev. ed. New York, Cortina, 1969. 250 p. $2

Provides many patterns and dialogs to learn Portuguese. Includes notes and vocabularies.

1987
Cowles Book Co., eds. *How to pass graduate record examination advanced test: Spanish.* Chicago, Cowles Book Corp., 1973. 200 p. $2.95

This is a helpful book for students preparing for the graduate record exam.

1988
Craig, Ruth P. *Diccionario de 201 verbos ingleses conjugados en todos sus tiempos y personas.* Woodbury, N.Y., Barron's Educational Series, 1972. xxiv, 432 p. $3.95

Intended to aid Spanish-speaking persons to perfect their skills in mastering English. A very useful and important reference and learning tool.

1989
Crow, John Armstrong, and Edward J. Dudley, comps. *El cuento.* New York, Holt, Rinehart and Winston, 1966. 380 p. $5.50

Contains 43 selections by the most important Spanish and Spanish American short story writers mostly of the 20th century. Includes biographic sketches of each author, as well as notes and vocabulary.

1990
Curcio, Louis L., and Carlos M. Terán, eds. *Cultural graded readers.* New York, Van Nostrand Reinhold, 1973. 4 v. $1.35 each

Volume 1 includes a history of Ponce de León; volume 2 deals with De Soto; volume 3 deals with the exploits of Coronado; and volume 4 chronicles the Caballeros de la Cruz. Intended for use in Spanish classes, with notes and vocabularies.

1991
Da Cal, Ernesto Guerra, ed. *New Appleton-Cuyas English-Spanish and Spanish-English dictionary.* Abridged ed. New York, Doubleday, 1973. 499 p. $2.50

This is an abridged version of the well-known Appleton-Cuyas bilingual dictionary.

1992
D'Ans, André Marcel. *Le créole français d'Haiti; études des unités d'articulation, d'expansion et de communication.* New York, Humanities Press, 1973. 213 p. $18.50

A thorough scholarly study of Haitian Creole, with a good bibliography.

1993
Day, Christopher. *The Jacaltec language.* New York, Humanities Press, 1974. 144 p. (Language science monographs) $7

Descriptive grammar of Jacaltec, a Mayan language of Guatemala. Includes notes and vocabularies. Of great interest to those specializing in Amerindian linguistics.

1994
Dixson, Robert James. *The blue book of Spanish; a simplified text for review.* New York, Regents Pub. Co., 1970. 192 p. illus. $1

A useful review of Spanish intended for travelers and students.

1995
Dixson, Robert James. *The blue book of Spanish; a simplified text for review.* New York, Regents Pub. Co., 1960. 192 p. $1

1996
Dixson, Robert James. *Curso completo en inglés,* by Robert J. Dixson in collaboration with Maria D. Andújar. New York, Regents Pub. Co., 1972. unpaged. $1

Intended for native Spanish speakers this is a helpful and clear English grammar, concentrating on phonetics, structure, and grammar.

1997
Dixson, Robert James. *Diner's Club basic Spanish for travelers.* New York, Regents Pub. Co., 1972. 186 p. $.85

Intended for travelers, this book contains most of the useful phrases and idioms that a traveler might encounter in a Spanish-speaking country.

1998
Dixson, Robert J., and Herbert Fox. *Mi primer diccionario ilustrado de inglés.* New York, Regents Pub. Co., 1960. unpaged. $.60

A simplified and illustrated dictionary of English for Spanish speakers.

1999
Dixson, Robert James, and Julio I. Andújar. *Resúmen práctico de la gramática inglesa.* New York, Regents Pub. Co., 1971. 185 p. $.85

An English grammar intended for native Spanish speakers. It is a practical and succinct presentation, with notes and vocabulary.

2000
Dobrian, Walter A., and C.R. Jefferson, eds. *Spanish readers for conversation.* Boston, Houghton, Mifflin, 1971. 212 p. $3.75

Contains short stories with notes and vocabulary.

2001
Donnel, Albert. *Vamos a conversar.* Skokie, Ill., National Textbook Corp., 1972. 243 p. illus. $1.60

A Spanish conversation manual, with brisk dialog and exercises.

2002
Dreyer, F.C. *Catolicismo romano a la luz de las escrituras*. Chicago, Moody Press, 1960. 256 p. $.85

> *Roman Catholicism in the light of the scriptures* is presented here in Spanish translation.

2003
Duff, Charles. *The basis and essentials of Spanish*. Totowa, N.J., Littlefield, Adams, 1972. xviii, 152 p. $1.95

> A good overview of essential structures of the Spanish language. The original edition was published in 1936.

2004
Duff, Charles. *Spanish for beginners*. Rev. American ed. New York, Barnes and Noble, 1968. 384 p. (Everyday handbooks, 271) $2.50

> Intended as a teaching aid for beginning Spanish students.

2005
Durán, Manuel. *Programmed Spanish dictionary*. Englewood Cliffs, N.J., Prentice-Hall, 1969. 216 p. $1.95

> A very useful and well-planned Spanish dictionary.

2006
Eaton, Helen S. *English, French, German, Spanish word frequency dictionary; a correlation of the first six thousand words in single-language frequency lists*. New York, Dover Publications, 1961. xvii, 440 p. tables. $3

> This book was originally published under the title *Semantic frequency lists* (1940). It is a scholarly contribution to linguistics.

2007
Espinosa, Aurelio M., Richard L. Franklin, and Klaus A. Mueller. *Cultura hispánica; temas para hablar y escribir*. 2d ed. rev. Lexington, Mass., Heath, 1972. xvii, 325 p. illus. $4.95

> Originally published in 1967 under the title *Cultura, conversación y repaso*, this is a useful selection of short readings intended for students of intermediate Spanish. Includes notes and vocabularies.

2008
Falconieri, John Vincent, ed. *Los duendes deterministas y otros cuentos*. Edited, with an introd., notes and exercises by John V. Falconieri. Englewood Cliffs, N.J., Prentice-Hall, 1965. 192 p. $3.95

> Includes short stories designed to teach Spanish language courses, with an extensive vocabulary of words and idioms. Most of the stories have been drawn verbatim from Enrique Anderson Imbert's *El grimbrio*.

2009
Feldman, D.M., and G.L. Boarino, eds. *Lecturas contemporáneas*. Boston, Ginn, Blaisdell, 1970. 180 p. $3.75

> Selections from contemporary Spanish and Spanish American short stories, with notes and vocabulary.

2010
Flores, Ángel, ed. *First Spanish reader; a beginner's dual language book*. New York, Bantam Books, 1964. 167 p. (The Bantam language library, 9) $.95

A bilingual edition of Spanish and Spanish American writings.

2011

Friar, John G., and George Kelly. *Practical Spanish grammar.* Garden City, N.Y., Doubleday, 1971. 184 p. $2.95

This edition was adapted from *A practical Spanish grammar for border patrol officers* (1959) prepared for the U.S. Immigration and Naturalization Service.

2012

Fuchs, Anna. *Morphologie des Verbs im Cahuilla.* New York, Humanities Press, 1970. 76 p. (Janua linguarum. Series practica, 87) $11

A scholarly study of Cahuilla verbs, with a thorough bibliography.

2013

Fucilla, Joseph Gurin. *World-wide Spanish dictionary.* New York, Fawcett, 1964. 2 v. in 1. $1.25

Includes words used in different Spanish-speaking countries.

2014

García-Prada, Carlos, and William E. Wilson, eds. *Cuentos de Alarcón.* Boston, Houghton, Mifflin, 1970. 210 p. $2.95

Contains short stories by Pedro Alarcón for Spanish courses, with notes and vocabulary.

2015

García-Prada, Carlos. *Entendámonos; manual de conversación.* 2d ed. Boston, Houghton, Mifflin, 1970. 250 p. $2.95

This is a rather extensive manual to acquaint students with Spanish dialog. Contains notes and vocabulary, as well as exercises.

2016

García-Prada, Carlos, and William E. Wilson, eds. *Tres cuentos.* 2d ed. Boston, Houghton, Mifflin, 1959. 193 p. illus. $2.95

Contains three annotated short stories intended for classroom use. The three fast-moving mystery stories are intended for use as soon as the tenses of the indicative mood have been studied. Includes notes, exercises, and vocabulary.

2017

Gerrard, A. Bryson, and J.D. Heras. *Cassell's beyond the dictionary in Spanish; a handbook of everyday usage.* 2d ed. rev. and enl. New York, Funk & Wagnalls, 1972. xxi, 226 p. $1.95

Presents a bilingual English and Spanish handbook for proficiency in Spanish conversation and writing.

2018

Gillhoff, Gerd Aage. *University Spanish-English and English-Spanish dictionary.* New York, Apollo, 1966. xii, 1261 p. $4.49

Originally published in a hard-cover edition under the title *Crowell's Spanish-English and English-Spanish Dictionary* (1963). This is a very complete and useful reference tool.

2019

Glover, Bobby Ray. *A history of six Spanish verbs meaning "to take, seize, grasp."* New York, Humanities Press, 1973. 115 p. $8

This is an exhaustive, scholarly analysis of six Spanish verbs. Contains an excellent bibliography.

2020

Gode, Alexander. *Portuguese at sight.* New York, F. Ungar, 1962. 102 p. illus. $1.25

A succinct grammar for beginning Portuguese students.

2021

Goldin, Mark G. *Spanish case and function.* Washington, Georgetown University Press, 1968. 83 p. $2.25

This is a thorough study of case and function in Spanish grammar. Includes a good bibliography.

2022

Gómez-Gil, Orlando, and Irene E. Stanslawczyk, eds. *Tierras, costumbres y tipos hispánicos; vistos por grandes escritores.* New York, Odyssey Press, 1970. xvi, 377 p. maps. $2.75

The editors have compiled a literary reader for Spanish-language students.

2023

González Muela, Joaquín. *Manual de composición española.* Englewood Cliffs, N.J., Prentice-Hall, 1969. x, 231 p. $5

This work is designed to teach Spanish composition to intermediate-level students of Spanish. It is a well-organized and useful textbook.

2024

Gooch, Anthony. *Diminutive, augmentative and pejorative suffixes in modern Spanish.* Elmsford, N.Y., Pergamon Press, 1970. xii, 385 p. (The Commonwealth and international library. Pergamon Oxford Spanish series) $14.50

Provides a thorough examination of suffixes in Spanish. Includes bibliographies.

2025

Goodman, Morris F. *Comparative study of Creole French dialects.* New York, Humanities Press, 1964. 143 p. map. $8.25

This is a very thorough comparative study of several French Creole dialects in the Caribbean area. It contains vocabularies and a bibliography.

2026

Graded Spanish readers; alternate series. Books 1-5. General editors, Otto F. Bond and Carlos Castillo. Boston, Heath, 1961. 305 p. $3.85

Includes selections from Riva Palacio, Lizardi, Quiroga, Sarmiento, and stories from Alto Peru, with notes, and vocabulary.

2027

Green, Jerald R. *Spanish phonology for teachers.* Philadelphia, Center for Curriculum Development, 1972. 196 p. $3.60

Intended for teachers of Spanish, this is a thorough review of phonological constructs and drills.

2028

Greenfield, Eric Viele. *Spanish grammar.* 4th ed. New York, Barnes & Noble, 1971. 236 p. $1.95

A succinct grammar, which will be very useful for beginning and intermediate students of Spanish.

2029

Grismer, Raymond L., and Doris Arjona. *Pageant of Spain; a graded reader with simplified arrangements of favorite selections from well known Spanish writers.* New York, Appleton-Century-Crofts, 1967. 202 p. illus. $2.65

Introduces Spain to the student of Spanish from a cultural and historical viewpoint. Contains vocabularies.

2030

Grosset, Charles A. *Grosset's universal Spanish phrase book for travelers.* New York, Grosset and Dunlap, 1973. 224 p. $1.25

Contains much useful information and useful phrases for those traveling through Spanish-speaking countries.

2031

Gruber, Edward C. *Spanish grammar with ease.* New York, Arco, 1967. 186 p. $1.95

Intended chiefly for review purposes for those preparing themselves for examinations.

2032

Gruber, Edward C. *Teacher of Spanish, jr. high school & high school.* New York, Arco, 1972. 253 p. $6

Intended as review exercises for junior high and high school students of Spanish.

2033

Hadlich, Roger L. *A transformational grammar of Spanish.* Englewood Cliffs, N.J., Prentice-Hall, 1971. 253 p. illus. $7.95

Transformational grammar can provide valuable insights into the whole fabric of linguistic structure. The author gives the reader a better understanding of how Spanish works. Includes an extensive bibliography.

2034

Hall, Eugene J. *Estudios de inglés; intermedio-avanzado.* New York, Regents Pub. Co., 1973. 215 p. $1.50

Recommended for Spanish-speaking students who wish to learn intermediate to advanced English.

2035

Hamilton, Carlos Depassier. *¡Conversemos! Manual de conversación para ' cursos avanzados de español.* Boston, Heath, 1972. 131 p. $3.50

This is a well-constructed conversation manual intended for advanced Spanish courses on the college level. Includes vocabularies.

2036

Hampares, Katherine J., and William Jassey. *Graduate school foreign language tests: Spanish.* New York, Arco Pub. Co., 1971. 301 p. $3.95

This is a useful practice manual to prepare for the Spanish graduate record examination.

2037

Hampares, Katherine J. *Spanish 2400: a programmed review of Spanish grammar.* New York, Harper & Row, 1973. 367 p. $7

A thorough review of Spanish grammar with many examples and a vocabulary.

2038

Hansen, Terrence Leslie, and Ernest J. Wilkins, comps. *Por los senderos de lo hispánico; cuentos y teatro minúsculo.* Waltham, Mass., Xerox College Publishing, 1971. 138 p. $3.25

> Intended as an intermediate reader, it includes short stories by some of the best 19th- and 20th-century writers, such as Borges, Horacio Quiroga, Manuel Gutiérrez Nájera, Juan Bosch and several others. Includes notes and vocabulary.

2039

Harvard, Joseph. *Bilingual guide to business and professional correspondence (Spanish-English). Guía bilingüe (inglés-español de correspondencia profesional y de negocios).* Spanish text by I.F. Ariza. New York, Oxford University Press, 1970. xiii, 224 p. (The Commonwealth and international library. Bilingual guides to business correspondence) $4

> This is a useful, up-to-date guide to business correspondence in Spanish and English. Recommended for public and junior college libraries.

2040

Herzfeld, A. *Notas y ejercicios de composición.* Edited by L.D. Mills. Englewood Cliffs, N.J., Prentice-Hall, 1970. 349 p. $3.95

> Presents a useful series of exercises in Spanish compositions. Includes vocabularies.

2041

Hirschhorn, Howard H. *Spanish-English and English-Spanish medical guide. Guía médica español-inglés, inglés-español.* New York, Regents Pub. Co., 1968. 120 p. $1

> This is a welcome addition to specialized bilingual dictionaries.

2042

Holder, Preston, ed. *Introduction to the handbook of American Indian languages,* by Franz Boas. *Indian linguistic families of America north of Mexico,* by J.V. Powell. Lincoln, University of Nebraska Press, 1966. 221 p. $1.85

> These two remarkable works study American Indian languages from the linguistics and geographic points of view. Of great interest to the specialist.

2043

Holt, Marion P., and Julianne Dueber. *One thousand and one pitfalls in Spanish.* Woodbury, N.Y., Barron's Educational Series, 1973. 221 p. $2.95

> Intended as an aid and exercise book in reviewing difficult portions for Spanish examinations.

2044

Howley, Michael, and Carmen Sanguinetti. *How to prepare for the high school equivalency test in Spanish.* New York, Barron's Educational Series, 1973. 399 p. $4.50

> This will be of special interest for Spanish-speaking high school students or for foreign students wishing to practice the U.S. test formats in their native language.

2045

Huebener, Theodore. *Así es Puerto Rico.* New York, Holt, Rinehart and Winston, 1960. 122 p. illus. $3.80

> This is a textbook in Spanish intended for use in a classroom situation. It describes the history, culture, society, and environment of Puerto Rico. Includes notes and vocabulary.

2046

Hughes, Dorothy. *Conchita de Cuba.* Francestown, N.H., Marshall Jones, 1970. 101 p. $1.40

This is a middle-level reader for Spanish language courses.

2047

Hughes, Dorothy. *Niños de España.* Francestown, N.H., Marshall Jones, 1970. 275 p. $1.75

This attractive reader is aimed at the junior high and high school level.

2048

Hughes, Dorothy. *Pedro; introducción al español.* Francestown, N.H., Marshall Jones, 1969. 99 p. $.50

An imaginative text for those studying elementary Spanish.

2049

Jackson, Eugene, and Antonio Rubio. *Spanish made simple.* New York, Made Simple Books; Distributed by Doubleday, Garden City, N.Y., 1965. 191 p. $1.95

An attempt to present basic Spanish to the student.

2050

Jassey, William. *Advanced tests for the graduate record examination: Spanish.* New York, Arco, 1968. 300 p. $3.95

This book will be of interest to those desiring to practice for the graduate record examination.

2051

Jiménez, Emma Holguín, and Conchita Puncel. *Cancioncitas para chiquitines.* Illustrated by Jacques Rupp.   Glendale, Calif., Bowmar, 1970. 69 p. $2.29

A collection of popular children's songs in Spanish.

2052

Jiménez, Emma Holguín, and Conchita Puncel, comps. *Juegos para meñiques.* Illustrated by Gilbert T. Martínez. Glendale, Calif., Bowmar, 1970. 76 p. $2.29

Presents popular Latin American games. Of interest to teachers and counselors of Spanish-language camps.

2053

Jiménez, Emma Holguín, and Conchita Puncel, comps. *Versitos para chiquitines.* Illustrated by Gilbert T. Martínez. Glendale, Calif., Bowmar, 1971. 69 p. $2.29

Presents poems, principally rhymes, for young people. Of interest to Spanish-language classes as well as for audiovisual resource centers.

2054

Johnson, J.L. *Spanish prose today; composition and conversation.* New York, Barnes and Noble, 1970. 275 p. $1.75

Contains numerous examples and exercises to perfect the students' skills in Spanish composition and conversation.

2055

Jones, Malcolm Bancroft. *Spanish idioms.* Boston, Heath, 1955. 87 p. $1.95

Contains listings, explanations, and guides to usage of a large number of commonly used Spanish idioms.

2056
Kahane, Henry Romanos, and Angelina Pietrangeli, eds. *Structural studies on Spanish themes,* by Sol Saporta, and others. Urbana, University of Illinois Press, 1973. 414 p. $7.50

> First published in 1959, in Salamanca, Spain, this work contains studies by a group of linguists at the University of Illinois. Topics include morpheme alternants, redundancy, the function of classes, and the transfer of linguistic methods to literature. Contains bibliographies.

2057
Kany, Charles Emil. *Advanced Spanish conversation.* Boston, Heath, 1969. 320 p. $1.25

> Originally published in 1939, this is a new edition of a book on advanced Spanish conversation.

2058
Kany, Charles Emil. *Spoken Spanish for students and travelers.* Rev. ed. Boston, Heath, 1961. 296 p. illus. $2.50

> A convenient guide to which the author has added vocabularies intended for travelers.

2059
Kendris, Christopher. *Beginning to write Spanish.* Woodbury, N.Y., Barron's Educational Series, 1972. 198 p. $1.75

> Presents a helpful guide to learn Spanish composition with notes and appendixes.

2060
Kendris, Christopher. *Diccionaire de 201 verbes espagnols conjugés a toutes les personnes.* Great Neck, N.Y., Barron's Educational Series, 1968. 224 p. $2.95

> A review of Spanish verbs intended primarily for French-speaking students. Useful in simultaneous translation drills.

2061
Kendris, Christopher. *Diccionario de 201 verbos franceses conjugados en todos sus tiempos y personas.* Great Neck, N.Y., Barron's Educational Series, 1968. 225 p. $2.95

> The author has assembled a review of the most frequently used French verbs for Spanish-speaking students. This work may also be helpful in courses on simultaneous translation. Also available in hard cover.

2062
Kendris, Christopher. *Dictionary of five hundred one Spanish verbs; fully conjugated in all the tenses, alphabetically arranged.* Woodbury, N.Y., Barron's Educational Series, 1971. xxxvii, 532 p. $2.95

> This is a revised and expanded edition of the 1963 title, *201 Spanish verbs; fully conjugated in all the tenses.* It will be useful for all who study Spanish, as well as for libraries.

2063
Kercheville, Francis M. *Practical spoken Spanish.* 7th ed. rev. Albuquerque, University of New Mexico Press, 1969. 258 p. $1.75

> First published in 1959, this is a practical guide to Spanish conversation. Includes notes and vocabularies.

2064
Labbé Barros, Eduardo, and José R. Fernández-Romero. *Listening comprehension drills for Spain and the Spaniards series.* New York, Regents Pub. Co., 1971. 301 p. $.95

2065
Laín, M. Milagro, and C. María Seoane. *Gramática española: curso intermedio.* New York, Harper & Row, 1973. 292 p. $2.20

This is a clear and well presented intermediate Spanish grammar in an attractive edition. Contains notes and a brief bibliography.

2066
Larra, Mariano José de. *En este país y otros artículos.* With notes by J. Campos. Philadelphia, Center for Curriculum Development, 1969. 195 p. $1.20

Includes a selection of articles by Larra in which he describes Spanish manners and customs.

2067
Lastra, Yolanda. *Cochabamba Quechua syntax.* New York, Humanities Press, 1968. 104 p. $8

This important work summarizes Quechua syntax as it it used in Bolivia. It will be of great interest to linguists and to students of Quechua.

2068
Leslie, John Kenneth. *Cuentos y risas; a first reader in Spanish,* illustrated by John Teppich. New York, Oxford University Press, 1952. 161 p. illus. $2.50

This is a delightful Spanish language-reader complete with exercises, vocabulary, and questions. The stories are humorous and the illustrations are both instructive and witty. Highly recommended.

2069
Lipton, Gladys, and Olivia Muñoz, comps. *Beginner's Spanish and English dictionary; Spanish-English, English-Spanish.* Woodbury, N.Y., Barron's Educational Series, 1973. 301 p. $3.95

Intended for use in secondary schools and for beginners in the study of Spanish.

2070
Lobos, Amílcar, and Leland Mellot. *Quetzal.* Edited by Rolando Castellón and Carlos Pérez. Millerton, N.Y., Glide Publications, 1974. 269 p. $3

Contains readings in Latin American civilization.

2071
Lopes, Albert Richard. *Bom dia! One minute dialogues in Portuguese.* New York, Appleton-Century-Crofts, 1964. 33 p. $1.25

This is a supplementary text containing dialogs in Portuguese.

2072
López, Carmen. *Beginning Spanish self-taught.* New York, Cambridge Book Co., 1973. 213 p. $.95

A well-organized and easy-to-follow book on learning Spanish.

2073
López, Norbert. *El rey Pancho y el primer reloj.* Escrito por Norberto C. López; ilustraciones de Marianne Gutiérrez. Mankato, Minn., Oddo, 1970. 32 p. col. illus. $1.75

This charming story can be synthesized as "in the second race between the tortoise and hare the hare runs twelve times faster and farther than the tortoise and in doing so creates the world's first clock."

2074

López-Morillas, Juan. *New Spanish self-taught; the quick, practical way to reading, writing, speaking, understanding.* Rev. by Juan López-Morillas. New York, Funk and Wagnalls, 1959. 340 p. (The Language phone series) $1.95

Contains much helpful information on how to master Spanish without a teacher.

2075

Loubotka, Cestmir. *Classification of South American languages.* Los Angeles, Latin American Center, University of California, 1971. 126 p. $10

Originally published in 1935, this is an updated edition of this classic listing and location of South American languages and language groups.

2076

Luce, Allena, ed. *Vamos a cantar, songs of Spain and the Americas; together with a supplement of songs popular in the Americas.* Boston, Heath, 1966. 104 p. $2

Designed primarily for high school and college students of Spanish in English-speaking countries. Contains scores for one to four voices with and without piano accompaniment. This is a welcome addition to the college or public library shelf, as well as a valuable classroom aid.

2077

Madrigal, Margarita. *First steps in Spanish; a beginner's book for children.* New York, Regents Pub. Co., 1971. 111 p. illus. $1

This is an attractive and well-organized book for children learning Spanish, aimed at the elementary and junior high school level. Includes notes and exercises.

2078

Madrigal, Margarita. *Invitación al inglés.* New York, Regents Pub. Co., 1971. 201 p. $1.50

This textbook is aimed at the Spanish-speaking student attempting to learn English as a second language. Contains notes and vocabularies.

2079

Madrigal, Margarita, and Ezequías Madrigal. *An invitation to Spanish.* New York, Simon and Schuster, 1971. 196 p. illus. $1.75

First published in 1943, this work teaches the student to think in Spanish from the very beginning without the use of translation. The system is designed to acquire quickly a speaking knowledge of Spanish.

2080

Madrigal, Margarita. *Open door to Spanish.* New York, Regents Pub. Co., 1970. 2 v. $1.50 each

This is a helpful and attractive textbook for intermediate Spanish classes, with notes, exercises, and vocabularies.

2081

Madrigal, Margarita. *Open door to Spanish.* New York, Regents Pub. Co., 1971. 202 p. illus. $2.95

This beginning language book can be purchased with four records for $9.95 and with four tapes for $22.50. Either combination provides a direct and well-organized audiovisual method to learn Spanish. Of great interest for high school, college, and public libraries.

2082
Madrigal, Margarita. *See it and say it in Spanish.* New York, New American Library, 1961. 255 p. illus. (A Signet language book, D-2001) $.75

Features exercises to learn Spanish for beginners.

2083
Mármol, José. *Amalia;* graded Spanish reader. Edited by J.C. Babcock and M.B. Rodríguez. Boston, Houghton, Mifflin, 1970. 231 p. $1.50

This important historical novel by a 19th-century Argentine author deals with the Rosas period. It presents an accurate historical and political picture of the period. This is an annotated textbook edition with vocabularies.

2084
Maronpot, Raymond P. *Fifty units of basic Spanish grammar.* Alhambra, Calif., Lawrence Pub. Co., 1972. 291 p. $1.55

Presents essential elements of Spanish grammar aimed at classroom instruction as well as private study. Contains notes and vocabulary.

2085
Martín-Gaite, Carmen. *Balneario.* Philadelphia, Center for Curriculum Development, 1969. 129 p. $.90

An annotated, textbook edition of a contemporary Spanish novel. Contains notes and vocabulary.

2086
Mason, K.L.J. *Advanced Spanish course.* New York, Pergamon Press, 1967. 377 p. $5

A thorough and useful Spanish course for the student with knowledge of the language.

2087
Mason, K.L.J., and M.J. Lawrence. *Key to advanced Spanish course.* New York, Pergamon Press, 1970. 101 p. (The Commonwealth and international library) $3

This is a well-organized book for students of advanced Spanish language courses, with helpful notes.

2088
Mason, K.L.J., and Juan C. Sager. *Spanish oral drill book.* New York, Pergamon Press, 1969. xi, 280 p. (The Commonwealth and international library. Pergamon Oxford Spanish series) $4.75

Provides drills and exercises for students of intermediate Spanish courses. Of great interest to professors and students alike.

2089
Mayers, Marvin Keene, ed. *The languages of Guatemala.* New York, Humanities Press, 1966. 318 p. $19.50

This collection of studies deals with indigenous languages of Guatemala. Includes a good bibliography.

2090
Mickle, M.M., and Francisco da Costa. *Say it in Portuguese.* New York, Dover Publications, 1971. 128 p. (Dover "say it" series, T-809) $.95

This is a useful and thorough phrase book containing Portuguese dialog and notes for those desiring to achieve fluency in Portuguese.

2091

Miller, J. Dale, comp. *1,000 Spanish idioms.* Provo, Utah, Brigham Young University Press, 1972. xii, 185 p. illus. $5

To know a language well one must know its idioms. This listing presents a significant compilation of Spanish idioms listed in the order of frequency of usage and therefore in the order of usefulness. A valuable tool.

2092

Milor, J.H. *Historietas en español.* Skokie, Ill., National Textbook Corp., 1969. 267 p. $2.75

A compilation of Spanish and Spanish-American short stories intended for beginning and intermediate students of Spanish. Contains notes and vocabularies.

2093

Mitchell, B., and N.J. Margetts. *La caza del lobo.* Illus. by Charles Keeping. New York, St. Martin's Press, 1972. 195 p. illus. $1

Includes adventures, written in a lively style, providing readings for intermediate students of Spanish. Includes notes and vocabulary and outstanding silk screen illustrations.

2094

Mitchell, B. *Viaje a Madrid.* New York, St. Martin's Press, 1971. 212 p. illus. $2

This reader is designed to acquaint students of Spanish with the social and cultural setting of the Spanish capital. Includes notes and vocabularies.

2095

Modern Language Association of America. *Handbook of foreign language classroom testing: French, German, Italian, Russian, Spanish.* New York, 1973. 431 p. $6

Includes material for tests in modern languages.

2096

Muirden, Sydney J., and others. *Cartas de Luis,* by Sidney J. Muirden, Roger M. Peel and Silvia Arron. Under the general editorship of Robert G. Mead, Jr. New York, Harcourt, Brace & World, 1968. xx, 168 p. maps (on inside covers) $4.50

This unique exercise book is systematically structured to introduce the student to correctly written Spanish. The book is divided into letters from Luis, an Argentine university student, to Ken, his American counterpart. A questionnaire follows each letter, and a paragraph of dictation is also included. Toward the end of the book the student is encouraged to write his own letters to Luis on various suggested themes. An extensive vocabulary makes this volume most worthwhile.

2097

Narvaez, Ricardo A. *Instruction in Spanish morphology: derivational lists.* St. Paul, Minn., EMC Corp., 1969. 74 p. tables. $4.75

This is a well-organized work explaining Spanish morphology. Contains notes and an index.

2098

Narvaez, Ricardo A. *Instruction in Spanish pronunciation: segmentals.* Rev. ed. St. Paul, Minn., EMC Corp., 1970. 64 p. illus., tables. $3

A useful guide for the study of Spanish pronunciation, with extensive notes.

2099
Nassi, Robert J. *Reviewing Spanish, first year.* New York, AMSCO School Publications, 1972. 165 [21] p. illus., maps. $1.95

Reviews first-year Spanish in a useful and organized manner, with many notes, exercises, illustrations, and maps.

2100
Nassi, Robert J. *Reviewing Spanish, three years.* New York, AMSCO School Publications, 1970. 170 [27] p. illus., maps. $2.20

A compact review of three years of Spanish instructions with helpful exercises.

2101
Nassi, Robert J. *Reviewing Spanish, two years.* 2d ed. New York, AMSCO School Publications, 1972. 171 [27] p. illus., maps. $3.10

Provides exercises to review the first two years of Spanish language courses, with notes and vocabulary, as well as maps of countries where Spanish is spoken.

2102
Nassi, Robert J. *Workbook in Spanish; three years.* New York, AMSCO School Publications, 1972. 399 p. $3.10

Contains appropriate exercises for three progressive years of Spanish instruction.

2103
Navarro Hinojosa, Ida. *Follett world-wide dictionaries: Spanish-English, English-Spanish (American English).* Based on the 1964 rev. ed. of the Fucilla Spanish dictionary, by Joseph G. Fucilla. Newly rev. by Ida Navarro Hinojosa. Edited by Richard J. Wiezell. With a traveler's conversation guide containing hundreds of expressions and items of information useful to tourists, students, and businessmen. Rev. ed. Chicago, Follett Pub. Co., 1966. 640 p. $2.95

A convenient and quite complete dictionary for the student and traveler.

2104
N'Daiaye-Correard, Genevieve. *Structure du dialect basque de Maya.* New York, Humanities Press, 1971. 249 p. $20

The dialect described in this scholarly work is the one spoken in the village of Maya in the Baztan valley in Spain. It analyzes the phonology and morphosyntax of this particular dialect. Contains a thorough bibliography.

2105
Newmark, Maxim. *Spanish: first year.* Woodbury, N.Y., Barron's Educational Series, 1971. 201 p. $1.50

Presents basic Spanish grammar and vocabulary for beginning students.

2106
Nitti, John J. *201 Portuguese verbs fully conjugated in all the tenses.* Woodbury, N.Y., Barron's Educational Series, 1968. xxx, 212 p. $2.95

This English and Portuguese compilation of Portuguese verbs, conjugated in all tenses, is a valuable aid to practice proficiency in Portuguese. Includes notes.

2107
Norman, Jill, and María V. Alvarez. *Spanish phrase book.* Baltimore, Penguin Books, 1973. 215 p. $.95

A useful, compact Spanish phrase book.

2108
O'Connor, Patricia, and Ernest F. Haden. *Oral drill in Spanish.* Boston, Houghton, Mifflin, 1967. 196 p. $4.75

Presents a useful and compact series of drills for the practice of intermediate-level Spanish.

2109
Olmo, Laura. *La camisa.* Edited by A.K. Ariza, and I.F. Ariza. New York, Pergamon Press, 1968. 125 p. illus. $2.50

An annotated textbook edition of a popular Spanish novel.

2110
Ortega, Wenceslao, and Alberto Sampere. *Mecanografía cien; curso avanzado.* New York, Harper & Row, 1973. 296 p. $3

This is an advanced manual for learning typing.   Intended for Spanish-speaking students and adults.

2111
Palfrey, Thomas R., Joseph Fucilla, and William C. Holbrook, comps. *A bibliographic guide to the Romance languages and literatures.* 8th ed. Evanston, Ill., Chandler's, 1971. 122 p. $3

Originally compiled as a brief list of references for graduate students, it is presented here in the form of a very useful bibliography.

2112
Papalia, Anthony, and José A. Mendoza, comps. *Lecturas de ahora y del mañana.* New York, AMSCO School Publications, 1973. 201 p. $2.10

Presents readings for intermediate Spanish courses, with notes and vocabularies.

2113
Payne, William H. *Programación en lenguaje de máquina, ensamblador y de sistemas con el IBM.* New York, Harper & Row, 1973. 250 p. $3.60

A Spanish translation of *Machine assembly and systems programming for the IBM.* It is a useful edition for those desiring to study computer programming.

2114
Pei, Mario Andrew, and Eloy Vaquero. *Getting along in Spanish,* . . . with the editorial collaboration of José Martel and John Fisher. New York, Bantam Books, 1957. 225 p. illus. (A Holiday magazine language book) $.75

A useful, detailed study by the famous linguist Mario Pei.

2115
Pemberton, R.A., comp. *The Penguin Spanish reader.* Harmondsworth, England, Penguin Books, 1971. 231 p. $1.75

Includes selections in Spanish by Rubén Darío, Juan Ramón Jiménez, Alfonso Reyes, Pío Baroja, Fernán Caballero, Gerardo Diego, Octavio Paz Gustavo Adolfo Bécquer, Gabriel García Márquez, Miguel Angel Asturias, Pablo Neruda, Benito Pérez Galdós, Mario Vargas Llosa, Juan Goytisolo, and many others, as well as selections from newspaper articles. All the selections are brief.

2116
Pérez-Sala, Paulino. *Interferencia del inglés en la sintaxis del español hablado en Puerto Rico; un estudio sobre la sintaxis de los puertorriqueños.* Hato Rey, P.R., Inter-American University Press, 1973. 132 p. $3.95

Presents a linguistic analysis of the influence of English on the syntax of Spanish spoken in Puerto Rico. This is a scholarly work on a problem of interest to sociolinguists. It was originally published as the author's thesis at the University of Puerto Rico. Includes a bibliography.

2117
Phillips, Robert N., and Olga Márquez. *Visiones de Latinoamérica; a cultural reader.* New York, Harper & Row, 1972. 199 p. illus. $5.95

Provides readings on the culture of Latin America, with attractive illustrations.

2118
Pimsleur, Paul, ed. *Sol y sombra; lecturas de hoy.* New York, Harcourt Brace Jovanovich, 1972. xvii, 206 p. illus. $3.50

Presents readings intended for intermediate to advanced students of Spanish. Includes extensive notes and vocabularies.

2119
Pittaro, John Michael, ed. *Cuentecitos.* Chicago, Regents Pub. Co., 1969. 224 p. $1.25

Contains short stories and folk tales.

2120
Pittaro, John Michael. *Mosaico hispánico.* New York, Bantam Books, 1972. 171 p. $.95

Contains vignettes and essays on Spanish and Latin American life and culture.

2121
Pope, Francis, and Edward Medina. *Spanish phonetic reading.* Champaign, Ill., Research Press, 1972. 192 p. $1.80

This is book 1 of a progressive program of Spanish phonetic reading, accompanied by English notes and translations.

2122
Portilla, Marta de la, and Thomas Colchie, eds. *Textbooks in Spanish and Portuguese; descriptive bibliography, 1939-1970.* New York, Clearinghouse on Languages and Linguistics, 1972. 120 p. $7.50

This is a thorough selection of the most useful textbooks in Spanish and Portuguese, with good annotations and other pertinent bibliographical data.

2123
Powell-Froissard, Lilly. *Spanish-English, English-Spanish crossword puzzle book.* New York, Citadel Press, 1973. 96 p. $1.75

Provides progressively more complicated puzzles in Spanish and in English.

2124
Prado, C. del, and J. Calvo. *Primeras lecturas: una historia incompleta.* New York, Odyssey Press, 1970. 282 p. $1.95

Contains short stories and readings intended for classroom use. Includes notes and vocabularies.

2125
Prista, Alexander R. *Essential Portuguese grammar.* New York, Dover Publications, 1966. 114 p. $1.25

This is a well-designed grammar which includes vocabularies.

2126
Rallides, Charles. *The tense aspect system of the Spanish verb; as used in cultivated Bogotá Spanish.* New York, Humanities Press, 1971. 66 p. $6

Describes the semantic structure of the grammaticized morphemes of the spoken Spanish verb used in the oral expression employed by cultivated speakers of Bogotá, Colombia. The term tense refers to forms whose content is time, and aspect refers to forms whose content is the speaker's point of view. Includes a bibliography.

2127
Ramboz, Ina W., ed. *Canciones de navidad.* Edited by the National Textbook Corp. Skokie, Ill., National Textbook Corp., 1969. 45 p. $1; 5 or more copies $.85 each

Provides a good selection of Christmas carols and seasonal songs from Spain and Latin America. This useful booklet should be acquired by public and school libraries as it would provide a good supplement for Spanish classes.

2128
Ramondino, Salvatore, ed. *New World Spanish-English, English-Spanish dictionary.* Prepared under the supervision of Mario A. Pei. Salvatore Ramondino, editor. New York, New American Library, 1969. xvi, 257 p. $.95

This dictionary of Spanish concentrates on Spanish American words and expressions, although it is based on standard Spanish.

2129
Redondo, Susana. *Spanish in a nutshell.* Montclair, N.J., Institute for Language Study; exclusive distributors to the book trade: Garden City Books, Garden City, N.Y., 1968. 128 p. illus. $1.25

A succinct handbook for beginning Spanish students, with notes, vocabularies, and exercises.

2130
Reedy, Daniel R., and Joseph R. Jones, comp. *Narraciones ejemplares de Hispanoamérica.* Edited, with introd., notes, and vocabulary by Daniel R. Reedy and Joseph R. Jones. Englewood Cliffs, N.J., Prentice-Hall, 1967. 241 p. $4.50

This representative anthology includes full length selections from the works of Esteban Echeverría, Rafael Arévalo Martínez, Horacio Quiroga, Agustín Yañez, and Alejo Carpentier. They span the literary styles of the cuento largo. Each selection contains commentaries on the author and his work.

2131
Reyes Orozco, Carlos. *Spanish-English/English-Spanish. Diccionario de comercio español-inglés, inglés-español.* Oxford, New York, Pergamon Press, 1969. 199 p. (Pergamon Oxford Latin American series; The Commonwealth and international library) $5.25

Presents an extremely useful compilation of everyday business terminology in a convenient pocketbook edition.

2132
Riccio, Guy J. *Introduction to Brazilian Portuguese: a grammar and conversation text.* Annapolis, Md., United States Naval Institute, 1957. 299 p. $4.50

A thorough introduction to Portuguese as it is spoken in Brazil.

2133
Rice, Frank A., ed. *Study of the role of second languages in Asia, Africa, and Latin America.* Washington, Center for Applied Linguistics, 1962. 123 p. $2.50

An important analysis of how essential second languages have become in the Third World. Includes bibliographies.

2134

Richard, Frederick S. *Hispanoamérica moderna.* New York, Harcourt Brace Jovanovich, 1972. x, 276 p. illus. $5.95

A Spanish language text to study the civilization of Spanish America divided into four parts: Mexico and Central America, the Antilles, the Andes, and the River Plata region. Includes notes and vocabulary. Intended for intermediate Spanish, or for Latin American survey courses.

2135

Richards, Ivor Armstrong, and others. *First workbook of Spanish.* New York, Washington Square Press, 1973. 199 p. $.75

Provides exercises and drills for first-year students of Spanish, with extensive notes on dialog and grammar.

2136

Richards, Ivor Armstrong. *Second workbook of Spanish.* New York, Washington Square Press, 1973. 187 p. $.75

Contains exercises, notes, and vocabulary for second-year Spanish students.

2137

Richards, Ivor Armstrong, and others, comps. *Spanish self-taught through pictures,* by I.A. Richards, Ruth L. Metcalf, and Christine Gibson. New York, Pocket Books, 1972. xiv, 270 p. illus. (Pocket books, 720) $1.25

This is a beginner's book for learning Spanish in a visual way. Contains notes and drills.

2138

Richardson, W.A.R., comp. *Modern Spanish unseens.* Selected by W.A.R. Richardson. Oxford, New York, Pergamon Press, 1964. xvii, 164 p. (Pergamon Oxford Spanish series) $2.95

The compiler has chosen a brief selection from modern Latin American and Spanish prose to provide material for reading and translation. The notes in the book include only such words and phrases as are unlikely to be found in a standard dictionary. One section contains selections from nonliterary, mainly modern, press material.

2139

Roach, Eloise. *Siete piezas fáciles.* Skokie, Ill., National Textbook Corp., 1970. 40 p. $1.25; 5 or more $1 each

Presents six short one-act plays and one pageant including music, simple enough for first-year students of Spanish. This work could also be useful for Spanish clubs as the rehearsals and the making of costumes would develop a close association with the country represented.

2140

Robe, Stanley Linn, ed. *Hispanic riddles from Panama; collected from oral tradition.* Berkeley, University of California Press, 1963. 94 p. (University of California publication. Folklore studies, 14) $2.50

These riddles were obtained orally from Panamanian informants. All regions of Panama are represented, especially villages and rural sections where riddling is an active diversion. This is a well-organized work with a vocabulary of unusual terms and an index to solutions.

2141
Robles, José. *Cartilla Española.* New York, Appleton-Century-Crofts. 1969. 110 p. illus. $2.30

This reader presents a good picture of daily life in Madrid.

2142
Rodriguez, Mario B. *Cuentistas de hoy.* Boston, Houghton, Mifflin, 1952. 208 p. illus. $3.60

Presents selections from prominent Spanish and Spanish American short story writers. This is an annotated textbook edition.

2143
Rodriguez, Mario B. *Cuentos de ambos mundos.* Boston, Houghton Mifflin, 1960. 161 p. $1.80

Includes short stories by Spanish and Spanish-American writers. Contains notes, questionnaires, and vocabulary.

2144
Rodriguez, P. César. *Bilingual dictionary of the graphic arts.* Edited by George A. Humphrey. Rev. ed. Farmingdale, N.Y., G.A. Humphrey, 1966. 448 p. $15

A useful and welcome compilation of Spanish and English terms used in the graphic arts.

2145
Rodriguez, T. Manuel, et al. *Spanish verbs and review of expression patterns; verb key method.* New York, D. McKay Co., 1966. 1 v. (unpaged) $1.50

Includes the most essential Spanish verb patterns. A useful book for the student of Spanish speech and grammar. Includes notes and questionnaires.

2146
Rosensweig, Jay B. *Caló; gutter Spanish.* New York, Dutton, 1974. 123 p. $2.95

A useful dictionary of words which are not found in standard dictionaries and words which have completely different meaning when used by the underworld. It will be helpful to those who speak Spanish fluently and especially to police who are dealing with Spanish-speaking minorities who use slang.

2147
Rosenthal, Oscar, and José Martel. *Spanish; three years.* New York, Cambridge Book Co., 1972. 265 p. illus. $.75

This textbook covers three years of Spanish instruction. It is intended for classroom use. Contains notes and vocabularies.

2148
Rosenthal, Oscar, and José Martel. *Spanish; two years.* New York, Cambridge Book Co., 1971. 211 p. $.60

Presents material for the first two years of classroom Spanish, with notes and drills.

2149
Rubin, Joan. *National bilingualism in Paraguay.* New York, Humanities Press, 1969. 135 p. $15

In Paraguay, Spanish and Guarani have coexisted for the past 300 years in relative equilibrium. Over half of the population is bilingual and 92 percent can speak the aboriginal language. This important monograph analyzes attitudes, extra-linguistic behavior, awareness of linguistic norms, and other variables. Includes a bibliography.

2150

Rudman, Jack. *Exámen de equivalencia para el diploma de escuela superior.* Plainview, N.Y., National Learning Corporation, 1971. 451 p. $5.95

Intended as a practice tool for the high school equivalency examination.

2151

Rudman, Jack. *National teacher examination passbook: Spanish.* Plainview, N.Y., National Learning Corp., 1970. 401 p. $5

Contains examples of questions which may appear in examinations for Spanish teachers.

2152

Sallese, Nicholas Francis, and Oscar Fernández de la Vega. *Audiolingual Spanish; a laboratory manual.* New York, Van Nostrand Reinhold Co., 1973. 345 p. $3.50

This is a multimedia guide to aid the student in studying Spanish.

2153

Sallese, Nicholas Francis, and J.A. Pérez. *España: vida y literatura,* por Nicholas F. Sallese y José A. Pérez. New York, Van Nostrand, 1969. xii, 271 p. $4.95

Includes a brief outline of Spanish culture and literature for students of intermediate Spanish.

2154

Savaiano, Eugene, and Lynn W. Winget, comps. *Dictionary of Spanish and English idioms.* Woodbury, N.Y., Barron's Educational Series, 1972. 301 p. $2.95

Presents a useful compilation of Spanish and English idiomatic expressions.

2155

Scarr, J.R. *Present-day Spanish.* Illustrated by Francis King. Oxford, New York, Pergamon Press, 1966-67. 2 v. illus. (The Commonwealth and international library) vol. 1, $1.95; vol. 2, $3

Designed for the beginning Spanish-language student, these volumes contain stories, conversation drills, vocabularies, and questions which aid in studying. This is a concise and well-written Spanish grammar.

2156

Schoemaker, William Hutchinson, ed. *Cuentos de la joven generación,* por José Luis Acquaroni, et al. New York, Holt, 1959. 165 p. $4.60

This anthology is unusual in that all the authors are writing after the Spanish Civil War, and none of the stories date before 1950. The editor chose representative works which are arranged for study purposes, in ascending order of difficulty. Recommended for second-year students. The introduction is in English and the biographical sketches on each author, as well as the texts themselves, are in Spanish.

2157

Schulz, Charles M. *Hay que ayudarte Charlie Brown.* Cartoons by the author. New York, Holt, Rinehart and Winston, 1970. 128 p. illus. $1.50

This is the Spanish version of *You need help, Charlie Brown,* featuring the characters of the Peanuts comic strip.

2158
Schulz, Charles M. *Siempre a flote, Charlie Brown*. New York, Harcourt, Brace & World, 1971. 1 v. (chiefly illus.) $1.50

The *Unsinkable Charlie Brown* (1967) has been translated into Spanish for those learning the language and also for those who do not read English.

2159
Schulz, Charles M. *Te vas a desnucar Charlie Brown*. New York, Harcourt, Brace & World, 1972. 1 v. (chiefly illus.) $1.50

This is a Spanish version of *You've had it, Charlie Brown* which was first published in 1969.

2160
Schulz, Charles M. *Snoopy vuelve a casa*. New York, Harcourt, Brace & World, 1973. 1 v. (chiefly illus.) $1.50

Presents a Spanish translation of the charming Peanuts classic, *Snoopy, come home* (1963). Intended for those learning Spanish.

2161
Schwartz, Isidore Adolphe, and Jennie Stanger. *Español conversado*. New York, Oxford University Press, 1972. 198 p. $.80

Includes conversation drills for Spanish classes, with notes and vocabulary.

2162
Scofield, Cyrus Ingerson. *Trazando bien la palabra de verdad; Rightly dividing the word of truth*. Chicago, Moody Press, 1971. 89 p. $.50

Outlines in Spanish divisions of scripture.

2163
Sedwick, Frank, comp. *Conversation in Spanish; points of departure*. New York, Van Nostrand Reinhold Co., 1973. 295 p. $2.75

This is a compilation of Spanish dialogs, with notes, questionnaires, and vocabulary for the beginning student.

2164
Shaw, L., and C. Ibañez. *Cartas de Zaragoza*. New York, St. Martin's Press, 1971. 321 p. illus. $1.80

2165
Silverstein, Ruth, and Allen Pomerantz. *Spanish; level one*. Woodbury, N.Y., Barron's Educational Series, 1972. 211 p. $2.95

Sketches basic Spanish grammar and presents a dialog for the beginner of Spanish. Contains notes and vocabulary.

2166
Solé, Carlos A. *Bibliografía sobre el español en América, 1920-1967*. Washington, Georgetown University Press, 1970. 175 p. $3.95

Contains 1,500 works on Spanish spoken in Latin America. Some of them are annotated. The work is divided into several general sections and into individual countries. This is a very important contribution.

2167
Solé, Carlos A. *Morfología del adjetivo con -ál, -éro, -ico, -óso*. Washington, Georgetown University Press, 1966. 135 p. $1.95

Originally presented as the author's doctoral dissertation, this work studies the morphology of Spanish adjectives with the endings mentioned in the title, to investigate the constant models in this type of derivation within the structure of Spanish. Includes appendixes and a bibliography.

2168
Solé, Yolanda R. *Hacer: verbo funcional y lexical*. Washington, Georgetown University, Institute of Languges and Linguistics, 1973. 112 p. $1.50

This monograph analyzes the functional and lexicological facets of the Spanish verb which is the equivalent of "to do." Contains notes and a bibliography.

2169
Soto, Osvaldo N., comp. *España e Hispanoamérica*. Edited by Osvaldo N. Soto. Indianapolis, Odyssey Press, 1972. xvi, 412 p. maps. $4.50

This textbook describes 20 Spanish-American countries and Spain in brief essays. It is intended for the intermediate student of Spanish as a two-semester text. Includes notes and vocabulary.

2170
Spaulding, Robert Kilburn. *Syntax of the Spanish verb*. New York, Harcourt, Brace, and World, 1970. 225 p. $2.80

This is an exhaustive study of Spanish verbs.

2171
Spurgeon, Charles Haddon. *Todo de gracia; palabra seria a todos cuantos buscan la salvación por el Señor Jesu-Cristo*. Translated by Arboleda. Chicago, Moody Press, 1969. 128 p. (Moody Colportage library, 139) $.50

This is a Spanish-language book about salvation through Christ.

2172
Stevenson, C.H. *The Spanish language today*. London, Hutchinson University Library, 1970. xi, 146 p. illus. (Modern languages) $2.50

Seeks to explain some of the greater complexities of Spanish which is a verb-centered language of free word order. Spanish is the most faithful descendant of classical Latin. This is a succinct survey of the language rather than a grammar. This important work should be acquired by most university and large public libraries. Contains a select bibliography.

2173
Stillman, Clark, and Alexander Gode. *Spanish at sight*. New York, Ungar Pub. Co., 1972. 102 p. illus. $1.25

A traditional visual book for learning the essentials of Spanish through pictures with the elementary and junior high school student in mind. Contains notes and a vocabulary.

2174
Stockewell, Robert P., Donald Bowen, and John W. Martin. *The grammatical structures of English and Spanish*. Chicago, University of Chicago Press, 1965. xi, 328 p. (Contrastive structure series) $3.75

Compares basic sentence structures, morphological characteristics, verb forms, simple and complex sentence transformations, lexical differences, and other features. Intended for English-speaking students. Contains a bibliography.

2175
Stoner, Peter Winebrenner. *La ciencia habla.* Chicago, Moody Press, 1971. 92 p. $.50

Spanish translation of *Science speaks; an evaluation of certain Christian evidences.*

2176
Sullivan, M. W. *Introductory Spanish.* Palo Alto, Calif., Behavioral Research Laboratories, 1972. 7 v. $18.70

This is a Spanish grammar and conversation aid. It uses the most modern methods of language instruction.

2177
Tardy, William T. *Composiciones ilustradas.* Rev. ed. Skokie, Ill., National Textbook Corp., 1972. 231 p. $1.75

Contains exercises and readings for learning Spanish composition, with notes and vocabulary.

2178
Taylor, Kenneth Nathaniel. *Meditaciones; devotions for the children's hour.* Chicago, Moody Press, 1968. 175 p. illus. $.95

Contains devotional readings in Spanish.

2179
Timms, Wilfred W. *A first Spanish reader for adults.* With illus. by A. C. Eccott. New York, McKay, 1960. 96 p. illus. $1.50

A book of short readings for high school and college intermediate Spanish classes. The readings are humorous and well written. Contains vocabularies.

2180
Tsuzaki, Stanley M. *English influence on Mexican Spanish in Detroit.* New York, Humanities Press, 1970. 92 p. $8.50

A scholarly linguistic study of the English syntactic, verbal, and other influences on the spoken Spanish of people of Mexican extraction. This detailed study includes a bibliography.

2181
Turk, Laurel Herbert, and Aurelio M. Espinosa, eds. *Lecturas hispánicas.* Lexington, Mass., Heath, 1972. 244 p. illus. $4.95

Provides readings for intermediate Spanish classes, with notes, vocabulary, glossary, and attractive illustrations.

2182
Turner, Paul R., and Shirley Turner, comps. *Chontal to Spanish-English, Spanish to Chontal, Dictionary.* Tucson, University of Arizona Press, 1971. xx, 364 p. illus., map. $3.95

The Lowland Chontals live in the valley towns of Huamelula and Astata, and the Highland Chontals live in the southeastern corner of Oaxaca. The languages of these two groups have changed over the years so that speakers of each group communicate in Spanish rather than in the two Chontal languages. Highland Chontal has changed less radically and is considered to be a Hokan language by linguists. This dictionary is intended for linguists as well as for native speakers of the Chontal languages and Spanish. Contains a bibliography.

2183
Valdman, Albert. *Basic course in Haitian Creole.* New York, Humanities Press, 1971. 345 p. $15.75

Analyzes common features of Creole and the West European languages (French, Spanish, English, and Dutch). Creole is a hybrid of lower class French and Afro-Portuguese Pidgin. The book contains vocabularies of regular usage and is intended for the professional linguist and language teacher.

2184

Vasi, Susan, and Joseph Tomasino. *Auditory and reading comprehension exercises in Spanish.* New York, Regents Pub. Co., 1968. 213 p. $1.95

Contains Spanish reading exercises for the beginning student. Includes vocabularies.

2185

Vázquez, Máximo L. *Commercial correspondence dictionary: Spanish-English, English-Spanish.* New York, Regents Pub. Co., 1971. 314 p. $1.50

Contains most terms and phrases used in commercial correspondence.

2186

Vocolo, Joseph M., and Enrique H. Miyares. *Bosquejos de México y Centroamérica.* New York, Holt, Rinehart and Winston, 1972. 159 p., xlviii p. illus. $2.40

This textbook contains vignettes and descriptions of the civilization and culture of Middle America. Intended for intermediate students of Spanish. Contains notes and vocabularies.

2187

Vogan, Grace Dawson. *Merry-go-around of games in Spanish.* Skokie, Ill., National Textbook Corp., 1962. 22 p. illus. $1

Contains games in Spanish intended for beginning Spanish classes.

2188

U.S. Dept. of Defense. *The Armed Forces dictionary of spoken Spanish words; words, phrases, sentences.* Garden City, N.Y., Doubleday, 1968. 384 p. $2.45

Contains words and sentences needed to acquire fluency in everyday Spanish.

2189

U.S. Dept. of Defense. *Dictionary of spoken Spanish: Spanish-English, English-Spanish.* New York, Dover, 1967. 349 p. $2.50

This is a helpful and concise bilingual dictionary for the student and the traveler.

2190

Vos, Howard Frederic. *Breve historia de la iglesia cristiana.* Chicago, Moody Press, 1971. 113 p. $.60

Presents the Spanish translation of *Highlights of church history.*

2191

Vos, Howard Frederic. *Introducción a la arqueología bíblica.* Chicago, Moody Press, 1970. 109 p. $.50

This is the Spanish version of *An introduction to Bible archaeology.*

2192

Walsh, Donald Devenish, and Harlan Gary Sturm. *Repaso; lectura, explicación, práctica.* Rev. ed. New York, Norton, 1971. 246 p. $5.95

Provides useful exercises for the study of Spanish, with notes and vocabulary.

2193

Walsh, Donald Devenish, comp. *What's what; a list of useful terms for the teacher of modern languages.* 3d ed. New York, Modern Languages Association, 1965. 34 p. $4

The romance languages are well represented in this useful list. Contains a brief bibliography.

2194

Wenger, John Christian. *Compendio de historia y doctrina menonitas.* Traducido por Ernesto Suárez. Scottdale, Pa., Herald Press, 1973. 250 p. illus., ports. $2

This is the Spanish version of *Glimpses of Mennonite history and doctrine* (1972).

2195

Wiener, Solomon. *Manual de modismos americanos más comunes.* Spanish translations by Mélida Macía. New York, Handy Book Press, 1958. 144 p. $.75

Lists the most common idioms used in Spanish America in a bilingual format. Contains notes and references.

2196

Willes, Burlington. *Games and ideas for teaching Spanish.* Palo Alto, Calif., Fearon Publishers, 1967. 33 p. illus. $2

An imaginative and creative manual for teaching Spanish which will also be useful for teachers.

2197

Williams, Edwin Bucher. *Diccionario español.* New York, Pocket Books, 1972. 411 p. $1.25

This is a useful Spanish dictionary containing many Spanish-American idioms.

2198

Williams, Edwin Bucher. *New college Spanish and English dictionary.* New York, Bantam Books, 1969. xi, 353, 370 p. $.95

One of the most complete Spanish-English and English-Spanish dictionaries, of interest to students as well as travelers.

2199

Wilson, Norman Scarlyn. *Teach yourself Spanish.* Greenwich, Conn., Fawcett World Library, 1973. xiv, 242 p. $.95

An updated edition of a work published in 1946, intended as an aid for studying Spanish. Includes vocabularies.

2200

Wofsy, Samuel Abraham. *Diálogos entretenidos.* New York, Scribner's, 1962. 207 p. illus. $2.95

Contains sparkling dialogs intended for Spanish-language courses, with notes and vocabulary.

2201

Wolfe, David L. *Structural course in Spanish*. New York, Macmillan, 1972. 231 p. $4.95

The original Spanish edition of 1970 was entitled *Curso básico de español para alumnos de habla inglesa*. Intended for students on the intermediate level.

2202

Zayas y Sotomayor, María de. *Novelas ejemplares y amorosas*. Philadelphia, Center for Curriculum Development, 1969. 212 p. $1

Contains Spanish short stories in an annotated, textbook format.

List of Publishers
and Booksellers

Abrams, Harry N., Inc., 110 East 59th St., New York, N.Y. 10022
Academic Press, Inc., 111 Fifth Ave., New York, N.Y. 10003
Airmont Pub. Co., Inc.; orders to: Associated Booksellers, 147 McKinley Ave.,
  Bridgeport, Conn. 06606
Aldine Pub. Co., 529 South Wabash Ave., Chicago, Ill. 60605
Allyn & Bacon, Inc., 470 Atlantic Avenue, Boston, Mass. 02210
American Bibliographical Center-Clio, Inc., Riviera Campus, 2040 Almeda Padre Serra,
  Santa Barbara, Calif. 93103
American Philosophical Society, 104 South Fifth St., Philadelphia, Pa. 19106
American Universal Artforms Corp., P.O. Box 2442, Austin, Tex. 78767
American Universities Field Staff, Inc., 3 Lebanon St., Hanover, N.H. 03755
Ancient City Bookshop, P.O. Box 5401, Santa Fe, N.M. 87501
Apollo Editions, Inc., 666 Fifth Ave., New York, N.Y. 10019
Appleton-Century-Crofts; *see* Prentice-Hall, Inc.
Arco Pub. Co., Inc., 219 Park Ave. South, New York, N.Y. 10003
Arizona State University, Center for Latin American Studies, Tempe, Ariz. 85281
Associated Booksellers, 147 McKinley Ave., Bridgeport, Conn. 06606
Atheneum Publishers; orders to: Book Warehouse, Inc., Vreeland Ave., Boro of Totowa,
  Paterson, N.J. 07512
Avon Books, 959 Eighth Ave., New York, N.Y. 10019
Ballantine Books, Inc.; orders to: Random House, Inc., Order Dept., Westminster, Md.
  21157
Bantam Books, Inc., 666 Fifth Ave., New York, N.Y. 10019
Barnes & Noble Books; orders to: Harper & Row Publishers, Keystone Industrial
  Park, Scranton, Pa. 18512
Barron's Educational Series, Inc., 113 Crossways Park Dr., Woodbury, N.Y. 11797
Bauhan, William L., Publisher, Dublin, N.H. 03444
Beacon Press, 25 Beacon St., Boston, Mass. 02108
Between Hours Press, 29 East 63d St., New York, N.Y. 10021
Binford & Mort, 2536 South East 11th Ave., Portland, Ore. 97202
B'nai B'rith Great Book Series, 1640 Rhode Island Ave., N.W., Washington, D.C. 20036
Bobbs-Merrill Co., Inc., 4300 West 62d St., Indianapolis, Ind. 46268
Borden Pub. Co., 1855 West Main St., Alhambra, Calif. 91801
Bowker, R. R., Co.; orders to: Order Dept., P.O. Box 1807, Ann Arbor, Mich. 48106
Bowmar, 622 Rodier Dr., Glendale, Calif. 91201
Branden Press, Inc., 221 Columbus Ave., Boston, Mass. 02116
Braziller, George, Inc., 1 Park Ave., New York, N.Y. 10016
Brookings Institution, 1775 Massachusetts Ave., N.W., Washington, D.C. 20036
Cambridge Book Co., 488 Madison Ave., New York, N.Y. 10022
Canfield Press, 850 Montgomery St., San Francisco, Calif. 94133
Capricorn Books; *see* G. P. Putnam's Sons
Carnegie Endowment for International Peace; orders to: Taplinger Pub. Co., Inc., 200
  Park Ave. South, New York, N.Y. 10003
Center for Applied Linguistics, 1611 North Kent St., Arlington, Va. 22209
Center for Curriculum Development, 401 Walnut St., Philadelphia, Pa. 19106
Chandler Pub. Co.; orders to: Oak St. & Pawnee Ave., Scranton, Pa. 18512
Chilton Book Co., Sales Service Dept., Chilton Way, Radnor, Pa. 19089
Chips Bookshop, P.O. Box 123, Planetarium Station, New York, N.Y. 10024
Citadel Press (NYC), 222 Park Ave. South, New York, N.Y. 10003

City Lights Books, Inc., 1562 Grant Ave., San Francisco, Calif. 94133
Clarion Books; *see* Simon & Schuster, Inc.
Collier Books; *see* Macmillan, Inc.
Columbia University Press; orders to: 136 South Broadway, Irvington-on-Hudson, N.Y. 10533
Compsco Pub. Co., 663 Fifth Ave., New York, N.Y. 10022
Cornell University Press, 124 Roberts Place, Ithaca, N.Y. 14850
Corner Book Shop, 102 Fourth Ave., New York, N.Y. 10003
Cornerstone Library, Inc.; orders to: Simon & Schuster, Inc., 1 West 39th St., New York, N.Y. 10018
Creative Press, P.O. Box 89, Claremont, Calif. 91711
Crowell, Thomas Y., Co., Inc., 666 Fifth Ave., New York, N.Y. 10019
Delano, Lucille K., P.O. Box 2474, Cherry Road Station, Rock Hill, S.C. 29730
Dell Pub. Co., Inc., 1 Dag Hammarskjold Plaza, 245 East 47th St., New York, N.Y. 10017; 1900 Sacramento St., Los Angeles, Calif. 90021
Dodd, Mead & Co., 79 Madison Ave., New York, N.Y. 10016
Doubleday & Co., Inc., 501 Franklin Ave., Garden City, N.Y. 11530
Douglas Books; orders to: World Pub. Co., Order Dept., 2080 West 117th St., Lakewood, Ohio 44111
Dover Publications, Inc., 180 Varick St., New York, N.Y. 10014
Dow Jones-Irwin, Inc., 1818 Ridge Rd., Homewood, Ill. 60430
Dufour Editions, Inc., Chester Springs, Pa. 19425
Dumbarton Oaks, 1703 32d St., N.W., Washington, D.C. 20007
Dutton, E. P., & Co., Inc., 201 Park Ave. South, New York, N.Y. 10003
Eerdmans, William B., Pub. Co., 255 Jefferson Ave., S.E., Grand Rapids, Mich. 49502
EMC Corp., 180 East Sixth St., St. Paul, Minn. 55101
Essandess Special Editions; orders to: Simon & Schuster, Inc., 1 West 39th St., New York, N.Y. 10018
Facts on File, Inc., 119 West 57th St., New York, N.Y. 10019
Farrar, Straus & Giroux, Inc., 19 Union Square West, New York, N.Y. 10003
Fawcett World Library, 1515 Broadway, New York, N.Y. 10036
Fearon Publishers, 6 Davis Dr., Belmont, Calif. 94002
Fernhill House, Ltd.; orders to: Humanities Press, Inc., Atlantic Highlands, N.J. 07716
Fides Publisher, Inc., P.O. Box F, Notre Dame, Ind. 46556
Follett Corp., 1010 West Washington Blvd., Chicago, Ill. 60607
Free Press; orders to: Macmillan, Inc., Riverside, N.J. 08075
Friendship Press, 475 Riverside Dr., New York, N.Y. 10027
Frommer-Pasmantier Pub. Corp., 70 Fifth Ave., New York, N.Y. 10011
Frontier Book Co., P.O. Box 805, Fort Davis, Tex. 79734
Funk & Wagnalls Pub. Co., Inc.; distributed by Thomas Y. Crowell Co., Inc., 666 Fifth Ave., New York, N.Y. 10019
Gary Press, P.O. Box 655, Brownsville, Tex. 78520
Ginn and Co., 191 Spring St., Lexington, Mass. 02173
Glencoe Press; orders to: Macmillan, Inc., Riverside, N.J. 08075
Glide Publications, 330 Ellis St., San Francisco, Calif. 94102
Green Mountain Press, P.O. Box 16628, Denver, Colo. 80216
Grosset & Dunlap, Inc., 51 Madison Ave., New York, N.Y. 10010
Grossman Publishers; orders to: Viking Press, 625 Madison Ave., New York, N.Y. 10022
Grove Press, Inc.; orders to: Random House, Inc., Order Dept., Westminster, Md. 21157
Hafner Press; orders to: Macmillan, Inc., Riverside, N.J. 08075
Harcourt Brace Jovanovich, Inc., 757 Third Ave., New York, N.Y. 10017
Harian Publications; orders to: Grosset & Dunlap, Inc., 51 Madison Ave., New York, N.Y. 10010
Harper & Row, Publishers; orders to: Keystone Industrial Park, Scranton, Pa. 18512
Heath, D.C., & Co., College Dept., 125 Spring St., Lexington, Mass. 02173
Hill & Wang 19 Union Square West, New York, N.Y. 10032
Hispanic Society of America, 613 West 155th St., New York, N.Y. 10032
Holt, Rinehart and Winston, Inc., 383 Madison Ave., New York, N.Y. 10017
Hoover Institution Press, Stanford University, Stanford, Calif. 94305
Houghton Mifflin Co., 2 Park St., Boston, Mass. 02107
Humanities Press, Inc., 171 First Ave., Atlantic Highlands, N.J. 07116

Humphrey, George A., P.O. Box 81, Farmingdale, N.Y. 11735
Huntington, Henry E., Library & Art Gallery, 1151 Oxford Rd., San Marino, Calif. 91108
Image Books; see Doubleday & Co., Inc.
Indiana University School of Business, Bureau of Business Research, Bloomington, Ind. 47401
Institute for Cross-Cultural Research; see Operations and Policy Research, Inc.
Institute for the Comparative Studies of Political Systems; see Operations and Policy Research, Inc.
International Publications Co., Inc., 381 Park Ave. South, New York, N.Y. 10016
International Publications Service, 114 East 32d St., New York, N.Y. 10016
Island Press, 175 Bahia Via., Fort Myers Beach, Fla. 33931
Jenkins Pub. Co., P.O. Box 2085, Austin, Tex. 78767
Johns Hopkins University Press, 5820 York Rd., Baltimore, Md. 21218
Jones, Marshall, Co.; distributed by The Golden Quill Press, Francestown, N.H. 03043
Kallman Pub. Co., P.O. Box 14076, 1614 West University Ave., Gainesville, Fla. 32601
Kent State University Press, Kent, Ohio 44242
King, Dale Stuart, Publisher, 2002 North Tucson Blvd., Tucson, Ariz. 85716
Knapp, Robert R., P.O. Box 7234, San Diego, Calif. 92107
Knopf, Alfred A., Inc.; orders to: Order Dept., 400 Hahn Rd., Westminster, Md. 21157
Knox, John, Press, 801 East Main St., Box 1176, Richmond, Va. 23209
Kodansha International/USA; orders to: Harper & Row, Publishers, Keystone Industrial Park, Scranton, Pa. 18512
Kraus Reprint Co., Rte. 100, Millwood, N.Y. 10546
Las Americas Pub. Co., Inc., 152 East 23d St., New York, N.Y. 10010
La Siesta Press, P.O. Box 406, Glendale, Calif. 91209
Lawrence Pub. Co.; orders to: Borden Pub. Co., 1855 West Main St., Alhambra, Calif. 91801
Lippincott, J. B., Co., East Washington Square, Philadelphia, Pa. 19105
Little, Brown and Co.; orders to: 200 West St., Waltham, Mass. 02154
Littlefield, Adams & Co., 81 Adams Dr., Boro of Totowa, Paterson, N.J. 07512
Liveright; orders to: E. P. Dutton & Co., Inc., 201 Park Ave. South, New York, N.Y. 10003
Los Angeles County Museum of Art, 5905 Wilshire Blvd., Los Angeles, Calif. 90036
Loyola University Press, 3441 North Ashland Ave., Chicago, Ill. 60657
M.I.T. Press, 28 Carleton St., Cambridge, Mass. 02142
McGilvery, Laurence, P.O. Box 852, La Jolla, Calif. 92037
McGraw-Hill Book Co., 1221 Avenue of the Americas, New York, N.Y. 10036
McKay, David, Co. Inc., 750 Third Avenue, New York, N.Y. 10017
Macmillan, Inc.; orders to: Riverside, N.J. 08075
McNally & Loftin, Publishers, P.O. Box 1316, Santa Barbara, Calif. 93102
Marquette University Press, 1131 West Wisconsin Ave., Milwaukee, Wis. 53233
Maryknoll Publications; orders to: Orbis Books, Maryknoll, N.Y. 10545
Merit Pubs.; see Pathfinder Press
Merrill, Charles E., Pub. Co., 1300 Alum Creek Dr., Columbus, Ohio 43216
Metropolitan Museum of Art; orders to: New York Graphic Society Ltd., 140 Greenwich Ave., Greenwich, Conn. 06830
Metropolitan Press; see Binford & Mort
Michigan State University Press, 25 Manly Miles Bldg., 1405 South Harrison Rd., East Lansing, Mich. 48824
Monarch Press; orders to: Simon & Schuster, Inc., 1 West 39th St., New York, N.Y. 10018
Monthly Review Press, 62 West 14th St., New York, N.Y. 10011
Moody Press, 820 North LaSalle St., Chicago, Ill. 60610
Museum of Primitive Art, 15 West 54th St., New York, N.Y. 10019
Nash Pub. Corp.; orders to: E. P. Dutton & Co., Inc., 201 Park Ave. South, New York, N.Y. 10003
National Academy of Sciences, Print. and Pub. Office, 2101 Constitution Ave., N.W., Washington, D.C. 20418
National Learning Corp., 20 DuPont St., Plainview, N.Y. 11803
National Textbook Co., 8259 Niles Center Rd., Skokie, Ill. 60076

Natural History Press; orders to: Doubleday & Co., Inc., 501 Franklin Ave., Garden City, N.Y. 11530
New American Library, Inc., 1301 Avenue of the Americas, New York, N.Y. 10019
New York Graphic Society Ltd., 140 Greenwich Ave., Greenwich, Conn. 06830
New York Teacher's College; *see* Teachers College Press
New York University Press, Washington Square, New York, N.Y. 10003
Newberry Library, 60 West Walton St., Chicago, Ill. 60610
Nijhoff, Martinus, The Hague, Netherlands
Nitty Gritty Productions, P.O. 5457, Concord, Calif. 94524
Noon House; *see* Bauhan, William L., Publisher
Norton, W.W., & Co., Inc., 500 Fifth Ave., New York, N.Y. 10036
Oak Publications; orders to: Quick Fox, 33 West 60th St., New York, N.Y. 10023
Oceana Publications, Inc., Dobbs Ferry, N.Y. 10522
Ocelot Press, P.O. Box 504, Clarement, Calif. 91711
October House, Inc., 160 Avenue of the Americas, New York, N.Y. 10013
Oddo Pub., Inc., Beauregard Blvd., Fayetteville, Georgia 30214
Ohio State University Press, 2070 Neil Ave., Columbus, Ohio 43210
Operations & Policy Research, Inc.; orders to: Institute for the Study of Political Systems, 4000 Albermarle St., N.W., Washington, D.C. 20016
Orbis Books, Maryknoll, N.Y. 10545
Oregon State University Press, P.O. Box 689, Corvallis, Ore. 97330
Oxford University Press, Inc., 16-00 Pollitt Dr., Fair Lawn, N.J. 07410
Pacific Coast Publishers, 4085 Campbell Ave. at Scott Dr., Menlo Park, Calif. 94025
Pathfinder Press, Inc., 410 West St., New York, N.Y. 10003
Pegasus, 4300 West 62d St., Indianapolis, Ind. 46268
Pemberton Press; *see* Jenkins Pub. Co.
Penguin Books, Inc.; orders to:7100 Ambassador Rd., Baltimore, Md. 21207
Pergamon Press, Inc.; orders to: Maxwell House, Fairview Park, Elmsford, N.Y. 10523
Philadelphia Book Co., Inc., 116 Fountain St., Philadelphia, Pa. 19127
Pittsburgh University Press, 4200 Fifth Ave., Pittsburgh, Pa. 15213
Pocket Books; *see* Simon & Schuster, Inc.
Praeger Publishers, Inc., 111 Fourth Ave., New York, N.Y. 10003
Prentice-Hall, Inc., Englewood Cliffs, N.J. 07632
Princeton University Press, Princeton, N.J. 08540
Putnam's, G. P., Sons, 200 Madison Ave., New York, N.Y. 10016
Pyramid Communications, Inc., 919 Third Ave., New York, N.Y. 10022
Quadrangle/The New York Times Book Co., 10 East 53d St., New York, N.Y. 10022
Rand McNally & Co., P.O. Box 7600, Chicago, Ill. 60680
Random House, Inc.; orders to: Order Dept., 457 Hahn Rd., Westminster, Md. 21157
Red Hill Press; orders to: Serendipity Books, 1790 Shattuck Ave., Berkeley, Calif. 94709
Redwood City Tribune, Redwood, Calif. 94062
Regents Pub. Co., Inc., 2 Park Ave., New York, N.Y. 10016
Regnery, Henry, Co., 1500 S. Western Ave., Chicago, Ill. 60608
Research Press, P.O. Box 3177, County Fair Station, Champaign, Ill. 61820
Ritchie, Ward, Press, 474 South Arroyo Pkwy., Pasadena, Calif. 91105
St. John's University Press, Grand Central & Utopia Pkwys., Jamaica, N.Y. 11439
St. Louis University Press, 220 North Grand Blvd., St. Louis, Mo. 63103
St. Martin's Press, Inc., 175 Fifth Ave., New York, N.Y. 10010
Savile Bookshop, 3226 P St., N.W., Washington, D.C. 20007
Schenkman Pub. Co., Inc., 3 Mt. Auburn Place, Harvard Sq., Cambridge, Mass. 02138
Schocken Books, Inc., 200 Madison Ave., New York, N.Y. 10016
Schram, Abner, 1860 Broadway, New York, N.Y. 10023
Scribner's, Charles, Sons; orders to: Shipping & Service Center, Vreeland Ave., Boro of Totowa, Paterson, N.J. 07512
Shields Pub. Co., Inc., 325 Ninth St., San Francisco, Calif. 94103
Siesta, La, Press; *see* La Siesta Press
Simon & Schuster, Inc.; orders to: 1 West 39th St., New York, N.Y. 10018
Soccer Associates, P.O. Box 634, New Rochelle, N.Y. 10802
Southern University Press, Second Ave. & 19th St., Birmingham, Ala. 35233
Stanford University Press, Stanford, Calif. 94305
Steck-Vaughn Co., P.O. Box 2028, Austin, Tex. 78767
Stein & Day, Publishers, 7 East 48th St., New York, N.Y. 10017

Sterling Pub. Co., Inc., 419 Park Ave. South, New York, N.Y. 10016
Stipes Pub. Co., 10-12 Chester St., Champaign, Ill. 61820
Stryker Post Publications, 888 17th St., N.W., Washington, D.C. 20006
Swallow Press, Inc., 1139 South Wabash Ave., Chicago, Ill. 60605
Taplinger Pub. Co., Inc., 200 Park Ave. South, New York, N.Y. 10003
Tate Gallery Publications, P.O. Box 428, Truchas, N.M. 87578
Teachers College Press, Columbia University, 1234 Amsterdam Ave., New York, N.Y. 10027
Texas Christian University Press, T.C.U. Station, Fort Worth, Tex. 76129
Texas Western Press, University of Texas at El Paso, El Paso, Tex. 79999
Trail-R Club of America, P.O. Box 1376, Beverly Hills, Calif. 90213
Transatlantic Arts, Inc., North Village Green, Levittown, N.Y. 11756
Travel Digest, Paul Richmond Publisher, Suite 1517, 1100 Glendon Ave., Los Angeles, Calif. 90024
Tudor Pub. Co.; orders to: Harlem Book Co., 221 Park Ave. South, New York, N.Y. 10003
Tuttle, Charles E., Co., Inc., 28 South Main St., Rutland, Vt. 05701
Twayne Pubs., Inc., 70 Lincoln St., Boston, Mass. 02111
Twentieth Century Fund, Inc., 41 East 70th St., New York, N.Y. 10021
Ungar, Frederick, Publishing Co., Inc., 250 Park Ave. South, New York, N.Y. 10003
Unicorn Press, Inc., P.O. Box 3307, Greensboro, N.C. 27402
U.S. Naval Institute, Annapolis, Md. 21402
Universe Books, 381 Park Ave. South, New York, N.Y. 10016
University of Alaska Press; orders to: University of Washington Press, Seattle, Wash. 98195
University of Arizona Press, P.O. Box 3398, College Station, Tucson, Ariz. 85722
University of California, Art Museum, Berkeley, Calif. 94720
University of California at Los Angeles, Latin American Center, 405 Hilgard Ave., Los Angeles, Calif. 90024
University of California Press, 2223 Fulton St., Berkeley, Calif. 94720
University of Florida Press, 15 N.W. 15th St., Gainesville, Fla. 32601
University of Georgia Press, Waddel Hall, Athens, Ga. 30602
University of Illinois Press, Urbana, Ill. 61801
University of Michigan Press, 615 East University, Ann Arbor, Mich. 48106
University of Minnesota Press, 2037 University Ave., S.E., Minneapolis, Minn. 55455
University of New Mexico Press, Albuquerque, N.M. 87131
University of North Carolina Press, Box 2288, Chapel Hill, N.C. 27514
University of Notre Dame Press; orders to: Harper & Row, Publishers, Keystone Industrial Park, Scranton, Pa. 18512
University of Oklahoma Press, 1005 Asp Ave., Norman, Okla. 73069
University of Oregon Books, Eugene, Ore. 97403
University of Puerto Rico, Institute of Caribbean Studies, Rio Piedras, Puerto Rico 00928
University of Texas Press, P.O. Box 7819, University Station, Austin, Tex. 78712
University of Toronto Press; orders to: 33 East Typper St., Buffalo, N.Y. 14208
University of Wisconsin Press, P.O. Box 1379, Madison, Wis. 53701
University Place Book Shop, 821 Broadway, New York, N.Y. 10003
University Press of Kansas, 366 Watson Library, Lawrence, Kan. 60045
University Press of Virginia, P.O. Box 3608, University Station, Charlottesville, Va. 22903
Vanderbilt University Press, Nashville, Tenn. 37235
Van Nostrand Reinhold Co.; orders to: 300 Pike St., Cincinnati, Ohio 45202
Viking Press, Inc., 625 Madison Ave., New York, N.Y. 10022
Warner Paperback Library; distributed by Independent News Co., 75 Rockefeller Plaza, New York, N.Y. 10020
Washington, Square Press, 630 Fifth Ave., New York, N.Y. 10020
Wayne State University Press, Wayne State University, 5980 Cass Ave., Detroit, Mich. 48202
Wiley, John, & Sons, Inc., 605 Third Ave., New York, N.Y. 10016
Wittenborn, George, Inc., 1018 Madison Ave., New York, N.Y. 10021
World Pub. Co., 110 East 59th St., New York, N.Y. 10022
Yale University Press, 92A Yale Station, New Haven, Conn. 06520

subject index

culture, 17, 50, 182, 199, 485, 716, 756, 777, 819, 832, 857, 1027A, 1033, 1092, 1224
economic conditions, 142, 170, 227, 291, 702
education, 297, 427, 579, 652, 872, 1215, 1366
history, 858, 987, 1027A
literature, 199, 921, 945-946, 1086, 1260
social conditions, 154, 185, 291, 427, 479, 481, 571-572, 607, 661, 797, 804, 857, 1270
see also Braceros
Chile, 103
description and travel, 94
economic conditions, 412, 511, 906, 1067
foreign relations, with the U.S., 352
history, 1360
politics and government, 98, 228, 311, 370, 375, 385, 408, 650, 681, 975
Christian Democrats, Latin America, 973
Church and state
Brazil, 43, 1014
fiction, 502, 504-505
Latin America, colonial period, 508, 829, 980-981, 1266
see also Catholic church
Cinematography
educational, 775
Latin America, 157A
Mexico, 648
Spain, 1464, 1854
Clarín (pseud.), *see* Alas, Leopoldo
Codex Hall, 327
Codex Vienna, 704
Codices Alcobacenses, 1392
Coffee, 1177
Coins, Spain, 1737-1739
Colombia
description and travel, 1200
economic conditions, 631
history, national period, 92
Columbus, Christopher, 237, 860, 1201, 1236
Communism
bibliography, 1083-1084
Brazil, 816
Chile, 650
Cuba, 335-336, 377, 500, 514-516, 518, 520, 601, 1197, 1329
Latin America, 5, 56, 313-314, 329, 515-522, 636, 812, 989, 1011
Venezuela, 14
Constitutions, Latin America, 396
Cookery
Caribbean, 682
Central American, 1372
Latin American, 682
Mexican, 26, 298, 387, 922, 1013, 1204, 1221, 1273, 1297, 1372-1373
Peruvian, 60A
Spanish, 1625, 1752, 1927
Coronado y Valdés, Francisco Vásquez de, 111, 310
Corrêa, Gaspar, 1425
Costa Rica
politics and government, 320
social conditions, 473
Cortés, Hernán, 475
Couto, Diogo do, 1422
Cuba
bibliography, 947, 1259
culture, 925

hispanic foundation
bibliographical series

1. Latin American belles-lettres in English translation;
   a selective and annotated guide. 2d rev. ed. 1943. 33 p.   Out of print

2. A provisional bibliography of United States books
   translated into Portuguese. 1957. 182 p.
      Superseded by no. 8.   Out of print

3. A provisional bibliography of United States books
   translated into Spanish. 1957. 471 p.
      Superseded by no. 8.   Out of print

4. William Hickling Prescott; an annotated bibliography
   of published works. 1958. 275 p. illus.   Out of print

5. Latin America in Soviet writings, 1945-1958; a
   bibliography. 1959. 257 p.   Out of print

6. Works by Miguel de Cervantes Saavedra in the
   Library of Congress. 1960. 120 p. illus.   Out of print

7. Ladino books in the Library of Congress; a
   bibliography. 1963. 44 p.   Out of print

8. Spanish and Portuguese translations of United States
   books, 1955-1962; a bibliography. 1963. 506 p.
      Supersedes nos. 2 and 3.   Out of print

9. Latin America; a bibliography of paperback books.
   1964. 38 p.
      Superseded by nos. 11, 13, and 14.   Out of print

10. National directory of Latin Americanists; bio-
    bibliographies of 1,884 specialists in the social
    sciences and humanities. 1966. 351 p.
       Superseded by no. 12.   Out of print

11. Latin America; an annotated bibliography of paperback
    books. 1967. 77 p.
       Superseded by nos. 13 and 14.   Out of print

12. National directory of Latin Americanists.
    2d ed. 1972. 683 p.
       Revision of no. 10. $7.50

13. Latin America, Spain, and Portugal; an annotated
    bibliography of paperback books. 1971. 180 p.
       Supersedes nos. 9 and 11. $1.50

☆ U.S. GOVERMENT PRINTING OFFICE: 1976 O— 588-334